Depressive illness

Received in
C. N. S. Division

Thomas

Depressive illness

Diagnosis, assessment, treatment

Edited by P. Kielholz, Basle

Hans Huber Publishers
Bern Stuttgart Vienna

An international symposium
St. Moritz, 10th-11th January 1972

Manuscripts coordinated and translated under the supervision of:

Dr. C. ADAMS
Mr. I. C. W. BIGLAND, M.A.
Dr. W. JOCHUM
Dr. H. KARRER
Dr. R. LUDWIG
Mr. H. D. PHILPS, M.A.

ISBN 3–456–00324–2

Contents

Address of chief coordinator:
Dr. C. ADAMS, Head of the Medical and Pharmaceutical Information Service,
CIBA-GEIGY LIMITED, Steinengraben 42, Basle, Switzerland

List of authors

Dr. S.P. AFEICHE, CIBA-GEIGY LIMITED, Klybeckstrasse 141, Basle (Switzerland)

Prof.J. ANGST, Forschungsdirektor der Psychiatrischen Universitätsklinik, Lenggstrasse 31, Zurich (Switzerland)

Dr. ESTHER BARTHOLINI, CIBA-GEIGY LIMITED, Klybeckstrasse 141, Basle (Switzerland)

Prof. H.J. BEIN, Head of the Research Department, Pharmaceutical Division, CIBA-GEIGY LIMITED, Klybeckstrasse 141, Basle (Switzerland)

Prof. P. BERNER, Vorstand der Psychiatrischen Universitätsklinik, Lazarettgasse 14, Vienna (Austria)

Prof. W. BIRKMAYER, Leiter des Ludwig Boltzmann-Instituts für Neurochemie, Versorgungsheimplatz 1, Vienna (Austria)

Dr. A. COPPEN, M.R.C. Neuropsychiatry Unit, Medical Research Council Laboratories, Woodmansterne Road, Carshalton, Surrey (England)

Dr. W. R. DARROW, CIBA-GEIGY CORPORATION, 556 Morris Avenue, Summit, N.J. 07901 (U.S.A.)

Dr. ALEXANDRA DELINI-STULA, CIBA-GEIGY LIMITED, Schwarzwaldallee 215, Basle (Switzerland)

Dr. F. FREYHAN, Director of Research, St. Vincent's Hospital, 153 West Eleventh Street, New York, N.Y. 10011 (U.S.A.)

Prof. L. GEISLER, Oberarzt, Medizinische Kliniken und Polikliniken der Justus-Liebig-Universität, Friedrichstrasse 27, Giessen (Germany)

Prof. W. GRÜTER, CIBA-GEIGY LIMITED, Steinengraben 42, Basle (Switzerland)

Dr. I. GUZ, Médico Chefe das Unidades Masculinas de Adultos da Clínica Psiquiátrica do Departamento de Neuropsiquiatría, Hospital das Clínicas, Faculdade de Medicina da Universidade Federal de São Paulo, São Paulo (Brazil)

Prof. M. HAMILTON, M.D., F.R.C.P., D.P.M., Department of Psychiatry, University of Leeds, 15 Hyde Terrace, Leeds LS2 9LT (England)

Priv.-Doz. Dr. E. HEIM, Chefarzt, Psychiatrische Klinik "Schlössli", Oetwil am See (Switzerland)

Prof. H. HEIMANN, Centre de recherches psychopathologiques, Clinique psychiatrique universitaire, Hôpital de Cery, Prilly-Lausanne (Switzerland)

Prof. H. HIPPIUS, Direktor der Universitäts-Nervenklinik, Nussbaumstrasse 7, Munich (Germany)

Doz. Dr. U.J. JOVANOVIĆ, Universitäts-Nervenklinik und Poliklinik, Röntgenring 12, Würzburg (Germany)

Prof. C. R. B. Joyce, CIBA-GEIGY LIMITED, Klybeckstrasse 141, Basle (Switzerland)

Dr. H. Keberle, CIBA-GEIGY LIMITED, Klybeckstrasse 141, Basle (Switzerland)

Prof. P. Kielholz, Direktor der Psychiatrischen Universitätsklinik, Wilhelm-Klein-Strasse 27, Basle (Switzerland)

Prof. R. Kuhn, Direktor der Kantonalen Psychiatrischen Klinik, Münsterlingen (Switzerland)

Dr. Verena Kuhn-Gebhardt, Oberärztin, Kantonale Psychiatrische Klinik, Münsterlingen (Switzerland)

Prof. J. J. López Ibor, Clínica López Ibor, Av. Nueva Zelanda 78, Puerta de Hierro, Madrid-20 (Spain)

Dr. M. Lorgé, CIBA-GEIGY LIMITED, Klybeckstrasse 141, Basle (Switzerland)

Dr. P. Loustalot, Head of the Clinical Trials Department, CIBA-GEIGY LIMITED, Klybeckstrasse 141, Basle (Switzerland)

Priv.-Doz. Dr. N. Matussek, Universitäts-Nervenklinik, Nussbaumstrasse 7, Munich (Germany)

Prof. R. Oberholzer, Head of the Medical Department, CIBA-GEIGY LIMITED, Klybeckstrasse 141, Basle (Switzerland)

Prof. P. Pichot, Faculté de médecine Cochin-Port-Royal, Centre psychiatrique Sainte-Anne, 1 rue Cabanis, Paris 14e (France)

Priv.-Doz. Dr. W. Pöldinger, Oberarzt, Psychiatrische Universitätsklinik, Lazarettgasse 14, Vienna (Austria)

Dr. B. Popkes, Chefarzt der Neurologischen Abteilung, Albertinen-Krankenhaus, Süntelstrasse 11a, Hamburg 61 (Germany)

Prof. A. Reale, Divisione Cardiologica, Istituto di Chirurgia del Cuore, University of Rome (Italy)

Prof. K. Rickels, M.D., Department of Psychiatry, University of Pennsylvania, University Hospital, 3400 Spruce Street, Philadelphia, Pa 19104 (U.S.A.)

Dr. H.-D. Rost, Medizinische Kliniken und Polikliniken der Justus-Liebig-Universität, Friedrichstrasse 27, Giessen (Germany)

Prof. I. Sano, Department of Neuropsychiatry, Osaka University Medical School, Dojima Hamadori, Fukushima-ku, Osaka (Japan)

Dr. P. Schmidlin, CIBA-GEIGY LIMITED, Klybeckstrasse 141, Basle (Switzerland)

Doz. Dr. W. Walcher, Oberarzt, Psychiatrisch-Neurologische Universitätsklinik, Auenbruggerplatz 1, Graz (Austria)

Dr. J. Welner, Chief of Psychiatric Department, Kommunehospitalet, Farimagsgade 5, Copenhagen (Denmark)

Dr. M. Wilhelm, CIBA-GEIGY LIMITED, Schwarzwaldallee 215, Basle (Switzerland)

Opening address:
Diagnostic aspects in the treatment of depression

by P. KIELHOLZ*

In all the industrialised countries, especially among people living in urban communities, depressive disorders have been encountered during the past two decades on a steadily increasing scale. This increase in recorded cases of depression is attributable partly to improved methods of diagnosis, and partly to the fact that since the discovery of therapeutically active antidepressant drugs more and more persons suffering from depression have, on their own initiative, been consulting doctors in the expectation of receiving effective treatment. In various publications it is pointed out that psychogenic and masked forms of depression are particularly on the increase.

Parallel with the rise in the incidence of depression, the last 20 years have witnessed in all civilised countries an increase not only in the number of attempted suicides but, to some extent, also in the number of successful suicides. Several authors, including RINGEL, STENGEL, SAINSBURY, and PÖLDINGER, have furnished consistent evidence to the effect that some 50% of all subjects who attempt or commit suicide are suffering from depression. The greater frequency of suicidal acts is thus yet a further sign of the growing prevalence of depressive illnesses.

During the last 15 years a *change in the symptomatology of depression* has also been observed, a change characterised by an increasing tendency towards *somatisation*.

Despite improvements in diagnosis, many cases of depression are not recognised in good time, because the underlying depressive condition is masked by a wide variety of somatic and autonomic nervous symptoms.

Essential for the success of treatment in depressive states is the establishment of an *accurate nosological and phenomenological diagnosis*. Although transitional forms of depression occur in all possible guises, an attempt should be made in every depressive syndrome to arrive at a differential diagnosis based on identification of the main elements contributing to the multifactorial aetiology of the condition. Correct nosological classification of a case can only be achieved by a conjoint study of the patient's heredity, pre-morbid personality structure, and life history, the psychic and somatic findings he presents, as well as his occupational, familial, and economic situation.

In accordance with their nosological classification, we broadly divide depressive syndromes into the various groups outlined in Figure 1. This method of differentiating between forms of depression according to whether they are of organic, endogenous, or psychogenic aetiology has proved useful in practice. It enables conclusions to be drawn regarding not only the type of pharmacotherapy or psychotherapy indicated, but also the clinical course and the prognosis.

* Director of the Psychiatrische Universitätsklinik, Basle, Switzerland.

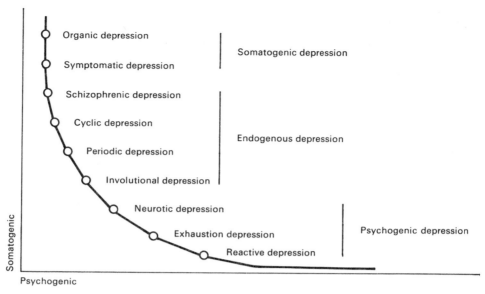

Fig. 1. Nosological classification of depressive states.

The diagnosis of depression, however, must not be confined to a mere nosological classification, but should take the form of a dual analysis in which the phenomenological aspects, i.e. what FREYHAN refers to as the target symptoms, are also included. It may be taken as a general rule that the *nosological diagnosis* plays a decisive role in determining the indication for psychopharmacotherapy and psychotherapy, whereas it is on the *phenomenological aspects* of the depressive syndrome that the choice of antidepressant to be employed depends. Which psycho-active drug should be selected is conditioned by the three target symptoms of "diminished drive", "depressed mood", and "anxiety". The antidepressant prescribed must be one displaying an activity pattern appropriate to the nature of the target symptom.

It is from this largely subjective twofold diagnostic analysis that the type of treatment indicated in a case of depression is deduced. The problem of quantifying depressive symptoms and syndromes has not yet been satisfactorily solved. One of the most urgent tasks now confronting those engaged on *biological research* is therefore to provide the wherewithal for a new classification of depression and for causal therapy based on biological principles.

Biochemical aspects of depression

by N. Matussek*

Since 1959, when Everett and Toman[25] first postulated that catecholamines and serotonin (5-hydroxytryptamine) may play an important role in connection with depression, it is upon these substances that research on the biochemical aspects of depression has been concentrated (Bunney and Davis[13]; Schild-kraut[49]; Matussek[37]; van Praag[46]; Schildkraut and Kety[51]; Lapin and Oxenkrug[33]; Coppen and Shaw[19]). The catecholamine and serotonin hypotheses of depression were founded chiefly on the observation that reserpine and methyldopa are liable to provoke depression, as well as on the antidepressant effects exhibited by monamine-oxidase inhibitors and the tricyclic thymoleptic agents. But I do not propose here to discuss once again the mechanisms of action of such drugs, since these mechanisms have already been described in detail on numerous previous occasions. Instead, I should simply like to refer to certain more recent studies on depression which are primarily devoted to clinical and biochemical aspects of the problem, with particular reference to catecholamine and serotonin metabolism (cf. Figures 1 and 2).

Analysis of brain tissue

If it were possible to obtain biopsy material from certain regions of the brain in man, examination of this material would probably provide the best evidence by which to verify the two hypotheses I have just mentioned. For ethical reasons, however, i.e. because of the irreparable damage which might be inflicted in such biopsy studies, this approach is, of course, out of the question. Consequently, we have to fall back upon an analysis of brain tissue obtained at autopsy. In the brains of deceased depressive patients, smaller concentrations of 5-hydroxy-indole-acetic acid (the principal metabolite of serotonin) have been found than in controls, whereas no differences could be demonstrated with respect to the serotonin and noradrenaline concentrations (Bourne et al.[8]). Since, in these depressive patients, only the levels of 5-hydroxyindole-acetic acid were reduced, and no significant decrease in the concentration of the amine itself was apparent, this finding might be indicative of a diminution in the rate at which serotonin is broken down. The catecholamine metabolites were not analysed in this study, which therefore sheds no light on catecholamine metabolism in the brains of depressive patients. In view of the fact that not enough is yet known about changes occurring in the brain post mortem, and that in most cases quite a long time elapses between death and removal of the brain, these autopsy findings should be interpreted with caution.

* Universitäts-Nervenklinik, Munich, Germany.

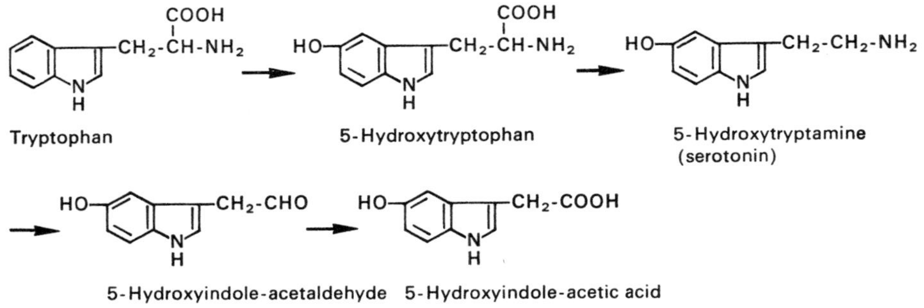

Fig. 1. Biosynthesis and breakdown of serotonin.

Analysis of the cerebrospinal fluid

From an analysis of the metabolites present in the C.S.F., various research teams have therefore attempted to draw inferences regarding the metabolism of the respective transmitter in the brain. On the basis of studies which BULAT and ŽIVKOVIĆ[11] have recently undertaken on the origin of the 5-hydroxyindole-acetic acid present in the C.S.F., however, these two authors conclude that the 5-hydroxyindole-acetic acid detectable in the C.S.F. can chiefly be ascribed to serotonin metabolism in the spinal cord. Nevertheless, there is some evidence to suggest that metabolic processes occurring in the brain are also reflected, a few hours later, in the lumbar C.S.F. [D. ECCLESTON (personal communication); F. K. GOODWIN (unpublished findings)]. I believe that, to avoid misinterpretations, the connections between cerebral metabolism and the metabolites appearing in the C.S.F. should be more thoroughly investigated than has hitherto been the case. C.S.F. analyses carried out several years ago (ASHCROFT et al.[1]; DENCKER et al.[24]; BOWERS et al.[10]) had already disclosed reduced 5-hydroxy-indole-acetic acid levels in the C.S.F. of depressive patients, so that the above-mentioned autopsy findings thus tally with the results obtained by analysing the C.S.F. More recent investigations, in which the transport of 5-hydroxy-indole-acetic acid from the C.S.F. was inhibited by treatment with probenecid, have yielded data pointing in the same direction; under these conditions, i.e. following the administration of probenecid, the rise in the 5-hydroxyindole-acetic acid levels in the C.S.F. of depressives (VAN PRAAG et al.[48]), as well as of manic patients (SJÖSTRÖM and ROOS[52]), was significantly less marked than in controls. This once again suggests that serotonin is metabolised at a reduced rate both in depressive and in manic patients. On the other hand, it has also been found that even when the depressive phase has abated, i.e. when the pa-

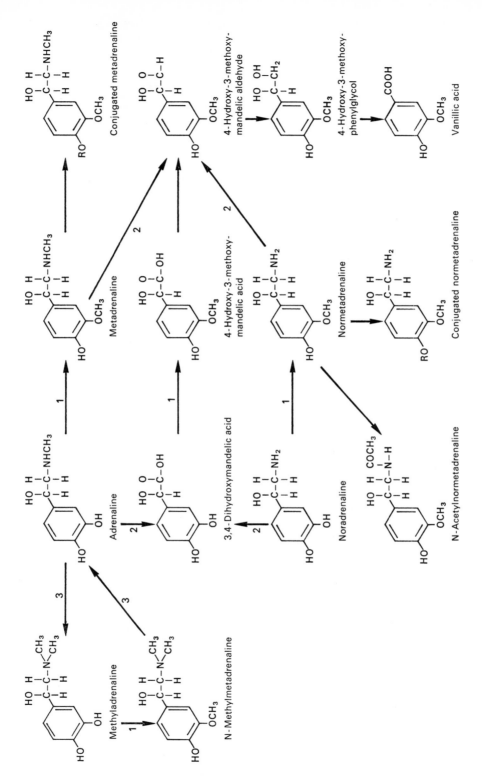

Fig. 2. Pathways in the breakdown of noradrenaline and adrenaline.

tient's affective status has reverted to normal, the 5-hydroxyindole-acetic acid concentration in the C.S.F. is still lower than in controls (COPPEN et al.[18]). In patients whose depression has improved under treatment with amitriptyline, the 5-hydroxyindole-acetic acid levels likewise fail to rise (BOWERS et al.[10]).

There thus seems to be no direct connection between a low 5-hydroxyindole-acetic acid concentration in the C.S.F. and the presence of depressive symptoms, particularly since reduced 5-hydroxyindole-acetic acid levels have also been found in the C.S.F. of manic patients. To what extent these interesting findings are indicative of a specific personality disorder—or possibly of some genetic defect—in patients subject to endogenous depression, will have to be determined in the light of further study.

Now let us turn to the question of the catecholamine metabolites present in the C.S.F. of depressive patients. In the case of homovanillic acid, which is the principal metabolite of dopamine, such differences as have been observed in its concentrations in depressive patients, as compared with patients suffering from neurological diseases or with normal subjects, have been only slight and of no statistical significance (DENCKER et al.[24]; BOWERS et al.[10]). In cases of retarded depression, however, the rise in the homovanillic acid concentration following treatment with probenecid is significantly smaller than in non-retarded depressive patients (VAN PRAAG and KORF[47]), who in this respect do not differ significantly from controls. From these findings VAN PRAAG and KORF rightly conclude that it is above all motor activity, and not a specific nosological entity, which is reflected in dopamine metabolism, especially since a reduction in the homovanillic acid level is also a feature of Parkinson's disease (OLSSON and ROOS[42]).

Of particular interest in this connection are the results of recent investigations concerned with the concentration of methoxyhydroxyphenylglycol in the C.S.F., which provides a clue to the noradrenaline turnover. In "longitudinal" studies on patients suffering from bipolar depression, BUNNEY et al.[12,14] found that in the depressive phase the methoxyhydroxyphenylglycol values are lower, and in the manic phase higher, than in the normothymic state. On the other hand, when groups of depressive, manic, and normothymic patients were compared, no such differences could be detected in the C.S.F. concentrations of methoxyhydroxyphenylglycol (WILK et al.[58]; ASHCROFT et al.[2]). It should be pointed out, however, that so far these determinations of methoxyhydroxyphenylglycol have been undertaken only in small groups of patients. Consequently, before any final conclusions can be drawn, further investigations in this field must be carried out and, in particular, the aforementioned question of the relationships between cerebral metabolism and the metabolites occurring in the C.S.F. will also have to be analysed more closely.

Analysis of the urine

For several years now, interest has also centred upon the methoxyhydroxyphenylglycol concentrations in connection with the analysis of catecholamine metabolites in the urine. Of all the noradrenaline metabolites excreted in the urine, it is methoxyhydroxyphenylglycol which—to some extent, at least—is alleged to provide the most reliable indicator of the noradrenaline turnover in the brain (MAAS et al.[35], who also give details of further literature on this topic). Only recently, however, some doubts have been expressed as to the correctness of this allegation (CHASE et al.[17]). Nevertheless, in my opinion these findings relating to the levels of methoxyhydroxyphenylglycol in the urine deserve close attention, even though it has not yet been determined with certainty how much of the methoxyhydroxyphenylglycol is of central, and how much of peripheral origin.

In depressive patients, the normetadrenaline and metadrenaline concentrations in the urine do not differ from those measured in controls, whereas the methoxy-hydroxyphenylglycol concentrations are reported to be significantly lower (MAAS et al.[34, 35]). Under conditions of stress, on the other hand, the methoxy-hydroxyphenylglycol values in depressive patients rise to almost normal levels. Highly interesting correlations between the psychic state of patients and their urinary excretion of methoxyhydroxyphenylglycol have been found by SCHILD-KRAUT[50]: following electroconvulsive therapy, as well as during recovery from the abuse of amphetamines, the excretion of methoxyhydroxyphenylglycol increased *pari passu* with the improvement in the patients' depression. But, since the quantity of methoxyhydroxyphenylglycol produced is also influenced by the patient's physical activity [F. K. GOODWIN (unpublished results)], these findings, too, must be interpreted with caution.

The noradrenaline hypothesis postulates that in manic states increased quantities of noradrenaline become available at the receptor sites. The question as to what happens during the so-called "switch process", i.e. during the period of transition from a depressive to a manic phase, has recently been comprehensively investigated by BUNNEY et al.[12,14]. In "longitudinal" studies an increase in the urinary concentration of noradrenaline has already been found to occur on the day preceding the onset of mania, whereas no changes were detected in the concentrations of dopamine, methoxyhydroxyphenylglycol, or 5-hydroxyindole-acetic acid measured in the urine. Since the noradrenaline level already undergoes a rise before the outbreak of mania, it is certain that this rise cannot be attributable to the increase in motor activity with which manic states are associated. Of major importance in this connection are also the investigations reported by TISSOT and GEISSBUHLER[56] who, when they analysed the arteriovenous difference in the brain, found that a higher consumption of labelled dopa occurred in manic states than in the depressive phase. These findings, coupled with the results yielded by analysis of the methoxyhydroxyphenylglycol levels in the C.S.F. of manic patients (BUNNEY et al.[12,14]; WILK et al.[58]) reveal that mania is associated with an enhanced catecholamine turnover.

That increased quantities of noradrenaline and normetadrenaline are excreted in hypomanic, as opposed to normothymic and depressive, phases was already reported by GREENSPAN et al.[27] in 1969. From their findings these authors conclude that the elevated output of noradrenaline and normetadrenaline is due to heightened activity on the part of the peripheral sympathetic nervous system and the adrenal medulla. In view of the fact that during the "switch process" no increase in the methoxyhydroxyphenylglycol values was found (BUNNEY et al.[12,14]), and that the noradrenaline recovered in the urine originates mainly from the peripheral regions of the body, the rise occurring in the urinary excretion of noradrenaline on the day before the onset of mania is presumably likewise related to an activation of the peripheral sympathetic nervous system. Also of considerable interest in this context are findings relating to the excretion of cyclic adenosine monophosphate in the presence of depression and mania. It is precisely because cyclic adenosine monophosphate is known to have close connections with noradrenaline metabolism in the nervous system, and also because it is involved in the regulation of other central and peripheral mechanisms, that this nucleotide has been so intensively studied. The excretion of cyclic adenosine monophosphate is highest in manic patients and lowest in depressive patients (for details, including further literature, see PAUL et al.[44]). Here once again, however, the interpretation of these findings is far from easy.

Peripheral factors and blood analyses

In recent years the question has repeatedly been raised as to the extent to which peripheral factors may influence the metabolism of serotonin and noradrenaline in the brain, thereby possibly provoking the onset of a depressive phase. In the light of results he obtained in animal experiments, CURZON[23] postulates that less serotonin is synthesised in the brains of depressive patients owing to activation of tryptophan-pyrrolase by the pituitary-adrenocortical system. In the presence of enhanced tryptophan-pyrrolase activity, more tryptophan becomes broken down into kynurenine, with the result that the tryptophan concentration in the body diminishes. Since tryptophan-hydroxylase in the brain is governed by the Michaelis constant, the cerebral synthesis of serotonin depends upon the concentration of tryptophan in the brain (JÉQUIER et al.[29,30]; McGEER et al.[41]). It is thus quite possible that peripheral factors affecting the tryptophan levels may exert a considerable influence on serotonin metabolism in the brain. Only recently, TAGLIAMONTE et al.[53,54] demonstrated that, for example, lithium salts and monamine-oxidase inhibitors, as well as electroconvulsive therapy [G. L. GESSA (personal communication)], step up the metabolism of serotonin by raising the tryptophan content in the brain. Further research will have to be undertaken, however, in order to determine to what extent this mechanism is responsible for the antidepressant activity of monamine-oxidase inhibitors and electroconvulsive therapy and for the prophylactic effect of lithium salts. No differences have so far been found in the plasma tryptophan concentrations in depressive patients as compared with controls (BIRKMAYER and LINAUER[7]), but it must be pointed out that the plasma concentrations do not necessarily provide any indication of the tryptophan levels in the brain (TAGLIAMONTE et al.[53,54]). Moreover, the circadian plasma tryptophan concentrations in depressive patients have not yet been investigated; that it would be desirable to do this is suggested by the following observation. When we measured the fasting plasma levels of tyrosine in the morning, we—in contrast to BIRKMAYER and LINAUER[7]— found no significant difference between patients suffering from endogenous depression and other groups of cases. It was not until we investigated the circadian rhythm of the plasma tyrosine concentrations that we were able to discern significant differences between patients with endogenous depression on the one hand and neurotic depressives, schizophrenics, and healthy controls on the other (BENKERT et al.[4, 5]). Changes in the diurnal rhythm of the tyrosine levels such as occur in the presence of endogenous depression can also be observed in manic phases, as well as during periods of remission; they are not affected either by treatment with tricyclic thymoleptics or by long-term lithium medication (CROMBACH et al.[22]). Certain parallels would thus seem to exist between the circadian plasma tyrosine levels and the 5-hydroxyindole-acetic acid concentrations in the C.S.F., which, as already mentioned, are likewise independent of the depressive phase (COPPEN et al.[18]). Whether, on the basis of these findings, it may be possible to begin tentatively analysing the biochemistry of pre-morbid depressive personality structures, is a question which only further investigations can answer.

The reason for the difference in the diurnal rhythm in patients suffering from endogenous depression is as yet unknown, but the possibility that it may be due to an hormonally controlled activation of enzymes in the periphery is one which should be considered. In view of the fact that the Michaelis constant governs tyrosine-hydroxylase, the change in the plasma tyrosine rhythm does not in our opinion have any influence on catecholamine synthesis in the brain.

Administration of tryptophan and dopa

In order to determine whether depression is associated with a deficiency of serotonin or catecholamines, clinical investigations have also been carried out with the precursors of these neurohormones in depressive patients. It was found that tryptophan—a precursor of serotonin—potentiates the antidepressant effect of monamine-oxidase inhibitors (COPPEN et al.[20]; PARE[43]); and it has also been reported that, when administered alone to depressive patients, tryptophan is just as effective as electroconvulsive therapy (COPPEN et al.[21]). Other studies, however, failed to confirm that tryptophan and electroconvulsive therapy are equally effective (CARROLL et al.[16]; BOWERS[9]; BUNNEY et al.[12,14]).

Clinical research has also been undertaken with L-dopa, which is a catecholamine precursor (KLERMAN et al.[31]; TURNER and MERLIS[57]; INGVARSSON[28]; MATUSSEK et al.[39, 40]; GOODWIN et al.[26]; MALITZ and KANZLER[36]). The results thus far obtained in these studies, in which L-dopa was also given in combination with monamine-oxidase and decarboxylase inhibitors, can be summarised as follows: even in patients suffering from retarded depression, antidepressant therapy with L-dopa elicits good responses only in a few cases.

Though treatment with L-dopa often exerts an activating effect on depressed patients, it usually fails to brighten their mood. In cases of bipolar depression, dopa may also provoke manic states. Experiments on animals have shown that, in response to doses of dopa, a particularly marked increase occurs in the supply of dopamine to the brain [BENKERT et al.[3, 6] (further literature is contained in these papers)]—a finding which incidentally would account for the success of dopa in the treatment of parkinsonism. On the other hand, it is very questionable whether the administration of dopa also produces a notable increase in the levels of physiologically active noradrenaline present in the brain (for a further discussion of this topic, including details of relevant literature, see MATUSSEK[38]). Additional clinical as well as animal-experimental studies will be required in order to provide for a fuller understanding of the processes by which dopamine becomes converted in the brain to noradrenaline. It is conceivable that an activation of the enzymes involved in the biosynthesis of noradrenaline—an activation similar to that occurring under stress (KVETŇANSKÝ et al.[32]; THIERRY et al.[55])—may be one of the main factors responsible for the antidepressant effect which the new method of treatment based on deprival of sleep has been found to exert. From the investigations which have so far been carried out with dopa it may at all events be concluded that a deficiency of dopamine in the brain can virtually be excluded as a cause of depression, because, if the depression were indeed due to lack of dopamine, then treatment with dopa would—as in cases of parkinsonism—prove more effective. Consequently, it would now seem preferable to abandon the so-called catecholamine hypothesis in favour of a more restricted noradrenaline hypothesis—an hypothesis, however, which still remains to be verified or disproved.

Summary

1. The quantity of 5-hydroxyindole-acetic acid present in the nervous system of depressive and manic patients is smaller than in the case of mentally healthy controls, i.e. such patients are suffering from a functional deficiency of 5-hydroxytryptamine, although—according to findings obtained in initial studies—this deficiency is independent of the phase in which the patient happens to be. To what extent the deficiency in 5-hydroxytryptamine metabolism in the nervous system has to be corrected by various measures (pharmacotherapy and electroconvulsive treatment) in order to achieve an antidepressant effect, has not yet been fully clarified.

2. Evidence has been found that, in the depressive phase and in states of depression following the abuse of amphetamines, the catecholamine turnover in general and the noradrenaline turnover in particular are reduced. It cannot at present be stated with certainty, however, whether the decrease in the noradrenaline turnover is of peripheral or central origin, or to what degree motor activity exerts an influence on the findings obtained in the depressive and in the normothymic state.

3. During the manic phase the catecholamine turnover is increased. The fact that administration of dopa is capable of provoking manic phases also points to the existence of close correlations between the catecholamines and mania.

4. Peripheral factors, such as hormones and certain enzyme systems, are variously affected in depression, but no proof of any causal connection between these factors and depression has yet been forthcoming.

Although considerable progress has been made in the field of biochemical research on depression, thanks to which a number of important questions concerned with methodology in particular have been clarified, we are still far from having found a biochemical solution to the problem of depression. Interpretation of the sometimes conflicting results of urinalyses and C.S.F. analyses continues to present great difficulties. The causes responsible for some of the metabolic disorders whose occurrence in depression has been postulated are also still awaiting experimental confirmation. Little or nothing is yet known about many of the biochemical reactions taking place in the normal nervous system, and the same applies particularly to the regulation of the cyclic processes which play such an important role in depression.

More extensive research efforts, which it is hoped will prove more rewarding, will have to be made before the serotonin and noradrenaline hypotheses that sound so simple and plausible can be confirmed or refuted.

References

1 ASHCROFT, G.W., CRAWFORD, T.B.B., ECCLESTON, D., SHARMAN, D.F., MAC-DOUGALL, E.J., STANTON, J.B., BINNS, J.K.: 5-Hydroxyindole compounds in the cerebrospinal fluid of patients with psychiatric or neurological diseases. Lancet *ii*, 1049 (1966)

2 ASHCROFT, G.W., CUNDALL, R.L., ECCLESTON, D., MURRAY, L.G., PULLAR, I.A.: Changes in the glycol metabolites of noradrenaline in affective illness. Vth World Congr. Psychiat., Mexico 1971; Abstr., p. 189 (Prensa méd. mex., Mexico 1971)

3 BENKERT, O., GLUBA, H., MATUSSEK, N.: Dopamine, norepinephrine and 5-hydroxytryptamine in relation to motor activity, fighting and mounting behavior. I. L-Dopa and DL-threo-dihydroxyphenylserine in combination with Ro 4-4602, pargyline and reserpine. Neuropharmacology (printing)

4 BENKERT, O., MATUSSEK, N.: Change in tyrosine level in affective disorders. Proc. VIIth int. Congr. Coll. int. neuro-psycho-pharmacol. (C.I.N.P.), Prague 1970 (printing)

5 BENKERT, O., RENZ, A., MARANO, C., MATUSSEK, N.: Altered tyrosine daytime plasma levels in endogenous depressive patients. Arch. gen. Psychiat. *25*, 359 (1971)

6 BENKERT, O., RENZ, A., MATUSSEK, N.: Dopamine, norepinephrine and 5-hydroxytryptamine in relation to motor activity, fighting and mounting behavior. II. L-Dopa and DL-threo-dihydroxyphenylserine in combination with Ro 4-4602 and parachlorphenylalanine. Neuropharmacology (printing)

7 BIRKMAYER, W., LINAUER, W.: Störung des Tyrosin- und Tryptophanmetabolismus bei Depression. Arch. Psychiat. Nervenkr. *213*, 377 (1970)

8 BOURNE, H.R., BUNNEY, W.E., Jr., COLBURN, R.W., DAVIS, J.M., DAVIS, J.N., SHAW, D.M., COPPEN, A.J.: Noradrenaline, 5-hydroxytryptamine, and 5-hydroxyindoleacetic acid in hindbrains of suicidal patients. Lancet *ii*, 805 (1968)

9 BOWERS, M.B., Jr.: Cerebrospinal fluid 5-hydroxyindoles and behavior after L-tryptophan and pyridoxine administration to psychiatric patients. Neuropharmacology *9*, 599 (1970)

10 BOWERS, M.B., Jr., HENINGER, G.R., GERBODE, F.: Cerebrospinal fluid 5-hydoxyindoleacetic acid and homovanillic acid in psychiatric patients. Int. J. Neuropharmacol. *8*, 255 (1969)

11 BULAT, M., ŽIVKOVIĆ, B.: Origin of 5-hydroxyindoleacetic acid in the spinal fluid. Science *173*, 738 (1971)

12 BUNNEY, W.E., Jr., BRODIE, H.K.H., MURPHY, D.L., GOODWIN, F.K.: Studies of alpha-methyl-para-tyrosine, L-dopa, and L-tryptophan in depression and mania. Amer. J. Psychiat. *127*, 872 (1971)

13 BUNNEY, W.E., Jr., DAVIS, J.M.: Norepinephrine in depressive reactions. Arch. gen. Psychiat. *13*, 483 (1965)

21

14 BUNNEY, W. E., Jr., GORDON, E. K., GOODWIN, F. K., MURPHY, D. L.: Psycho-
biology of mania. Amer. psychiat. Ass., Washington 1971

15 BUNNEY, W. E., Jr., MURPHY, D. L., GOODWIN, F. K., BORGE, G. F.: The switch
process from depression to mania: relationship to drugs which alter brain amines.
Lancet i, 1022 (1970)

16 CARROLL, B. J., MOWBRAY, R. M., DAVIES, B.: Sequential comparison of L-
tryptophan with E.C.T. in severe depression. Lancet i, 967 (1970)

17 CHASE, T. N., BREESE, G. R., GORDON, E. K., KOPIN, I. J.: Catecholamine metabolism in the dog: comparison of intravenously and intraventricularly administered (^{14}C)dopamine and (^{3}H)norepinephrine. J. Neurochem. 18, 135 (1971)

18 COPPEN, A., PRANGE, A. J., WHYBROW, P. C., NOGUERA, R.: Abnormalities of
indoleamines in affective disorders. Arch. gen. Psychiat. (printing)

19 COPPEN, A., SHAW, D. M.: Biochemical aspects of affective disorders. Pharmakopsychiat. Neuro-Psychopharmakol. 3, 36 (1970)

20 COPPEN, A., SHAW, D. M., FARRELL, J. P.: Potentiation of the antidepressive
effect of a monoamine-oxidase inhibitor by tryptophan. Lancet i, 79 (1963)

21 COPPEN, A., SHAW, D. M., HERZBERG, B., MAGGS, R.: Tryptophan in the treatment of depression. Lancet ii, 1178 (1967)

22 CROMBACH, G., BERTHOLD, A., BENKERT, O., MATUSSEK, N.: Further studies regarding altered tyrosine plasma level in endogenous depressive patients. Vth
World Congr. Psychiat., Mexico 1971

23 CURZON, G.: A relationship between brain serotonin and adrenocortical secretion
and its possible significance in endogenous depression. Pharmakopsychiat.
Neuro-Psychopharmakol. 2, 234 (1969)

24 DENCKER, S. J., MALM, U., ROOS, B.-E., WERDINIUS, B.: Acid monoamine metabolites of cerebrospinal fluid in mental depression and mania. J. Neurochem. 13,
1545 (1966)

25 EVERETT, G. M., TOMAN, J. E. P.: Mode of action of Rauwolfia alkaloids and
motor activity. In Masserman, J. H. (Editor): Biological psychiatry, Vol. I, p. 75
(Grune & Stratton, New York/London 1959)

26 GOODWIN, F. K., BRODIE, H. K. H., MURPHY, D. L., BUNNEY, W. E., Jr.: Administration of a peripheral decarboxylase inhibitor with L-dopa to depressed
patients. Lancet i, 908 (1970)

27 GREENSPAN, K., SCHILDKRAUT, J. J., GORDON, E. K., LEVY, B., DURELL, J.:
Catecholamine metabolism in affective disorders. Arch. gen. Psychiat. 21, 710
(1969)

28 INGVARSSON, C. G.: Orientierende klinische Versuche zur Wirkung des Dioxy-
phenylalanins (l-Dopa) bei endogener Depression. Arzneimittel-Forsch. 15, 849
(1965)

29 JÉQUIER, E., LOVENBERG, W., SJOERDSMA, A.: Tryptophan hydroxylase inhibition:
the mechanism by which p-chlorophenylalanine depletes rat brain serotonin.
Molec. Pharmacol. 3, 274 (1967)

30 JÉQUIER, E., ROBINSON, D. S., LOVENBERG, W., SJOERDSMA, A.: Further studies
on tryptophan hydroxylase in rat brainstem and beef pineal. Biochem. Pharmacol. 18, 1071 (1969)

31 KLERMAN, G. L., SCHILDKRAUT, J. J., HASENBUSH, L. L., GREENBLATT, M.,
FRIEND, D. G.: Clinical experience with dihydroxyphenylalanine (DOPA) in
depression. J. psychiat. Res. 1, 289 (1963)

32 KVETŇANSKÝ, R., WEISE, V. K., KOPIN, I. J.: Elevation of adrenal tyrosine hydroxylase and phenylethanolamine-N-methyl transferase by repeated immobili-
zation of rats. Endocrinology 87, 744 (1970)

33 LAPIN, I. P., OXENKRUG, G. F.: Intensification of the central serotoninergic
processes as a possible determinant of the thymoleptic effect. Lancet i, 132 (1969)

34 MAAS, J. W., DEKIRMENJIAN, H., FAWCETT, J.: Catecholamine metabolism, depression and stress. Nature (Lond.) 230, 330 (1971)

35 MAAS, J.W., FAWCETT, J., DEKIRMENJIAN, H.: 3-Methoxy-4-hydroxy phenyl-glycol (MHPG) excretion in depressive states. Arch. gen. Psychiat. *19*, 129 (1968)

36 MALITZ, S., KANZLER, M.: L-Dopa in depression. In Malitz, S. (Editor): L-Dopa and behavior (Raven Press, New York; in preparation)

37 MATUSSEK, N.: Neurobiologie und Depression. Med. Mschr. *20*, 109 (1066)

38 MATUSSEK, N.: L-Dopa treatment of depression, loc. cit.[4]

39 MATUSSEK, N., BENKERT, O., SCHNEIDER, K., OTTEN, H., POHLMEIER, H.: Wirkung eines Decarboxylasehemmers (Ro 4-4602) in Kombination mit L-Dopa auf gehemmte Depressionen. Arzneimittel-Forsch. *20*, 934 (1970)

40 MATUSSEK, N., POHLMEIER, H., RÜTHER, E.: Die Wirkung von Dopa auf gehemmte Depressionen. Klin. Wschr. *44*, 727 (1966)

41 MCGEER, E.G., PEETERS, G.A.V., MCGEER, P.L.: Inhibition of rat brain tryptophan hydroxylase by 6-halotryptophans. Life Sci. *7/II*, 605 (1968)

42 OLSSON, R., ROOS, B.-E.: Concentrations of 5-hydroxyindoleacetic acid and homovanillic acid in the cerebrospinal fluid after treatment with probenecid in patients with Parkinson's disease. Nature (Lond.) *219*, 502 (1968)

43 PARE, C.M.B.: Potentiation of monoamine-oxidase inhibitors by tryptophan. Lancet *ii*, 527 (1963)

44 PAUL, M.I., CRAMER, H., GOODWIN, F.K.: Urinary cyclic AMP excretion in depression and mania. Arch. gen. Psychiat. *24*, 327 (1971)

45 PFLUG, B., TÖLLE, R.: Therapie endogener Depressionen durch Schlafentzug. Nervenarzt *42*, 117 (1971)

46 PRAAG, H.M. VAN: Antidepressants, catecholamines and 5-hydroxyindoles. Trends towards a more specific research in the field of antidepressants. Psychiat. Neurol. Neurochir. (Amst.) *70*, 219 (1967)

47 PRAAG, H.M. VAN, KORF, J.: Retarded depression and the dopamine metabolism. Psychopharmacologia (Berl.) *19*, 199 (1971)

48 PRAAG, H.M. VAN, KORF, J., PUITE, J.: 5-Hydroxyindoleacetic acid levels in the cerebrospinal fluid of depressive patients treated with probenecid. Nature (Lond.) *225*, 1259 (1970)

49 SCHILDKRAUT, J.J.: The catecholamine hypothesis of affective disorders: a review of supporting evidence. Amer. J. Psychiat. *122*, 509 (1965)

50 SCHILDKRAUT, J.J.: Norepinephrine metabolism in affective disorders: recent clinical studies, loc. cit.[2], p. 80

51 SCHILDKRAUT, J.J., KETY, S.S.: Biogenic amines and emotion. Science *156*, 21 (1967)

52 SJÖSTRÖM, R., ROOS, B.-E.: Measurement of 5-HIAA and HVA in manic depressive patients after probenecid application, loc. cit.[4]

53 TAGLIAMONTE, A., TAGLIAMONTE, P., PEREZ-CRUET, J., GESSA, G.L.: Increase of brain tryptophan caused by drugs which stimulate serotonin synthesis. Nature new Biol. (Lond.) *229*, 125 (1971)

54 TAGLIAMONTE, A., TAGLIAMONTE, P., PEREZ-CRUET, J., STERN, S., GESSA, G.L.: Effect of psychotropic drugs on tryptophan concentration in the rat brain. J. Pharmacol. exp. Ther. *177*, 475 (1971)

55 THIERRY, A.M., BLANC, G., GLOWINSKI, J.: Effect of stress on the disposition of catecholamines localized in various intraneuronal storage forms in the brain stem of the rat. J. Neurochem. *18*, 449 (1971)

56 TISSOT, R., GEISSBUHLER, F.: Valeur de quelques troubles du métabolisme des mono-amines observés dans les syndromes dépressifs et maniaques, loc. cit.[2], p. 79

57 TURNER, W.J., MERLIS, S.: A clinical trial of pargyline and DOPA in psychotic subjects. Dis. nerv. Syst. *25*, 538 (1964)

58 WILK, S., SHOPSIN, B., GERSHON, S.: Cerebrospinal fluid levels of MHPG in affective disorders: a test of the catecholamine hypothesis. Nature (Lond.) (printing)

Discussion

A. COPPEN: I should like to congratulate Dr. MATUSSEK on the extremely lucid outline he has given of a very difficult subject. May I perhaps just enlarge on one or two points he made.

There are now three brain studies which suggest that in depression some deficiency in 5-hydroxytryptamine or 5-hydroxyindole-acetic acid exists. Autopsy studies in which brain tissue has been quickly assayed after obtaining the specimen show a significantly lower concentration of 5-hydroxytryptamine in the brains of depressed subjects as compared with controls. SHAW and his colleagues* from our unit indicated that there was a significant lowering of the 5-hydroxytryptamine concentrations in the case of depressed subjects whose brains were assayed two to three days after death. When, as mentioned by Dr. MATUSSEK in his paper, the brains are stored longer**, such differences between the amine concentrations are no longer found; but there is still a difference in the metabolite 5-hydroxyindole-acetic acid, the concentration of which is lower in the brains of depressed suicides. I think these results are borne out in a paper by PARE et al.*** from London; here again, the brains were assayed very soon after death, and significantly lower brain 5-hydroxytryptamine levels were found in suicides, whereas there were no differences in brain noradrenaline levels. In the small number of specimens in which PARE et al. assayed 5-hydroxyindole-acetic acid, a tendency towards lower concentrations was likewise observed in suicides. So I think that, taken together, these three investigations do afford definite evidence of a decrease in brain 5-hydroxytryptamine.

Summarised in Table 1 are the results of our studies on the concentrations of 5-hydroxyindole-acetic acid in cerebrospinal fluid. Here we have demonstrated—and I think several other groups have found the same thing—that there is a lowering of the C.S.F. 5-hydroxyindole-acetic acid levels both in depression and in mania. As Dr. MATUSSEK said, no change in these levels occurs with clinical recovery. It would therefore seem that the anomaly affecting brain hydroxytryptamine does not vary in the course of the illness, but is a consistently present predisposing factor. Nevertheless, I think there is evidence that tryptophan combined with a monamine-oxidase inhibitor is a better type of treatment than the use of a monamine-oxidase inhibitor alone—which indicates that increasing brain 5-hydroxytryptamine reduces the symptoms of a depressive illness****. The role of tryptophan by itself still seems to be debatable at the moment, but in due course we hope to have further results from other investigators which may shed light on this point.

To conclude these few brief remarks, I should like to show another slide (Table 2), which presents what I consider to be one of the most interesting observations we have made in the last few years. This slide relates to a group of patients suffering from re-

---

* SHAW, D. M., CAMPS, F. E., ECCLESTON, E. G.: 5-Hydroxytryptamine in the hindbrain of depressive suicides. Brit. J. Psychiat. *113*, 1407 (1967)

** BOURNE, H. R., BUNNEY, W. E., Jr., COLBURN, R. W., DAVIS, J. M., DAVIS, J. N., SHAW, D. M., COPPEN, A. J.: Noradrenaline, 5-hydroxytryptamine, and 5-hydroxyindoleacetic acid in hindbrains of suicidal patients. Lancet *ii*, 805 (1968)

*** PARE, C. M. B., YEUNG, D. P. H., PRICE, K., STACEY, R. S.: 5-Hydroxytryptamine, noradrenaline, and dopamine in brainstem, hypothalamus, and caudate nucleus of controls and of patients committing suicide by coal-gas poisoning. Lancet *ii*, 133 (1969)

**** COPPEN, A., SHAW, D. M., FARRELL, J. P.: Potentiation of the antidepressive effect of a monoamine-oxidase inhibitor by tryptophan. Lancet *i*, 79 (1963)

PARE, C. M. B.: Potentiation of monoamine-oxidase inhibitors by tryptophan. Lancet *ii*, 527 (1963)

GLASSMAN, A. H., PLATMAN, S. R.: Potentiation of a monoamine oxidase inhibitor by tryptophan. J. psychiat. Res. *7*, 83 (1970)

Table 1. Lumbar C.S.F. 5-hydroxyindole-acetic acid concentration (ng./ml.) in controls and in patients with affective disorders.

	Groups			
	Control	Depressive	Manic	Recovered depressive
N	20	31	18	8
Mean	42.3	19.8*	19.7*	19.9*
S.D.	14.2	8.5	6.0	7.2

* Difference from control: $P < 0.001$

Table 2. Affective illness during trial.

Group	N	% time as in-patient	% time with out-patient episode	
All lithium	28	4.9*	7.0*	11.9*
All placebo	37	26.8	19.2	46.0
Unipolar, lithium	11	1.0	3.7**	4.7**
Unipolar, placebo	15	8.7	21.6	30.3
Bipolar, lithium	17	7.5*	9.2***	16.7*
Bipolar, placebo	22	39.2	17.5	56.7

Lithium superior to placebo at   *$P < 0.001$
   **$P < 0.01$
   ***$P < 0.05$

current depression, whom we followed up over a period of two and a quarter years*. Some of these patients were given lithium during this time, and some received a placebo instead of lithium. In every other respect they could have any further treatment that was considered necessary. We found that giving lithium, in fact, reduced the morbidity to about one-fifth—that is, it had a very profound effect on the course of the affective disorder. What is more, this response was not paralleled by any other type of treatment. Now, as Dr. MATUSSEK suggested, there might be some link between this observation and serotonin metabolism, because evidence has now been obtained by two groups working independently of each other in the United States that lithium, given in therapeutic doses, does indeed increase the serotonin synthesis rate by about 20%, which is just about the degree of deficiency that one is finding in depressives. So, perhaps, one of the explanations for the effects of lithium might be that it acts on the biogenic amines. In my view, the mode of action of lithium poses at all events one

* COPPEN, A., NOGUERA, R., BAILEY, J., BURNS, B. H., SWANI, M. S., HARE, E. H., GARDNER, R., MAGGS, R.: Prophylactic lithium in affective disorders. Lancet ii, 275 (1971)

of the most challenging problems and offers one of the most intriguing opportunities for those of us who are interested in the biological aspects of depression.

I. Sano: I felt that it was particularly important to test the l-form of 5-hydroxytryptophan in cases of depression, but it was not until November 1970 that I had sufficient quantities of this substance available for the purpose. The results I obtained in 207 patients, whom I observed for at least five weeks, were reported in four publications. The response displayed by manic-depressive patients undergoing a depressive phase was so surprisingly good that I could hardly believe it. Dramatic improvements set in within only a few days, most often on the third day. The depressive phase lifted completely, or almost completely, within a week. Close on 90% of the patients treated with l-5-hydroxytryptophan showed a very good response to the medication. It is highly unlikely that this effect could have been due to the suggestibility of the patients, because depressive subjects do not as a rule respond to psychotherapy. A double-blind trial was not carried out because of the risk of suicide. One striking feature of these results was that manic episodes—which, in our experience, quite often occur after the depressive phase has lifted—were not observed following treatment with l-5-hydroxytryptophan.

Endogenous depression seems to be associated with a periodical reduction in the biosynthesis of serotonin in the brainstem. This reduction can rapidly be corrected by administering small amounts of l-5-hydroxytryptophan. Depression would thus appear to be due basically to a metabolic defect.

N. Matussek: It has been reported by Kline that dl-5-hydroxytryptophan, at least, does not exert a good antidepressant effect. Physiologically, 5-hydroxytryptophan is not involved in serotonin metabolism in the brain to the same extent as tryptophan. The rate of serotonin synthesis is determined by hydroxylase, which is present only in serotoninergic neurones, and the turnover of this enzyme is governed by the amount of tryptophan in the brain. 5-Hydroxytryptophan also influences the other neurone systems which make use of decarboxylase, an enzyme that is less specifically distributed. I should like to refer once again to the publications by Tagliamonte et al. which I mentioned in my paper and in which it is reported that serotonin metabolism was accelerated not only during medication with lithium and monamine-oxidase inhibitors but also in response to electroconvulsive therapy. In my opinion, further studies must be undertaken in this direction in order to find out whether an increase in serotonin metabolism plays a decisive role in the various forms of antidepressant therapy. I believe that, even in depressive patients in whom the risk of suicide has to be taken into account, double-blind studies can still be conducted without any misgivings of an ethical nature, provided the control group receives another antidepressant.

J. Angst: May I comment briefly on the question of tryptophan therapy. Two years ago we carried out an open trial in which we administered daily dosages of 3.0 g. l-tryptophan to hospitalised depressive patients; the results were not really very impressive. We then undertook a double-blind study involving three groups of patients: 10 patients, serving as controls, were given 150 mg. imipramine daily, 10 patients received combined treatment with amitriptyline and l-tryptophan, and a third group was given isocarboxazid, i.e. a monamine-oxidase inhibitor, together with l-tryptophan. The Hamilton scale was employed as one of the means of assessing the effect of the 20-day period of treatment. Easily the best results were obtained in the imipramine group. Not far behind came, to our surprise, the isocarboxazid/l-tryptophan group; we had expected lower values in this group. The worst results—i.e. values not much higher than those encountered with placebo—were recorded in the patients treated with a combination of amitriptyline and l-tryptophan. It should, however, be pointed out that we had restricted the dosage of amitriptyline to 75 mg. daily, which is a very low dose for hospitalised patients.

This trial showed, then, that combined treatment with a monamine-oxidase inhibitor and l-tryptophan exerts a good effect, but is not quite so beneficial as imipramine.

W. BIRKMAYER: In 1961, immediately after having obtained positive results with L-dopa in parkinsonian patients, we gave this drug a trial in cases of endogenous depression. Neither L-dopa nor combined treatment with L-dopa and a monamine-oxidase inhibitor produced anything more than a non-specific increase in drive, an effect already mentioned by Dr. MATUSSEK. Today we know that L-dopa is of no value in the treatment of depression. I expect you are familiar with the published reviews indicating that two out of 200 cases showed a good response. The good response in these two cases, however, is due to mere chance, and must be regarded in exactly the same light as the alleged "sexually stimulating effect" of L-dopa. Depressive mood virtually never lifts in response to L-dopa.

Genetic aspects of depression

by J. ANGST*

I. Causes of depressive diseases

In the pathogenesis of depressive syndromes whole clusters of causes are usually involved. In this connection, discussion tends to centre most frequently upon the causes responsible for reactive, neurotic, and endogenous forms of depression. It is therefore with this gamut of depressive diseases that the following review will be concerned.

Our theoretical concept of the causes underlying them postulates that in every case of depressive disease a role is played by the patient's constitution itself as well as by environmental factors of varying specificity. It is thus assumed that symptom-provoking environmental factors in the broadest sense of the term participate in the causation of all affective psychoses (e.g. endogenous depression); from this it follows that there is no such thing as a purely endogenous disease to the manifestation of which the environment makes no contribution. Conversely, it is postulated that, in cases of reactive, neurotic, or exhaustion depression, constitutional factors within the wider meaning of the term also serve as a contributory element—in addition, of course, to the main causes in the form of psychoreactive upheavals. *With regard to their specificity, constitutional and environmental factors seem to be mutually complementary.* Thus, the more specifically a reactive depression, for example, can be ascribed to environmental factors, the more unspecific the contribution made by the patient's constitution; conversely, the greater the extent to which constitutional factors are demonstrably and specifically inculpated in the causation of endogenous depression, the more unspecific the role played by environmental factors.

It is against the background of this hypothesis that the following observations on the genetic aspects of depressive diseases should be considered.

II. Aetiological findings in psychoreactive forms of depression

1. Environment

There exist numerous well-known descriptions of the obvious connections existing between traumatic experiences and psychoreactive forms of depression. And it is indeed true that, when assessed in terms of their content, distressing experiences having their origin in the patient's environment can be regarded as more or less specific causes for this type of depression; examples of such experiences may include deprival of interpersonal relationships (resulting from the death of a loved one, from separation, or from loneliness), as well as radical

28   * Psychiatrische Universitätsklinik, Zurich, Switzerland.

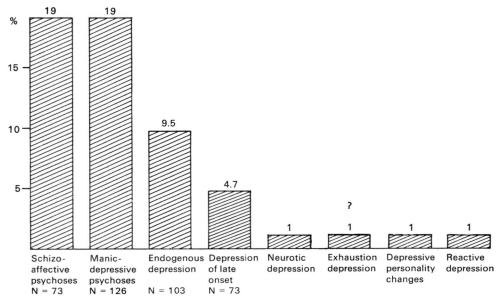

Fig. 1. Risk of depressive psychoses and suicide in the parents and siblings of patients belonging to various diagnostic categories.

changes at the patient's place of work, in his living conditions, in his family life, or in his other personal contacts. Probably the most detailed presentation of the long catalogue of such possible causes is that given by Brown and Birley[3].

2. Constitution

Investigations into the families of patients suffering from *psychoreactive depression* (i.e. reactive depression, neurotic depression, or exhaustion depression) have yielded negative findings, inasmuch as no abnormally high incidence of depressive diseases was apparent among other members of the family (cf. Figure 1). In the case of exhaustion depression, however, the picture has not yet been fully clarified from the familial angle. Although, in a total of 72 such families investigated, Martin[7] discovered only two with manic-depressive psychoses and eight with schizophrenia, he found six with suicide and 11 with depression of indeterminate aetiology. In other words, leaving aside the families with schizophrenia, there were nevertheless 19 in which evidence was found of affective diseases, including suicide.

From a study on psychoreactive depression in twins Shapiro[10] concluded that such distinctive personality traits as these twins exhibited tended to take the form, not so much of a disposition to depressive disease, but rather of other personality changes. Although he found no concordance with respect to reactive depression, he did observe quite an impressive degree of concordance with respect to disorders affecting the development of the personality, i.e. neuroses. *Thus, in depressive neuroses and reactive forms of depression in the broader sense of the*

29

term, it is possible to distinguish a constitutional tendency towards pathological personality changes, but no specific predisposition to depression.

III. Aetiological findings in affective psychoses

1. Environment

Despite all the attempts that have been made, using the same methods as for the study of psychoreactive depression, it has not yet been demonstrated on a convincing scale that equally specific environmental causes are also involved in the aetiology of *endogenous depression*. Though evidence can sometimes be found to suggest that an episode of endogenous depression has initially been triggered off by some upsetting experience, in the case of phasic, recurrent forms of depressive illness such traumatic experiences become less frequent and less relevant, with the result that the condition often assumes what appears to be a purely endogenous character.

2. Constitution

On the other hand, what the results of research have largely succeeded in proving is that hereditary factors do contribute to the causation of these particular forms of disease. The chief purpose of the following observations is to show that in such cases the patient's inherited predisposition is of a sufficiently specific nature to enable a more or less clear distinction to be drawn between three groups of diseases, i.e. endogenous depression*, manic-depressive psychoses, and schizo-affective disorders. What, then, are the genetic features which these affective psychoses share in common, and what are the differences between them?

a) *Genetic findings common to the three groups*

Common to all the three types of disease is the increased familial prevalence of affective disorders. Particularly frequent in each of the three groups is the occurrence of suicide, as well as reactive depression and endogenous forms of depression without manic episodes. One consistent finding is thus a whole gamut of variously diagnosed psychiatric conditions embracing all kinds of affective disorder. Where the three groups do differ, however, is in the severity of the familial taint with respect to the individual diagnostic categories.

b) *Depressive psychoses and suicides*

Reproduced in Figure 1 are the *global figures for the familial risk of depressive psychoses and suicide* among subjects of first-degree kinship, listed separately for the various diagnostic categories, i.e.: depression of late onset (involutional melancholia), endogenous depression, manic-depressive psychoses (bipolar psychoses), and schizo-affective disorders. Although a distinction is drawn here between endogenous (i.e. recurrent) depression and depression of late onset, this has been done merely for didactic and historical reasons, because in point of fact

---

* The term "endogenous depression" is applied here to recurrent forms of depression (also known as "periodic depression").

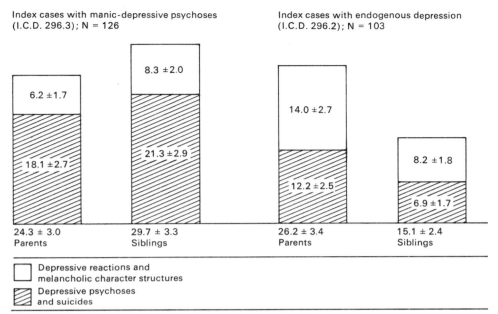

Index cases with manic-depressive psychoses
(I.C.D. 296.3); N = 126

Index cases with endogenous depression
(I.C.D. 296.2); N = 103

8.3 ±2.0

6.2 ±1.7

14.0 ±2.7

21.3 ±2.9

18.1 ±2.7

8.2 ±1.8

12.2 ±2.5

6.9 ±1.7

| 24.3 ± 3.0 | 29.7 ± 3.3 | 26.2 ± 3.4 | 15.1 ± 2.4 |
| Parents | Siblings | Parents | Siblings |

☐ Depressive reactions and
melancholic character structures

▨ Depressive psychoses
and suicides

Fig. 2. Risk (expressed in %) of depressive psychoses and suicide, as well as of depressive reactions and melancholic character structures, in the parents and siblings of patients with manic-depressive psychoses or endogenous depression. (I.C.D. = International Classification of Diseases, 1965 Revision, Vol. 1, W.H.O., Geneva 1967)

the two constitute a continuum passing from early, through middle, to late forms of purely depressive psychosis. In the forms of late onset an important role is played by environmental factors in promoting manifestations of the disease. As shown in Figure 1, it is in these late forms that the factor of heredity is least apparent; second in order of the degree of familial risk are the endogenous forms of depression; finally, the risk is greatest in the case of manic-depressive psychoses and schizo-affective diseases.

c) *Psychoreactive depression and depressive personality types*
Whether the morbidity in persons related to manic-depressive patients is indeed significantly higher than in those related to patients suffering from endogenous depression, is a question that remains to be examined. It is true that, as indicated by Figure 2, depressive psychoses occur far more frequently in the families of manic-depressives than in those of endogenous depressives. But, as further revealed by Figure 2, when *the morbidity figures for depressive reactions and melancholic character structures* are also taken into account, the risk is seen to be likewise fairly high among the relatives of endogenous depressives. Here, however, the tendency to depressive disorders manifests itself more frequently in the form of depressive reactions, depressive changes, and depressive personality traits than in the form of depressive psychoses, whereas in the families of manic depressives this is much less often the case, the incidence of psychoses being higher in these

31

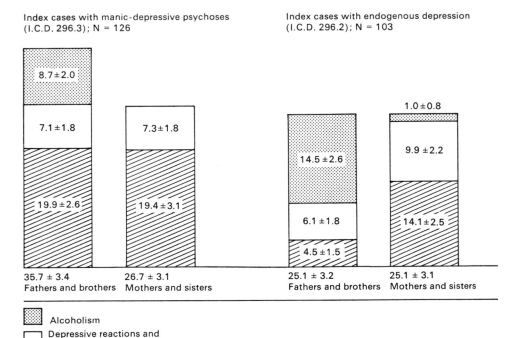

Index cases with manic-depressive psychoses
(I.C.D. 296.3); N = 126

Index cases with endogenous depression
(I.C.D. 296.2); N = 103

8.7±2.0

7.1±1.8   7.3±1.8

1.0±0.8

14.5±2.6   9.9±2.2

19.9±2.6   19.4±3.1

6.1±1.8   14.1±2.5

4.5±1.5

35.7 ± 3.4   26.7 ± 3.1   25.1 ± 3.2   25.1 ± 3.1
Fathers and brothers   Mothers and sisters   Fathers and brothers   Mothers and sisters

Alcoholism

Depressive reactions and
melancholic character structures

Depressive psychoses
and suicides

Fig. 3. Risk (expressed in %) of depressive psychoses and suicide, depressive reactions and melancholic character structures, and alcoholism in the parents and siblings (classified according to sex) of patients with manic-depressive psychoses or endogenous depression.

families. When the aforementioned milder types of depressive illness—i.e. depressive reactions, etc.—are taken into consideration, it thus appears that the morbidity in parents of endogenous depressives is just as high as in those of manic depressives! In the siblings, by contrast, a distinct difference is still found with respect to endogenous as compared with manic depression.

d) *Morbidity in terms of sex*

A far clearer distinction appears when the *morbidity risk for the two sexes* is compared in manic-depressive and endogenous depressive diseases. Indicated in Figure 3 is the morbidity risk in fathers and brothers as compared with mothers and sisters. An analysis confined to depressive psychoses and suicides fails to reveal any difference in the morbidity for the two sexes among members of the families of manic depressives. Among those of endogenous depressives, by contrast, a high incidence of depressive psychoses and suicides is particularly apparent in the females. This holds true regardless of whether the respective index cases are female or male. When the analysis is extended to include not only depressive psychoses and suicides but also depressive reactions and melancholic character structures, no alteration occurs in the proportions (Figure 3). In the case of manic-depressive psychoses, an equally high morbidity in male and female members of the family is still observed even when the whole gamut of depressive disorders—excluding alcoholism—is taken into account; in the case of endogenous forms of depression, on the other hand, the morbidity in the female members of the family then becomes considerably higher, i.e. more than twice as high as in the males. Another point worth noting is that in some 50% of cases the depressive disorders occurring in the families of endogenous depressives do not assume the proportions of a frank psychosis, whereas in the families of manic depressives the percentage of frank psychoses is much higher. *From the statistical material which has just been reviewed, it is clearly evident that endogenous depression—in contrast to manic-depressive diseases—is at least twice as frequent in women as in men.*

e) *Alcoholism*

WINOKUR et al.[11] were the first to point out that alcoholism is a particularly common finding in the fathers of women with endogenous depression as opposed to those with bipolar psychoses; these authors suggest that alcoholism, too, might perhaps be a manifestation of a depressive constitution. For this reason, Figure 3 also includes the incidence of alcoholism, which does in fact reveal a certain difference between the family patterns of manic depressives and endogenous depressives. Among the families of endogenous depressives, alcoholism (in the patient's father and/or brothers) accounts for a figure of no less than 14.5%, whereas the corresponding figure in the case of families of manic depressives is only 8.7%. Since—as in the general population too—it is men rather than women who usually suffer from alcoholism, in both diagnostic groups alcoholism makes a far bigger contribution to the overall morbidity figures in the male than in the female members of the families.

From this it can be concluded that, viewed globally, the familial morbidity figures in the case of both types of psychosis tend to become increasingly similar the broader the range of the diseases that are taken into account. It still seems doubtful, however, whether the alcoholism encountered in the families of endogenous depressives is indeed at least partly attributable to genetic factors, particularly since here various possible sources of error must be borne in mind and such questions considered as: Were the parents or siblings in the two diagnostic groups living during the same decades? Were differences in social status perhaps responsible for differences in drinking habits? Allowance must also be made for the fact that male members of the families of endogenous depressives, since they are less susceptible to affective disorders, may well show a fortuitously higher rate of alcoholism than those of manic depressives.

But even if alcoholism is left out of account, the findings obtained do seem to suggest that, by analogy with the approach advocated by ROSENTHAL[9] in the case of schizophrenia, a whole gamut of diagnoses also has to be taken into consideration as indicators of constitutional factors when carrying out genetic studies on depressive disorders. Investigations on twins of identical constitution, but with differing diagnoses, might prove particularly helpful in this connection.

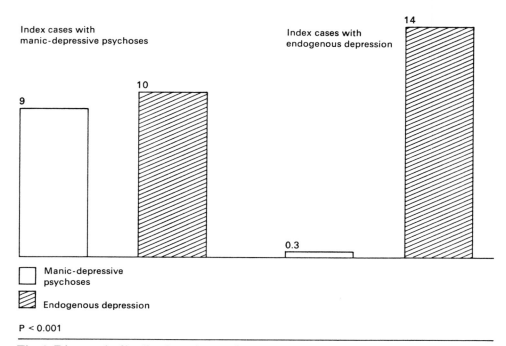

Index cases with
manic-depressive psychoses

Index cases with
endogenous depression

14

10

9

0.3

Manic-depressive
psychoses

Endogenous depression

P < 0.001

Fig. 4. Diagnostic distribution of secondary cases (expressed in %) among members of the families of index patients suffering from manic-depressive psychoses or endogenous depression.

f) *Diagnosis of secondary cases*

A further important criterion serving to distinguish endogenous forms of depression from manic-depressive psychoses is to be found in the *diagnostic distribution of secondary cases among members of the patient's family*. In the families of manic-depressive index cases the incidence of bipolar manic-depressive diseases amounts to 9%, whereas in the families of endogenous-depressive index cases it works out at only 0.3%—a figure which probably corresponds to the morbidity risk for bipolar manic-depressive illness in the average population. These findings show that an increased constitutional predisposition towards mania is encountered only in the families of manic-depressive index patients, but not in those of patients suffering from endogenous depression (Figure 4). Persons belonging to the families of endogenous depressives, in fact, have a morbidity risk for manic-depressive disease which, at 0.3%, does not differ from that of the average population. If the German concept of *"manisch-depressives Kranksein"* (i.e. "manic-depressive illness") were indeed a uniform entity embracing both unipolar and bipolar psychoses, then manic conditions and manic-depressive psychoses could be expected also to show a higher-than-normal incidence among members of the families of endogenous depressives; but this is not the case.

g) *Additional criteria*

Additional criteria for the differentiation of these two forms of disease include: manifestation of manic-depressive illness at an earlier age; disease characterised by a more severe clinical course; differences in the patient's pre-morbid personality; and perhaps also differences in the psychopathology of the condition. Recently it would seem that this differentiation, arrived at along clinical lines, has also proved of value in connection with basic somatic research on affective psychoses. DUNNER et al.[5], using the method of AXELROD and COHN[2], have succeeded in demonstrating reduced catechol-O-methyltransferase activity in the erythrocytes of women suffering from affective disorders. This reduction is even more clearly marked in women with endogenous depression than in those with manic depression. In contrast to what might have been expected in the light of clinical experience, patients suffering from pure forms of depression thus deviate more strongly from the norm than do those with bipolar disease. According to LANGE[6], endogenous depressives can frequently be identified among members of the average population on the basis of serological evidence (post-albumin), whereas this is not possible in the case of manic depressives. Finally, PERRIS[8] states that patients with bipolar diseases display a lower threshold for the flicker and fusion frequency, while BUCHSBAUM et al.[4] report that in such patients the evoked potentials are also stronger.

IV. Conclusions

All the above-mentioned studies show quite clearly how important it is to undertake thorough genetic investigations in the field of affective disorders. Genetic studies help to ensure a better classification of affective diseases; in this way, they not only enable sharper dividing lines to be drawn, but at some later stage they may perhaps also make it possible to subsume clinically differing forms of disease into broader categories of illnesses that are liable to present varying phenotypic manifestations. It is quite conceivable that, from the constitutional standpoint, at least some forms of so-called reactive or neurotic depression, for example, or certain types of exhaustion depression may be indistinguishable from endogenous psychoses. In this case, we should be confronted with a gamut of depressive diseases that are biologically of the same nature. In the psychopathological differentiation of depressive conditions we have now reached a point beyond which it is difficult to proceed any further; it may even be that such differentiation according to psychopathological criteria has resulted in far too great a variety of nosological classifications for conditions which are sometimes pathogenetically indistinguishable from one another. It will be the task of those engaged on clinico-genetic and biological research to introduce new criteria of classification based upon biological principles.

References

1 ANGST, J.: Zur Ätiologie und Nosologie endogener depressiver Psychosen (Springer, Berlin/Heidelberg/New York 1966; Monogr. Neurol. Psychiat. No. 112)
2 AXELROD, J., COHN, C.K.: Methyl transferase enzymes in red blood cells. J. Pharmacol. exp. Ther. (printing)

3 BROWN, G.W., BIRLEY, J.L.T.: Crises and life changes and the onset of schizophrenia, J. Hlth soc. Behav. *9*, 203 (1968)

4 BUCHSBAUM, M., GOODWIN, F.K., MURPHY, D.L.: Average evoked responses in affective disorders (submitted for publication)

5 DUNNER, D.L., COHN, C.K., GERSHON, E.S., GOODWIN, F.K.: Differential catechol-O-methyltransferase activity in unipolar and bipolar affective illness (printing)

6 LANGE, V.: Die Verteilung erblicher Serumgruppen bei manisch-depressiver Krankheit. Int. Pharmacopsychiat. *4*, 1 (1970)

7 MARTIN, J.: Zur Ätiologie der Erschöpfungsdepression. Arch. Neurol. Neurochir. Psychiat. *102*, 193 (1968)

8 PERRIS, C.: A study of bipolar (manic-depressive) and unipolar recurrent depressive psychoses. Acta psychiat. scand. *42*, Suppl. 194 (1966)

9 ROSENTHAL, D.: Two adoption studies of heredity in the schizophrenic disorders. In Bleuler, M., Angst, J. (Editors): The origin of schizophrenia, Akt. Probl. Psychiat. Neurol. Neurochir. Vol. V, p. 21 (Huber, Berne/Stuttgart/Vienna 1971)

10 SHAPIRO, R.W.: A twin study of non-endogenous depression. Acta jutland. *42*, No. 2 (1970)

11 WINOKUR, G., CADORET, R., DORZAB, J., BAKER, M.: Depressive disease. A genetic study. Arch. gen. Psychiat. *24*, 135 (1971)

Discussion

N. MATUSSEK: Additional evidence that unipolar and bipolar forms of affective illness constitute two different groups of diseases has been provided by BUNNEY et al. These authors showed that in the depressive phase lithium produced an improvement only in cases of bipolar depression, and not in patients with the unipolar form. From this finding, as well as from other studies, they concluded that these two forms must also differ considerably both biochemically and in their response to drug therapy.

J. ANGST: The reason why I did not dwell on the findings reported by BUNNEY et al. was that they seem to me still to require confirmation. So far as I know, Dr. COPPEN is the only person to have carried out a proper double-blind trial with lithium and placebo and, at the same time, to have analysed his patients in terms of bipolar and unipolar depression. Moreover, his trial lasted two years and was conducted in a large number of patients. Dr. COPPEN, did you really find that the two diagnostic groups differed in their response to lithium, as BUNNEY et al. thought they would?

A. COPPEN: We did in fact examine the effect of lithium on the clinical course both in cases of unipolar, i.e. recurrent, depression as well as in bipolar manic-depressive patients, and we found that prophylactically lithium was equally effective in both groups. We have no data on the effect of lithium upon the actual treatment of depression, either in unipolar or in bipolar cases.

J. WELNER: May I say how much I appreciated Dr. ANGST's very clear account of the genetics of affective disorders. I have just a few questions to put to him. Firstly, it would interest me to know if anybody has tried to review the earlier results reported from Sweden by STENSTEDT, who found that, regardless of whether the material studied consisted of depressed patients or of manic patients, the secondary cases occurring in their families were exactly the same. My second query concerns WINOKUR's hypothesis of the X-link mode of inheritance of manic-depressive disease. Two days before I left Denmark I got back some results relating to 55 carefully selected male manics, all of whom were typical cases presenting no schizophrenic or schizoid features. Among the parents of these patients there were just as many fathers with manic-depressive or manic disease as there were mothers. When we looked at the total incidence of affective disorders in the parents, we found that, if anything, the incidence was slightly higher among the fathers than among the mothers. These very preliminary findings of ours would thus not seem to confirm WINOKUR's hypothesis. The same applies to his hypothesis about alcoholism in the fathers of manics. In our series of 55 male manics, we found only one father with a confirmed diagnosis of alcoholism.

J. ANGST: I'm afraid I can't remember now all the data presented in STENSTEDT's two monographs. But I did analyse the material once for the purposes of a paper on endogenous depression which was published in 1966. In his index cases STENSTEDT didn't really draw a clear enough distinction between the purely depressive and the bipolar form. According to his tables, the incidence of psychotic illness differed from one sex to the other in the two sub-groups, though not to a very marked extent.
I cannot confirm WINOKUR's results. In view of the higher incidence of purely depressive disorders among women, I would rather tend to think that sex-specific factors might be involved here. This was why, on a previous occasion, I expressed the opinion that the X chromosome might be implicated in *unipolar* depression. Hence, this hypothesis is the very opposite of WINOKUR's. His postulate concerning the X-link mode of inheritance of *bipolar*, i.e. manic-depressive, disease has not yet been confirmed.
I would also agree with you, Dr. WELNER, as regards alcoholism. The high incidence of alcoholism among the average population tends to obscure subtle differences in familial morbidity. The inclusion of alcoholics in the analysis almost always either cancels out many differences there may be between the sexes, or else it creates differences which do not exist—for the simple reason that men drink more than women.

Masked depression and depressive equivalents

by J. J. López Ibor*

The terms "affective or depressive equivalents" and "masked depression" are being used more and more often nowadays, especially in the Anglo-Saxon literature. Careful analysis of these two terms immediately reveals that, as KIELHOLZ[7] has aptly observed, it is possible to draw a distinction between them.

Masked depression would seem to be a form of the disease resembling the classic *depressio sine depressione;* it is being encountered in a steadily growing number of cases, not because its actual incidence is on the increase but simply because physicians have now learnt to recognise it**. To give an example, we once had to deal with a woman who came to our clinic accompanied by her husband. She accused him of no longer paying any attention to her, and this accusation of hers had given rise to difficulties in their marriage. She did not feel at all melancholy and she refused to admit that she had any symptoms referable to depression. Nevertheless, her face belied her words, and when, with the husband's help, we had pieced together her clinical history, we were able to confirm that she was in fact suffering from depression. She was given appropriate treatment, and when the depressive phase lifted, her marital problems disappeared as well. Three years later she had a second phase of typical depression, which likewise cleared in response to treatment. After a further three years had passed, a third depressive phase ensued, but was not recognised as such by her doctor even though her husband repeatedly told him about the previous phases—and the patient committed suicide by throwing herself from a balcony. In this case, weight loss was the only detectable sign of a mental disorder.

The term "affective or depressive equivalent" implies the presence of a predominant symptom which claims the patient's—and even the unwitting physician's—entire attention. But this attention-riveting symptom, which drives the patient to seek medical advice in the first place, is accompanied by a depressive state of mind that is difficult to detect. For example, the patient may complain initially of headaches, which mask, as it were, his depression.

In 1950 I published a book on "Vital anxiety"[9], the sub-title of which was "General psychosomatic pathology". In this book, I put forward the thesis that certain forms of anxiety neurosis and of so-called psychosomatic disease were

---

* Clínica Psiquiátrica, University of Madrid, Spain.
** The following synonyms are employed in English to denote this condition: "masked depression", "hidden depression", "missed depression", "depressive equivalent", "affective equivalent". It should also be mentioned that the term *"larvierte Depression"* has long been used in German, as has *"depresión larvada"* in Spanish, and "latent depression" in English.

superimposed on a phasic alteration in the *endothymic background* of the patient's personality. I singled out a group of patients displaying relatively well-defined features which I described as indicative of *anxious thymopathy;* at that time, I was not aware that FRANK[4] had brought out a book in which he used the term "thymopathy" instead of "neurosis". My basic contention was as follows: just as there is a "vital sadness" typical of so-called endogenous depression—as pointed out by SCHNEIDER[16], who based his approach on SCHELER's classification of the emotions[15]—so is there also a vital anxiety.

Subsequently, the term "vital anxiety" came to be widely used in Spanish to denote the normal anxiety engendered by conflict situations arising as a result of our modern way of life; for this reason, I abandoned the expression and replaced it by "endothymic anxiety", using the word "endothymic" in the sense in which LERSCH employs it.

As far as psychiatry is concerned, clinical observation has shown me that the psychodynamic mechanisms underlying neuroses are very often based on an anxiety which is not reactive in the strict meaning of the word, but endothymic. When SCHULTE[17] said that patients suffering from melancholia cannot feel sadness, he was undoubtedly referring to two different types of sadness—the sadness of the healthy person who is afflicted by some misfortune which makes him sad, and the sadness of the patient with melancholia. The problem becomes even more complicated if fluctuations in mood and in mood structure, as well as, for example, the role played by sadness in the clinical picture of anxiety, are also taken into account.

It should be remembered that SCHELER never included sadness among the normal vital emotions. In his stratification of affective life, sadness figures among the psychic—i.e. reactive—emotions. Pain is classified under the heading of sensory emotions. Although other phenomenologists may disagree with SCHELER's classification, the exclusion of vital sadness from the category of the vital emotions demonstrates that the distinctions drawn between the various strata of emotional experience do alter *under pathological conditions*.

Acceptance of the thesis that there is an endothymic background in neuroses and in the group of masked depressions and affective equivalents does not imply that psychodynamic factors are not involved in the clinical morphology of these disorders, especially in the case of neurotic patients. In all such instances, one problem which has to be faced is that of the patient's personality and of the way in which his personality reacts to any upset he may encounter*. When SCHNEIDER[16] described his "underground depressions", he was referring to depressions superimposed on a background that could not be experienced by the patient. The important thing is to find out to what extent a painstaking analysis of the symptomatology can reveal the role played by the endothymic background in these cases—a background which apparently cannot be experienced by the patient himself and which is expressed by him in the guise of symptoms. By way of example, let me mention the case of a woman who one day, for no

---

* Cf. PÖLDINGER's classification of anxiety[14] and KIELHOLZ's classification of depression[7].

apparent reason, tried to hang herself at home, but whose life was eventually saved by treatment in an intensive care unit. Nothing in this patient's past history would have led one to think that she was suffering from depression; she had never complained of any symptoms, apart from mild headaches for which she had taken some drug she had seen advertised on television. There was no conflict situation. Nevertheless, we realised that she was suffering from deep depression immediately we saw her facial expression, even though questioning failed to reveal any of the usual symptoms, whether of the nuclear or of the peripheral type. It was only our determination to discover the exact structure of the headaches experienced by the patient that put us on the right track (this case was subsequently used as the theme for an instructional film entitled "The case of Antonia L.").

Psychiatrists are steadily improving their knowledge of depression in all its forms. Moreover, doctors working in general, non-psychiatric hospitals are surprised to see that suicide is much more common among the patients in non-psychiatric wards than among those treated in psychiatric departments. In the University Psychiatric Clinic in Madrid we have had only one case of suicide in five years, as compared with six to eight cases in other departments. This fact provides considerable food for thought.

Posthumous re-examination of these patients' clinical histories with the assistance of their relatives suggested that almost all of them had been suffering from unrecognised depression and that they had presented with one predominant symptom; the department to which they were sent for examination and treatment had been selected in the light of this predominant symptom. Most of these patients had committed suicide during their first six or seven days in hospital— i.e. during the period devoted to exhaustive clinical tests. All this demonstrates that in the field of depression today there is a peripheral zone which deserves to be extensively studied; it is highly important that general practitioners and non-psychiatric specialists should always bear the possibility of masked depression in mind.

We have been investigating this problem in detail for a number of years and we have succeeded in many cases in persuading our colleagues in internal medicine or surgery to keep a look-out for this possibility and to refer any suspect patients to us before deciding on diagnosis or treatment. With this aim in view, moreover, we are planning to organise seminars for general practitioners (the University Clinic in Madrid belongs to the Social Insurance Scheme). These seminars will be run along the lines suggested by BALINT[1], but with certain modifications. BALINT adopted a psychoanalytical approach, but we intend to tackle the matter from another angle.

A number of authors have pointed out that somatic disorders often coincide with depressive phases. SCHULTE, for example, has drawn attention to the relationship between depression and certain forms of cardiac arrhythmia, cerebrovascular accidents, infectious mononucleosis, etc. Other authors have reported a similar relationship between depression and thyrotoxicosis, rheumatoid arthritis, diabetes, alopecia areata, and lupus erythematosus (McCLARY, MEYER, and WEITZMAN[13]; COHEN and LICHTENBERG[2]). This problem, as well as that of the "syndrome shift", has been studied in particular by Spiegelberg[18,19] and Groen et al.[6] from two different aspects*.

It is very difficult to estimate, even approximately, the incidence of such disorders. Some authors—such as Dowling and Knox[3], and Lesse[8]—suggest that 20 % of the patients treated in a general medical hospital fall into this category. These authors only consider the question of whether masked depression is a primary disorder or whether it is secondary to some organic disease for which the patients concerned have been admitted to hospital; in the majority of cases, however, a physician who has received adequate training in both general medicine and psychiatry will not find it all that difficult to distinguish between the two.

The problem of depressive equivalents has to be viewed in relation to psychosomatic disturbances. It is also important that we should discuss here the relationship between depressive equivalents and such clinical pictures as anorexia nervosa, anaclitic depression, and forms of hysteria which run a phasic course. Another point to be borne in mind is that depression does not display the same pattern in adolescents as in adults. An analysis of this whole problem would inevitably draw us into a long discussion on whether or not all these groups of disorders are of endothymic origin.

When singling out and describing many depressive equivalents—a subject which I do not intend to go into today—the basic criteria I employ are as follows: firstly, the absence of any lesions which would justify the signs and symptoms in question, and, secondly, the clinical connection between the symptomatology and depressive phases. Nuchal pain might be taken as an example of the first criterion; nuchal pain is often attributed to osteoarthritic changes in the cervical vertebrae, changes which persist unaltered in follow-up X-ray pictures even when the pain itself has completely disappeared. In cases of meralgia paraesthetica I have noticed that sometimes the symptoms fail to respond to neurosurgical operations on the external cutaneous femoral nerve; in these instances, the symptoms seem to be related to depressive phases and they disappear in response to appropriate treatment. I could quote many other examples of this type. It is therefore my belief that this sector provides a new approach to the clinical assessment of certain psychic, neurological, and psychosomatic disturbances, and should be carefully investigated; the extensive clinical material I have collected, which is based on very long follow-up periods, is extremely demonstrative in this connection.

In patients suffering from pain the physician bases his diagnostic approach on the peripheral and radicular distribution of the nervous pathways, except in cases of referred pain or of so-called thalamic pain. In its distribution, as well as in the manner in which it is elicited and experienced, thalamic pain most closely resembles thymopathic pain, although it also differs from the latter in some respects. As a rule, the patient complains of a "dull ache" which he finds very difficult to describe; one can spend hours or even days observing and questioning the patient and still not succeed in obtaining a detailed description of

---

* Cf. the thesis on "Depressive equivalents" by J. J. López-Ibor Aliño[12].

his sensations. The pain, moreover, may not follow the expected pattern; it may change its site not only from day to day, but even while the physician is carrying out his examination. Meralgia paraesthetica, for example, sometimes fails to correspond in its extent to the distribution of the external cutaneous femoral nerve and may even assume an alternating form in which it affects the left thigh for a few days and then switches to the right thigh.

More than a hundred years ago, in one of his inaugural lectures at the Berlin Clinic, GRIESINGER[5] gave a masterly description of thymopathic frontal headaches which he designated as "frontal anxiety" or "frontal dysthymia". "The patients complain", he said, "of a sensation in the frontal part of the head. Their entire disease consists solely of this sensation. They search for words to describe it. They all say it is not a pain, and some add: 'If only it were a pain'. Many of them refer to it as a torment, a weight, etc. To indicate the localisation of the disorder, many patients draw lines across the root of the nose. When they experience this sensation, they are incapable of thinking and are prostrate with anxiety. The sensation is much more impressive than any other pain and exerts a much more marked effect on the patient's psyche. One elderly patient who consulted me after his second attack told me he had been so despondent as a result of this painful sensation in the head that he had attempted to commit suicide, but had fortunately been stopped in time."

It is possible in some cases to analyse the peculiar nature of these forms of paraesthesia and to conclude that they represent a sensation equivalent to the fear of dying evinced by some patients usually diagnosed as suffering from anxiety neuroses. Such an analysis, however, which might be described as a "transphenomenological analysis", is only feasible if the patient possesses a certain capacity for self-observation and if the psychiatrist has sufficient patience and psychological insight. I have often seen cases of "paraesthetic brachialgia" which, as WARTENBERG[20] has reported, occurs in the morning and disappears again as soon as the patient begins to move his arms. Akinesia algera and a whole series of similar manifestations are likewise commonly encountered. Even akathisia, in cases where it is not due to treatment with neuroleptic drugs, may often be included among these thymopathic equivalents.

A long time ago, when the only treatment for depression was electroconvulsive therapy, I was faced with the problem of treating a severely depressed patient. He improved a little in response to the first two E.C.T. sessions, but after the third he developed such marked akathisia that he could no longer stay in bed. He insisted on getting up not only during the day but also during much of the night, despite the fact that he was given hypnotics to help him sleep. I was extremely puzzled by this behaviour, but as neither the patient's past history nor the results of current examinations provided any clue to the cause of the akathisia, I decided to continue the treatment. In response to the fourth E.C.T. session an improvement set in, and after the fifth the akathisia disappeared completely. Following two more E.C.T. applications the patient's depression also lifted. I have followed up this patient ever since, and he has never had any recurrence of akathisia. Fortunately, moreover, his depression has not returned

either.

More common than this major form of akathisia is the phenomenon described as "restless legs", which has recently been much discussed in the literature. Its cause has been interpreted in a number of different ways. Although I certainly do not deny that this symptom may be due to various aetiopathogenic factors, I can affirm, in the light of my long experience, that many patients with restless legs belong to the group we are concerned with here.

We are at present studying other similar neurological syndromes, all of them relatively rare ones. I should like to point out, for example, that what is often diagnosed as vertigo of the Ménière type is simply another thymopathic equivalent which should really be called agoraphobic vertigo or thymopathic vertigo. I have seen a number of cases of this kind in which the patient has even undergone a surgical operation. The operation failed to elicit a response because the patient's condition had not been correctly diagnosed.

It is important that general practitioners should be fully aware of the existence of latent or masked depression, which manifests itself exclusively in the form of non-depressive symptoms or depressive equivalents, and that they should in general be familiar with this marginal zone of classic depression, because they probably encounter even more cases of this type than do psychiatrists. This sector constitutes, as it were, a bridge between general medicine as practised by family doctors, and psychiatry.

References

1   BALINT, M.: The doctor, his patient and the illness (Pitman, London 1957)
2   COHEN, I. H., LICHTENBERG, J. D.: Alopecia areata. Arch. gen. Psychiat. *17*, 608 (1967)
3   DOWLING, R. H., KNOX, S. J.: Somatic symptoms in depressive illness. Brit. J. Psychiat. *110*, 720 (1964)
4   FRANK, L.: Affektstörungen. Studien über ihre Ätiologie und Therapie (Springer, Berlin 1913; Monogr. Gesamtgeb. Neurol. Psychiat., No. 4)
5   GRIESINGER, W.: Vortrag zur Eröffnung der Klinik für Nerven- und Geisteskrankheiten in der Königl. Charité in Berlin. Arch. physiol. Heilk. 7, 338 (1866); Wilhelm Griesinger's Gesammelte Abhandlungen, Vol. I, p. 107 (Hirschwald, Berlin 1872)
6   GROEN, J., BASTIAANS, J., VALK, J. M. VAN DER: Psychosomatic aspects of syndrome shift and syndrome suppression. In Booij, J. (Editor): Psychosomatics. A series of five lectures, p. 33 (Elsevier, Amsterdam/London/New York/Princeton 1957)
7   KIELHOLZ, P.: Diagnose und Therapie der Depressionen für den Praktiker, 3rd Ed. (Lehmanns, Munich 1971)
8   LESSE, S.: The multivariant masks of depression. Amer. J. Psychiat. *124*, Suppl. to No. 11:35 (1968)
9   LÓPEZ IBOR, J. J.: La angustia vital (Paz Montalvo, Madrid 1950)
10 LÓPEZ IBOR, J. J.: Las neurosis como enfermedades del ánimo (Gredos, Madrid 1966)
11 LÓPEZ IBOR, J. J.: Depressive Äquivalente. Das depressive Syndrom, Int. Symp., Berlin 1968, p. 403 (Urban & Schwarzenberg, Munich/Berlin/Vienna 1969)
12 LÓPEZ-IBOR ALIÑO, J. J.: Thesis, Madrid 1972 (printing)

13 McClary, A. R., Meyer, E., Weitzman, E. L.: Observations on the role of the mechanism of depression in some patients with disseminated lupus erythematosus. Psychosom. Med. *17*, 311 (1955)

14 Pöldinger, W.: Aspects of anxiety. Anxiety and tension—new therapeutic aspects, Int. Symp., St. Moritz 1970, p. 7

15 Scheler, M.: Der Formalismus in der Ethik und die materiale Wertethik (mit besonderer Berücksichtigung der Ethik Immanuel Kants). Jb. Philos. phänom. Forsch. *1*, 405 (1913) and *2*, 21 (1916)

16 Schneider, K.: Klinische Psychopathologie, 9th Ed. (Thieme, Stuttgart 1971)

17 Schulte, W.: Über das Wesen melancholischen Erlebens und die Möglichkeiten der Beeinflussung (Hippokrates, Stuttgart 1965)

18 Spiegelberg, U.: Über Beziehungen endogener Psychosen zu körperlichen Krankheiten. Fortschr. Neurol. Psychiat. *23*, 221 (1955)

19 Spiegelberg, U.: Zyklothymie, Neurose und Psychosomatische Störung. In Colmant, H. J. (Editor): Vitalität (Enke, Stuttgart 1968; Forum Psychiat. No. 20)

20 Wartenberg, R.: Neuritis, sensory neuritis, neuralgia (Oxford Univ. Press, New York 1958)

Discussion

P. KIELHOLZ: I should like to thank Dr. LÓPEZ IBOR for his excellent paper. I am particularly grateful to him for emphasising the frequency with which masked depression escapes detection and for pointing out, as Dr. KUHN also did many years ago, that these depressive equivalents respond to treatment with antidepressants.

W. WALCHER: May I comment on several of the points raised by Dr. LÓPEZ IBOR. First of all, a word or two about the incidence of masked depression. Even psychiatrists hold widely varying views on this subject. The hospital psychiatrist either does not see patients of this type at all, or else he sees them only at a very late stage after all the other medical departments have failed to find any evidence of an organic lesion. The sad thing about these patients, in fact, is that they are shuttled from one doctor to another, and that nobody is capable of dealing with them properly; as a result, they tend to be labelled simply as cases of hysteria. I believe that the incidence of masked depression has increased not only relatively—that is, because we are becoming more skilled at diagnosing it—but also in absolute terms; this is because psychodynamic stress factors—which, in addition to constitutional predisposition, play a part in the development of these states—loom much larger now than they did perhaps ten or twenty years ago. The more exacting demands which our society makes in respect of performance are partly to blame here.

As regards symptomatology, most patients with masked depression complain of headache; other common symptoms are cardiac disturbances, abdominal upsets, and neuralgia-like pain. The symptomatology may, indeed, faithfully imitate that of virtually any organic disease. When faced with a patient who complains of a large number of symptoms that are constantly changing, the physician is more likely to think in terms of a psychogenic disorder, though not necessarily in terms of endogenous or reactive depression. Often it is precisely the somatic "vitalisation symptoms"—or "devitalisation symptoms" as Dr. KIELHOLZ prefers to call them—that manifest themselves at the site of least resistance in the autonomic nervous system, a site referable perhaps to some organic disease suffered many years previously.

Why is it so difficult to diagnose these states? In Austria we may possibly have made some progress in this field, thanks to the fact that various psychiatrists, such as Dr. BIRKMAYER and also myself, have always endeavoured in our lectures to general practitioners to make them realise how common these clinical pictures really are. The reason why they are so hard to diagnose is that, unlike other psychiatric conditions, they do not display a distinctive hierarchy of clinical signs and symptoms and that the depression, which remains completely hidden behind the somatic equivalents, can only be brought to light by specific questioning. One should try to find out, for example, whether the patient suffers from sleep disturbances, whether his mental or physical efficiency has declined, whether he fails to get any enjoyment out of life, whether he has a poor appetite, and whether his symptoms decrease to some extent in the evening. The term *depressio sine depressione* is certainly not a good one, because depressive mood is invariably present, but is concealed by somatic equivalents.

J. J. LÓPEZ IBOR: There can be no doubt that even the psychiatrist often has difficulty in diagnosing masked depression. When we talk about the incidence of masked depression, we are usually referring to those patients who attend psychiatric clinics or who consult specialists. If, however, it were possible to examine systematically all the patients who go to general practitioners because of various disorders which might be relevant in this connection, we should find many more cases of depression.

When you talk to patients suffering from masked depression, you are often inclined to feel that their depression is of a reactive nature, but if you enquire more deeply, you discover time and again that there is a family history of endogenous depression. Genuine depressive moods are often difficult to recognise, and only time and experience can help here. I myself find that I can detect such cases more often now than I used to be able to, simply because I have meanwhile acquired more experience. In this context, I should also like to quote G. A. GERMAN, who is a professor at the Mankerere University of Kampala in Uganda. In the Goldman Memorial Lecture he gave in New York recently, he stated that among his depressive patients only 2% actually complained of sadness.

W. BIRKMAYER: As Dr. KIELHOLZ has already pointed out, we are agreed that depression is a metabolic disorder. Whether the disorder concerns catecholamine metabolism or serotonin metabolism does not alter the fact that it is unlikely to be confined to the brain. Thus, for example, it is not surprising that a depressive patient should suffer from constipation, because this disturbance, too, can reflect a deficiency of serotonin.

The many different symptoms of masked depression which Dr. LÓPEZ IBOR described, and to which European investigators at least are devoting an increasing amount of attention, are likewise to be regarded as metabolic disorders affecting biogenic amines. A typical case in point is meralgia paraesthetica. Patients with this symptom are frequently operated on for the removal of an intervertebral disc, but the operation proves a complete failure. If, however, they are given Tofranil® or some other antidepressant with activating properties, their pain disappears. And we know today that this is not a placebo effect. What happens is that the resultant rise in the concentration of biogenic amines leads to activation of the gamma loop, to an increase in muscle tone, to an improvement in posture, and, consequently, to elimination of the pain.

J.J. LÓPEZ IBOR: That is perfectly correct. An American colleague has reported that quite an appreciable degree of improvement can sometimes be elicited in refractory cases of nuchal pain by administering Tofranil orally, combined with a local injection of hydrocortisone. We have just started a study of our own on this problem.

B. POPKES: Dr. WALCHER, I feel that I must contradict you on one point. You said that when questioning patients with masked depression one can always discover several depressive symptoms. In my experience, however, this is usually not the case; on the contrary, it seems to me that in many patients with masked depression there is virtually only one symptom. What I have almost always found, though, is that these patients are retarded; although the degree of retardation may be slight, it can be detected in the patient's general behaviour. The patient himself will often admit it in response to direct questioning, and his relatives are invariably aware of it.

W. WALCHER: There may be various reasons why interrogation fails to reveal symptoms of masked depression:
1. The patient may not have noticed the symptoms himself. However, once the depressive phase has subsided, he frequently realises retrospectively that he has been suffering from depressed mood.
2. The patient may be retarded and say very little about himself. This reticence, of course, might be due in part to national characteristics. In Austria most patients with masked depression are anxious hypochondriacs and tend to be talkative.
3. The questions put to the patient may not have been specific enough.

J.J. LÓPEZ IBOR: We have noticed that loss of appetite can also be a predominant symptom. In fact, we treat cases of loss of appetite with antidepressants. During the last three years we have obtained good results with Anafranil®, administered in high doses, in a large number of patients suffering from anorexia nervosa.

P. BERNER: The problem of masked depression can only be elucidated, in my opinion, by undertaking extensive basic research. This research would have to involve much more than the customary enumeration of clinical observations. It would have to be preceded, in the clinical field, by an attempt to clarify certain terms and concepts. Moreover, when dealing with masked depressions, one has to decide whether the disease is of a bipolar or unipolar type. It is also particularly important in the case of masked depressions to assess the depth of the depression. Finally, it should be borne in mind that loss of drive is not invariably the cardinal sign of depression; in some cases it is motility that is chiefly affected, in others depressed mood is the principal symptom, and in certain instances the most striking features are those reminiscent of an "affective psychosis" (such as Leonhardt's "anxiety-happiness psychosis"). Even if one does not agree with Leonhardt that these forms of depression represent disease entities in their own right, one cannot deny that they do exist. In such cases, it is by no means uncommon to use the term "masked depression" or *depressio sine depressione* to describe patients whose predominant symptoms are loss of drive and retardation. On the other hand, in bipolar forms of depression in particular one very frequently encounters mixed states or dysphoric pictures which are generally not recognised for what they really are, but are once again classified as "masked depression". These clinical pictures are usually marked by a plethora of neurotic symptoms. There is good reason to believe that, by analogy with learning theories, the neurotic symptoms masking the depression show a pronounced tendency to become generalised, whereas genuine depression is as a rule concealed by only one major neurotic symptom. The mixed states I have just referred to are often characterised by the fact that they differ from typical depression in respect of autonomic reactivity. In these mixed states, the constipation associated with genuine depression is often replaced by diarrhoea, and dryness of the skin by marked sweating—which accounts for the term "wet depression". Finally, the answer to the question why neurotic defence mechanisms are mobilised only in some forms of depression may be sought in Janzarik's dynamic constellation model: in shallow depressions, as in hypomanic moods, the patient still has reserves of dynamism which are capable of generating neurotic defence mechanisms. When, on the other hand, depression reduces the patient's dynamism to such a marked extent that he loses interest even in his personal problems—i.e. in unsolved psychic conflicts which had previously troubled him—then defence mechanisms are no longer necessary or even possible. In conclusion, however, it must be emphasised that only psychobiological and biochemical studies can provide objective evidence of the existence of these shifts in dynamism occurring in cases of so-called masked depression.

J.J. López Ibor: I am not sure whether depressive equivalents or masked depressions are more frequently associated with bipolar or with unipolar disease. It is my impression that the underlying depression is more often unipolar. None the less, there are certainly cases in which masked depression manifests itself in the form of neuroses. In these cases, a thorough analysis of the psychopathology will reveal that the psychic disorders concealed behind the somatic symptoms are due not only to melancholia but also to anxiety.
As far as these psychic disorders are concerned, I would stress that in my experience anxiety is more common in the first half of life, whereas melancholia predominates in the second. I also have statistics to confirm this.

M. Hamilton: Concerning masked depressions, I think it is important that in every case we should consider why the patient is emphasising or magnifying certain symptoms, and why others are being minimised or hidden. It is only when we understand the patient's reasons for the attitude he or she adopts towards the symptoms that we can obtain a clear picture of the condition. Once we have done this, there is no need to talk of a masked depression, but simply of a depression. "Depressive equivalents" are even more doubtful. Many cyclical, remittent conditions are seen in general medicine. Psychiatrists should not try to tackle these cases without very convincing evidence that they fall within the province of psychiatry, e.g. that they are of depressive origin. Disorders of this type are remittent and their response to antidepressants means nothing more than that they responded to all sorts of other treatments in the past!

I. Sano: Has masked depression anything to do with endogenous depression? And what percentage of patients suffering from depression in the strict sense of the term complain of headaches? Headache is rare among our depressive patients, who are far more apt to complain of a sensation of cloudiness or woolliness in the head.

J. J. López Ibor: As regards the incidence of headache in patients suffering from endogenous depression, the answer depends on how the patients are examined. Headache will be found to be less common in cases where only spontaneous complaints are recorded; if, however, you ask the patients specifically about this symptom, as we did in one of our studies, you will find that headache is in fact one of the commonest depressive equivalents.

In reply to Dr. Hamilton, I should like to say that I agree with him that not all the cyclic syndromes met with in general medicine can be assigned to the category of depressive illness. But in this connection I think it is important to distinguish between non-depressive and depressive cyclic conditions. Besides the nature of the symptomatology as such, another point to which major attention must be devoted in depressive cases is the question of genetic factors. Perhaps you remember once telling me, Dr. Hamilton, that the most frequent symptom in depression was anorexia? But anorexia is also encountered in other diseases that have nothing to do with depression. Anorexia, in fact, is unspecific. It may or may not be a depressive equivalent. Incidentally, much the same applies to epileptic equivalents as well. A great deal has been written about so-called epileptic equivalents, particularly in the form of temporal epilepsy. Speaking from my own clinical experience, I would say that this temporal form really has nothing to do with genuine epilepsy, despite the fact that in such cases some minor anomalies are observed in the electro-encephalogram. In the United States a book has been published* in which all these electro-encephalographic anomalies are interpreted as evidence of ictal neurosis, whereas I am sure that in fact they are not.

P. Kielholz: May I add something to Dr. Sano's comment. We have recorded the somatic symptoms in a large number of depressive patients, and we have found that the most common are cardiac and respiratory disturbances; second in order of frequency are sensations of pressure; and sweating occupies third place. Headache—and here it should be pointed out that we also included under this heading patients who complained of a feeling of pressure in the forehead—was encountered in 40% of patients, the percentages being lower in the case of gastro-intestinal symptoms and sleep disturbances.

To sum up, we undoubtedly all agree with Dr. López Ibor on one point—namely, that depression may manifest itself not only as melancholia, anxiety, inhibition of thought, or loss of vitality, but also in the form of autonomic nervous and somatic disturbances. It is certainly true that in the past too little attention has been paid to the possibility that somatic symptoms may be the principal feature in some cases of depression. These forms of depression are only diagnosed at a very late stage, if at all, because the physician allows himself to be led astray initially by the somatic symptoms.

* Jonas, A.D.: Ictal and sub-ictal neuroses (Thomas, Springfield, Ill. 1965)

The current status of treatment for depression

by H. Hippius*

The present symposium has two objectives: firstly, it features a series of eight papers serving to review the situation to date with regard to research on depression, and, secondly, it is intended to provide an opportunity to present the initial results of studies with a new antidepressant, Ludiomil®, so that these results can be discussed in relation to the latest developments in the field of research on depression. One outcome of this symposium should therefore be to enable us to assign to Ludiomil its appropriate place in the gamut of the antidepressant drugs.

In a report on the treatment of depression it might appear tempting to limit oneself solely to *drug therapy*. For various reasons, however, this is not justifiable, and I should therefore like to begin this brief review of mine with a few *general remarks* on the management of depression.

After the introduction of electroconvulsive therapy in the treatment of endogenous depression, it became the widely accepted view—a view which owed much to the nosological categories in which psychiatrists are wont to think—that somatic convulsive therapy should be chiefly reserved for endogenous forms of depression; that in cases of psychogenic depression treatment should be confined to psychotherapeutic methods; and that, in types of depression apparently attributable to physical causes (symptomatic and organic depression), treatment should be aimed at the underlying somatic disease (for a review of this subject, see KALINOWSKY and HIPPIUS[26]). Such was still the general consensus of opinion even after the start of the psychopharmaceutical era of antidepressive therapy in 1957.

Today, however, this notion—based as it was upon sharply differentiated fields of indications established on monocausal nosological premises—can be regarded as outdated. It has meanwhile been recognised that depression is usually not due to any single cause, but is of multifactorial origin, and that the *predominant feature in the multifactorial aetiology of the syndrome* should be regarded merely as the decisive factor determining the diagnostic category to which a given case is assigned. Though this may sound highly theoretical and abstruse, it is in point of fact of major practical importance. The concept of the multifactorial aetiology of depressive syndromes implies with regard to therapy that, when drawing up *overall treatment programmes*, it is essential that *somatotherapeutic, psychotherapeutic,* and *sociotherapeutic* factors should always be considered collectively and conjointly[1].

If we consider the situation today in terms of the multifactorial aetiology of depressive syndromes, we find that, although endogenous types of depression

* Universitäts-Nervenklinik, Munich, Germany.

still constitute the domain for somatic methods of treatment, there is a steadily growing tendency to combine somatic therapeutic principles with psychotherapeutic and sociotherapeutic measures. Furthermore, somatic forms of treatment are likewise indicated in psychogenic types of depression, firstly as an adjunct to psychotherapy, and, secondly, whenever psychotherapeutic methods have failed to elicit a convincing response. Finally, the somatic therapeutic procedures which have proved so successful in cases of endogenous depression are also employed in forms of depression due to physical causes, especially where—as in degenerative processes affecting the brain, for example—no effective treatment for the underlying disease is available[1].

Against the background of these general introductory observations, I now propose to present a summary review of the *current status* of somatic therapeutic methods used in depression, after which I shall conclude with a few remarks on possible future developments.

As I have already emphasised, it would be unjustifiable to deal only with drug treatment in a review of somatic therapy for depression. This has become particularly obvious since PFLUG and TÖLLE[35] published last year their initial observations on the good therapeutic effects produced by sleep deprival at SCHULTE's clinic. So far only a few clinical reports on this form of therapy have appeared, and the findings obtained are anything but consistent. Systematic studies and experiments designed to elucidate the mechanism of action of this seemingly paradoxical method of treatment have yet to be undertaken. One thing, however, is already clear: in certain cases it proves strikingly effective. Moreover, the example offered by sleep-deprival therapy suggests that there are valuable possibilities inherent in somatic therapeutic methods which would never be exploited if treatment for depression were to be confined solely to the use of drugs. The neglect of such possibilities would certainly be unjustified, if only because—despite the successes yielded by drugs—the fact must be acknowledged that the failure rate with all tricyclic antidepressants and all monamine-oxidase inhibitors is still generally in the region of some 10–30%. These figures alone afford compelling proof that in the management of depression there is still also a place for *electroconvulsive therapy*, at least in patients who have proved resistant to attempts at drug treatment[20, 25, 26]. Admittedly, there are certain authors who repeatedly express the view that it is now possible to dispense completely with convulsive therapy in the treatment of depression. But an enquiry conducted in German hospitals has revealed that almost all psychiatric clinics without exception resort to electroconvulsive treatment in cases of refractory depression. The only differences of opinion concern the length of time during which drug treatment should be continued before the decision is taken to employ electroconvulsive therapy. Incidentally, whether a case of depression should already be considered resistant after a few days or weeks of medication, or not until the treatment has been in progress for several months, depends not so much on psychiatric evidence of the generally accepted type yielded by systematic research on the course taken by depressive illnesses, but rather on socio-medical factors, such as whether the patient's health-insurance arrangements provide coverage for only a short or for a long period of illness. It is apparently for reasons of this kind that in the United States, for example, even in patients undergoing ambulant treatment, recourse is had to electroconvulsive therapy at a relatively early stage.

During recent years various research groups, including in particular the teams headed by OTTOSSON and by FINK, have reintensified their efforts to achieve further advances with convulsive therapy. Attempts to elicit convulsions by administering new drugs, e.g. hexafluorodiethyl ether, have demonstrated the feasibility of this approach, but have not brought any decisive progress[29, 42]. On the other hand, most authors acknowledge that so-called unilateral electroconvulsive therapy possesses certain advantages. It has been shown by D'ELIA, from OTTOSSON's group, that this new method of electroconvulsive therapy is superior to the classic procedure, particularly insofar as it minimises the amnesia which is liable to result from such treatment[19]. A number of investigators have confirmed that memory is less impaired if the electroconvulsive therapy is confined to the non-dominant hemisphere, but they state at the same time that the therapeutic results in endogenous depression were not so good as with the usual bilateral method[16]. Other authors, though, maintain that there is no difference in the response elicited by these two forms of electroconvulsive therapy[8]. One point that is still unclear is whether "electro-sleep" (transcranial electric stimulation for the purpose of inducing sleep), a method which the Russians use on a comparatively large scale and which ROSENTHAL and WULFSOHN have investigated in the U.S.A., constitutes a useful therapeutic procedure[40].

Finally, the third non-medicinal form of somatic antidepressive therapy to which reference should be made is that consisting of psychosurgical interventions, which—chiefly in Great Britain—are now once again being advocated on a limited scale in the management of depression. The interventions in question take the form of bimedial leucotomy or, more recently, of stereotactic operations on the anterior thalamic nuclei[26, 30, 36].

Drug therapy for depression now has almost 15 years of experience behind it. As the prototype of the so-called tricyclic antidepressants, imipramine—the drug with which KUHN's investigations[28] ushered in the era of pharmacotherapy—still embodies the most important therapeutic principle. Since 1957 the family of the tricyclic antidepressants has steadily grown (see Table 1); the spectrum encompassed by their action has to some extent also increased in range—but no fundamentally new types of compound differing radically from imipramine have yet been developed from this group of drugs.

Still valid as a means of taking into account the varying prominence of the three main properties characterising the activity of the different tricyclic antidepressants is the triple-component classification as described by KIELHOLZ[27], who distinguishes between their depression-relieving, their drive-enhancing, and their anxiety and excitation reducing effects.

All the tricyclic antidepressants known to date, including those introduced only recently, such as doxepine[3, 9, 10], noxiptiline[2, 5, 6], dimethacrin[44], and iprindole[4], can be readily allocated to their respective categories in KIELHOLZ's classification, on the basis of which it is possible to distinguish between three groups of antidepressants[27]:

1. An intermediate group of the imipramine type, in which the depression-relieving component predominates.
2. A group displaying particularly marked excitation-reducing activity, as exemplified by amitriptyline. To this group may also be assigned neuroleptic agents of the thioridazine and levomepromazine type.
3. Preparations endowed with a pronounced drive-enhancing effect, i.e. drugs of the desmethylimipramine (desipramine) type, whose action resembles that of the monamine-oxidase inhibitors.

From this threefold grouping the differential indications for the various tricyclic antidepressants can be deduced. Although I have emphasised here the differences in the activity patterns of the various preparations, the fact must not be overlooked that in the last analysis the similarities in their therapeutic effects far outweigh the differences. These differences may sometimes be due not so much to genuine differences in pharmacological activity, but rather to variations in the dosage required to produce an equivalent response or to variations in the mode of administration. A typical example in point are the two drugs imipramine and clomipramine, the latter of which is preferentially employed for infusion therapy in cases where prior oral treatment with a drug such as imipramine has proved unsuccessful[7, 12, 14].

Many of the original dimethyl compounds have meanwhile become available in the form of desmethyl derivatives known as nor-compounds. In pairs of substances of this kind, the nor-compound regularly exhibits a more potent drive-enhancing effect. Whether these nor-compounds also have a more rapid onset of action has not yet been established with certainty.

The delayed onset of action common to all tricyclic antidepressants is a by no means negligible disadvantage of these preparations. In suicidal patients, particularly if they are receiving treatment on an ambulant basis, a delay of one or two weeks in the onset of the drug's effect represents a serious risk, a risk which may be aggravated by a disparity in the time at which the preparation begins to exert its action on drive as compared with mood.

Another shortcoming in the activity pattern of the tricyclic antidepressants is the absence, or virtual absence, of any anxiolytic properties. Drive-enhancing tricyclics often actually have the effect of provoking anxiety. On the other hand, tricyclic or polycyclic drugs which do exert an anxiolytic effect—such as Tacitin®, for example—generally display rather a weak antidepressant action. In view of the inadequate anxiolytic activity of most antidepressants, it is advisable, in order to fulfil the practical requirements of treatment for depression, to resort to *combinations*—either with a minor tranquilliser (e.g. amitriptyline + chlordiazepoxide) or with small doses of a more potent major tranquilliser (e.g. amitriptyline + perphenazine[32] or melitracen + flupentixol[13]). Scandinavian investigators, incidentally, reported a few years ago that the major tranquilliser flupentixol is also effective in depressive illness when used *alone*[39]. It has likewise recently been stated that potent major tranquillisers belonging to the group of the butyrophenones display some degree of antidepressant activity.

Another approach, based on different premises, has been to combine tricyclic antidepressants with stimulants. In the U.S.A., for example, favourable reports

Table 1. Drugs used in the treatment of depression.

Chemical designation	Type of clinical effect	Trade mark	Dosage range (oral daily dosages)
Tricyclic and tetracyclic antidepressants (in square brackets: minor and major tranquillisers with antidepressant properties)			
Amitriptyline	III	Laroxyl®, Roche	
		Saroten®, Tropon	25–350 mg.
		Tryptizol®, Merck, Sharp and Dohme	
		[● Limbatril®/Limbitrol®, Roche] (combination with chlordiazepoxide)	15–120 mg.
[Benzoctamine]	V	[Tacitin®, CIBA]	15–150 mg.
Clomipramine	II	Anafranil®, GEIGY	50–200 mg.
[Chlorprothixene]	IV	Taractan®, Roche Truxal®, Tropon, Lundbeck	30–150 mg.
Desipramine	I	Pertofran®, GEIGY	50–200 mg.
Dibenzepine	II	Noveril®, Wander	200–600 mg.
Dimethacrin	II	Istonil®, Siegfried	100–500 mg.
Doxepine	III	Aponal®, Boehringer Mannheim	
		Sinquan®, Pfizer	50–300 mg.
Imipramine	II	Tofranil®, GEIGY	50–300 mg.
Iprindole	II	Galatur®, Wyeth	
		Prondol®, Wyeth	45–180 mg.
[Levomepromazine]	IV	Neurocil®, Bayer Nozinan®, Specia	25–150 mg.
Maprotiline	?	Ludiomil®, CIBA	30–150 mg.
Melitracen	II	Trausabun®, Byk-Gulden Lomberg	
		Dixeran®, Lundbeck	30–200 mg.
Nortriptyline	I	Acetexa®, Lilly	
		Nortrilen®, Tropon, Lundbeck	30–250 mg.
		Sensival®, Pharmacia	
Noxiptiline	II	Agedal®, Bayer	50–450 mg.
[Opipramol]	V	[Insidon®, GEIGY]	50–300 mg.
Protriptyline	I	Concordin®, Merck, Sharp and Dohme	
		Maximed®, Sharp und Dohme	30–150 mg.
[Thioridazine]	IV	[Melleril®, Sandoz]	25–200 mg.
Trimipramine	III	Stangyl®, Rhodia	
		Surmontil®, Specia	50–250 mg.
Monamine-oxidase inhibitors			
Isocarboxazid	I	Marplan®, Roche	30– 90 mg.
Nialamide	I	Niamid®, Pfizer	75–500 mg.
Trancylpromine	I	● Jatrosom®, Röhm and Haas (combination with trifluoperazine)	10– 30 mg.
Lithium salts			
Acetate	VI	Quilonum®, Dauelsberg	Individualised
Carbonate	VI	Hypnorex®, Delalande	dosage (based
		Quilonum retard®, Dauelsberg	on serum lith-
Sulphate	VI	Lithium-Duriles®, Pharma-Stern	ium levels of 0.7–1.3 mEq./l.)

Types of clinical effect:
 I = depression-relieving and strongly psychomotor-activating
 II = depression-relieving and activating
 III = depression-relieving and sedative
 IV = major tranquillisers with antidepressant properties
 V = minor tranquillisers with antidepressant properties
 VI = for prophylactic use in depression (● = combined preparations)

53

have been published on the combination of tricyclic antidepressants with methylphenidate, a drug which slows down the degradation of the tricyclics [21, 46]. Finally, it should be mentioned that VAN PRAAG et al. recently reported good therapeutic results with p-chloromethylamphetamine and p-chloro-amphetamine, thereby drawing attention once again not only to the serotonin hypothesis of endogenous depression, but also to the practical possibilities offered by psychostimulants of the amphetamine type [37].

At the beginning of the pharmacotherapeutic era, tricyclic antidepressants were also given in combination with monamine-oxidase inhibitors, a practice which soon resulted in increasingly numerous reports of complications. It was these reports, among other things, which led for some time to the almost complete abandonment of treatment with monamine-oxidase inhibitors in Central Europe. In Great Britain, however, they continued to be prescribed, and during the past few years they have once again come to be used on a larger scale in Central Europe as well, mainly in the form of a fixed combination consisting of trancylpromine and trifluoperazine [24]. This combination has proved effective particularly in the treatment of involutional depression and chronic depression; another of its advantages is the fact that the time-lapse preceding its onset of action is very short. Anglo-Saxon investigators in particular have pointed out that, provided they are employed cautiously, it is even possible to combine tricyclic antidepressants with monamine-oxidase inhibitors. But, where such medication is administered, the antidepressant should be given first, followed afterwards by the monamine-oxidase inhibitor. In cases refractory to treatment, this form of combined medication may serve as a penultimate resort prior to falling back upon electroconvulsive therapy.

For the purposes of clinical practice, the following procedure can perhaps be recommended: if a case of depression proves resistant to oral or intramuscular medication with tricyclics, the next step should be to try intravenous infusions; where these too are of no avail, one can resort to a monamine-oxidase inhibitor, which—provided the patient is kept under careful surveillance—can if necessary be combined with a tricyclic antidepressant; only if this fails is there then no alternative but to institute electroconvulsive therapy.

Basic research in the biochemical field has recently yielded further findings indicating how the success rate with tricyclic antidepressants might possibly be improved. PRANGE et al.[38] and EARLE[18] have shown that better results can be obtained by adding doses of *tri-iodothyronine* to the treatment. COPPEN et al.[15] recommend additional medication with L-tryptophan, which according to them and to other authors also possesses antidepressant properties of its own. In Great Britain L-tryptophan has now been officially approved as a drug suitable for use in the treatment of depression (Optimax®, which contains L-tryptophan, pyridoxine, and ascorbic acid). Moreover, L-hydroxytryptophan is considered by one author[41] to be outstandingly effective as an antidepressant.

Finally, combined treatment with L-dopa (possibly L-dopa plus a decarboxylase inhibitor) also appears to hold out some promise [11, 23, 31, 34]. Since it can be expected to elicit favourable results chiefly in forms of depression running a bipolar course, this combination may also even prove of value in facilitating a differential diagnosis[33]. Speaking quite generally, careful attention should always be paid to differences encountered in the effects of antidepressant drugs under differing circumstances. The effects may vary, for example, depending on:

1. Hereditary factors.
2. Course of the disease.
3. Configuration of the psychopathological syndrome (e.g. a drug may be effective only in retarded depression and not in agitated forms).
4. Sex of the patient. This point was recently referred to by WHYBROW[47] in a comparison of the antidepressant effect of tryptophan and imipramine.

It is conceivable that the systematic use of antidepressant drugs in combination with substances such as tri-iodothyronine, tryptophan, and L-dopa may enable the activity patterns of the tricyclic antidepressants to be more sharply differentiated. Pharmacological and biochemical investigations have in fact shown that the tricyclic antidepressants exert differing effects on the re-uptake of noradrenaline or serotonin. It is thus possible that antidepressants which display no differences in their action when given alone may exhibit varying activity patterns when administered together with the appropriate amine-precursors. Here we perhaps have a line which could be successfully followed up and so contribute to further developments in the field of treatment with the tricyclic compounds that have now gained acceptance as classic antidepressants.

Incidentally, it would also be a valuable acquisition for us if tricyclic antidepressants could be made available in the form of *depot preparations* comparable with the tricyclic neuroleptic depot drugs which have meanwhile rendered such good service.

The most decisive advance achieved in the management of depression since 1957 has been the introduction of prophylactic *lithium therapy*[17, 22]. Only three years ago there were still frequent arguments as to whether continuous treatment with lithium salts really was in fact capable of preventing relapses. The evidence in favour of such medication is now unquestionable, and it has been convincingly confirmed in double-blind withdrawal studies, too, that lithium therapy offers a highly effective means of guarding against relapses[43]. In this area of antidepressant treatment it would be desirable, firstly, if salts other than the acetate, carbonate, and sulphate could be produced (because certain patients have such difficulty in tolerating lithium in its present forms that long-term medication sometimes proves impossible), and, secondly, if long-acting depot preparations could be developed for the purpose of lithium prophylaxis. Whether and, if so, to what extent beneficial drug interactions are likely to result from the combined administration of lithium and other psycho-active agents, is a question that has so far hardly been studied at all[48]. It is also not yet clear whether carbonic anhydrase inhibitors may really be preferable to lithium in view of their better tolerability[45].

To sum up, it may be said that treatment for depression as it now stands already constitutes one of the most satisfactory fields in which somatic methods of therapy are being practised in psychiatry. This is chiefly because, on the one hand, overt symptoms of depression can be effectively combated and because, on the other hand, recourse to lithium prophylaxis also makes it possible to prevent the reappearance of depressive symptoms.

The purpose of this paper has been not only to describe the achievements that have already been attained, but also to highlight those areas in which further progress in the treatment of depression would be most welcome. I also wanted to show how the data acquired in recent years on the pathophysiology—and especially the biochemistry—of endogenous depression have provided a foundation for the continued development and differentiation of antidepressive treatment.

References

1 ANGST, J., HIPPIUS, H.: Pharmakotherapie depressiver Syndrome. In Schulte, W., Mende, W. (Editors): Melancholie in Forschung, Klinik und Behandlung, p. 188 (Thieme, Stuttgart 1969)

2 ANGST, J., JAENICKE, U., PETER, J., PÖLDINGER, W.: Vergleichende Studie mit den tricyclischen Antidepressiva Noxiptilin und Dibenzepin. Arzneimittel-Forsch. *21*, 635 (1971)

3 AYD, F.J., Jr.: A clinical evaluation of doxepin (Sinequan). (A new psychotherapeutic agent). Dis. nerv. Syst. *30*, 396 (1969)

4 AYD, F.J., Jr.: Clinical evaluation of a new tricyclic antidepressant iprindole. Dis. nerv. Syst. *30*, 818 (1969)

5 BERICHT über das Symposium anläßlich der Einführung des Antidepressivums Agedal, Basle/Cologne 1968. Arzneimittel-Forsch. *19*, 833 (1969)

6 BERNER, P., GUSS, H., HOFMANN, G., KRYSPIN-EXNER, K., KÜFFERLE, B.: Doppelblindprüfung von Antidepressiva (Noxiptilin – Imipramin). Arzneimittel-Forsch. *21*, 638 (1971)

7 BIEBER, H., KUGLER, J.: Die Behandlung von depressiven Kranken mit Chlorimipramin-Infusionen. Arch. Psychiat. Nervenkr. *212*, 329 (1969)

8 BORDELEAU, J.-M., TÉTREAULT, L., ST-HILAIRE, J., PINARD, G., BERGERON, R., ROBILLARD, L.: Etude comparative de l'électrochoc unilatéral et bilatéral chez les malades traités pour dépression. Laval méd. *40*, 825 (1969)

9 BOYSEN, K.-H.: Behandlung depressiver Zustandsbilder mit Doxepin. Wien. med. Wschr. *118*, 1095 (1968)

10 BOYSEN, K.-H., HACKL, H., LACKNER, M.: Doppelter Blindversuch mit Doxepin und Opipramol an Patienten mit vegetativ-depressiver Symptomatik. Schweiz. Rdsch. Med. (Praxis) *59*, 1242 (1970)

11 BUNNEY, W.E., Jr., BRODIE, H.K.H., MURPHY, D.L., GOODWIN, F.K.: Studies of alpha-methyl-para-tyrosine, L-dopa, and L-tryptophan in depression and mania. Amer. J. Psychiat. *127*, 872 (1971)

12 BURNER, M.: Traitement ambulatoire des états dépressifs par perfusions intraveineuses de thymoleptiques. Schweiz. Rdsch. Med. (Praxis) *60*, 338 (1971)

13 CERMAK, I., RINGEL, R.: Klinische Erfahrungen mit dem neuen Psychoaktivator Deanxit (Melitracen und Flupenthixol). Schweiz. Rdsch. Med. (Praxis) *60*, 757 (1971)

14 COLLINS, G.H.: Intravenous chlorimipramine in the treatment of severe depression. Brit. J. Psychiat. *117*, 211 (1970)

15 COPPEN, A., SHAW, D.M., HERZBERG, B., MAGGS, R.: Tryptophan in the treatment of depression. Lancet *ii*, 1178 (1967)

16 CRONIN, D., BODLEY, P., POTTS, L., MATHER, M.D., GARDNER, R.K., TOBIN, J.C.: Unilateral and bilateral ECT: a study of memory disturbance and relief from depression. J. Neurol. Neurosurg. Psychiat. *33*, 705 (1970)

17 DIDING, N., OTTOSSON, I.-O., SCHOU, M. (Editors): Lithium in psychiatry. Acta psychiat. scand. Suppl. 207 (1969)

18 EARLE, B.V.: Thyroid hormone and tricyclic antidepressants in resistant depressions. Amer. J. Psychiat. *126*, 1667 (1970)

19 D'ELIA, G. (Editor): Unilateral electroconvulsive therapy. Acta psychiat. scand. Suppl. 215 (1970)

20 FINK, M. (Editor): Convulsive therapy. Seminars in Psychiat. *4*, No. 1 (1972)

21 FLEMENBAUM, A.: Methylphenidate: a catalyst for the tricyclic antidepressants? Amer. J. Psychiat. *128*, 239 (1971); Corresp.

22 FREYHAN, F.A. (Editor): Lithium: clinical and biological aspects. Int. Pharmacopsychiat. *5*, 77 (1970)

23 GOODWIN, F.K., MURPHY, D.L., BRODIE, H.K.H., BUNNEY, W.E., Jr.: L-DOPA, catecholamines, and behavior: a clinical and biochemical study in depressed patients. Biol. Psychiat. *2*, 341 (1970)

24 HARRER, G.: (Editor): Therapie mit Jatrosom, Symp., Salzburg 1969 (Thieme, Stuttgart 1970)

25 HEINRICH, K., KRETSCHMAR, J.H., KRETSCHMAR, C.: Vergleichende Untersuchungen über die Ergebnisse der Pharmakotherapie und der älteren somatischen Behandlungsverfahren bei endogenen Depressionen. Pharmakopsychiat. Neuro-Psychopharmakol. *3*, 50 (1970)

26 KALINOWSKY, L.B., HIPPIUS, H.: Pharmacological, convulsive and other somatic treatments in psychiatry (Grune & Stratton, New York/London 1969)

27 KIELHOLZ, P.: Diagnose und Therapie der Depressionen für den Praktiker, 3rd Ed. (Lehmanns, Munich 1971)

28 KUHN, R.: Über die Behandlung depressiver Zustände mit einem Iminodibenzylderivat (G 22355). Schweiz. med. Wschr. *87*, 1135 (1957)

29 LAURELL, B. (Editor): Flurothyl convulsive therapy. Acta psychiat. scand. Suppl. 213 (1970)

30 MARK, V.H., BARRY, H., McLARDY, T., ERVIN, F.R.: The destruction of both anterior thalamic nuclei in a patient with intractable agitated depression. J. nerv. ment. Dis. *150*, 266 (1970)

31 MATUSSEK, N., BENKERT, O., SCHNEIDER, K., OTTEN, H., POHLMEIER, H.: Wirkung eines Decarboxylasehemmers (Ro 4-4602) in Kombination mit L-DOPA auf gehemmte Depressionen. Arzneimittel-Forsch. *20*, 934 (1970)

32 MOLČAN, I., MOTÝLOVÁ, A., POLÁK, L.: Ein Beitrag zur Pharmakotherapie depressiver Störungen mittels der Kombination von Amitriptylin und Perphenazin. Int. Pharmacopsychiat. *4*, 77 (1970)

33 MURPHY, D.L., BRODIE, H.K.H., GOODWIN, F.K., BUNNEY, W.E., Jr.: Regular induction of hypomania by L-dopa in "bipolar" manic-depressive patients. Nature (Lond.) *229*, 135 (1971)

34 PERSSON, T., WÅLINDER, J.: L-DOPA in the treatment of depressive symptoms. Brit. J. Psychiat. *119*, 277 (1971)

35 PFLUG, B., TÖLLE, R.: Therapie endogener Depressionen durch Schlafentzug. Nervenarzt *42*, 117 (1971)

36 POST, F., REES, W.L., SCHURR, P.H.: An evaluation of bimedial leucotomy. Brit. J. Psychiat. *114*, 1223 (1968)

37 PRAAG, H.M. VAN, SCHUT, T., BOSMA, E., BERGH, R. VAN DEN: A comparative study of the therapeutic effects of some 4-chlorinated amphetamine derivatives in depressive patients. Psychopharmacologia (Berl.) *20*, 66 (1971)

38 PRANGE, A.J., Jr., WILSON, I.C., RABON, A.M., LIPTON, M.A.: Enhancement of imipramine antidepressant activity by thyroid hormone. Amer. J. Psychiat. *126*, 457 (1969)

39 REITER, P.J.: On flupentixol, an antidepressant of a new chemical group. Brit. J. Psychiat. *115*, 1399 (1969)

40 ROSENTHAL, S.H., WULFSOHN, N.L.: Electrosleep. A preliminary communication. J. nerv. ment. Dis. *151*, 146 (1970)

41 SANO, I.: L-5-Hydroxytryptophan-(L-5-HTP)-Therapie. Münch. med. Wschr. (printing)

42 SMALL, J.G., SMALL, I.F.: Indoklon versus ECT – clinical results. Seminars in Psychiat. *4*, 13 (1972)

43 SMALL, J.G., SMALL, I.F., MOORE, D.F.: Experimental withdrawal of lithium in recovered manic-depressive patients: a report of five cases. Amer. J. Psychiat. *127*, 1555 (1971)

44 SPIEGELBERG, U., PETRILOWITSCH, N.: Dimetacrin – ein neues trizyklisches Antidepressivum. Med. Welt *21* (N.F.), 227 (1970)

45 TANIMUKAI, H., INUI, M., KANEKO, Z.: Treatment and prophylaxis of manic states with a carbonic anhydrase inhibitor. Int. Pharmacopsychiat. *5*, 35 (1970)

46 WHARTON, R., PEREL, J.M., DAYTON, P.G., MALITZ, S.: A potential clinical use for methylphenidate with tricyclic antidepressants. Amer. J. Psychiat. *127*, 1619 (1971)

47 WHYBROW, P.C.: On melancholia and models of madness – recent psychobiologic research in depressive illness. Dartmouth med. School Quart. (printing)

48 ZALL, H.: Lithium carbonate and isocarboxazid – an effective drug approach in severe depressions. Amer. J. Psychiat. *127*, 1400 (1971)

Discussion

F. Freyhan: It is always a pleasure for me to listen to the concise papers presented by Dr. Hippius. He hasn't raised a single theoretical or clinical point on which I would disagree with him. But I am afraid I cannot share his optimistic view that the management of depressive disorders represents "one of the most satisfactory fields in which somatic methods of therapy are being practised in psychiatry". Whenever a group of experts, such as we have here, gathers together, it tends to reflect a strong feeling of accomplishment—a feeling founded upon the great wealth of investigative experience in which we all share. We have what we believe to be valid data. But we cannot afford to ignore the fact that lately there has been a rapidly growing disparity between what might be called academic guide-lines for the treatment of depressive disorders and the actual facts of life as encountered in psychiatric practice. In the United States, for example, a phenomenal increase in the use of electroconvulsive therapy has occurred over the past 15 years during which antidepressant drugs have been available. There are two factors which account for this. Firstly, the health insurance schemes operating in the United States cover the patient only for a period of three to four weeks; this means that the most rapid-acting method of treatment has to be selected. Secondly, despite all our scientific efforts to communicate our findings to those engaged in the day-to-day practice of medicine, a certain degree of disillusionment and confusion seems to have arisen. We are in fact witnessing a game of pharmacotherapeutic roulette. The majority of patients referred to us have been receiving five or six drugs, each of a different type. In addition, they are also given electroconvulsive therapy. Thus, it becomes more and more difficult to find a rationale for the therapeutic management of these patients. We need sound guide-lines not only for the G.P. but also for the psychiatric practitioner so that they can make better use of what they read in the literature. I think this poses a challenge to a gathering such as is assembled here. We have to realise that even for the majority of psychiatrists the criteria for effective drug treatment are still poorly understood. The combinations of drugs employed are often quite astonishing, and the ever-increasing dependence on electroshock treatment reflects, I think, a lack of confidence in the use of drugs because of their slow onset of action. While I certainly share with Dr. Hippius the conviction that we have made great progress, I feel it necessary to introduce these rather sobering thoughts into the discussion. The present scene, particularly in the U.S.A., is one that doesn't seem to me to inspire all that much optimism. Part of the trouble lies in problems of communication; but I think that we must ask ourselves why, despite the existence of better and better antidepressants, the use not only of electroconvulsive therapy, but also of such other therapeutic measures as electro-sleep, etc., is still on the increase.

L. Geisler: One question, Dr. Hippius, concerning side effects: patients under treatment with lithium may develop euthyroid goitre. How is this side effect to be accounted for in pathophysiological terms, and how common is it?

W. Walcher: May I say a few words about the electro-sleep method of treatment mentioned by Dr. Hippius? Our anaesthesiologists in Graz have found that this method is not even capable of exerting a sleep-promoting effect. Electronarcosis is another matter; electron-microscope studies conducted in animals have shown that electronarcosis depletes all the synapses of both the cholinergic and the adrenergic systems. It produces a massive, albeit transient, neuroleptic effect, and cannot therefore be expected to have an antidepressant action.

J. J. López Ibor: I should like to draw attention to the results obtained with psychosurgical operations in depressive patients displaying suicidal tendencies—especially young depressives aged between 20 and 30 years who are quite often obsessed with the idea of suicide. In these cases, psychosurgical interventions—i.e. stereotactic operations—frequently yield excellent results.

M. Lorgé: Dr. Hippius, you said in your paper that depot preparations of tricyclic antidepressants would be a valuable acquisition. But wouldn't the action of such preparations be too uncontrollable, and wouldn't this loss of control over the drug's effect be a disadvantage in the treatment of depression? I am, of course, not referring to long-acting preparations which could be given once a day.

A. Coppen: I should like to support what Dr. Freyhan has said about the need for a cautious appraisal of the efficacy of our methods of treatment for affective disorders. As I mentioned earlier, in patients who had recovered from a period of affective disorder, we have had an opportunity of carrying out follow-up studies over two and half years. In these cases we have discovered that—though what are regarded as the best forms of conventional treatment had been given, i.e. electroconvulsive therapy and/or antidepressant drugs—the patients continued to suffer from a considerable amount of illness. We have found, for example, that they spent about 46% of their time with an affective episode and 26% of their time as in-patients, that 43% of them needed one or more courses of electroconvulsive therapy, and that they required antidepressant and antimanic drugs, although these didn't apparently prove all that effective. I think that, if one looks at such patients over a period of time, as I feel one should do, one is bound to conclude that the treatment we are now giving for affective disorders is really still at quite a primitive stage. I don't believe we have grounds for too much self-congratulation, because, as I have tried to show, if we follow these patients up over a fair period of time, the effects of our treatment don't look all that impressive.

J. Welner: I'm sorry that I have to share Dr. Freyhan's and Dr. Coppen's lack of optimism. I say this especially because we are very dissatisfied with the antidepressants we are now using in our everyday psychiatric practice. This dissatisfaction has also been a feature of our trial with Ludiomil. We found that although two-thirds of the patients reacted positively to each of the two drugs—amitriptyline or Ludiomil—only about one-fifth really responded satisfactorily in the sense that the improvement bore comparison with the results obtained in patients given electroconvulsive therapy. I think this is the main reason why electroconvulsive treatment has been resorted to on such a large scale in our country during the last six years or so; we have lost confidence in the drugs available, and we don't have any really rational guide-lines enabling us to judge what dosages we should use and which drugs deserve preference. I don't think that even Dr. Kielholz's system of drug classification offers us a great deal of help in this respect.

P. Kielholz: May I call upon Dr. Hippius to conclude this discussion?

H. Hippius: The principal objection to my paper seems to be that it was too optimistic. Drs. Freyhan, Coppen, and Welner have expressed their scepticism on the subject of the methods currently employed in the management of depressive illness. I think, though, that optimism is justified as regards the somatic treatment of depression. If we compare, for example, the overall results it yields with those obtained by neuroleptic therapy in schizophrenia, we are bound to admit that the situation is much more favourable in the case of depression. As far as depressive illness is concerned, we not only possess the means of treating the signs and symptoms of the disease, but we also have the possibility of carrying out effective prophylaxis. In schizophrenia, prophylaxis of this type is only possible to a limited extent; it is true that recurrences can sometimes be avoided by the long-term administration of neuroleptic drugs, but as a rule all that this achieves is to postpone for a few years the development of so-called residual and terminal states and the appearance of irreversible schizophrenic deficiency symptoms. By comparison, the five years' experience I have now had in the prophylactic use of lithium in depression has been much more encouraging. Hence, I do not hesitate to describe the introduction of lithium as a decisive advance.

Now, of course, I didn't wish to give the impression of believing that drug therapy has solved the entire problem of depression. In fact, it was in an attempt to prevent such a misunderstanding from arising that I dealt in detail with the aetiology of depressive syndromes. I emphasised that in every case of depression account must also be taken of psychological and social factors which, naturally, cannot be successfully tackled with drugs alone.

Finally, I must stress that basic pathophysiological research has yielded more extensive and more differentiated findings in the field of depression than in that of schizophrenia. Consequently, close collaboration between biochemists engaged in basic research, on the one hand, and clinicians, on the other, may well lead to further discoveries of value for the treatment of depression. That, too, strikes me as giving cause for optimism; here, once again, the situation in the case of schizophrenia is not so favourable. The biochemical findings that have been obtained in research on schizophrenia are much more contradictory and therefore cannot yet be used as a basis for new developments in the realm of therapy.

When discussing the use of drugs in the management of depression, we must not lose sight of the fact that the success rate achieved in the relatively short-term treatment of depressive phases does not usually exceed 60–80%. The data so far available on the incidence of relapses in patients given prophylactic treatment with lithium are not consistent, but it is safe to assume that this incidence, if assessed over a five-year follow-up period, will also amount to some 20–40%.

As for the mechanism by which euthyroid goitre develops during lithium treatment, I'm afraid I cannot supply you with any information on this point. This side effect, at all events, is a comparatively harmless one. Viewed in their totality, however, the side effects of lithium are such that we must make every effort to improve upon this method of treatment. Time and again, lithium medication, though effective *per se*, has to be discontinued because the patient concerned cannot tolerate any of the lithium preparations currently available.

As regards Dr. WALCHER's comments, I would remind you that in my paper I adopted a very cautious approach to the subject of electro-sleep. However, with your reference to electronarcosis, Dr. WALCHER, you touched upon an important question. We should submit all methods of treatment to investigations of the kind that have been carried out with electronarcosis. This applies in particular to sleep deprival and electroconvulsive therapy. The current state of our knowledge demands that we should always endeavour to establish links with basic biochemical research. Otherwise we run the risk of constructing, on the basis of the results obtained with drug therapy, theories that will promptly collapse as soon as these results are compared with those yielded by other methods of treatment. This demand, by the way, also holds good for general clinical research on depression and not only for treatment-oriented research. Masked depression is a case in point: it would certainly not be a good thing if we were to go on investigating masked depression only from the psychopathological and clinical angle. On the contrary, it is urgently necessary that the masked depressions, too, should be included in genetic and biochemical basic research programmes. If they are not, attempts to solve the problem of masked depression will continue to be based only on the study of case records, and possibly only on clinical anecdotes and speculations.

As for psychosurgical interventions, stereotactic operations are definitely indicated in certain exceptional cases, e.g. in cases of depression associated with severe obsessional syndromes. In the United States, incidentally, operations of this kind have been performed even in patients displaying no obsessional symptoms.

On the subject of depot preparations, I would agree that the diminished control which one would have over the effects of such drugs does pose a difficult problem—a problem, however, that is also encountered with the use of neuroleptic agents in depot form in the treatment of schizophrenia. But one advantage of depot preparations, particularly where patients are being treated on an ambulant basis, is that the physician knows that the drug has actually been taken. Whether the use of a depot preparation is really indicated is a question that has to be weighed up in each individual case. There will always be patients who should be given a depot preparation because they cannot otherwise be depended upon to take their tablets. This lack of reliability on the patient's part is very often met with in long-term lithium treatment. I must admit, though, that in depressive illness in particular, the use of depot preparations does raise one special problem—and that is the risk of their causing the patient to swing from depression into mania. Due account must be taken of this risk from the very outset when developing depot preparations. A similar problem exists with the neuroleptic depot preparations—namely, the problem of drug-induced depression, which, incidentally, can be quite successfully combated by administering L-dopa. Thus, despite what Dr. BIRKMAYER said in the discussion following Dr. MATUSSEK's paper, there *are* depressive syndromes that respond to L-dopa. Perhaps this response is linked with the fact that in drug-induced depression the depressive symptomatology is associated with extrapyramidal motor disturbances. One further brief remark in this connection: impressive though all the findings corroborating the serotonin hypothesis of endogenous depression undoubtedly are, it would be inadvisable—precisely because of the observations I have just mentioned concerning L-dopa—to abandon the catecholamine hypothesis completely at this stage. It is perfectly conceivable that both hypotheses are justified; it may even be that some sort of interaction between serotonin and catecholamines is responsible for the development of depression.

P. KIELHOLZ: Thank you, Dr. HIPPIUS. We all seem to be agreed that there are a very large variety of refractory and chronic depressive states, that—to revert to a point mentioned previously—many cases of masked depression are not diagnosed in good time, that one great disadvantage of the antidepressants in current use is their slow onset of effect, and that basic research in pathophysiology and biochemistry, as well as the development of new drugs by the research-based pharmaceutical industry, could be of considerable help to us.

Suicidal tendencies, anxiety, and depression

by W. PÖLDINGER*

The past 20 years have witnessed an intensification of research on depression. One of the reasons for this is no doubt the fact that, since it has quite a high mortality, depression can certainly be regarded as one of the so-called "serious" diseases. The vast majority of the fatalities occurring in cases of depression are due to suicide; and attempts at suicide also constitute grave complications of this illness.

Thanks to the development of the modern antidepressant drugs, major progress has recently been made in the management of depression and, in particular, it has now become possible to resort on a wide scale to ambulant treatment for depressive conditions; but at the same time—owing once again to the risk of suicide—the burden of responsibility resting on the shoulders of the physician treating such cases has correspondingly increased.

Turning first of all to the question as to the frequency of suicidal acts among depressed patients, we have outlined in Table 1 the results of several studies on the incidence of depression as a cause of suicide. These studies confirm the general conclusion emerging from many other similar investigations, i.e. that some 30–50 % of suicides are attributable to depressive disease.

Table 2, which deals with attempted suicide, shows that here the percentages reported in the papers in question have a somewhat wider scatter. It should be added that, in these statistical reviews, no account has been taken of the nosological classifications of the various depressive mood disorders.

Tables 3 and 4 have been adapted from compilations in which LUNGERS-HAUSEN[19] has endeavoured to determine the percentage incidence of endogenous psychosis as a cause of suicide or attempted suicide. It is very important to single out endogenous psychosis, because "depression" is a diagnosis certainly subject to greater differences of interpretation than the more clearly definable diagnosis of "endogenous depression" or "depression of the manic-depressive type".

Table 1. Percentage figures for cases of suicide in which "depression" was diagnosed.

Authors	Year of publication	No. of cases	"Depression" diagnosed (%)
Robins et al.[25] (U.S.A.)	1959	139	45
Dorpat and Ripley[8] (U.S.A.)	1960	108	30
Capstick[6] (Great Britain)	1960	351	38.7
Sainsbury[28] (Great Britain)	1968	409	47.6

* Psychiatrische Universitätsklinik, Vienna, Austria.

Table 3 lists the percentages of suicides, and Table 4 the percentages of attempted suicides, accounted for by endogenous psychoses. Although the figures in these two tables relate to all forms of endogenous psychosis, various studies have revealed that, compared with endogenous depression, schizophrenic psychoses are responsible for only a very small proportion of suicidal acts. Incidentally, the percentages attributable to endogenous psychoses tend to be higher the more recent the publication, particularly in the case of the suicides; but this can to some extent undoubtedly be ascribed to a progressive refinement of diagnostic methods.

It seems at all events safe to assume that *endogenous* depression is not the only condition entailing a high risk of suicide. Owing to methodological difficulties,

Table 2. Percentage figures for cases of attempted suicide in which "depression" was diagnosed.

Authors	Year of publication	No. of cases	"Depression" diagnosed (%)
Batchelor and *Napier*[3] (Great Britain)	1953	200	47
Ettlinger and *Flordh*[10] (Sweden)	1955	500	30.8
Sclare and *Hamilton*[31] (Great Britain)	1963	180	70
Krupinski et al.[15] (Australia)	1965	358	31.6
Achté and *Ginman*[1] (Finland)	1966	100	21
Blanc et al.[5] (France)	1966	500	48
Kapamadžija[13] (Jugoslavia)	1966	180	13
Pöldinger[22] (Switzerland)	1968	450	47.7

Table 3. Percentage figures for the incidence of endogenous psychosis as a cause of suicide.

Authors	Year of publication	Percentage
Delannoy[7] (Austria)	1927	9
Bingler[4] (Germany)	1930	6
Weichbrodt[34] (Germany)	1937	3
Säker[27] (Germany)	1938	12
Gruhle[12] (Germany)	1940	15
Parnitzke[20] (Eastern Germany)	1961	36
Yessler et al.[36] (U.S.A.)	1961	22
Ringel[24] (Austria)	1961	34
Lungershausen[18] (Western Germany)	1968	40

Table 4. Percentage figures for the incidence of endogenous psychosis as a cause of attempted suicide.

Authors	Year of publication	Percentage
Schneider[29] (Germany)	1933	11
Feudell[11] (Eastern Germany)	1952	10
Ringel[23] (Austria)	1953	14
Ettlinger and Flordh[10] (Sweden)	1955	10
Parnitzke[20] (Eastern Germany)	1961	14
Yessler et al.[36] (U.S.A.)	1961	10
Rüegsegger[26] (Switzerland)	1963	25
Blanc et al.[5] (France)	1966	22
Lungershausen[18] (Western Germany)	1968	15
Pöldinger[22] (Switzerland)	1968	15

Table 5. Follow-up studies on the risk of suicide in patients with endogenous depression.

Authors	Year of publication	Start of case history	No. of patients	Deaths during follow-up period	Percentage of deaths due to suicide	Percentage of suicides in each series of patients
Slater[32] (Germany)	1938	1904–1922	138	59	15.3	6.5
Langelüddeke[16] (Germany)	1941	1904–1913	341	268	15.3	12.0
Lundquist[17] (Sweden)	1945	1912–1931	319	119	14.3	5.4
Schulz[30] (Western Germany)	1949	1904–1927	2,004	492	13.4	3.3
Stenstedt[33] (Sweden)	1952	1919–1948	216 288*	42 ?	14.3	2.8 6.3*
Ringel[24] (Austria)	1961	1951	126	?		10.3
Angst[2] (Switzerland)	1966	1959–1963	331	14	85.6	3.6
Perris[21] (Sweden)	1966	1950–1963	797	102	22.6	2.9
Pöldinger[22] (Switzerland)	1968	1950–1955	136	50	16.0	5.9

* Including secondary cases

however, no precise figures relating to the population as a whole are at present obtainable. Here, it would be possible to form a clearer impression only by resorting to collaborative research involving the application of uniformly defined terms and standardised methods of statistical analysis.

A further assessment of the risk of suicide in the presence of endogenous depression can also be made on the basis of follow-up studies in patients suffering from this form of depression. Presented in Table 5 are the findings reported in a series of such follow-up studies covering relatively long periods. These findings confirm once again that individuals subject to endogenous depression run a much higher risk of committing suicide than do members of the general population. One striking feature of the statistics given in Table 5 is the fact that—at least during the past 30 years or so—the percentage of deaths due to suicide has remained roughly constant; though the suicide quota reported by ANGST is exceptionally high, it has to be viewed in relation to the small total number of deaths that had occurred among the patients he studied, the reason for which was presumably the comparative shortness of the follow-up period.

Following this brief review in which the correlations between suicidal acts and depressive diseases have been examined with reference to nosological classification, we must now take a closer look at these same correlations from the symptomatological standpoint as well, particularly in view of the fact that—thanks to the scope offered by modern pharmacotherapy in the treatment of depressive conditions—it has become a matter of the utmost importance also to pay due attention to the phenomenological classification in terms of "target symptoms" or "target syndromes". The various drugs currently available for the treatment of depression differ from one another not only so far as the potency of their "antidepressant" properties is concerned, but also with regard to their spectra of activity, inasmuch as some tend rather to suppress anxiety and agitation while others have a predominantly disinhibiting and activating effect. Thus, for example, in an anxious and agitated patient suffering from depression the use of a monamine-oxidase inhibitor might well aggravate his anxiety and so initially activate his suicidal tendencies—an effect which of course should at all costs be avoided.

With a view to systematically analysing the widely accepted clinical impression that a close connection exists between depression, anxiety, and suicidal tendencies, we—together with BLASER*, GEHRING**, and SUTTER***, with whom we were then still working in Basle—carefully studied certain specific variables in 364 patients admitted to the University Psychiatric Clinic in Basle to receive treatment for depression. The total was made up of: 129 patients with endogenous depression (i.e. periodic, involutional, or cyclic depression); 216 cases of psychogenic depression (i.e. reactive depression, exhaustion depression, or neurotic depression), and 19 patients with symptomatic or organic depression. Our statistical analysis covered the following variables: sex and age, main nosological diagnosis and syndromal classification, attempts at suicide and presence of suicidal thoughts, as well as anxiety and sleep disturbances.

---

* Psychologist, ** biologist, and *** sociologist at the Department for Research on Depression, University Psychiatric Clinic, Basle, Switzerland.

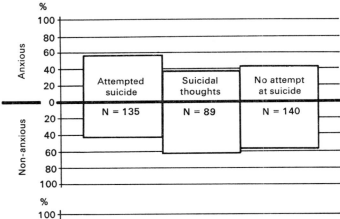

Fig. 1.
Correlation between anxiety and attempted suicide. Correlation significant (P<0.01).

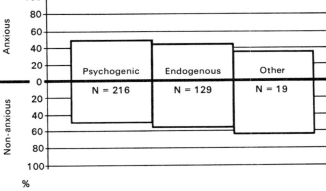

Fig. 2.
Correlation between anxiety and nosological diagnosis. Correlation not significant.

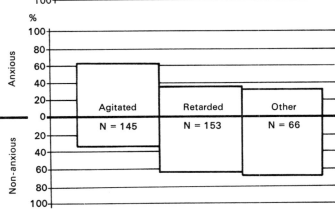

Fig. 3.
Correlation between anxiety and syndromal classification. Correlation significant (P<0.001).

In an initial analysis the distribution of each of these variables was first compared using punched cards, and the χ^2 test was performed to determine the statistical significance of the differences in their distribution.

Figure 1 reveals that anxious patients differed from non-anxious ones with respect to the incidence of suicidal attempts and suicidal thoughts.

The next question of interest to us was whether any significant differences in the incidence of anxious mood disorders could be found in the various nosologically classified forms of depression. Figure 2 shows that none were apparent.

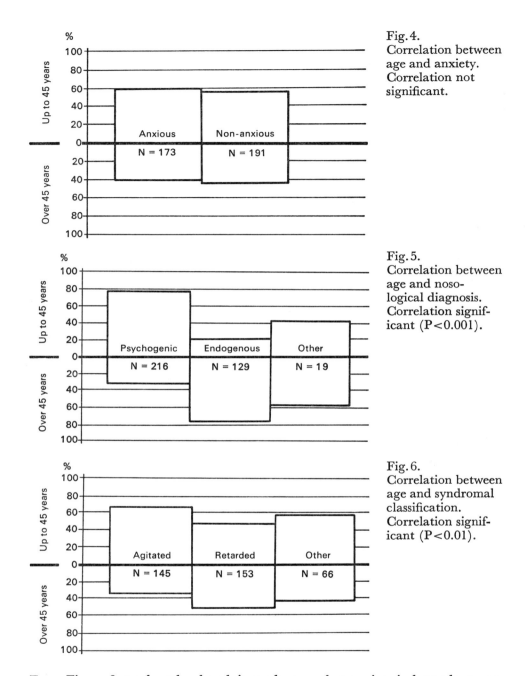

Fig. 4.
Correlation between age and anxiety. Correlation not significant.

Fig. 5.
Correlation between age and noso-logical diagnosis. Correlation signif-icant (P<0.001).

Fig. 6.
Correlation between age and syndromal classification. Correlation signif-icant (P<0.01).

From Figure 3, on the other hand, it can be seen that anxiety is dependent upon the syndromal characteristics of the various forms of depression insofar as psychomotor status is concerned. This is in line with clinical experience, which indicates that anxious patients are often also agitated (KIELHOLZ[14]).

In addition, we were interested in the relationship between age and anxiety. Here, as shown in Figure 4, we were unable to find any difference between patients under 45 years of age and those aged over 45.

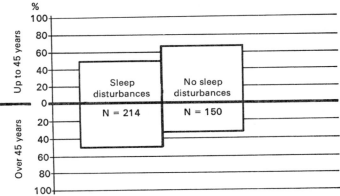

Fig. 7.
Correlation between age and sleep disturbances. Correlation significant (P<0.01).

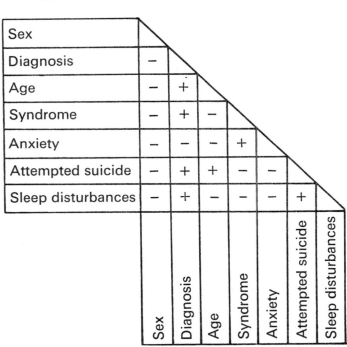

Fig. 8.
Significant correlations (+) between pairs of variables when the influence of all other variables is excluded (r ⩾0.20).

	Sex	Diagnosis	Age	Syndrome	Anxiety	Attempted suicide	Sleep disturbances
Sex							
Diagnosis	−						
Age	−	+					
Syndrome	−	+	−				
Anxiety	−	−	−	+			
Attempted suicide	−	+	+	−	−		
Sleep disturbances	−	+	−	−	−	+	

From Figure 5, by contrast, it becomes evident that the age factor does influence the nosological category to which patients are assigned. In this connection, however, it must be borne in mind that the "endogenous depression" group also included cases of involutional depression; in the patients under 45 years of age psychogenic forms of depression predominated. As revealed by Figure 6, age was likewise found to exert an influence on the syndromal classification.

Since sleep disturbances tend to occur with particular frequency in elderly patients, we also studied this factor in our analysis. When the incidence of sleep disorders was examined in relation to age, yet another difference became apparent: patients over 45 complain more often of sleep disorders than do patients under 45 (Figure 7).

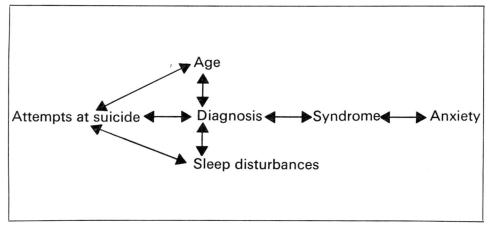

Fig. 9. Working hypothesis indicating the mutual interdependence of variables (r ≫ 0.20).

Numerous further examples could be added to those that have been cited here. When comparing and contrasting two sets of variables in this manner, however, one is inevitably faced with the question whether, in view of the complex inter-relationships that are liable to exist between one variable and another, such comparisons are really permissible. Consequently, when determining the degree to which one variable is dependent on the other, attempts should also be made to ensure the statistical elimination of such influence as further variables might exert on the relationship between the two under study. Having completed our initial analysis, we therefore then investigated the partial correlations between pairs of variables when the influence of all the other variables had been excluded. The findings obtained are presented graphically in Figure 8, from which it can be seen that partial correlations existed between attempted suicide on the one hand and nosological diagnosis, age, and sleep disturbances on the other. The nosological diagnosis, too, showed partial correlations with age, syndromal classification, and sleep disturbances. Finally, the syndromal classification was also found to be correlated with anxiety.

These findings provide the basis for the working hypothesis outlined in Figure 9, which indicates the mutual interdependence of the variables in question.

In depressive conditions it is chiefly via the syndromal classification in terms of psychomotor status that the connections between anxiety and suicidal tendencies operate, the syndromal classification being dependent on the manifestation of anxiety. But these studies of ours also indicated that the nosological classification is dependent upon the syndromal classification. The example of sleep disturbances shows that the nosological classification likewise depends on how the patient happens to feel at the time. Age, too, must be regarded as exerting a considerable influence on the diagnosis of depression.

It is therefore essential that one should always pay particular attention to the age factor when undertaking research on depression. As also evidenced by clinical experience, much the same applies to suicidal tendencies as well, studies having shown that attempted suicide is more common among younger patients and successful suicide more common among older patients.

Compared with our first analysis, this second study of partial correlations has the advantage that, when examining the connections between two variables, we were also able to make allowance for the influence exerted by other variables. Its chief disadvantage lies in the fact that, in contrast to the first method we employed, it did not provide us with any detailed information on the type of the connection existing between the variables.

To sum up, it may thus be said that there are close correlations between suicidal tendencies, depression, and anxiety. In cases of depression, the risk of suicide, however, depends not so much upon the nosological classification of the clinical picture presented by the patient, but to a far greater degree upon the character of the syndrome, including especially the extent to which such distinguishing features as anxiety and agitation are present.

Manifestations of this kind—referred to as "target symptoms" or "target syndromes"—are likewise of cardinal significance in connection with drug therapy for depressive diseases. When investigating a new antidepressant agent, it is therefore important not only to record the percentage of improvements occurring in depressive conditions, but in particular also to note in each case the type of syndrome from which the patient is suffering, because only in this way is it possible to draw valid conclusions concerning the precise pattern of activity displayed by the drug. A knowledge of the latter is also of major importance with regard to the problem of suicide prevention, a problem to the solution of which the modern antidepressants have made a decisive contribution.

References

1 ACHTÉ, K. A., GINMAN, L.: Suicidal attempts with narcotics and poisons. Acta psychiat. scand. *42*, 214 (1966)
2 ANGST, J.: Zur Ätiologie und Nosologie endogener depressiver Psychosen (Springer, Berlin/Heidelberg/New York 1966; Monogr. Neurol. Psychiat. No. 112)
3 BATCHELOR, I. R. C., NAPIER, M. B.: Broken homes and attempted suicide. Brit. J. Delinq. *4*, 99 (1953)
4 BINGLER, N.: Statistische Betrachtungen über den Selbstmord im Reichsheere in den Jahren 1921–1929. Veröff. Heeressan.wes. No. 84:74 (1930)
5 BLANC, M., BOURGEOIS, M., HENRY, P.: La tentative de suicide. Aspects actuels (A propos de 500 observations). Ann. méd.-psychol. *124*, 554 (1966)
6 CAPSTICK, A.: Recognition of emotional disturbance and the prevention of suicide. Brit. med. J. *i*, 1179 (1960)
7 DELANNOY, R. M.: Selbstmorde und Selbstmordversuche in Wien im Jahre 1926. Statist. Mitt. Stadt Wien, 3. Sonderheft (1927)
8 DORPAT, T. L., RIPLEY, H. S.: A study of suicide in the Seattle area. Comprehens. Psychiat. *1*, 349 (1960)
9 DOTZAUER, G., GOEBELS, H., LEGEWIE, H.: Selbstmord und Selbstmordversuch. Münch. med. Wschr. *105*, 973 (1963)
10 ETTLINGER, R. W., FLORDH, P.: Attempted suicide: experience of five hundred cases at a general hospital. Acta psychiat. scand. Suppl. 103 (1955)
11 FEUDELL, P.: Epikrise zu 700 Selbstmordversuchen. Psychiat. Neurol. med. Psychol. (Lpz.) *4*, 147 (1952)

12 GRUHLE, H.W.: Selbstmord (Thieme, Leipzig 1940)

13 KAPAMADŽIJA, B.: Stoosamdeset slučajeva pokušaja samoubistva tretiranih na našoj klinici od 1952–1966 godine (One hundred and eighty cases of attempted suicide treated at our clinic from 1952 to 1966). Med. Pregl. *19*, 261 (1966)

14 KIELHOLZ, P.: Diagnose und Therapie der Depressionen für den Praktiker, 3rd Ed. (Lehmanns, Munich 1971)

15 KRUPINSKI, J., POLKE, P., STOLLER, A.: Psychiatric disturbances in attempted and completed suicides in Victoria during 1963. Med. J. Aust. *52/ii*, 773 (1965)

16 LANGELÜDDEKE, A.: Über Lebenserwartung und Rückfallhäufigkeit bei Manisch-Depressiven. Z. psych. Hyg. *14*, 1 (1941)

17 LUNDQUIST, G.: Prognosis and course in manic-depressive psychoses. A follow-up study of 319 first admissions. Acta psychiat. (Kbh.) Suppl. 35 (1945)

18 LUNGERSHAUSEN, E.: Selbstmorde und Selbstmordversuche bei Studenten (Hüthig, Heidelberg 1968; Theoretische und klinische Medizin in Einzeldarstellungen, Vol. 38)

19 LUNGERSHAUSEN, E.: Zum Problem des Suizids bei endogenen Psychosen. In Huber, G. (Editor): Schizophrenie und Zyklothymie, p. 197 (Thieme, Stuttgart 1969)

20 PARNITZKE, K.H.: Bemerkungen zum Selbstmordgeschehen der letzten Jahre. Psychiat. Neurol. med. Psychol. (Lpz.) *13*, 397 (1961)

21 PERRIS, C.: A study of bipolar (manic-depressive) and unipolar recurrent depressive psychoses. Acta psychiat. scand. *42*, Suppl. 194 (1966)

22 PÖLDINGER, W.: Die Abschätzung der Suizidalität, Akt. Probl. Psychiat. Neurol. Neurochir., Vol. I (Huber, Berne/Stuttgart 1968)

23 RINGEL, E.: Der Selbstmord. Abschluss einer krankhaften psychischen Entwicklung (Maudrich, Vienna/Düsseldorf 1953)

24 RINGEL, E.: Neue Untersuchungen zum Selbstmordproblem. Unter besonderer Berücksichtigung prophylaktischer Gesichtspunkte (Hollinek, Vienna 1961)

25 ROBINS, E., MURPHY, G.E., WILKINSON, R.H., Jr., GASSNER, S., KAYES, J.: Some clinical considerations in the prevention of suicide based on a study of 134 successful suicides. Amer. J. publ. Hlth *49*, 888 (1959)

26 RÜEGSEGGER, P.: Selbstmordversuche. Psychiat. et Neurol. (Basle) *146*, 81 (1963)

27 SÄKER, G.: Ärztliches zum Selbstmordproblem. Münch. med. Wschr. *85*, 782 (1938)

28 SAINSBURY, P.: Suicide and depression. In: Recent developments in affective disorders; Special Publ. No. 2 (Roy. med.-psychol. Ass. 1968)

29 SCHNEIDER, K.: Selbstmordversuche. Dtsch. med. Wschr. *59*, 1389 (1933)

30 SCHULZ, B.: Sterblichkeit endogen Geisteskranker und ihrer Eltern. Z. menschl. Vererb.- u. Konstit.-Lehre *29*, 338 (1949)

31 SCLARE, A.B., HAMILTON, C.M.: Attempted suicide in Glasgow. Brit. J. Psychiat. *109*, 609 (1963)

32 SLATER, E.: Zur Erbpathologie des manisch-depressiven Irreseins. Die Eltern und Kinder von Manisch-Depressiven. Z. ges. Neurol. Psychiat. *163*, 1 (1938)

33 STENSTEDT, Å.: A study in manic depressive psychosis. Clinical, social and genetic investigations. Acta psychiat. scand. Suppl. 79 (1952)

34 WEICHBRODT, R.: Der Selbstmord (Karger, Basle 1937)

35 WORLD HEALTH ORGANISATION. Prevention of suicide. Publ. Hlth Papers No. 35 (W.H.O., Geneva 1968)

36 YESSLER, P.G., GIBBS, J.J., BECKER, H.A.: On the communication of suicidal ideas. II. Some medical considerations. Arch. gen. Psychiat. *5*, 34 (1961)

Discussion

I. SANO: For some years now I have been coming across patients with endogenous depression who sleep more than usual and display a good appetite. They put on weight during the depressive phase. I describe these patients as suffering from an "appetite-sleep" form of endogenous depression. Some 10% of my cases fall into this category. Is your experience, Dr. PÖLDINGER, similar to mine in this respect?

H. HEIMANN: I have a question for Dr. PÖLDINGER on the subject of "age and the diagnosis of endogenous versus psychogenic depression": do you not think that the results obtained in this connection are due to artifact? After all, in younger patients presenting with depression, eliciting factors are usually clearly apparent and the clinician tends to classify the depression in such cases as being of a psychogenic or neurotic type. Not until he has had to treat the same patients on several subsequent occasions does he realise that their depression has probably always been of the endogenous type.

P. KIELHOLZ: I was also intending to ask the same question. It often happens that patients are classified initially as cases of reactive depression, then as cases of neurotic depression, and later still as cases of periodic depression; not until they display their first manic phase are they finally labelled as cases of cyclic depression. I think that this is a very important question. The World Health Organisation is planning transcultural studies on this subject, using a standardised terminology and classification. Only in this way can comparable results be obtained in the various countries.

W. PÖLDINGER: May I deal first of all with the point raised concerning age. I am very grateful for the questions put to me on this subject, because they highlight a factor which, I believe, we are all too apt to forget—namely, ourselves. The process of diagnosis invariably involves an interaction between the patient, in whom the diagnosis is established, and the psychiatrist, who establishes the diagnosis. We carried out a very large number of reliability studies in Basle, and we found that cardinal importance must be attached to such studies.

As regards masked depression, we have to realise that the frequency with which it is diagnosed depends on how much psychiatric training the G.P.s and specialists in the district concerned have had. If a specialist in internal medicine diagnoses depression and refers the patient to a hospital, that patient is generally regarded thereafter as, in fact, suffering from depression. But if the specialist refers a case to hospital for further investigation because he suspects the patient of having a cholecystopathy but doesn't know whether it may be of psychogenic or hysterical origin, and if *we* then diagnose depression, we call it masked depression. For this reason, I feel that we should take as our starting point not the diagnoses noted on the patients' cards, but the incidence of psychopathological and somatic features. As Dr. HEIMANN rightly implied, it is very important to know who made the diagnosis; it is perhaps true that the correlations between the variables shed light not only on the categories to which the patients belong, but also to some extent on the doctors who make the diagnosis. This, I think, is a point which we should always bear in mind.

As for Dr. SANO's question concerning the increase in appetite sometimes observed in depressive patients, this feature is of course by no means uncommon. In German-speaking countries it is so familiar that even ordinary people refer to it. They call it "*Kummerspeck*", which means, literally, "the fat that comes from worrying". Moreover, I have heard patients in Vienna saying "When I feel bad, I just have to eat". We have also observed on many occasions the increase in sleep requirement you mentioned. Sometimes, however, we have the impression that we are putting the wrong interpretation on what the patients tell us. These patients are simply retarded and have little drive. They don't want to do anything. Their chief desire is to go to bed and to hear nothing and see nothing. But they don't sleep, they just lie there and worry. And then, because they go to bed during the day, they usually cannot sleep at night.

The problem of quantifying the symptomatology of depression

by P. Pichot*

The first practical methods of quantifying the symptomatology of psychiatric disease were devised more than 50 years ago, the first rating scale (the Phipps Psychiatric Clinic Rating Chart) having been described by Kempf[10] in 1915 and the first self-rating questionnaire (Personal Data Sheet) by Woodworth[28] in 1917.

It was not until much later, however, that these documentary aids came to be applied to the specific problem of depression. As regards physician rating scales, mention must be made of the pioneering studies conducted by Moore[19], who in 1930 assessed 41 different signs and symptoms in 367 psychotic patients on the basis of clinical observations and submitted the resultant scores to a factorial analysis. He was thus able to distinguish between two groups of symptoms, one of which could be used as a measure of the factor "retarded depression" and the other as a measure of the factor "agitated depression". As for self-rating questionnaires, the first part of the Minnesota Multiphasic Personality Inventory (M.M.P.I.) was published in 1940, and the first M.M.P.I. manual appeared in 1943. The M.M.P.I. included a "depression scale" consisting of a selection of items by reference to which normal subjects could be differentiated to a significant extent from a group of patients diagnosed on the basis of clinical examination as suffering from depression. It was also back in 1930 that Jasper[9] published his "depression-elation" questionnaire. For various reasons, however, these documentary aids do not fall within the compass of the present paper. Moore was concerned with purely theoretical considerations. The M.M.P.I. depression scale has proved to be very unspecific because of its extreme sensitivity; it is in fact so sensitive that it yields a high score in the case of patients suffering from nothing more than anxiety states. As for Jasper's questionnaire, it was drawn up for the purpose of investigating normal subjects.

The development of the first practical rating scales, which are still in use today, coincided more or less with the advent of the psychotropic drugs, and was undoubtedly stimulated by the need to have a precise method of checking the therapeutic effects of these drugs.

These rating scales were of a very general type, because they were intended as a means of studying various aspects of the behaviour of hospitalised or ambulant mental patients, irrespective of the exact nature of the disease involved. Following his initial studies published in 1951[27], Wittenborn made his Psychiatric Rating Scales (P.R.S.) available to psychiatrists in 1955[25], and subsequently revised them in 1964[26]. In 1953, Lorr and his associates in the Veterans Ad-

* Clinique de la Faculté de médecine, Centre psychiatrique Sainte-Anne, Paris, France.

ministration presented their Northport Record, followed by a Multidimensional Scale for Rating Psychiatric Patients (M.S.R.P.P.)[14], which was revised in 1963 and re-issued under the title "In-patient Multidimensional Psychiatric Scale" (I.M.P.S.)[16]. The Wittenborn and Lorr scales contain items relating to the various aspects of depressive symptomatology, and it is possible by means of factorial analyses to pick out groups of these items and to use them as factorial scales for quantifying such factors as "depression" and "anxiety" (P.R.S.), "retarded depression" and "melancholic agitation" (M.S.R.P.P.), and "sluggishness and apathy" and "anxious intropunitivity" (I.M.P.S.)*.

In parallel to these scales, a group of university psychiatric clinics in Germany, Austria, Switzerland, and Jugoslavia has developed an optic scanner sheet based on norms established by the *Arbeitsgemeinschaft für Methodik und Dokumentation in der Psychiatrie* (A.M.P.)[1] and serving, among other things, to record a certain number of the signs and symptoms encountered in depressive patients.

During the late 1950s and early 1960s various rating scales intended specifically for use in depression were published. The first to appear was the one designed by LEHMANN[12] in 1958 for the purpose of studying the effect of imipramine. In 1960, HAMILTON[8] in England published his Rating Scale for Depression, which comprised 17 items and which is still the documentary aid most widely employed today in trials of antidepressant drugs. In 1961, GRINKER et al.[7] brought out their study entitled "The phenomena of depressions"; this was a particularly ambitious attempt to submit the symptomatology of depression to statistical analysis, inasmuch as the authors used two rating scales for each patient—a Feelings and Concerns Check-List, comprising 111 items, and a Current Behaviour Check-List, featuring 139 items. Further rating scales have since been published, including the Quantification of Depressive Reactions by CUTLER and KURLAND[5] in 1961, the Psychiatric Judgment Depression Scale by OVERALL et al.[21] in 1962, the Depression Rating Scale by H. WECHSLER et al.[24] in 1963, and the *Bewertungsskala der Depressionszustände* (Rating Scale for Depressive States) by BOJANOVSKÝ and CHLOUPKOVÁ[3] in 1966—to quote but a few.

In addition to these physician rating scales, self-rating questionnaires have also been devised. The M.M.P.I., for example, as already pointed out, included a depression scale, although the usefulness of this scale in psychiatric practice was limited. Furthermore, most "anxiety" questionnaires contain items relating to depressive symptomatology. Owing to their potential value for psychopharmacological investigations, attempts have also been undertaken to work out questionnaires suitable for assessing both anxiety and depression at the same time. Worthy of mention in this connection is the questionnaire of LIPMAN et al.[13] which was devised and validated in actual clinical practice.

The first questionnaire designed specifically for depression and intended for practical use is BECK's Inventory for Measuring Depression[2] which dates from 1961. This inventory, like ZUNG's Self-Rating Depression Scale (S.D.S.)[29] which appeared in 1965, is still very widely employed today. Reference should

*A review of this problem, as well as a comparison of the various scales in terms of the results yielded by factorial analysis, will be found in the book by LORR et al[15]. This book covers all studies published in English prior to 1963.

also be made here to the Hamburg Depression Scale published in German by von Kerekjarto[11] in 1969.

Very similar to the self-rating questionnaires are the lists of adjectives from which the patient has to pick out those that best describe his present state. The methods of correction employed vary; for example, some lists are virtually identical to questionnaires, whereas others, based on the "Q sort" technique, involve a complex scoring system which really calls for the use of a computer. The best known is the Clyde Mood Scale (1963)[4]. It is not designed specifically for depression and it yields six scores defined by factorial analysis and designated by the terms "friendly", "aggressive", "clear-thinking", "sleepy", "unhappy", and "dizzy". This scale has been used to study fluctuations in depressive symptomatology in response to treatment. The Depression Adjective Check-Lists (D.A.C.L.), drawn up by Lubin[17] in 1967, are concerned solely with depression and closely resemble a questionnaire.

This review of documentary aids is of necessity very incomplete. Incidentally, it is a pity that in the field of quantitative psychopathology we do not possess a full list of existing documentary aids accompanied by critical comments on their usefulness as instruments of measurement and by a bibliography of publications referring to them. In the case of mental tests, for example, a compilation of this type has been available for many years in the shape of the series of Mental Measurement Yearbooks edited by Buros. Some data on documentary aids used in the quantification of depressive symptomatology will be found in the studies published by Pichot[22] in 1964, Lyerly and Abbott[18] in 1966, and Gebhardt et al.[6] in 1969.

Rating scales versus questionnaires

As methods of quantifying depressive symptomatology, rating scales and questionnaires obviously each possess their own particular advantages and disadvantages. First of all, the symptoms covered by these two types of documentary aid are identical only in cases where the patient has actually experienced them and can express them in words. On the other hand, symptoms—or, rather, signs—which are not experienced by the patient but are observed by the physician (e.g. facial expression, slowing down of motor activity, or changes in tone of voice) can be recorded only by the use of rating scales. In theory, therefore, rating scales cover not only all the symptoms figuring in questionnaires, but also symptoms which questionnaires are incapable of registering.

This theoretical superiority of rating scales, however, deserves to be examined more closely. Rating scales imply the existence of an intermediary between the symptom such as it is experienced by the patient and the quantitative recording of that symptom. This intermediary is the observer who interprets what the patient says and evaluates the patient's general behaviour. There are not necessarily any drawbacks to such a procedure in cases where the observer is a trained, objective clinician. Hamilton[8] even maintains that it is essential to make use of relatively complex symptoms, the assessment of which is based on a more or less explicit integration of numerous elementary impressions that are probably incapable of analysis. The assessment of these symptoms depends also, to a considerable extent, on the investigator's ability to perceive a global picture or *Gestalt*, a picture which is difficult to describe in words. But one may also wonder how much reliance can be placed on an assessment of global symptoms which are incapable of operational definition. It may be, in fact, that such assessments are only valid if the rating scale in question is used by a physician of wide experience who possesses a highly developed clinical flair.

When, as often happens in practice (in many clinical trials, for example), the information is collected by observers with only a limited training in psychiatry—e.g. by general practitioners—it is certainly preferable to use a questionnaire, because the latter, even though it records only some of the patient's symptoms, is nevertheless extremely reliable. A rating scale, especially if it contains "global" items, could not be employed under these conditions.

Where circumstances permit, the most satisfactory solution is of course to combine a physician rating scale with a self-rating questionnaire. Even in cases where the symptoms covered by the two types of documentary aid are theoretically similar, the type of information obtained is never completely identical.

The scope of documentary aids

Physician rating scales and self-rating questionnaires have a very limited scope. The documentary aids employed by GRINKER comprise a total of 250 items, but they are unique, and none of the other scales so far devised—not even those used in research—is anything like as comprehensive. We all know of course how difficult it is to obtain answers to a questionnaire from a patient with retarded depression, even where the questionnaire is relatively short. Moreover, experience has shown that most clinicians are reluctant to use rating scales that are too complex. The documentary aids most widely employed—i.e. the Brief Psychiatric Rating Scale (B.P.R.S.) of OVERALL and GORHAM[20], derived from the I.M.P.S. but containing only 18 items instead of the original 75, the Hamilton Rating Scale for Depression (17 items), the Beck Inventory for Measuring Depression (21 questions), and the Zung Self-Rating Depression Scale (20 questions) owe much of their success to their brevity. If the work demanded of the observer is too laborious, there is usually a risk that its quality will suffer.

To sum up, it seems that, for practical reasons, the number of items in a questionnaire should be about 20. Longer questionnaires cannot in any event be employed in patients suffering from retarded melancholic depression. The number of items included in physician rating scales should likewise be about 20, in cases where the scales are intended for widespread use. For the purposes of intensive research carried out by highly motivated observers, rating scales containing about a hundred items (such as the P.R.S., I.M.P.S., and A.M.P. system) can be resorted to.

Selection of items and aim of the documentary aids

The number of possible symptoms that can be recorded with the aid of either a questionnaire or a rating scale is considerable, even if the choice is restricted to symptoms connected in some way or other with depression. Every documentary aid of this type, therefore, has to be selective, and the selection of the items must depend on the aim in view. This aim may fall, broadly speaking, into any one of the following categories:

a) Measurement of the general severity of depression.
b) Simultaneous measurement of several symptomatological dimensions in depression (factorial or dimensional model).
c) Measurement of symptomatological elements with a view to allotting each patient to a symptomatological sub-group (typological or syndromal model).
d) Measurement of symptomatological elements with a view to predicting a variable that is not directly related to symptomatology (e.g. exogenous or endogenous aetiology, response to treatment, etc.). Depending on the case, the model used may be of the factorial or of the typological type.

Account must also be taken of the situation in which the measurement is performed. Let us take as an example clinical trials with an antidepressant. Quantification of the symptomatology in this case might be designed to serve a number of different purposes which can be summarised as follows:

1. Initial classification of patients
   – using a dimensional model (e.g. factorial analysis) to divide up the patients on the basis of
     – symptomatology
     – aetiology and symptomatology;
   – using a syndromal model (e.g. typological analysis) to divide up the patients on the basis of
     – symptomatology
     – aetiology and symptomatology.
2. Measurement of changes in symptomatology
   – global measurement of severity
   – analytical measurement.
3. Search for prognostic indicators based on observations of the response to treatment.

Thus, at least seven types of measurement are possible, all of them different, and the conclusion to be drawn is that a multiplicity of specialised documentary aids must be available, each based on a selection of symptoms best suited to serve the specific purpose in view.

It is, of course, possible to devise documentary aids that are relatively "polyvalent" and suitable for use in different situations. It must, however, be borne in mind that existing rating scales do not always meet this requirement. For example, the Hamilton Rating Scale for Depression was designed to measure the general severity of depression. It can therefore be applied in a clinical trial before and after treatment in order to obtain an estimate of the global changes occurring in the severity of depression. It is much more questionable whether this documentary aid should be used, as it has been on numerous occasions, to measure variations in the dimensions of depressive symptomatology. If an investigator does employ the Hamilton scale for this purpose, he is forced to work either with isolated items (the measurement of which invariably gives unreliable results) or with groups of items submitted to a factorial analysis and yielding more reliable scores. But factorial analyses based on the Hamilton scale have produced divergent results and, consequently, shed little light on the dimensions of depressive symptomatology. On the other hand, depressive symptomatology factors obtained from the P.R.S., I.M.P.S., or B.P.R.S. are well established, and preference should therefore be given to these documentary aids in situations where it is desired to assess dimensions of depressive symptomatology.

Discussion and conclusions

Although more work has been done on the quantification of symptoms in depression than in any other field, the position is still far from satisfactory today. There are numerous "parallel" documentary aids—both rating scales and questionnaires—for the global measurement of the severity of depression, but comparative studies enabling one to choose between them are sadly lacking. What is more, no reliable procedures are available for assessing the validity of the results obtained with these documentary aids. Further attention should thus be paid, for example, to the development of documentary aids designed for analytical measurements and of those serving to facilitate a symptomatological or aetiological and symptomatological classification. Encouraging studies have already been carried out in this direction, but they have usually been unconnected with one another and have yielded no documentary aids of practical value.

It is perhaps instructive at this point to recall what happened in the development of mental tests, because the experience gained in this field may serve as a model for us. When D. WECHSLER [23] first published his Intelligence Scale in 1939, the elements it contained were not particularly original since they were all, in principle, more than ten years old; moreover, the need in adults for a grading system based on age had long been acknowledged. But the grouping of the subtests, the analysis of the interrelationships between them, and their grading were so good that the Wechsler scale is still, after 30 years, the standard documentary aid employed throughout the world for measuring intelligence in adults.

By way of conclusion, I should like to suggest that now, after a period of more than ten years during which the development of rating scales and questionnaires for use in depression has progressed in a somewhat anarchic fashion, the time is ripe for a coordinated effort, and I sincerely hope that our discussions today will lay the foundation for such an effort.

References

1 ANGST, J., BATTEGAY, R., BENTE, D., BERNER, P., BROEREN, W., CORNU, F., DICK, P., ENGELMEIER, M.-P., HEIMANN, H., HEINRICH, K., HELMCHEN, H., HIPPIUS, H., PÖLDINGER, W., SCHMIDLIN, P., SCHMITT, W., WEIS, P.: Das Dokumentations-System der Arbeitsgemeinschaft für Methodik und Dokumentation in der Psychiatrie (AMP). Arzneimittel-Forsch. *19*, 399 (1969)

2 BECK, A.T., WARD, C.H., MENDELSON, M., MOCK, J., ERBAUGH, J.: An inventory for measuring depression. Arch. gen. Psychiat. *4*, 561 (1961)

3 BOJANOVSKÝ, J., CHLOUPKOVÁ, K.: Bewertungsskala der Depressionszustände. Psychiat. et Neurol. (Basle) *151*, 54 (1966)

4 CLYDE, D.J.: Manual for the Clyde mood scale (Biometric Lab., Univ. of Miami; Coral Gables, Florida 1963)

5 CUTLER, R.P., KURLAND, H.D.: Clinical quantification of depressive reactions. Arch. gen. Psychiat. *5*, 280 (1961)

6 GEBHARDT, R., HELMCHEN, H., HIPPIUS, H., KEREKJARTO, M. VON, LIENERT, G.A., RENFORDT, E.: Beurteilungs-Skalen (Rating-Scales) und Merkmalslisten für depressive Syndrome. In Hippius, H., Selbach, H. (Editors): Das depressive Syndrom, Int. Symp., Berlin 1968, p. 603 (Urban & Schwarzenberg, Munich/Berlin/Vienna 1969)

7 GRINKER, R.R., MILLER, J., SABSHIN, M., NUNN, R., NUNNALLY, J.C.: The phenomena of depressions (Hoeber Med. Div., Harper & Row, New York/Evanston/London 1961)

8 HAMILTON, M.: A rating scale for depression. J. Neurol. Neurosurg. Psychiat. *23*, 56 (1960)

9 JASPER, H.H.: The measurement of depression-elation and its relation to a measure of extraversion-intraversion. J. abnorm. soc. Psychol. *25*, 307 (1930)

10 KEMPF, E.J.: The behavior chart in mental disease. Amer. J. Insan. *71*, 761 (1915)

11 KEREKJARTO, M. VON: Hamburger Depressions-Skala (HDS), loc. cit.[6], p. 640

12 LEHMANN, H.E., CAHN, C.H., VERTEUIL, R.L. DE: The treatment of depressive conditions with imipramine (G 22355). Canad. psychiat. Ass. J. *3*, 155 (1958)

13 LIPMAN, R.S., COVI, L., RICKELS, K., UHLENHUTH, E.H., LAZAR, R.: Selected measures of change in outpatient drug evaluation. In Efron, D.H., et al. (Editors): Psychopharmacology. A review of progress, 1957–1967. Publ. Hlth Serv. Publ. (Wash.). No. 1836: 249 (1968)

14 LORR, M.: Multidimensional scale for rating psychiatric patients; hospital form. Veterans Adm. techn. Bull. (TB 10-507) *6*, 1 (1953)

15 LORR, M., KLETT, C.J., McNAIR, D.M.: Syndromes of psychosis (Pergamon Press, Oxford/London/New York, 1963)

16 LORR, M., KLETT, C.J., McNAIR, D.M., LASKY, J.J.: Inpatient multidimensional psychiatric scale, manual (Consult. Psychol. Press, Palo Alto 1963)

17 LUBIN, B.: Manual for the depression adjective checklists (San Diego Educ. and Industr. Testing Serv. 1967)

18 LYERLY, S.B., ABBOTT, P.S.: Handbook of psychiatric rating scales (1950–1964). Publ. Hlth Serv. Publ. No. 1495 (Nat. Inst. ment. Health, Bethesda, Md 1966)

19 MOORE, T.V.: The empirical determination of certain syndromes underlying praecox and manic-depressive psychoses. Amer. J. Psychiat. *9*, 719 (1930)

20 OVERALL, J.E., GORHAM, D.R.: The brief psychiatric rating scale. Psychol. Rep. *10*, 799 (1962)

21 OVERALL, J.E., HOLLISTER, L.E., POKORNY, A.D., CASEY, J.F., KATZ, G.: Drug therapy in depressions. Clin. Pharmacol. Ther. *3*, 16 (1962)

22 PICHOT, P.: Les aspects symptomatiques des états dépressifs. Schweiz. Arch. Neurol. Neurochir. Psychiat. *94*, 392 (1964)

23 WECHSLER, D.: Manual for the Wechsler adult intelligence scale (Psychol. Corp., New York 1955)

24 WECHSLER, H., GROSSER, G.H., BUSFIELD, B.L., Jr.: The depression rating scale. A quantitative approach to the assessment of depressive symptomatology. Arch. gen. Psychiat. *9*, 334 (1963)

25 WITTENBORN, J.R.: Psychiatric rating scales (Psychol. Corp., New York 1955)

26 WITTENBORN, J.R.: Wittenborn psychiatric rating scales, Rev. Ed. (Psychol. Corp., New York 1964)

27 WITTENBORN, J.R., HOLZBERG, J.D.: The generality of psychiatric syndromes. J. cons. Psychol. *15*, 372 (1951)

28 WOODWORTH, R.S.: Personal data sheet (Stoelting, Chicago 1918)

29 ZUNG, W.W.K.: A self-rating depression scale. Arch. gen. Psychiat. *12*, 63 (1965)

Discussion

F. FREYHAN: One of the major advantages of prophylactic treatment with lithium is that it has led to a deeper and more extensive knowledge of mood fluctuations occurring during therapy. What we observe during lithium treatment are less severe variations of depressive or manic states which do not require hospitalisation. This prompts me to ask Dr. PICHOT what can be recommended today as adequate rating instruments to cover all parameters of mood, since present rating scales are limited to depressive states only. In other words, what is at present the most satisfactory method for assessing the kind of minor to major mood swings that occur over a period in patients, for example, under treatment with lithium?

W. BIRKMAYER: Dr. PICHOT, your paper will have gladdened the heart of every clinician here! I think we all realise that a clinician does not need either a record sheet or a rating scale in order to establish his diagnosis and to assess the effect of the treatment he prescribes. But without these documentary aids it would have been impossible to collect statistical data on the efficacy of, for example, dopa and to demonstrate that dopa has a good effect on akinesia, but no effect on tremor. We clinicians do not need these documentary aids, but they are indispensable for those who have to carry out or organise drug trials.

H. HEIMANN: I should like to make two comments on Dr. PICHOT's paper. Firstly, in our comparative studies with Ludiomil we worked with various scales. Besides the Hamilton scale, we also made use of VON ZERSSEN's subjective status rating scale* and the Structured Psychological Interview (S.P.I.)**. The S.P.I. consists of a series of standard questions which are put to the patient. It is a carefully calibrated instrument which differs fundamentally from both physician's rating scales and self-rating scales designed for the quantitation of psychiatric syndromes. The von Zerssen subjective status rating scale is filled up by the patient himself and is excellently suited for the assessment of depressive states. In the double-blind study in which we compared Ludiomil with amitriptyline, the Hamilton scale failed to reveal any differences in the response to the two drugs; but the S.P.I. and the von Zerssen subjective status rating scale both showed that the response elicited by Ludiomil after 14 and 21 days was significantly better than that produced by amitriptyline.
Secondly, we have on many occasions carried out reliability studies on assessments of the clinical items figuring in the A.M.P. system. It was found that emotional symptoms, assessed on the basis of the patient's behaviour, are much less reliable than symptoms reported by the patient himself (e.g. delusional symptoms). According to SARTORIUS, this also applies to the international scale for the assessment of patients suffering from schizophrenia. In his reliability studies, too, SARTORIUS found that assessments of emotional symptoms were invariably the least reliable.

M. HAMILTON: Dr. PICHOT has recommended the use of the P.R.S., the I.M.P.S., and the B.P.R.S. scales because of the reliability of the factors obtained from them; but he himself has pointed out that scales should have about 20 items, whereas the B.P.R.S. scale has only four that are directly related to depression. With four items the degree of reliability is insufficient. The I.M.P.S. has many more items, but most of them are irrelevant to depressive illness; consequently, using the I.M.P.S. involves asking questions and filling in items the majority of which do not apply to the condition of

---

* ZERSSEN, D. VON, KOELLER, D.-M., REY, E.-R.: Die Befindlichkeits-Skala (B-S) – ein einfaches Instrument zur Objektivierung von Befindlichkeitsstörungen, insbesondere im Rahmen von Längsschnittuntersuchungen. Arzneimittel-Forsch. 20, 915 (1970)
** BURDOCK, E.I., HARDESTY, A.S.: SCI-structured-clinical-interview-manual (Springer, New York 1969)

the patients concerned. I therefore agree with Dr. PICHOT that the need is for special scales specifically designed for the purpose they are required to fulfil. And it is for this reason that I feel I must disagree with him about the use of the I.M.P.S. and the B.P.R.S.

W. PÖLDINGER: I should like to raise one further point concerning both Dr. PICHOT's paper and Dr. HEIMANN's comments. In reliability studies conducted in Basle we found that, precisely in the case of depressives, no account was taken of the time of day at which the assessment was made. If the same patient is assessed by one or several doctors at different times of the day, the results obtained are bound to differ. Perhaps this is the reason—or, at least, one of the reasons—why reliability studies yield such a poor measure of agreement in the case of emotional symptoms. If one assessment is made six hours later in the day than another, it is just impossible, in our experience, to obtain any correlation between the two, because in the middle of the "morning trough" the patient naturally does not feel the same as in the evening. I think that, from the standpoint of practical clinical psychopharmacology, it might be a very good idea simply to note the time of day at which the assessment is made. If you assess a patient for the first time in the afternoon and then repeat the assessment three days later in the morning, I guarantee that you will find a considerable deterioration in his condition. But it would be quite wrong to say that this deterioration is due to the treatment you have prescribed for him.

P. PICHOT: In connection with the question Dr. FREYHAN raised, I must say that there are very few instruments for measuring what might be termed elation. Theoretically you could use the I.M.P.S.—bearing in mind, of course, the criticisms that Dr. HAMILTON has just levelled against it. BUNNEY's associates have recently developed a scale for mania which could be used, and which has in fact been employed in conjunction with a scale for depression. So far as I am aware, their special scale for manic symptomatology represents the only major attempt that has so far been made to elaborate a scale for rating elated mood.

My friend MAX HAMILTON is quite right about the B.P.R.S. I should not have recommended it for measuring depression. I meant to refer to the P.R.S. of WITTENBORN, which has a scale of about 10 items in depression. I do in fact agree with Dr. HAMILTON that the actual scales in the I.M.P.S. and in the Wittenborn P.R.S. are largely made up of redundant items. My argument was therefore that we need a really good scale for measuring several dimensions of depression, because the Hamilton scale—which provides an excellent instrument for making a global rating of depression—is, of course, too short to be broken down for the purpose of measuring different aspects in particular. In my opinion, the reliability of the factorial scales derived from it is not quite high enough, because the number of items is too small. So it was my conclusion that some sort of cooperative study ought to be undertaken to develop a form of standard instrument, by analogy with what DAVID WECHSLER has done for intelligence. I think that at present we don't need any new rating scales; it seems that nowadays a new rating scale for depression or a new inventory of depression is appearing every year, if not every month. What we want instead of these new scales is a study which would enable us to agree on the kind of standard instrument that could provide both a global appreciation of depression and at the same time some possibility of measuring several dimensions of the symptomatology.

Methodological aspects in the testing of antidepressant drugs

by K. RICKELS and R.W. DOWNING*

Methodological issues concerning the evaluation of drug efficacy in the treatment of depression may be thought of as the interface between, on the one hand, the specific problems and strategies for their solution with which those engaged on research into depressive illnesses have to deal and, on the other, the concerns which arise in the course of work designed to evaluate the effectiveness of psychiatric treatment in general. In the following paper the authors will attempt to highlight selected aspects of these two broad areas which they believe are of central importance to current research and which they feel carry implications for the future directions to be taken in the investigation of drug efficacy in depressive illness.

A recent publication sponsored by the American College of Neuropsychopharmacology and the National Institute of Mental Health probably constitutes what is currently the most up-to-date discussion of problems and principles of drug research in psychopharmacology[16]. Even more recently one of the authors (K.R.) had the privilege of participating in a Food and Drug Administration endeavour to develop guide-lines for the evaluation of psychiatric drugs. Once these guide-lines are published, they, together with the above-mentioned book, should prove an invaluable help to the clinician concerned with psychopharmacological trials in depression.

I. Problems of definition and selection

Those who conduct research dealing with depression are immediately confronted with the bewildering heterogeneity of clinical manifestations to which the term depression has been applied, with a chaos of competing attempts to conceptualise and identify clinical entities, and with a host of inconclusive, often conflicting, efforts to specify the causes, symptoms, and courses of postulated diagnostic entities. Data on drug efficacy which have been produced by individual investigators working with samples of depressed in-patients or out-patients, often selected solely because of their availability in local hospitals and out-patient clinics, have frequently been difficult to integrate into an overall picture indicating what compound or class of compounds is of particular use-

* Dr. RICKELS is Professor of Psychiatry, University of Pennsylvania, and Director of the Psychopharmacology Research Unit, Philadelphia General Hospital, Philadelphia, Pennsylvania, U.S.A.
Dr. DOWNING is Associate Professor of Psychology in Psychiatry, University of Pennsylvania, Philadelphia, Pennsylvania.
This work was supported by U.S.P.H.S. Grants MH-08957-8.

fulness in what form of depressive manifestation. In an attempt to deal with these difficulties several lines of approach have been adopted.

1. During recent years emphasis has been placed upon the conduct of *collaborative studies*, so that a broader sampling of clinical material, encountered in a wider range of treatment settings, might be available. Such an approach, for example, has been adopted with in-patients in the N.I.M.H. (National Institute for Mental Health) collaborative studies of depression, one of which involved 555 patients drawn from the psychiatric populations of two large metropolitan receiving hospitals, four state hospitals, and four private hospitals[25]. Other collaborative research endeavours in depression have been undertaken in England[29] as well as in continental Europe[11].

Collaborative research with depressed out-patients, for example, is being conducted in England by WHEATLEY[31], who draws upon the private practices of a large number of general practitioners, and in the U.S.A. by our own research team, which utilises patients from several large metropolitan hospital clinics and from a group of private general practitioners and private psychiatrists practising in the greater Philadelphia area[27]. The need to obtain patient samples from a diversity of treatment settings has also been documented by KLERMAN and PAYKEL[15].

Such undertakings make it possible to assemble large patient samples and to broaden the range of clinical content available for study. But studies of this kind also greatly increase the demand for rater training and are beset with all the problems resulting from differences in the rating patterns of psychiatrists and non-psychiatrists, i.e. of physicians who have had diverse forms of training and who are working in treatment settings with diverse philosophies and approaches to treatment.

2. An *operational approach* based upon readily observable or easily obtained information can be used in *selecting patients* for study. One such operational approach has been employed as a selection device by RASKIN et al.[25] (Table 1). Prospective cases for study were initially evaluated on three five-point scales, the first scale assessing the severity of the patient's depression as expressed in his verbal report, the second as evinced in his clinical behaviour, and the last as revealed by the presence and severity of such secondary symptoms as loss of appetite and sleep disturbance. Patients who received a total of nine or more points on this scale were considered by RASKIN to be sufficiently ill to warrant their inclusion in a drug study.

The third of these scales, i.e. that dealing with the severity of secondary symptomatology, seems to beg the question as to precisely what the secondary symptoms of depression are; at least it appears to be unaccompanied by any specification of how the list of secondary symptoms given was determined. Nevertheless, such a procedure does define a population that has sufficient depressive symptomatology to justify a study of drug effectiveness. However, since it takes neither the diagnosis nor any other contextual factors into consideration, it ignores issues related to the essential differences which may characterise depressive symptomatology as it appears in different syndromes. For this reason, the three

Table 1. The Raskin Depression Scale.

Severity of depression:
To what extent does the patient evince depression or despondency in verbal report, behaviour, and secondary symptoms of depression?

		Very much	Consid-erably	Moder-ately	Some-what	Not at all
Verbal report	Says he feels blue; talks of feeling helpless, hopeless, or worthless; complains of loss of interest; may wish he were dead; reports crying spells	5	4	3	2	1
Behaviour	Looks sad; cries easily; speaks in a sad voice; appears slowed down; lacking in energy	5	4	3	2	1
Secondary symptoms of depression	Insomnia; gastro-intestinal complaints; dry mouth; history of recent suicide attempt; lack of appetite; difficulty in concentrating or remembering	5	4	3	2	1
Total	Add the scale points checked for severity of depression in verbal report, behaviour, and secondary symptoms of depression . .					

scales must generally be supplemented by other information enabling the patients to be classified into more homogeneous sub-groups.

Thus, while RASKIN succeeded in showing that both imipramine and chlorpromazine were superior to placebo in his total patient group, he was able to demonstrate differences between the two active substances only when additional information about illness and non-illness factors was taken into account[23, 24, 25]. These factors included education, age, number of previous episodes, and initial severity of depression.

Another example illustrating how depressed patients selected for a given study can be defined in operational terms is given in Table 2. Such operational definitions do at least permit the selection of patients who are indeed depressed and suffer from a given minimum of symptomatology.

3. Multivariate statistical techniques have been employed in an effort to isolate *patient typologies* or *illness syndromes* which might replace conventional diagnostic classifications, and the responses shown by patients of a given type to various psychotropic agents have been studied.

a) *The endogenous versus reactive dichotomy*. The recognition of one form of depression which is based primarily upon factors internal to the individual (endog-

Table 2. Example of a depression check-list.

To be eligible for inclusion in the study, the patient must exhibit dysphoric mood (depressed, sad, despondent, hopeless, down in the dumps, discouraged) plus any five of the following associated symptoms:

Poor appetite and weight loss (2 lbs per week or 10 lbs per year, if not dieting)	1. No	2. Yes
Sleep difficulty (insomnia or hypersomnia)	1. No	2. Yes
Loss of energy (fatigability, tiredness)	1. No	2. Yes
Agitation or retardation	1. No	2. Yes
Recent loss of interest in usual activities and decreased libido	1. No	2. Yes
Self-reproach or guilt feelings	1. No	2. Yes
Complaints of (or actually diminished) thinking and concentration (slow thinking, mixed-up thoughts)	1. No	2. Yes
Recurrent thoughts of death or suicide, wish to be dead	1. No	2. Yes

Comments:

enous) and another form which is primarily related to factors in the individual's environment and to his difficulties in coping with them (reactive) is far from new. BECK[1] noted that the distinction between endogenous and exogenous depression was already beginning to emerge in the psychiatric literature of the 1920s. It is probably the continual clinical confrontation with such a distinction, combined with the conviction that a marked contrast in the basic nature of both depressive types does exist, which has led to a widespread effort over the past several years to legitimise the distinction through the use of multivariate and other statistical techniques[13, 14, 22, 32].

While some evidence has been obtained through factor analysis that certain clusters of symptoms and case-history data are associated with the two depressive types, many difficulties and inconsistencies[22, 32] continue to plague this effort at typology. Thus, quite diverse lists of symptoms characterising each type of illness have been drawn up by those working in this area; many patients have been encountered who manifest symptoms of both types of depressive illness (e.g. diurnal variation, psychomotor retardation, early morning awakening, illness course, family history); the question of whether a dichotomy or a continuum is involved has not been settled; and the influence of such major confounding factors as severity of depressive symptomatology and patient age has not yet been checked. It must therefore be concluded that the conviction that a dichotomy exists between endogenous and reactive depression is a persisting article of clinical faith which thus far lacks complete empirical validation. Stable and consistent criteria for determining to which of the two categories a patient should be assigned would seem a necessary prerequisite before attempts can be made to identify therapeutic agents which may be differentially effective in these forms of depression.

b) *Empirically based typology.* The work of OVERALL and associates [20, 21] probably represents the most rigorous attempt at using multivariate statistical procedures to establish a typology for depression. Basing their analysis on scores obtained using the Brief Psychiatric Rating Scale [19] in a heterogeneous group of depressed in-patients, and employing an empirical profile-analysis technique, these authors obtained three profile clusters which they called anxious depression, hostile depression, and retarded depression. When they studied drug effects in these patient types, OVERALL and HOLLISTER found, in a double-blind drug trial in which depressed patients were given either imipramine or thioridazine, that only when they took these three patient types into consideration were they able to distinguish significant differences between the two drugs. A significant interaction between drug and patient type was discerned inasmuch as thioridazine proved greatly superior to imipramine in anxious depressives, and imipramine greatly superior to thioridazine in retarded depressives, whereas hostile depressives responded well to both drugs. Similar findings were made in subsequent studies with other psychiatric drugs. The development and use of information concerning patient types thus clearly revealed the difference between the presence and absence of detectable differential treatment effects.

A simpler approach to the problem of categorising patients was adopted by our own group [28]. We divided depressed non-psychotic out-patients into four types (Figure 1) on the basis of their degree of depression and anxiety, and we were thus able for the first time to differentiate not only between an antidepressant and a tranquilliser, but also between the combination of both compounds and the two single agents. The drug combination was found to be most effective in the high-depression/high-anxiety patient, amitriptyline in the high-depression/low-anxiety patient, and chlordiazepoxide in the low-depression/high-anxiety patient.

c) *A strategy for the construction of outcome-related typologies.* Commenting on several papers presented at a symposium on "The Role and Methodology of Classification in Psychiatry and Psychopathology", held in 1965, LUBIN [17] argued that the best way of assuring that a typology will be related to the differential treatment response is to build the typology around the differential treatment response at the outset. To do this, it is necessary to assemble data on the treatment responses of large groups of patients, each patient having been treated with one of a representative set of medications selected for study. A body of data must also be assembled in the form of a vector of scores for each patient which are measures of patient attributes felt to be potentially relevant to the differential treatment response.

The actual statistical procedures to be employed are complex, but the objective is relatively straightforward. The aim is to establish quantitative criteria for defining patient type in terms of a profile of patient attributes, so that each type will include those patients who respond best to one drug or to a group of drugs

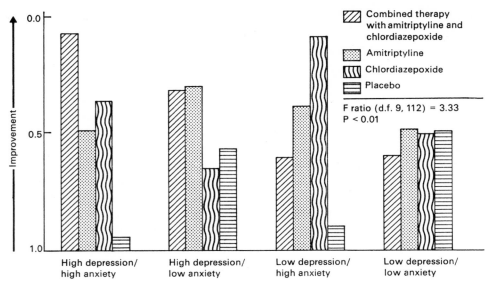

Fig. 1. Total adjusted scores for depression (physician's scale) after a four-week period of treatment in neurotic out-patients (N = 243), as a function of initial levels of depression and anxiety. (From: RICKELS et al.[28]. Reproduced by courtesy of Physicians Postgraduate Press)

from the set of therapeutic agents studied. The number of types will depend upon the number of different patterns of differential treatment effectiveness present in the samples of patients and medications under study. Unfortunately, rules for selecting the patient attributes and the measurements of improvement to be included in the analyses cannot be laid down in the same way as rules for conducting the analyses once these attributes and measurements of improvement have been selected. Although LUBIN suggests an analytical procedure to aid in the selection of improvement measurements, the burden of decision in selecting patient attributes rests with clinical experience, intuition, the results of previous research, and luck.

It cannot be expected that all patients will show an equally good fit to one of the types isolated. Extreme cases may occur in which it might be said that a patient is not classifiable into any of the types established. Such considerations emphasise the need for agreeing upon a decision rule by which to determine type membership. How dissimilar to a given type must an individual be before it is decided that he does not belong to that type? And what about those individuals whose attribute profiles are so dissimilar to all the types in question that they can be considered as belonging to none of them? In the first place, it would seem that some provision must be made for the existence of such persons. Criteria must be established for identifying individuals whose profiles are sufficiently different from those of the types specified that the system of typologies being used is unable to make predictions about their drug response. Further study of the attributes of these individuals in conjunction with information concerning the nature of their treatment response might serve the hypothesis-finding function of isolating new predictors.

Once a typology of the kind described above has been constructed with a given sample of patients, it is imperative that the predictive accuracy with which it can be applied to new patient samples should be checked and continually monitored. It can be expected that the degree of accuracy in predicting the treatment response with a new sample will be less than that obtained with the original sample. It is not only necessary to find out how much "shrinkage" from the original to new samples takes place but also advisable to study those new cases for which predictability appears particularly poor. The latter procedure may once again serve an hypothesis-finding function, i.e. that of determining additional patient characteristics which can be incorporated into the predictive model, thereby increasing the accuracy of prediction. Besides serving such an actuarial purpose, a procedure of this type may help to shed fresh light on the mechanisms of response to drug treatment and thus on the mode of operation of those predictors that prove effective.

II. Problems in dealing with patient heterogeneity

Once a particular illness entity has been selected for study, the traditional rationale for proceeding with a drug trial might be outlined as follows: a random sample representative of patients suffering from the illness under study is selected, a double-blind paradigm is followed in which each patient receives either a drug or placebo, and information about the treatment response is systematically assembled; if clear-cut drug-placebo or drug-drug differences are found, then the results relating to drug effectiveness may be extrapolated in general terms to the population from which the sample was drawn.

When drug efficacy is sufficiently great to enable the effects of treatment to be unambiguously demonstrated despite the heterogeneity of the non-illness characteristics typically present in such random samples, information is obtained which proves useful in establishing future treatment policies.

Further useful information about the treatment response may be obtained if it is possible to assess the effect exerted on the outcome of therapy by a number of "non-specific" factors which may be contributing to patient heterogeneity, regardless of whether or not these factors are illness-related. A first step in such a procedure should probably involve the use of some form of covariance technique to statistically eliminate such heterogeneity. This eliminating process may lead to an increase in the significance of the difference between treatment effects—thanks to an increase in the size of the treatment difference, to a decrease in the size of error, or both. Should this be the case, the investigator may merely content himself with the increase in experimental precision which has been achieved or, alternatively, he may conclude that he has found justification for an examination of the manner in which non-specific predictors are modifying the response to treatment. In the latter case, the application of an appropriate technique, such as multiple regression, might enable him to identify predictors or patient attributes which are systematically related to the treatment response, or to isolate patient sub-groups that are homogeneous with regard to some relevant characteristic in which the treatment response is particularly high or particularly low.

The usefulness of such a "predictor approach" is likely to vary with the effectiveness of the compound under study. Highly effective compounds (more frequently encountered in areas of medicine other than psychiatry) are probably so slightly affected by non-drug factors that little would be gained by a search for predictors. To take the other extreme, highly ineffective medications also appear to be only slightly affected by "non-specific" factors; this is very probably because the placebo response is very limited in patients suffering from depression of more than modest severity[3]. Therefore, therapeutic agents of moderate effectiveness, such as are usually applied in psychiatry, are probably the ones primarily affected by non-drug factors of this kind.

The data presented in Table 3 may serve as an example illustrating how several non-specific factors predict or affect the outcome of drug treatment. These findings—which represent the results of a search multiple-regression analysis[5] in which predictors for both amitriptyline and placebo treatment were assessed in non-psychotic depressed out-patients—indicate that several variables related to illness and social class, as well as physician liking of the patient, significantly affect the degree of improvement. In addition, although not selected by the search procedure, the response to previous drug treatment and the initial degree of psychomotor disturbance also had significant zero-order correlations with improvement. Besides helping to reinforce existing drug-placebo differences, several of the above variables also exert differential effects on the outcome of treatment with drug and placebo.

III. General methodological issues

1. Measuring instruments

a) *Problems of reliability and validity.* The soundness of the results of any study of drug effectiveness depends upon the reliability and validity of the criteria of improvement employed. Since the great majority of improvement measurements used in research with psychotropic drugs are based upon ratings of improvement or illness severity, lack of inter-rater reliability is a potentially important source of experimental error. Rater reliability increases with the training and experience of the raters, as well as with increasing specificity in the definition of the items to be rated.

Generalised and specific rater biases detract from the validity of improvement ratings recorded by the doctor. When such influences loom large in relation to the "size" of the treatment effects, preliminary work with a group of raters to be employed in a given drug-evaluation project may make it possible to estimate the biases which characterise their evaluations. Such biases may then be eliminated from the patient evaluations which these raters subsequently perform, or may be used in training sessions designed to increase the reliability and validity of rating procedures.

Table 3. Predictors of global improvement in depressed out-patients.

Predictors selected in search multiple-regression analysis	Amitriptyline (N = 120)	Placebo (N = 137)	P <
Treatment (amitriptyline)	More	Less	0.001
Illness-related variables: Higher initial depression (Total Zung scale)	Less	Less	0.10
Higher initial emotional symptomatology	More	Less	0.001
Duration of illness ($\leq$ 6 months)	More	More	0.01
Social-class related variables: Treatment setting (private psychiatric vs. all others)	Less	More	0.10
Realises problems are emotional (Yes)	More	Less	0.05
Race (White)	Less	Less	0.10
Physician likes patient (More)*	Less	Less	0.05

Multiple R = 0.53; percentage of predicted variance = 28

* This effect is significantly greater for placebo than for amitriptyline treated patients.

b) *Global, specific, and composite scores*. A global rating of improvement has the face value of a measurement which allows the treating physician to weight the varying components of change he has observed in a patient in accordance with his clinical understanding of the patient's condition. However, the selective nature of human attention makes it virtually certain that no two observers will include an identical set of observations in their evaluations. Also, an absence of basic rules for the combining of separate impressions makes it unlikely that any two clinicians, even if they had observed the same set of symptoms, would assign similar weights to them in arriving at a composite judgment.

A set of ratings of specific symptoms adds materially to the range of approaches which may be adopted in order to specify the effect of a particular drug and to contrast its effects with those of other agents. Methods are available for constructing profiles of pre-treatment symptomatology or profiles of symptom change. The former type of profile may be useful in isolating uniform patient types in whom drug effects may be studied, and the latter in specifying patterns of change resulting from treatment.

While composite scores may be constructed from the specific symptom measurements by grouping together those symptoms that can reasonably be said to constitute clinical clusters, a composite score arrived at in this way lacks the mathematical properties of the several statistical procedures available for forming weighted score combinations. Multiple regression, cluster analysis, factor analysis, discriminant analysis, and multivariate analysis of variance all generate weighted composite scores with well-defined properties that are useful in an appropriate research context.

Many rating scales, including those involving both physician ratings as well as patient self-ratings, have been used as criteria of measurement. The Hamilton Depression Scale[9], the Zung Depression Scale[33], and the Beck Depression Inventory[1] are representative of these scales. A depression scale used by our own research group for many years in out-patient research may serve as an example. We have employed the 23-item Physician Depression Scale in a number of clinical trials. Not only its total score, but also its four major clinical clusters (determined clinically, not statistically) (Table 4) and its six orthogonal factors (produced by factor analysis with varimax rotation) (Table 5) have consistently proved to be sensitive to differential treatment response. These factors and clusters reflect several dimensions of depressive symptomatology, dimensions which are often differentially affected by different therapeutic agents.

The complexity and poorly understood nature of psychiatric syndromes, and of the processes of change by which psychotropic agents bring about improvement, make it necessary to regard global and composite scores as being only partially adequate for the assessment of drug effects. For example, both global and composite scores may fail to focus sufficiently upon that symptom or group of symptoms around which a particular patient's illness is organised. The use of "target symptoms", or symptoms which the patient feels to be focal to his disorder, in the assessment of drug effectiveness represents one attempt to take those symptoms that are significant for the individual patient into consideration in evaluating the response to treatment[7, 8, 10, 12].

c) *Multiple sources of information.* The inclusion of patient self-ratings of improvement provides a measure of the extent to which a given therapeutic agent has been successful in alleviating subjective discomfort. However, the residual psychopathology of patients who have obtained some symptomatic relief may distort their view of the change in their condition. Also, their evaluations may be influenced by a desire to please, or to displease, the physician treating them. It is nevertheless true that an evaluation of the amount of improvement which is agreed upon by both patient and doctor is one worthy of considerable credence. In addition, the study of discrepancies between physician and patient ratings in distinctive patient groups may shed further light on the treatment-evaluation process and possibly on the nature of underlying drug effects.

In hospitalised psychotic patients, who frequently cannot make meaningful self-ratings, improvement is often evaluated not only by the physicians treating them but also by nurses or relatives. As in the case of neurotic patients, a comparison of nurse and relative ratings of psychotic patients with the ratings of treating physicians may provide additional useful information.

2. Sample size

The size of the patient sample to be employed in a drug trial has many critical implications for the interpretation of the results obtained. When the number of patients receiving each agent is "too small", the investigator may actually have "stacked the cards" so heavily against himself that his research effort will

Table 4. Physician Depression Scale: clinical clusters.

Mood:	*Pathological thinking:*
Mood	Suicidal ideation
Facial expression	Guilt, hopelessness
General appearance	Can't decide or concentrate
Crying	Paranoid thinking
Anxiety	
Hostile attitude	*Somatic:*
Irritability	Headaches
Elation	Sleep disturbances
	Poor appetite
Psychomotor:	Fatigue
Motor retardation	Loss of weight
Decrease in speech	Somatic complaints
Loss of interest	
Overactivity	
Agitation	

Table 5. Physician Depression Scale: rotated factors (N = 983).

I. *Anxiety/depression:*	IV. *Somatic:*
Agitation	Headaches
Can't decide or concentrate	Sleep disturbances
Guilt, hopelessness	Fatigue
Overactivity	
Anxiety	V. *Depressed mood:*
Suicidal ideation	Mood
Mood	Crying
	Facial expression
II. *Retardation:*	*Few* somatic complaints
Motor retardation	*Low* in elation
Decrease in speech	
Loss of interest	VI. *Hostile/paranoid:*
Facial expression	Hostile attitude
General appearance	Paranoid thinking
	Irritability
III. *Appetite:*	
Loss of weight	
Poor appetite	

have been wasted. The smaller the sample, the less the likelihood that significant treatment differences will be found *even when they are actually present.*

While an approximate rule-of-thumb recommendation for the minimum size of the patient sample for each therapeutic agent is frequently given as 30–40, the factors which contribute towards determining the best sample size for a given investigation are many and the decision process required is a complex one [2, 6]. Unless the investigator has the necessary statistical expertise, or the time and inclination to acquire it, he would be well advised to consult a statistician before beginning his drug trial.

Large patient samples have the advantage of increasing the sensitivity of treatment comparisons and of facilitating the use of a number of predictor variables in the fashion to which we have already referred. However, when the sample size is large, it is possible to obtain treatment differences of an impressively high significance level, even though the extent of the difference in treatment effects may actually be quite small. Consequently, it is extremely important that the investigator should give careful thought to the amount of treatment difference which will have practical significance and import.

3. Pitfalls of the predictor approach

Although the use of non-specific predictors may yield very useful information about specific aspects of the response to treatment, attention should be drawn to the pitfalls which it may create for the unwary. As already noted, large patient samples are required if the effects of a substantial number of predictors are to be determined with adequate reliability. Even when the sample sizes are large, the low reliability of some predictor variables and the often unavoidable overlap between many frequently used predictors cause the estimates of predictor effects to be unstable and difficult to replicate. Finally, when such techniques as multiple regression are employed, the underlying dimensions tapped by surface predictors may be so hard to identify that it becomes difficult to understand what the basic significance or meaning of even a large predictor effect may be [4, 6].

4. Problems in synthesising results across different sets of data

When either a clinician or a research worker attempts to synthesise the information available from the literature in order to form an impression of the effectiveness of a given medication, he frequently encounters a veritable jungle of diverse measuring instruments, patient material, research paradigms, statistical approaches, and treatment paradigms. We have discussed elsewhere [6] the techniques appropriate for combining results from studies at several levels of comparability. Obviously any movement towards the standardisation of procedures and measuring instruments used by the psychopharmacological research community would greatly facilitate the combination of cross-study results.

Collaborative studies represent the efforts of groups of individuals to achieve such standardisation for patient samples larger than those which it is usually feasible for a single individual working alone to assemble. If such studies are to realise their aim of ready comparability of results across a range of collaborating individuals and treatment settings, several requirements must be fulfilled. All data must be collected in accordance with a common protocol. This entails collection of the same information about all patients using the same assessment instruments. All raters must be carefully trained, and constant supervision of the data-collection process must be maintained.

The protocol for collaborative studies must include specific provision for the identification of patients eligible for study. The protocol may, for example, stipulate that schizo-affective patients should not be included in the sample, indicate that only patients with a specified amount of "core" depression (Table 6)[18] should be admitted, or use an operational procedure such as that devised by RASKIN et al.[25]. Such factors as prior treatment response, initial degree of psychopathology, or the presence or absence of core depressive features sometimes seem to have a more important bearing on the outcome of drug treatment than whether a patient is diagnosed as belonging to an endogenous or reactive depressive sub-type[26].

While the use of an exclusion rule would assure some degree of uniformity and objectivity in patient selection, it does not preclude subsequent analyses based upon less readily identifiable clinical entities. Thus, investigators may proceed to classify depressed patients in a collaborative study sample into such groups as bipolar/unipolar, endogenous/exogenous (reactive), psychotic/non-psychotic (neurotic), agitated/retarded, typical/atypical, hospitalised/non-hospitalised, and then look for differential drug effects across these classifications.

Finally, collaborative investigators must commit themselves to taking into consideration data from all patients, irrespective of the extent to which the treatment response of a particular patient may deviate from the typical treatment response seen in the total group. This does not, of course, mean that data from patients with deviant responses must automatically be fed into a final assessment of drug efficacy. The circumstances of data collection for such patients, as well as the characteristics of the patients themselves, should be carefully scrutinised. Should deviations from protocol or other forms of procedural error come to light, this will be a valid reason for discarding the data for these patients from a final analysis, although such a process must be completely documented when reporting the final results. While the absence of detectable artifacts necessitates the inclusion of these patients in the data analysis, an examination of their characteristics may bring to light hitherto unrecognised predictors of treatment response which may be taken into account both in qualifications made about the current results and in the planning of future work.

The specific set of analyses to be performed with the total set of data collected is highly dependent upon the particular circumstances of the study in question. However, it may be appropriate here to mention a few points concerning general procedures. It is usually necessary to begin with a factorial design in which the treatment settings from which samples were drawn form one factor or mode of classification and the treatments used form the other. A treatment times treatment-setting interaction term is also included. When the treatment times treatment-setting interaction is not significant, the treatment-setting factor can usually be dropped, so that total group estimates and tests of significance can be obtained. The course to be followed when the treatment times treatment-setting interaction *is* significant is more complex and situation-dependent, and a detailed discussion of the issues involved can be found elsewhere[6]. Significant interactions of this type may occur even when unanticipated[30]. Where meaningful causes for their occurrence can be found, they may provide new and important information concerning mechanisms which affect drug response. However, when such interpretation is not possible, these interactions may impose a recalcitrant stalemate upon the research effort at hand.

Table 6. "Core" depressive symptoms.

Low mood
Loss of interest and enjoyment
Unusual pessimism, irritability, self-depreciation
Social withdrawal
Impaired concentration
Disturbance in energy, appetite, and sleep pattern
Suicidal feelings
Feeling much different from usual

Summary

The authors have attempted to select what they believe to be several cardinal issues with which the clinical research worker must come to grips in attempting to assess the efficacy of psychotropic medication in the treatment of depressive illness. The difficulties encountered in defining the illness entities to be studied, and hence the patient populations to be sampled, have been described. The discussion here has focused on the distinction between endogenous and exogenous depression, on the operational approach to patient selection, on empirically derived typologies, and on a strategy for typology which builds outward from the treatment response itself. Some attention has also been given to the role of non-specific factors in predicting the treatment response, to strategies for combining results from different data, to the question of the requisite sample size, to the advantages and problems of collaborative studies, and to the qualities desirable for adequate measuring instruments.

References

1 BECK, A.T.: Depression: clinical, experimental, and theoretical aspects (Hoeber Med. Div., Harper & Row, New York/Evanston/London 1967)

2 DEROGATIS, L.R., BONATO, R.R., YANG, K.C.: The power of IMPS in psychiatric drug research. Arch. gen. Psychiat. *19*, 689 (1968)

3 DOWNING, R.W., RICKELS, K.: The prediction of placebo response in anxious and depressed outpatients. In Wittenborn, J.R., Goldberg, S.C., May, P.R.A. (Editors): Psychopharmacology and the individual patient, p. 160 (Raven Press, New York 1970)

4 DOWNING, R.W., RICKELS, K.: Predictors of response to amitriptyline and placebo in three outpatient treatment settings. Proc. A.C.N.P. Meet., San Juan/Puerto Rico 1970 (printing)

5 DOWNING, R.W., RICKELS, K.: Predictors of amitriptyline response in outpatient depressives. J. nerv. ment. Dis. (printing)

6 DOWNING, R.W., RICKELS, K., WITTENBORN, J.R., MATTSSON, N.B.: Interpretation of data from investigations assessing the effectiveness of psychotropic agents, loc. cit.[16], p. 321

7   FREYHAN, F.A.: Therapeutic implications of differential effects of new pheno-
    thiazine compounds. Amer. J. Psychiat. *115*, 577 (1959)
8   FREYHAN, F.A.: Depressionsforschung: Klärung oder Verdunklung? In Hippius,
    H., Selbach, H. (Editors): Das depressive Syndrom, Int. Symp., Berlin 1968,
    p. 211 (Urban & Schwarzenberg, Munich/Berlin/Vienna 1969)
9   HAMILTON, M.: A rating scale for depression. J. Neurol. Neurosurg. Psychiat. *23*,
    56 (1960)
10 HESBACHER, P.T., RICKELS, K., WEISE, C.: Target symptoms. A promising im-
    provement criterion in psychiatric drug research. Arch. gen. Psychiat. *18*, 595
    (1968)
11 HIPPIUS, H.: Zur Durchführung koordinierter pharmakopsychiatrischer Unter-
    suchungen in verschiedenen Ländern. Neuro-Psycho-Pharmacology, Proc. Vth
    int. Congr. Coll. int. neuro-psycho-pharmacol. (C.I.N.P.), Washington, D.C.
    1966, p. 11. Int. Congr. Series No. 129 (Excerpta med. Found., Amsterdam etc.
    1967)
12 HIPPIUS, H.: Die Grenzen und Mängel der derzeitigen Therapie mit Anti-
    depressiva. The present status of psychotropic drugs, Proc. VIth int. Congr. Coll.
    int. neuro-psycho-pharmacol. (C.I.N.P.) Tarragona/Spain 1968, p. 176. Int.
    Congr. Series No. 180 (Excerpta med. Found., Amsterdam 1969)
13 KILOH, L.G., GARSIDE, R.F.: The independence of neurotic depression and
    endogenous depression. Int. J. Psychiat. *1*, 447 (1965)
14 KLERMAN, G.L.: Clinical research in depression. Arch. gen. Psychiat. *24*, 305
    (1971)
15 KLERMAN, G.L., PAYKEL, E.S.: Depressive pattern, social background, and
    hospitalization. J. nerv. ment. Dis. *150*, 466 (1970)
16 LEVINE, J., SCHIELE, B.C., BOUTHILET, L. (Editors): Principles and problems in
    establishing the efficacy of psychotropic agents. Publ. Hlth Serv. Publ. (Wash.)
    No. 2138 (1971)
17 LUBIN, A.: Discussant's remarks. In Katz, M.M., Cole, J.O., Barton, W.E.
    (Editors): The role and methodology of classification in psychiatry and psycho-
    pathology. Publ. Hlth Serv. Publ. No. 1584: 322 (1965)
18 McCLURE, J.N., Jr.: Pharmacotherapy. In Hill, D., Hollister, L.E. (Editors):
    Depression, p. 43 (Medcom, New York 1970)
19 OVERALL, J.E., GORHAM, D.R.: The brief psychiatric rating scale. Psychol. Rep.
    10, 799 (1962)
20 OVERALL, J.E., HOLLISTER, L.E.: Studies of quantitative approaches to psy-
    chiatric classification, loc. cit.[17], p. 277
21 OVERALL, J.E., HOLLISTER, L.E., JOHNSON, M., PENNINGTON, V.: Nosology of
    depression and differential response to drugs. J. Amer. med. Ass. *195*, 946 (1966)
22 RASKIN, A.: The prediction of antidepressant drug effects: review and critique.
    In Efron, D.H., Cole, J.O., Levine, J., Wittenborn, J.R. (Editors): Psycho-
    pharmacology: a review of progress, 1957–1967. Publ. Hlth Serv. Publ. (Wash.)
    No. 1836: 757 (1968)
23 RASKIN, A., BOOTHE, H., SCHULTERBRANDT, J.G., REATIG, N., ODLE, D.: A
    model for drug use with depressed patients, loc. cit.[4]
24 RASKIN, A., SCHULTERBRANDT, J.G., BOOTHE, H., REATIG, N., McKEON, J.J.:
    Treatment, social and psychiatric history variables related to symptom reduc-
    tion in hospitalized depressions, loc. cit.[3], p. 135
25 RASKIN, A., SCHULTERBRANDT, J.G., REATIG, N., McKEON, J.J.: Differential re-
    sponse to chlorpromazine, imipramine, and placebo. Arch. gen. Psychiat. *23*, 164
    (1970)
26 RICKELS, K.: Drug combination therapy in neurotic depression: its advantages
    and disadvantages. Pharmakopsychiat. Neuro-Psychopharmakol. *4*, 308 (1971)
27 RICKELS, K., HESBACHER, P.T.: A working model of clinical research in private
    practice. Psychopharmacol. Bull. *7*, 3 (1971)

28 RICKELS, K., HESBACHER, P.T., DOWNING, R.W.: Differential drug effects in neurotic depression. Dis. nerv. Syst. *31*, 468 (1970)

29 SHEPHERD, M.: Implications of a multi-centred clinical trial of treatments of depressive illness. Anti-depressant drugs, Proc. 1st int. Symp., Milan 1966, p. 332. Int. Congr. Ser. No. 122 (Excerpta med. Found., Amsterdam etc. 1967)

30 UHLENHUTH, E.H., RICKELS, K., FISHER, S., PARK, L.C., LIPMAN, R.S., MOCK, J.: Drug, doctor's verbal attitude and clinic setting in the symptomatic response to pharmacotherapy. Psychopharmacologia (Berl.) *9*, 392 (1966)

31 WHEATLEY, D.: Some problems of collating multi-participant research results, loc. cit.[11], p. 509

32 WINOKUR, G., PITTS, F.N., Jr.: Affective disorder: I. Is reactive depression an entity? J. nerv. ment. Dis. *138*, 541 (1964)

33 ZUNG, W.W.K.: A self-rating depression scale. Arch. gen. Psychiat. *12*, 63 (1965)

Rating scales in depression

by M. HAMILTON*

There is a very close relationship between the use of rating scales and the level of medical practice. Most clinical research nowadays includes the use of one or more rating scales, and they are well accepted by physicians who are associated with clinical research. In contrast, the broad mass of clinicians does not use them and is even suspicious of them on the grounds that they are artificial, misleading, and irrelevant to clinical practice. Where the medical services are inadequate, not only is the use of formal ratings non-existent, but even straightforward clinical recording is also deficient.

In general, it may be said that the use of rating scales in clinical work is only just beginning, and here the first step has been made in association with the storage of data on computers. Unfortunately, it is not practicable at present to use computers for storing clinical information about patients unless the volume of data can be reduced. Some method of compression to an acceptable volume must be devised, and the simplest method is to code the data by means of rating scales. Of course, this is only one aspect of the problem, for ratings are concerned primarily with clinical state; but systematic standardised recording of clinical data is still only at a very early stage of development. Even the limited achievements attained so far must be regarded as a remarkable success in view of the intractability of the problem. It may be that we are witnessing a change as revolutionary as was the introduction of standardisation and mass production in manufacture. Both have their positive and negative sides.

The advantages will be obvious to anybody who has ever had to search through old case records; standardisation means completeness. We can thus always be sure that important information about patients will not be missing. The other obvious gain from standardisation is the decrease in the variability of the information available about patients. The use of rating scales and standardised schedules will ensure that the description of the patient's behaviour and symptoms can be easily categorised by any observer. Naturally, there will be some losses. It is very easy for the physician who is recording a standardised interview to get into the habit of thinking that an interview which results in a rating is completed and sufficient for all purposes. It will be easy also to believe that what information goes into the computer is important and what does not go in is not. Both these assumptions are quite untrue. The taking of a history is the first stage of psychotherapy, and all patients need some psychotherapy. Is psychiatry going to change its attitude here, and, if so, is this desirable? A case record which consists of standardised items, however elaborate and numerous, loses informa-

---

100   * Department of Psychiatry, University of Leeds, England.

tion related to the individuality of the patient. Even if we ignore the special case of psychotherapy, we are faced with the problem of deciding how important this loss is. This is a field of research which will have to be explored sooner or later, and it may even become an urgent matter in the near future. To the average overworked mental-hospital psychiatrist, this may seem a problem very remote from his day-to-day activities, but there is no doubt that it will impinge on him much sooner than he would think.

A further advance towards complete automation is the use of computers for taking psychiatric histories. The first steps that have been taken along these lines arouse the admiration of everybody, but I do not set much store by further advances in this direction. From the technical point of view, such automated history taking is based on the assumption that patients are capable of giving a coherent and consistent history of themselves and their illness. This is not only uncommon but is sometimes impossible. In any case, a patient is going to have to meet either a nurse or a doctor at some time or other, however much he may be dealt with by machines; and if this meeting is inevitable, it might just as well be at the beginning rather than at the end!

Use of rating scales

The commonest type of rating scale in use is that which is designed to record the patient's condition, and this has the special purpose of measuring any changes that may occur, for example, in response to treatment. There are other kinds of scales which will become increasingly important in the future. First is the diagnostic scale, which is concerned with providing data for making some sort of classification of the patient's illness. This will include many items which are not necessarily symptoms and which need not or cannot change in the course of illness. For example, body habitus would be included in any scale designed to distinguish between depressions and schizophrenias. A family history of mental illness is another such item. Scales designed for determining prognosis or response to treatment would also include items not amenable to change as a result of treatment, e.g. previous response to treatment. In the case of the depressions, it has been found that, on the whole, the response to E.C.T. diminishes with successive attacks.

Scales designed to assess personality should, ideally, contain items which do not change in the presence or in the absence of illness. This is a controversial matter and cannot be dealt with in detail here because the relationship between mental illness and personality is not at all clear. It is traditionally believed that the personality of patients suffering from affective disorders is not fundamentally changed, but the reverse is true when we come to consider the schizophrenias.

Scoring of rating scales

The simplest method of scoring is known as the "pass-fail" method. Examples are "died versus did not die", or "recovered versus not recovered". Almost as simple is the use of global categories: mild, moderate, and severe illness. Similar categories for improvement comprise: no improvement, some improvement but still in hospital, improvement with discharge from hospital but not working, and complete social recovery. Both of these methods of assessment are very crude and on the whole suitable only for large numbers of cases. In spite of this, their simplicity makes them useful and popular, and they form the basis of much important work[1].

Categorisation of an item as absent or present is really very unsatisfactory because of the existence of an intermediate state of "doubtful". For example, when one takes the family history of a patient, how does one assess the statement that an aunt of the patient is supposed to have had a nervous breakdown at one time? When there is insufficient information to permit a clear allocation to a dichotomous categorisation, the opportunity for bias is enormously increased. It is not difficult to find examples of this in the current literature on the depressions. It is therefore always desirable to convert a dichotomous assessment into a three-group assessment of "absent", "doubtful", and "present", which normally would be coded as 0, 1, and 2.

It is not difficult to improve the last category by converting it into a "present: mild", and "present: marked to severe". These would be coded as Grades 2 and 3. This is, in effect, what I do for my own rating of retardation. Although there is a fourth category, this is defined as being so severe that it is impossible to interview the patient. Further subdivision of Grade 3 could produce "marked or obvious 3", "severe 4", and "very severe 5". The disadvantage of having five grades of severity for a given symptom is that they have a mid-point. This encourages the "bias of central tendency"—i.e., if the rater has difficulty in making a judgment, he tends to go to Grade 3. Furthermore, when there are only slight changes in the severity of the symptom, he has great difficulty in moving away from this grade. It was to avoid this difficulty of central tendency that I decided to have only four grades of severity for symptoms in the rating scale I designed for the assessment of depressive illness. There is no question that the more grades available the better the categorisation of the severity of a symptom, but the trouble is that a multiplicity of grades makes it difficult for the assessor to decide between them.

Analogue scales

There is no need to consider at length the importance of defining the various grades clearly in order to achieve the highest reliability. In recent years there has been a renewed interest in "analogue" scales. In these, the rater is asked to locate the position of the symptom along a line which runs between the two extremes of the symptom—i.e. at one end the symptom is absent and at the other it is very severe. This makes for increased flexibility in rating, but the increased range of scores is accompanied by greater difficulty in defining the positions of a rating. Different raters give different values to the points on the line, and if the position of the various grades is indicated, then raters tend to locate symptoms at the specified positions. The most obvious use for analogue scales is to serve as a substitute for an overall global judgment. This means that instead of having three or four categories there can be anything up to 100. I have not been able to find any publication which compares the two methods of assessment, but I can report some work done in 1956 in a clinical trial of benactyzine. Three psychiatrists were involved and they assessed patients diagnosed as suffering from "anxiety state". They used a rating scale and also made a global judgment of severity on an analogue scale 10 cm. in length. The correlation (for 16 or 18 cases) between the two assessments was 0.85, 0.65, and 0.49, and for all three raters together it was 0.67. This is quite good, but probably represents a maximum value, as the two types of assessment were obviously not independent. The results of the clinical trial, using the analogue scale and the rating scale, were almost identical.

The conclusion from these data is that the use of an analogue scale offers no advantage over a total score on a rating scale, but it does lose information concerning the pattern of symptoms in the initial state and the pattern of responses to treatment. This can be very important[8, 9, 10].

Sums of scores

It is customary to add the scores on items of a rating scale to give a total score, and clinicians find this very difficult to understand and very puzzling. "How is it possible to add scores on completely different symptoms and to make a total from them? And how is it possible to decide what value should be given to the various items when they are scored?" The simple answer is that it works. If a group of clinicians divides a number of patients into, say, three groups of mild, moderate, and severely ill, and if these three groups are then assessed with a rating scale, it will be found that the average scores of these three groups differ considerably and increase in the natural order. Furthermore, if the rating scale is good, it will be found that the overlap in scores between the three groups is very small. In other words, the patients in the "moderate" group who have the highest scores will only overlap very slightly with the patients in the "severe" group who have the lowest scores.

A rational explanation which is not too technical is as follows: if a particular variable is measured in two different ways, then normally it will be found that the two measurements are positively correlated, but it is common to find that this correlation is less than perfect. Each method of measurement is subject to some error and this accounts for the decrease below perfect correlation. It may also be that the two methods of measuring the one variable each also measure other variables to some extent, or, at least, are affected by them. If these additional variables are independent of one another and also of the one variable which is being measured, then such a contribution to the measurement can be treated in exactly the same way as an error. If we take the average of these two measurements or the total, which comes to the same, the errors will tend to cancel out, but the measurements themselves of the particular variable will not. In this way, summing or taking the average of two measurements increases the accuracy or reliability of the measurement.

If, when we are assessing, say, depression, we make assessments on a large number of symptoms, each of which is a manifestation of depression, then by taking the average or the total of the scores we increase the accuracy of the measurement of the depressive illness and at the same time tend to cancel out individual variations of the particular symptom. All this depends on the fact that the individual symptoms are each positively correlated with one another. In this way, a total score gives a measure of what is common to all the symptoms or variables which are included. A certain amount of information is lost, because no single number can give all the information that is available in all the separate scores. More information can be retained if the separate scores are divided into two or more groups, thus giving two or more scores to represent the totality. If it is desired to retain all the information available, then all the individual scores must be retained.

In some cases, the information that is lost by using a total score may be particularly important. In a trial in which benactyzine was employed for the treatment of anxiety states, the total scores showed that there was no significant difference between the results of treatment with the drug and with a placebo[6]. But by using special group scores (derived from factor analysis), it was shown that this drug did indeed produce a highly significant change in the pattern of symptoms[2].

How to score particular items in relation to others is theoretically a very difficult problem. If some items are regarded as being of greater importance than others (for a particular purpose), the scores on them could be multiplied by some appropriate factor (strictly speaking, it is the standard deviation rather than the actual score which should be increased). In practice, the use of special "weights" makes little difference to the total, and this difference diminishes as the number of items that make up the total score increases. Once again, crude empirical methods lose very little when compared with the utmost theoretical refinements.

Types of scale

Scales can be divided into those suitable for use by unskilled raters and those requiring skill in their use. Alternatively, they can be divided into those which are used by the patient himself and those used by observers. Clearly, the patient must be regarded as an unskilled rater. Self-assessment scales save the physician's time, but they do have a number of limitations. The patient must be capable of understanding and filling in the scale properly, and this may not be possible if he is too ill. He has difficulty in interpreting such adjectives as "very", "mild", or "frequent". Finally, there are a number of items, such as "loss of insight", which the patient cannot complete himself. The skilled rater can use his experience of interviewing not only to diminish error but also to collate evidence from all sources. I think that the skilled interviewer should use his judgment and experience to interpret the interview with the patient in order to make a proper assessment. If he does not do so, he is throwing away the benefits of his experience and training.

Not much research has been done to compare the relative merits of different kinds of scales, but KELLNER[7] has carried out some work in this field and has reviewed that of others, especially in relation to the assessment of anxiety states. He concludes that check-lists and questionnaires appeared to be somewhat less effective than other methods, but also that the effectiveness of self-ratings and that of observer-ratings were similar. A close agreement between self-assessments and observer-ratings in the course of treatment for depressions was also found by SCHLEMPER et al.[12]. One objection to rating by physicians is that it takes up a good deal of time. This criticism is irrelevant, because in any case the physician should be spending sufficient time with his patients and the filling in of a rating scale makes only a negligible addition to the total time.

A brief review of some of the more popular scales for depressive illness has already been published[5], but there are two other scales which are worth considering. Although the Hamilton scale[4] is widely used, it has been said to be more suitable for the more severely ill patients and not very satisfactory for the milder cases encountered in an out-patients department. RICKELS et al.[11] have introduced a modification of this scale which they consider to be more appropriate for the assessment of neurotic out-patients. It is in the form of a questionnaire which provides four major clinical clusters, which together form a total score. In addition, two sub-clusters of agitation and anxiety are also derived from the questionnaire. The four major clusters are *mood* (mood, facial expression, general appearance, crying, anxiety, hostile attitude, irritability, elation); *psychomotor* (motor retardation, decrease in speech productivity, loss of interest or drive, agitation); *psychopathological thoughts* (suicidal ideation, feelings of guilt, worthlessness, hopelessness, can't make decisions, can't concentrate or remember, paranoid thinking), and *somatic* (headaches, sleep and appetite disturbances, fatigue, loss of weight since beginning of illness, hypochondriacal or somatic complaints). It would be highly desirable to have this scale tested out and compared with others, although many clinicians might be disturbed at the many different kinds of symptoms which are assembled into one group.

A new self-rating scale has recently been published: the Wakefield S.A.D.S.[13]. This is a modification of the Zung scale, and because it contains several items related to anxiety it would appear to me to be particularly useful for anxious depressives of the milder type.

Analyses of results

The usual procedure in most drug trials is to make an assessment of the patient before the start of the treatment and at the end. The effect of treatment is then measured by an "improvement score", which is the difference between the two scores obtained before and after treatment. An improvement score has a natural simplicity and also shows differences in the amounts of improvement. It indicates clearly absence of change, improvement, or worsening, but does not enable one to compare the state of one patient with another. Equal improvement scores are not equivalent qualitatively, and although they may appear to be equal quantitatively it is doubtful if this is true—i.e. a decrease from 60 to 50 points is not necessarily the same clinically as a decrease from 15 to five. Furthermore, patients who have a low initial score can show only a small amount of improvement compared with patients who have a high initial score[3]. Finally, improvement scores have a high standard deviation. The variance of such scores can be as much as the sum of the variances of initial and final scores.

A much better method of assessing the effects of treatment is to use the final scores of the patients, but in that case it is useful to ensure that the initial scores of the groups of patients subjected to the different treatments are very close to each other. An improvement on this is to use the method of analysis of covariance in which the correlation between final score and initial score is employed to correct for differences in the initial scores. The statistical test of analysis of covariance implies homogeneity of covariance and this should be tested first. In clinical terms, this means that patients given different treatments will tend to have a final score which has the same relation to their initial score whatever the difference in treatment. Another method is to use "residual scores". Using the correlation between initial and final scores, an estimated final score for each patient is obtained and this is subtracted from the actual final score. This last figure is the one used in the analysis.

The availability of computers has made more refined methods of analysis practicable. Of these, one of the most important uses the techniques of multiple correlation. With this method, the different treatment groups of patients are analysed separately. All the variables available at the start of treatment are correlated with the outcome of treatment, and those which contribute insignificantly to the multiple correlation are deleted. The results obtained with the different treatment groups are then compared. If the predicting variables are the same for all the groups, then it is clear that the characteristics of those patients who respond to the different treatments are the same. Any difference found between the various treatments is then purely quantitative. If the predicting variables differ between the groups, then the patients who respond to the treatments differ qualitatively. Any one investigation can only provide tentative conclusions; if the investigations can be repeated, however, the information obtained will not only signify a great advance theoretically, but will also be of the utmost practical importance in the treatment of patients. In this lies one of the most important uses of rating scales in clinical practice.

Summary

This paper is concerned with a number of problems relating to rating scales—problems about which the relevant literature has little to say. Rating scales are employed chiefly in research, but they can also be of value in clinical practice. They have many uses, but must be specifically designed for each particular one—e.g. for diagnosis, prognosis, or assessment of clinical state. The various ways of scoring are considered, as are also the problems and uses of total scores and group scores. A proper index of improvement is difficult to choose, and different indices are therefore considered. Finally, the use of multiple-correlation techniques is described, together with their application to clinical practice.

References

1   CARNEY, M.W.P., ROTH, M., GARSIDE, R.F.: The diagnosis of depressive syndromes and the prediction of E.C.T. response. Brit. J. Psychiat. *111*, 659 (1965)

2   HAMILTON, M.: Treatment of anxiety states. III. Components of anxiety and their response to benactyzine. J. ment. Sci. *104*, 1062 (1958)

3   HAMILTON, M.: Psychotropic drugs: general considerations. International Encyclopedia of Pharmacology and Therapeutics, Sect. 6, Vol. I, p. 181 (Pergamon Press, Long Island City, N.Y. 1966)

4   HAMILTON, M.: Development of a rating scale for primary depressive illness. Brit. J. soc. clin. Psychol. *6*, 278 (1967)

5   HAMILTON, M.: Standardised assessment and recording of depressive symptoms. Psychiat. Neurol. Neurochir. (Amst.) *72*, 201 (1969)

6   HARGREAVES, G.R., HAMILTON, M., ROBERTS, J.M.: Benactyzine as an aid in treatment of anxiety states. Preliminary report. Brit. med. J. *i*, 306 (1957)

7   KELLNER, R.: The improvement criteria in drug trials with neurotic patients. Psychol. Med. (1972; printing)

8   KLEIN, D.F., FINK, M.: Psychiatric reaction patterns to imipramine. Amer. J. Psychiat. *119*, 432 (1962)

9   OTTOSON, J.-O.: Electroconvulsive therapy of endogenous depression: an analysis of the influence of various factors on the efficacy of the therapy. J. ment. Sci. *108*, 694 (1962)

10 OVERALL, J.E., HOLLISTER, L.E.: Differential drug responses of different depressive syndromes. Neuro-Psycho-Pharmacology, Proc. Vth int. Congr. Coll. int. neuro-psycho-pharmacol. (C.I.N.P.), Washington, D.C. 1966, p. 711. Int. Congr. Series No. 129 (Excerpta med. Found., Amsterdam etc. 1967)

11 RICKELS, K., JENKINS, B.W., ZAMOSTIEN, B., RAAB, E., KANTHER, M.: Pharmacotherapy in neurotic depression. J. nerv. ment. Dis. *145*, 475 (1967)

12 SCHLEMPER, M.S.H., HUSTINX, A., KOOYMAN, M., JANSSEN, R.H.C.: Measurement of depression. Psychiat. Neurol. Neurochir. (Amst.) *72*, 225 (1969)

13 SNAITH, R.P., AHMED, S.N., MEHTA, S., HAMILTON, M.: Assessment of the severity of primary depressive illness: Wakefield self-assessment depression inventory. Psychol. Med. *1*, 143 (1971)

Discussion

P. PICHOT: I have a question arising from Dr. HAMILTON's paper. It concerns the problem of simple versus complex items. This is a matter that I have discussed privately with Dr. HAMILTON, and I don't think he has actually written about it. I think it's a very important point for the future, and I should be grateful if he would give us his opinion on this problem.

M. HAMILTON: When we try to assess the condition of a patient, we are taking a sample of his total behaviour and generalising from it. Strictly speaking, the only way to make such an assessment is to observe the patient over a long period of time, to note everything he does and says and feels. This is impossible, and we therefore have to be content with a sample. We take this sample at the interview, or we observe the patient over a few days. Even a sample of this kind is still too big. For instance, we cannot describe the way he walks into and out of a room every time he comes to see us over a period of one or two days. So we have to select representative examples, and, to do this, we must use our judgment and experience to guide us. We do this in deciding what we should include in the case history, and the same applies when we are making a rating. The skilled observer can use all sorts of information, and as soon as he has enough to make an assessment, he has no need to ask any further questions. But when working with a fixed schedule or scale, he has to ask all the prescribed questions. The fixed scale is therefore a clumsy and laborious instrument. To be effective, it has to be long, and it therefore introduces much unnecessary information which may not be relevant. There is thus a big difference between the assessment of a complex system, such as depression, insomnia, or loss of interest, and a simple behavioural one.
In the end, we have to go back to the empirical data. Is the loss of information resulting from the use of restricted items and scales important? The answer is that some research, and more still needs to be done, has shown that in drug trials the loss of information is not great, provided the number of patients is sufficiently large. In practice, these restricted instruments are therefore adequate for their purposes. But when one is exploring—for example, looking for differential indicators of treatment—then one should use everything that is available. This is the reason why I, as a clinician, prefer to rely upon skill and experience in making a judgment, rather than contenting myself with a simple check-list filled in by an unskilled person or by the patient himself.

The activity of two structurally analogous psycho-active compounds

by H.J. BEIN*

When WILHELM and SCHMIDT[6] synthesised the dibenzobicyclo-octadienes, they presented biologists with a tool that is helping them to gain a deeper insight into cellular processes taking place in the nervous system. On the one hand, each of the various compounds in this new chemical class has clearly circumscribed effects and a characteristic spectrum of activity under both experimental and clinical conditions, while on the other, they display unusual, and exceptionally well-defined, structure-activity relationships.

Two of these substances that are chemically very closely related to each other—Tacitin® and Ludiomil®—have been thoroughly investigated in laboratory experiments and in clinical studies. Both affect the function of various formations in the nervous system.

It is only in the length of their side chain that the chemical structures of Tacitin and Ludiomil differ (Figure 1); yet this comparatively minor structural modification gives rise to remarkable disparities in their pharmacological and therapeutic effects: in the non-anaesthetised animal, for example, Ludiomil lacks the muscle-relaxant and tranquillising action that is typical of Tacitin (BEIN[1]).

It is therefore not surprising that various neuropharmacological test systems should reveal one very notable difference between the two compounds (Table 1): Ludiomil, in contrast to Tacitin, inhibits neither the activity of the gamma-fibre system nor decerebrate rigidity.

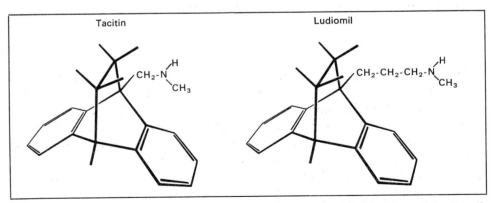

Fig. 1. Structural formulae of the active substances contained in Tacitin and Ludiomil.

---

* Research Department, Pharmaceutical Division, CIBA-GEIGY LIMITED, Basle, Switzerland.

Table 1. Effects of Tacitin and Ludiomil in neuropharmacological test systems.

Effect on:	Tacitin	Ludiomil
Polysynaptic reflex transmission	Marked inhibition	Very slight; occasionally facilitation
Tonic activity of gamma motoneurones	Marked inhibition	Very slight
Decerebrate rigidity	Marked inhibition	Very slight

Table 2. Influence of Tacitin and Ludiomil on components of catecholamine metabolism.

	Tacitin	Ludiomil
I. Inhibition of noradrenaline uptake		
a) *In situ*	Inactive	*Active*
b) In isolated granules	Slightly active	Slightly active
II. Change in noradrenaline content in the brain		
a) After repeated administration	Inactive	Slightly active (irregular)
b) After a single dose	Slight reduction	Inactive
III. Increase in noradrenaline and dopamine biosynthesis in the brain	*Active*	Inactive

This is an instance of how a specific action becomes lost as a result of chemical modification—a phenomenon that chemists and pharmacologists are all too familiar with. The following example, on the other hand, illustrates the qualitatively different effects of the two compounds in one and the same biological field, i.e. catecholamine metabolism, on which both Tacitin and Ludiomil have a marked and pharmacologically important influence (Table 2):

Tacitin stimulates, in particular, the biosynthesis of noradrenaline and dopamine in the brain; in this respect it bears a resemblance to chlorpromazine (MAÎTRE et al.[4]). Ludiomil inhibits the uptake of noradrenaline by the nerve cell and thus acts similarly to Tofranil® (MAÎTRE et al.[5]).

Owing to the marked effect many psycho-active compounds have on adrenergic functions and on catecholamine metabolism, the adrenergic system has assumed

Table 3. Activity of Tacitin and Ludiomil *in vitro* against biogenic substances (all concentrations expressed in mcg./ml.).

Organ	Antagonism torwards:	Effective concentration required for 50% inhibition	
		Tacitin	Ludiomil
Guinea-pig ileum	Histamine (0.03)	0.003	0.009
	Acetylcholine (0.1)	5	1
	Serotonin (0.1)	0.3	0.3
Guinea-pig seminal vesicle	Adrenaline (3.0)	0.4	4
Rat vas deferens	Noradrenaline (1.0)	0.05	*Enhancement* 0.01

a prominent place in both experimental and clinical research in the course of the last few years. We must, however, take care not to lose sight of the fact that we still know far too little about the function and the importance of noradrenaline in the brain. I find it impressive that the classic psycho-active compounds chlorpromazine and imipramine should both have risen from the ranks of the antihistamines; and it strikes me as being significant that they should antagonise histamine as well as exerting an unmistakably anticholinergic action.

Tacitin and Ludiomil are also histamine antagonists (Table 3). Whereas Tacitin counteracts the effect of histamine *in vitro* to a slightly greater extent than Ludiomil, Ludiomil has the more marked inhibitory action against acetylcholine; in the light of the biochemical findings already referred to, it was to be expected that there would also be marked differences in the activity of the two compounds against noradrenaline and adrenaline (JAQUES and RÜEGG [2, 3]).

We consider it a stroke of good luck that Tacitin and Ludiomil, which despite their fundamental dissimilarity do resemble each other in various respects, are both being studied clinically as well as experimentally. These studies should make a decisive contribution to our knowledge of the relationships between chemical structure and activity, especially as regards the more subtle aspects of specific actions and the extent to which effects observed in laboratory experiments are comparable with clinical effects.

References

1 BEIN, H.J.: Parmacological aspects of the activity of Tacitin. Anxiety and tension—new therapeutic aspects, Int. Symp., St.Moritz 1970, p. 36
2 JAQUES, R., RÜEGG, M.: Some peripheral pharmacological characteristics of benzoctamine. Pharmacology (Basle) *6*, 89 (1971)
3 JAQUES, R., RÜEGG, M.: Unpublished findings, 1972

4 MAîTRE, L., STAEHELIN, M., BEIN, H.J.: Effects of benzoctamine (30,803-Ba, Tacitin), a new psychoactive drug, on catecholamine metabolism. Biochem. Pharmacol. *19*, 2875 (1970)

5 MAîTRE, L., STAEHELIN, M., BEIN, H.J.: Blockade of noradrenaline uptake by 34,276-Ba, a new antidepressant drug. Biochem. Pharmacol. *20*, 2169 (1971)

6 WILHELM, M., SCHMIDT, P.: Synthese und Eigenschaften von 1-Aminoalkyldibenzo[b,e]bicyclo[2.2.2]octadienen. Helv. chim. Acta *52*, 1385 (1969)

The pharmacology of Ludiomil

by A. Delini-Stula*

The discovery of the therapeutic effectiveness of the first psychotropic compounds opened up a new era in the investigation and systematic analysis of the structural requirements upon which the specific central activity of such drugs depends. In connection with research on these compounds, pharmacologists have since also been faced with the task of determining possible relationships between their activity patterns as observed in animals and their therapeutic effects in man.

Such relationships as appear to exist are of a tenuous nature and permit only limited conclusions to be drawn. Pharmacologists have nevertheless learned one important lesson from their experience with psychotropic compounds, namely, that there is no single pharmacological property that can be regarded as *the* characteristic feature of any given psycho-active drug. On the contrary, each compound belonging to this category exhibits various effects which, viewed collectively, constitute a spectrum of activity that is distinctive of the substance in question. In order to evaluate a new psycho-active drug and to differentiate it from known compounds, it is therefore necessary to carry out comprehensive studies involving the use of a variety of methods.

Antidepressant properties of Ludiomil®

The main difficulty encountered when evaluating psychotropic drugs lies in the fact that there are no true animal equivalents to the psychic diseases occurring in man. The antidepressant activity of the tricyclic compounds, for example, was retrospectively demonstrated by reference to their mode of interaction with other centrally acting drugs. The finding that imipramine completely or partially suppresses the effects induced in animals by high doses of reserpine (Domenjoz and Theobald[8]; Garattini et al.[10,11]) was, for example, one of the first experimentally obtained clues to the drug's clinical antidepressant activity. Since then, a test based on the ability of antidepressants to antagonise reserpine-induced effects in animals has become widely used for the characterisation of such drugs.

Ludiomil as a reserpine antagonist

Findings on the interaction between Ludiomil and reserpine in rats are presented in Figure 1. From these it is evident that Ludiomil exerts a dose-dependent pro-

* Research Department, Pharmaceutical Division, CIBA-GEIGY LIMITED, Basle, Switzerland.

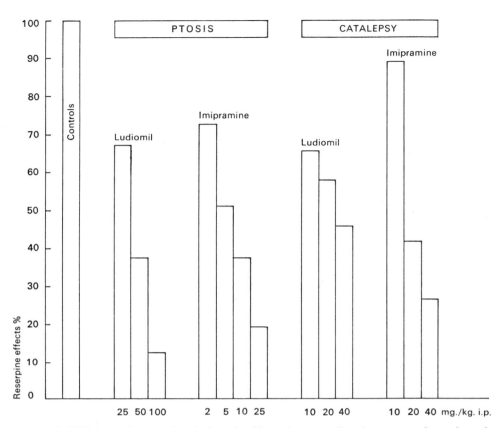

Fig. 1. Inhibition of reserpine-induced effects in rats. Ptosis was evaluated and rated as described by RUBIN et al.[17]. Each column represents the average of the individual scores for 10 rats, expressed as a percentage of the maximal response. Catalepsy was evaluated in terms of Stages III and IV as described by WIRTH et al.[22]. Again, each column represents the average of the individual scores for 10 animals, expressed as a percentage of the maximal cataleptic response. The test substances were given 30 minutes prior to the reserpine, which was administered intraperitoneally in doses of 2 mg./kg. (ptosis test) or 5 mg./kg. (catalepsy test). The effects of the substances were assessed four hours after reserpinisation of the animals.

tective effect against ptosis and catalepsy in rats treated with reserpine in intraperitoneal doses of 2 and 5 mg./kg., respectively. Compared with imipramine, Ludiomil had to be given in larger doses in order to prevent ptosis in reserpinised animals, whereas equal doses of both drugs were similarly effective in attenuating reserpine-induced catalepsy.

Ludiomil as a tetrabenazine antagonist

The tricyclic antidepressants not only characteristically suppress effects induced in animals by reserpine, but also antagonise the depressant activity of tetra-

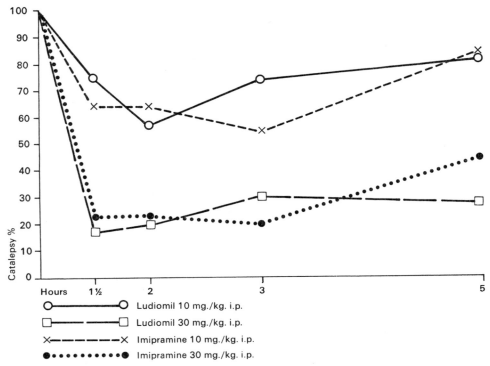

Fig. 2. Inhibition of tetrabenazine-induced catalepsy in rats. Each point in the curves represents the average cataleptic response of 10 rats. The catalepsy was rated as explained in Figure 1. The test substances were given at various time intervals (i.e. ½, 1, 2, and 4 hours) before tetrabenazine (20 mg./kg. i.p.). Their effects were always evaluated one hour after the tetrabenazine injection.

benazine (STILLE[18]), which is a short-acting depletor of the catecholamine stores. Shown in Figure 2 are curves in which the tetrabenazine-antagonising effect of Ludiomil is compared with that of imipramine. Both drugs proved to be equipotent in antagonising cataleptic immobility in rats treated with tetrabenazine in an intraperitoneal dose of 20 mg./kg.; Figure 2 indicates the dose-dependency of the effect of both compounds in this experiment, as well as their duration of action.

Interaction between Ludiomil and H 77/77

In another experimental procedure, Ludiomil was again found to display properties similar to those of imipramine, i.e. it considerably inhibited the rise in temperature induced by 4-α-dimethylmetatyramine (H 77/77), a substance which is able to penetrate into the brain and to deplete the catecholamine stores (CARLSSON et al.[4]). We had observed that, when administered to rats in an oral dose of 50 mg./kg., H 77/77 provokes a very marked increase in temperature

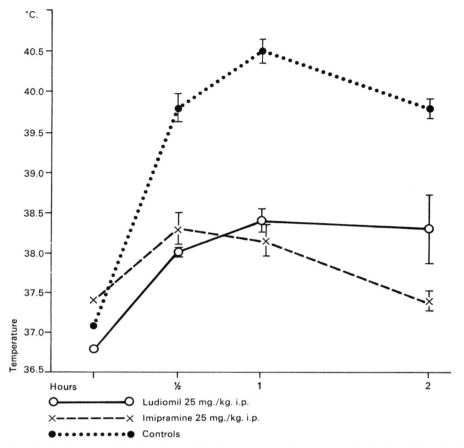

Fig. 3. Influence of Ludiomil and imipramine on hyperthermia induced by H 77/77 in rats. Each point in the curves represents the average rectal temperature of at least five rats (± S.E.M.). The noradrenaline-displacing agent H 77/77 was administered orally in a dose of 50 mg./kg. 30 minutes after an intraperitoneal injection (25 mg./kg.) of the test substance.

which can be counteracted by drugs that interfere with the uptake of catecholamines by the adrenergic neurones (DELINI-STULA[6]). In rats treated with H 77/77, Ludiomil—as revealed in Figure 3—diminished hyperthermia to about the same extent as imipramine, a finding which correlates well with the results of biochemical studies on the effect of Ludiomil in inhibiting the uptake of catecholamines.

Biochemical effects of Ludiomil

Experiments undertaken *in vivo* have shown that Ludiomil potently inhibits the uptake of noradrenaline in several sympathetically innervated organs of the rat, cat, and chick. These inhibitory effects, which proved to be very pro-

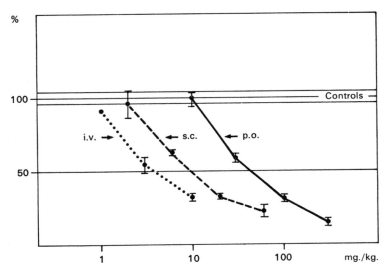

Fig. 4. Effect of Ludiomil on the uptake of H^3-noradrenaline in the rat heart. Dose-response relationships after intravenous (i.v.), subcutaneous (s.c.), and oral (p.o.) treatment. Abscissa: dose of Ludiomil. Ordinate: H^3-noradrenaline taken up, expressed as a percentage of the control values. Each point represents the mean value ($\pm$ S.E.) from four to nine experiments (for details and method, see MAÎTRE et al.[14]).

nounced both in the brain as well as in the peripheral tissues, were observed after oral, subcutaneous, and intravenous administration (Figure 4) (MAÎTRE et al.[14]). Ludiomil was likewise found to inhibit guanethidine-induced depletion of endogenous noradrenaline stores and also to reduce the uptake of radioactively labelled metaraminol in the rat myocardium (MAÎTRE et al.[14]). Although Ludiomil produced a marked and dose-dependent inhibition of the noradrenaline uptake in the brain and heart, it did not alter the concentration of noradrenaline in these organs, even after repeated daily administration.

The ability to inhibit catecholamine-uptake processes at the neural membrane is a typical property of imipramine-like compounds. In this respect Ludiomil exerts an effect qualitatively similar to that of imipramine. On the other hand, the quantitative differences we observed in these studies were dependent on the animal species employed and on the route of administration selected. Following intravenous injection, the degree to which the uptake of H^3-noradrenaline was inhibited in the rat heart was roughly the same with both Ludiomil and imipramine (Figure 5). When administered orally to rats, however, Ludiomil proved roughly ten times less potent in this respect than imipramine. In the cat, by way of contrast, no quantitative differences between the two drugs were apparent with regard either to the route of administration or to the organs examined (atria, ventricles, spleen, salivary gland). It could therefore be assumed that the quantitative differences observed in response to the variously administered doses were attributable merely to differences in absorption between the animal species used.

117

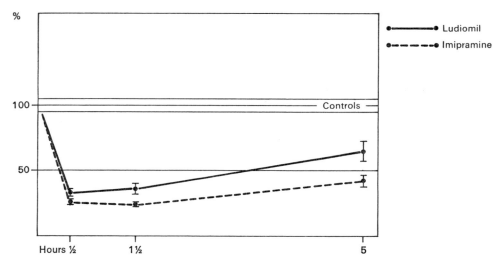

Fig. 5. Comparative effect of intravenous Ludiomil (10 mg./kg.) and imipramine (10 mg./kg.) on the uptake of H^3-noradrenaline in the rat heart. The rats received an intravenous injection of H^3-noradrenaline (100 μc./kg.) at different intervals of time after the drug pre-treatment. They were sacrificed one hour after the injection of radioactive noradrenaline. Abscissa: time elapsing between drug and H^3-noradrenaline injections. Ordinate: H^3-noradrenaline taken up, expressed as a percentage of the control values. The absolute values ($\pm$ S.E.) from eight control experiments were $95.7 \cdot 10^3 \pm 4.7 \cdot 10^3$ counts/min./g. heart (for details, see MAÎTRE et al.[14]).

Histochemical studies performed in order to determine the inhibitory effect of several drugs on the uptake of a-methyl-noradrenaline in reserpinised rats once again demonstrated the typical imipramine-like properties of Ludiomil. The degree to which Ludiomil inhibited the reserpine-resistant uptake of a-methyl-noradrenaline into the noradrenergic peripheral neurones was similar—at mg./kg. dosage levels—to that observed in response to cocaine (LOREZ[13]).

Interaction between Ludiomil and humoral neurotransmitters

In studies in which STONE[20] investigated the relationship between some of the effects of antidepressant drugs on the autonomic nervous system and their antidepressant activity, he demonstrated that a correlation appeared to exist between certain of their peripheral effects and their central antidepressant properties. Included among these peripheral effects were enhancement and prolongation of responses elicited by noradrenaline injections, an ability to antagonise indirectly acting sympathomimetic amines, and, finally, a capacity to offset the sympatholytic action of adrenergic blocking agents such as guanethidine.

Ludiomil displays all these effects. It enhances the action exerted by noradrenaline on the blood pressure (Figure 6) and on the nictitating membrane in the

118

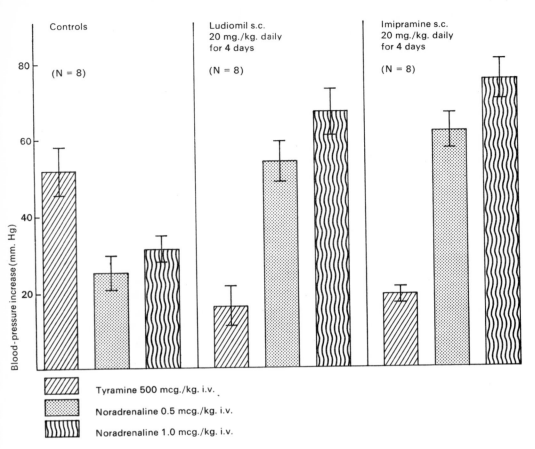

Tyramine 500 mcg./kg. i.v.

Noradrenaline 0.5 mcg./kg. i.v.

Noradrenaline 1.0 mcg./kg. i.v.

Fig. 6. Influence of Ludiomil and imipramine on blood-pressure changes induced by tyramine and noradrenaline. Direct measurement of blood pressure in the allobarbitone-urethane anaesthetised cat. Each column represents the mean increase in blood pressure following injection of the pressor substances; the bars represent the standard errors.

Table 1. Intensification of noradrenaline-induced spasm in the rat vas deferens by Ludiomil. The values listed represent the contractile response expressed as a percentage of the values obtained in controls (which were treated with noradrenaline only).

Concentration of Ludiomil (mcg./ml.)	N	Intensification of spasms (%)
0.01	4	53
0.1	10	107
1.0	8	150

cat, it prevents the rise in blood pressure induced by tyramine in the cat, and it also blocks the effect of guanethidine (BRUNNER et al.[3]). Furthermore, in studies undertaken *in vitro*, it has been found to produce a dose-dependent increase in the smooth-muscle contraction provoked by noradrenaline (Table 1).

The influence of Ludiomil on other humoral neurotransmitters was evaluated in various *in vitro* systems. Despite the dubieties involved in extrapolating from peripheral to central actions, it is a fact that these peripheral actions constitute important components in the spectra of activity of psychotropic drugs.

Ludiomil has been found to display strong antihistaminic activity. The contractile effects of serotonin in the isolated rat colon and the effects of acetylcholine on the rabbit intestine are also antagonised by Ludiomil (JAQUES and RÜEGG[12]).

The pharmacological and biochemical effects of Ludiomil as revealed in various tests and various animal species reflect the pattern of activity characteristic of antidepressant drugs. As already mentioned, Ludiomil resembles imipramine in that it antagonises the central effects of reserpine and tetrabenazine and diminishes the hyperthermia induced by 4-a-dimethylmetatyramine. It inhibits the uptake of noradrenaline in several organs of different animal species. It also potentiates the peripheral effects of noradrenaline *in vivo* and *in vitro*. Finally, it antagonises the contractile effect of various neurotransmitters *in vitro*.

However, just as the chemical structure of Ludiomil differs radically from that of the classic imipramine-like compounds, so its general pattern of activity displays clear differences as compared with the latter drugs. In this respect Ludiomil constitutes a genuinely new substance.

Sedative-tranquillising properties of Ludiomil

Ludiomil belongs to the category of central-acting drugs which in animals produce gross behavioural changes to only a minor degree. In mice, depending on the doses administered, initial signs of central nervous stimulation are followed by ataxia and hypoactivity of brief duration. When quantitatively evaluated using a photo-cell counting method (DEWS[7]), spontaneous locomotor activity in mice was found to diminish by about 50% in response to an intraperitoneal dose of about 20 mg./kg.; in this respect, Ludiomil was roughly twice as potent as imipramine. On the other hand, the depressant effect of Ludiomil, as studied also in other test procedures (Figure 7), was far less pronounced than that observed following major or minor tranquillisers.

Classic antidepressants usually induce signs of increased excitability and aggressiveness in rodents (STILLE[19]) and primates (BARUK et al.[1]); but in both these types of animal Ludiomil failed to elicit any such behavioural responses. On the contrary, in some forms of aggressiveness it actually exerted a taming influence in doses which did not appear to impair the animals' gross motor activity. In pairs of "fighting mice" (TEDESCHI et al.[21]) subjected to electrical foot-stimulation, it had a calming effect on the animals' belligerent behaviour. Vicious attacks by rats with electrolytic lesions of the septal brain nuclei ["septal rats" (BRADY and NAUTA[2])] were attenuated and the extreme irritability of the

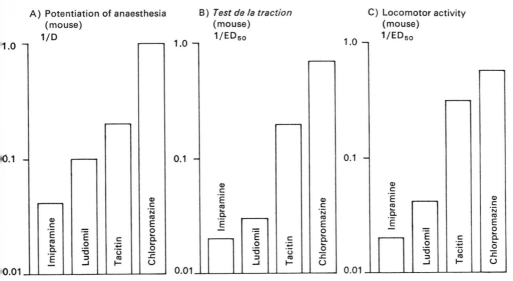

Fig. 7. Central nervous depressant activity of various psycho-active drugs. The potentiation of anaesthesia induced by a short-acting anaesthetic agent G 29,505 (DOMENJOZ and THEOBALD[8]), the effect in the *test de la traction* (COURVOISIER et al.[5]), and locomotor activity (DEWS[7]) were taken as measures of central nervous depressant activity. The degree of effect in the three respective tests is indicated on a logarithmic scale as the reciprocal of D and ED_{50}: A) $1/D$ (D = minimum dose which induced a significant prolongation of anaesthesia); B) $1/ED_{50}$ (ED_{50} = dose which impaired the holding reflex in 50% of animals); C) $1/ED_{50}$ (ED_{50} = dose which reduced locomotor activity by 50%).

animals counteracted in a dose-dependent manner. Here Ludiomil acted similarly to chlordiazepoxide (RANDALL et al.[16]), its activity as observed by us being in this instance only about two times weaker than that of chlordiazepoxide. Imipramine, on the other hand, clearly increased the irritability and aggressiveness of septal rats. When administered in oral doses as low as 5–10 mg./kg., Ludiomil markedly diminished inter-group aggressiveness in monkeys and facilitated social contact between them. Here, once again, the action of Ludiomil differed from that of imipramine.

Various types of aggressiveness are characteristically inhibited by tranquillising drugs (ZBINDEN and RANDALL[23]), but are not specifically attenuated by antidepressants (DUANE SOFIA[9]). In this connection Ludiomil thus behaves like the genuine tranquillisers. Nevertheless, it does not afford animals protection against experimentally induced convulsions, nor does it impair reflex transmission, and in other respects, too, it can be clearly differentiated from the tranquillisers.

Ludiomil differs from the classic antidepressants not only with regard to its sedative-tranquillising properties, but also by virtue of the fact that it lacks an amphetamine-potentiating effect. For example, the tricyclic antidepressants characteristically enhance and prolong amphetamine-induced hyperthermia in

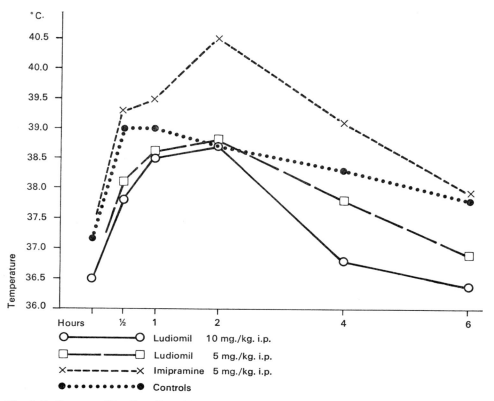

Fig. 8. Influence of Ludiomil and imipramine on amphetamine-induced hyperthermia in rats. The curves indicate the time course of rectal temperature changes occurring after treatment with the test substance and amphetamine. The amphetamine was given in a dose of 5 mg./kg. i.p. 30 minutes after intraperitoneal injection of Ludiomil (5 and 10 mg./kg.) or imipramine (5 mg./kg.). Each point in the curves represents the average rectal temperature of 10 rats.

rats (MORPURGO and THEOBALD[15]), whereas Ludiomil—as illustrated in Figure 8—tends if anything to suppress rather than to potentiate this effect of amphetamine in rats. In this particular respect, Ludiomil acts almost like a major tranquilliser. In contrast to the latter type of drug, however, it does not exert any intrinsic temperature-lowering effect in untreated animals.

Conclusions

Ludiomil constitutes a substance with a novel pharmacological profile. It has a clearly defined spectrum of activity and displays properties that are characteristic of an antidepressant drug. It differs from imipramine, however, in that it exerts a marked sedative and anti-aggressive action and exhibits no amphetamine-potentiating effect. The principal central effects of Ludiomil can thus be described as those of an antidepressant with tranquillising properties.

References

1 BARUK, H., LAUNAY, J., PERLÈS, R.: Dérivés de l'iminodibenzyle: l'imipramine. Expérimentation animale du G 22355 (Imipramine) chez le singe. Ann. Moreau Tours, Vol. I, p. 144 (Presses univ. France, Paris 1962)

2 BRADY, J.V., NAUTA, W.J.H.: Subcortical mechanisms in emotional behavior: affective changes following septal forebrain lesions in the albino rat. J. comp. physiol. Psychol. *46*, 339 (1953)

3 BRUNNER, H., HEDWALL, P.R., MEIER, M., BEIN, H.J.: Cardiovascular effects of preparation CIBA 34,276-Ba and imipramine. Agents and Actions *2*, 69 (1971)

4 CARLSSON, A., CORRODI, H., FUXE, K., HÖKFELT, T.: Effects of some antidepressant drugs on the depletion of intraneuronal brain catecholamine stores caused by 4,a-dimethyl-meta-tyramine. Europ. J. Pharmacol. *5*, 367 (1969)

5 COURVOISIER, S., DUCROT, R., JULOU, L.: Nouveaux aspects expérimentaux de l'activité centrale des dérivés de la phénothiazine. Psychotropic drugs, Proc. int. Symp. psychotrop. Drugs, Milan 1957, p. 373 (Elsevier, Amsterdam etc. 1957)

6 DELINI-STULA, A.: Pharmacological interaction of various antidepressants with noradrenaline-displacing agent 4-alpha-dimethyl-metatyramine (in preparation)

7 DEWS, P.B.: The measurement of the influence of drugs on voluntary activity in mice. Brit. J. Pharmacol. *8*, 46 (1953)

8 DOMENJOZ, R., THEOBALD, W.: Zur Pharmakologie des Tofranil (N-(3-Dimethylaminopropyl)-iminodibenzyl-Hydrochlorid). Arch. int. Pharmacodyn. *120*, 450 (1959)

9 DUANE SOFIA, R.: Effects of centrally active drugs on four models of experimentally-induced aggression in rodents. Life Sci. *8*, 705 (1969)

10 GARATTINI, S., GIACHETTI, A., JORI, A., PIERI, L., VALZELLI, L.: Effect of imipramine, amitriptyline and their monomethyl derivatives on reserpine activity. J. Pharm. Pharmacol. *14*, 509 (1962)

11 GARATTINI, S., GIACHETTI, A., PIERI, L., RE, R.: Antagonists of reserpine induced eyelid ptosis. Med. exp. (Basle) *3*, 315 (1960)

12 JAQUES, R., RÜEGG, M.: Personal communication

13 LOREZ, H.-P.: Histochemische Untersuchung der Wirkung von Pharmaka auf die Aufnahme von a-Methylnoradrenalin in Noradrenalin- und Dopamin-Neuren bei der reserpinisierten Ratte. Z. ges. exp. Med. *151*, 241 (1969)

14 MAÎTRE, L., STAEHELIN, M., BEIN, H.J.: Blockade of noradrenaline uptake by CIBA 34,276-Ba, a new antidepressant drug. Biochem. Pharmacol. *20*, 2169 (1971)

15 MORPURGO, C., THEOBALD, W.: Pharmacological modifications of the amphetamine-induced hyperthermia in rats. Europ. J. Pharmacol. *2*, 287 (1967)

16 RANDALL, L.O., SCHALLEK, W., HEISE, G.A., KEITH, E.F., BAGDON, R.E.: The psychosedative properties of methaminodiazepoxide. J. Pharmacol. exp. Ther. *129*, 163 (1960)

17 RUBIN, B., MALONE, M.H., WAUGH, M.H., BURKE, J.C.: Bioassay of Rauwolfia roots and alkaloids. J. Pharmacol. exp. Ther. *120*, 125 (1957)

18 STILLE, G.: Zur pharmakologischen Prüfung von Antidepressiva am Beispiel eines Dibenzodiazepins. Arzneimittel-Forsch. *14*, 534 (1964)

19 STILLE, G.: Pharmacological investigation of antidepressant compounds. Pharmakopsychiat. Neuro-Psychopharmakol. *1*, 92 (1968)

20 STONE, C.A.: Relationship of some autonomic actions of potential antidepressant activity among antidepressant drugs. Antidepressant drugs, Proc. 1st int. Symp., Milan 1966, p. 158. Int. Congr. Ser. No. 122 (Excerpta med. Found., Amsterdam etc. 1967)

21 TEDESCHI, R.E., TEDESCHI, D.H., MUCHA, A., COOK, L., MATTIS, P.A., FELLOWS, F.J.: Effects of various centrally acting drugs on fighting behavior of mice. J. Pharmacol. exp. Ther. *125*, 28 (1959)

123

22 WIRTH, W., GÖSSWALD, R., HÖRLEIN, U., RISSE, K.-H., KREISKOTT, H.: Zur
    Pharmakologie acylierter Phenothiazin-Derivate. Arch. int. Pharmacodyn. *115*,
    1 (1958)
23 ZBINDEN, G., RANDALL, L.O.: Pharmacology of benzodiazepines: laboratory
    and clinical correlations. In Garattini, S., Shore, P.A. (Editors): Advances in
    pharmacology, Vol. V, p. 213 (Acad. Press, New York/London 1967)

Discussion

F. FREYHAN: I was most impressed by the high scientific level of these two presentations. Both in the literature and at symposia there has been a great deal of discussion about the relevance of laboratory data in regard to predicting patterns of clinical effectiveness. For this reason I should like to ask two questions now, before the clinicians present their reports. Firstly, what sort of clinical activity pattern would you expect from this new compound in the light of your experimental data, and in what respect is the compound likely to introduce some new dimension of clinical value? Secondly, are there any data from your own laboratory work which would indicate that this new compound lowers the convulsive threshold? I ask this because in our initial series of 13 patients there were two instances of grand mal seizures.

W. PÖLDINGER: I, too, have a couple of questions for Dr. DELINI-STULA. The first concerns the diminution in aggressiveness which you observed in your animal experiments. In clinical use, antidepressants are liable to provoke symptoms in schizophrenic patients displaying signs of depression. Judging from the drug's pharmacological profile, this might perhaps not be the case with Ludiomil, and in that event the new compound would mark a step forward in the treatment of this particular group of patients.
My second question is as follows: if I understood you correctly, Dr. DELINI-STULA, you said that Ludiomil possesses certain fairly pronounced peripheral effects. One might therefore be entitled to expect the drug to elicit a particularly good response in masked depression or in psychosomatic disorders associated with depressive mood. Do the pharmacological data warrant this prediction?

N. MATUSSEK: I certainly believe that this category of substances differs quite considerably from the tricyclic thymoleptic agents, and that it will stimulate basic research in both the biochemical and pharmacological fields. Although there are many questions I would like to ask, I shall confine myself to just a few. Dr. BEIN, you mentioned that Tacitin® bears a resemblance to chlorpromazine in that it stimulates the biosynthesis of noradrenaline and dopamine. So far as I am informed, Tacitin has no cataleptic properties. The increased synthesis following chlorpromazine and other major tranquillisers is attributed to blockade of the dopamine receptors. Would you consider that mechanisms of this nature are involved in the case of Tacitin, i.e. does Tacitin block the receptors? Or is it more likely that the drug stimulates catecholamine biosynthesis via other mechanisms? Certain parallels may perhaps be drawn between Tacitin and amantadine. Have you carried out any further studies in this direction? I then have the following questions for Dr. DELINI-STULA:

1. As regards the antagonistic effect of Ludiomil on tetrabenazine-induced catalepsy, did you also find that the drug produced motor hyperactivity of the kind observed with tricyclic thymoleptics?
2. In what way does Ludiomil inhibit amphetamine-induced hyperthermia, and why does it not have an amphetamine-potentiating effect? Does it perhaps also inhibit the uptake of amphetamine?
3. Has any work been done on the question of how Ludiomil influences serotonin metabolism in the C.N.S.? Does the drug, like imipramine, inhibit the uptake of serotonin?
4. Does the noradrenaline turnover increase following prolonged administration of Ludiomil, as it did in SCHILDKRAUT's long-term experiments with imipramine?

H. HIPPIUS: When a clinician is confronted with these pharmacological findings, he is apt to consider what comparison substance he would choose if he had to carry out a double-blind trial in order to characterise a new antidepressant of this type as accurately as possible. I feel that in this case he would automatically think of taking a compound from the amitriptyline group as his comparison substance. What I would like to ask you, Dr. DELINI-STULA, is whether you have conducted any comparative pharmacological studies with amitriptyline?

Another question: when a clinician hears of a new antidepressant, he is also interested to learn whether the new substance possesses any one particular feature which completely distinguishes it from other known antidepressants.

W. BIRKMAYER: Clinicians know that parkinsonian patients may suffer attacks of hyperthermia which last for days and in which the body-temperature may rise to as much as 40 °C. In the past, patients used to die from this hyperthermia. Nowadays, we can arrest the attacks very rapidly by administering L-tryptophan in combination with a monamine-oxidase inhibitor. Ludiomil, given by the intravenous route, has the same effect. In fact, its effect is even quicker, because Ludiomil can be injected, whereas tryptophan has to be given by mouth.

R. KUHN: I should like to ask whether any conclusions as to the clinical effect of Ludiomil can be drawn from the difference between the doses of Ludiomil and imipramine required to inhibit reserpine-induced ptosis. Furthermore, I was struck by the fact that in the pharmacological experiments the drug was found to display only sedative properties. In clinical use, Ludiomil has definitely also been shown to exert a stimulant effect and even, in some cases, to induce aggressiveness. All antidepressants possess this property to some degree at least. Since this increase in aggressiveness is particularly liable to be encountered in children and adolescents, it may perhaps be connected with the patient's age. What comments can the pharmacologists make on this clinical fact?

P. KIELHOLZ: I have one more question for Dr. BEIN. Do the results of the pharmacological studies entitle us to draw any conclusions as to the drug's clinical profile, i.e. as to its inhibitory action on drive, and its ability to brighten the mood or to resolve anxiety? What clinical effects is the drug likely to have in view of its anti-aggressive properties?

H. J. BEIN: Dr. MATUSSEK, you asked about the extent to which Tacitin differs from chlorpromazine. We have found many points of difference between the two drugs. However, as regards their effect on catecholamine metabolism, I should perhaps have explained in somewhat greater detail that in this respect Tacitin behaves rather like a major tranquilliser of the chlorpromazine type and not like a minor tranquilliser of the chlordiazepoxide type. As far as serotonin metabolism is concerned, MAÎTRE's preliminary findings indicate that Ludiomil doesn't influence metabolism in the brain in the same way as imipramine does. In recent years, we have tended more and more not only to carry out biochemical analyses on the amines in the entire brain or in large portions thereof, but also to concentrate our attention chiefly on certain anatomically defined parts of the brain. In the course of these studies, we have found considerable differences between major tranquillisers, Tacitin, amantadine, and Ludiomil. Unfortunately, I am not able to give you any further details because these studies are still in progress. All I can say is that, in the light of MAÎTRE's investigations, the effect of the various compounds on catecholamine metabolism in the brain differs widely from one part of the brain to another. We feel that this is a fascinating approach because it may perhaps shed a little more light on the behaviour of various groups of substances in relation to catecholamine metabolism.

Several contributors to this discussion have raised the question of a correlation between pharmacological findings and clinical effects. To answer this question, I shall have to retrace briefly the history of the dibenzobicyclo-octadienes. We have tested a whole series of these substances. The first one had an unusual pharmacological profile, but, contrary to our expectations, it proved to be of no clinical value. Analogues of this substance, synthesised for the first time by Dr. WILHELM, were submitted to experimental tests and clinical trials. Following up a suggestion made by Dr. KUHN, we finally arrived at Tacitin and Ludiomil. But it was never our intention to tell the clinician what effects he could expect. Our aim was to move in the opposite direction, i.e. to take the clinical findings first and then to correlate them with the results of animal experiments, so as to be in a position to elaborate a better substance along more rational lines. The difficulties in this field are only too well known. It is perhaps possible in the case of anxiolytic drugs or drugs that reduce or increase muscle tone to establish positive correlations between the experimental procedures in animals and clinical equivalents, but in the case of the antidepressants we do not have this possibility and we must therefore rely on reports fed back to us by clinicians. Dr. DELINI-STULA has already pointed out that in psychopharmacology a single test is hardly meaningful, since what counts is the drug's overall spectrum or profile of activity. Nevertheless, we would of course agree with Dr. HIPPIUS that individual distinctive features are likewise important. I think that, as far as Ludiomil is concerned, Dr. DELINI-STULA also found some novel properties which she will tell you about.

A. DELINI-STULA: First of all, I should like to deal with the two questions raised by Dr. FREYHAN, although one of them has already been answered by Dr. BEIN. We pharmacologists already have a "feedback" from the clinic today, and we know that some pharmacological properties—or, to be more exact, some spectra of activity—can be correlated with clinical effects. The "antidepressant" profile of activity displayed by Ludiomil in animal experiments does enable us to make certain predictions about its antidepressant properties in clinical use. As regards Dr. FREYHAN's question about a lowering of the convulsive threshold, we found that in the mouse Ludiomil even exerted a mild anticonvulsive effect in the electroshock test, an effect similar to that observed with tricyclic antidepressants. Only in young rhesus monkeys did Ludiomil elicit convulsions, and then only when given in doses much larger than those required to produce a clear-cut taming effect.

As for Dr. PÖLDINGER's question concerning the use of Ludiomil in schizophrenia, I can imagine that the sedative, anti-aggressive, and anxiolytic properties observed in animals might feature certain components which could lead one to postulate that the drug may also exert a beneficial effect in schizophrenics displaying signs and symptoms of depression. But, as far as the practical use of the drug in such patients is concerned, extreme caution is indicated. It must not be forgotten that Ludiomil also exhibits properties typical of imipramine, and it is impossible to predict which component of the drug's activity would manifest itself first in a schizophrenic patient.

In reply to Dr. PÖLDINGER's second question, Ludiomil has marked peripheral effects, which can be compared with those of imipramine and other antidepressants. As regards its histaminolytic properties, Ludiomil is at least on a par with imipramine. Its anticholinergic properties differ from those of imipramine depending on the experimental procedure employed. Its peripheral anticholinergic effects on isolated organs are roughly similar to those of imipramine, but we have not been able to demonstrate that it has any central anticholinergic effects. This could suggest that the anticholinergic side effects of Ludiomil might be less pronounced in clinical use than those of imipramine.

Dr. MATUSSEK asked whether Ludiomil merely antagonised the catalepsy induced by tetrabenazine or whether it also reversed the inhibition of motor activity likewise seen after the administration of tetrabenazine. Our experimental procedure was designed primarily to enable us to assess the antagonistic effect of the drug on tetrabenazine-induced catalepsy. Of course, this procedure also provides some idea of the extent to which motor activity is influenced. Ludiomil did not reverse the inhibitory effect of tetrabenazine on motor activity—in other words, it did not give rise to hyperactivity of the kind observed with imipramine; but this might be a question of dosage.

As regards the lack of a potentiating effect on amphetamine-induced hyperthermia, I would point out that imipramine and desipramine probably owe their potentiating effect in this connection to the fact that they inhibit the breakdown of amphetamine. It is possible that Ludiomil does not possess this property, and therefore fails to cause any potentiation. It is also conceivable that other mechanisms are involved.

127

As to the question of an increase in noradrenaline turnover, we do not yet know how Ludiomil behaves in this respect.

To Dr. HIPPIUS I would reply as follows: since we pharmacologists have no psychotic animals to work with—and even if there were such animals, we could never be sure that the psychosis was genuine—we are unable to predict the therapeutic effect of a psycho-active agent with any degree of accuracy or to discover a completely new type of effect. To this extent, psychopharmacology is still what might be called a retrospective science. Nevertheless, differences in the overall spectrum of activity of Ludiomil do suggest that it may have novel properties. For example, we have sufficient data to be able to say that Ludiomil possesses certain properties which distinguish it from the classic antidepressants. Neither amitriptyline nor any other classic antidepressant exerts the same anti-aggressive effect as Ludiomil in septal rats. Moreover, in tests conducted in tupayas, which I did not mention in my paper, Ludiomil exhibited properties which imipramine does not have. In these easily excitable animals Ludiomil inhibits a stress-induced autonomic nervous reaction, as well as behavioural reactions, without influencing motor activity as a whole. However, to detect some entirely new type of effect, we should have to have an entirely new experimental model.

How can Ludiomil be differentiated from amitriptyline? Amitriptyline is an antidepressant with very marked sedative and relatively marked anticholinergic properties. Ludiomil has less of a sedative effect than amitriptyline (incidentally, one would expect an anti-aggressive effect to be part and parcel of a sedative effect, but this is not the case). The anticholinergic properties of Ludiomil are clearly less pronounced than those of amitriptyline. Thus, from the pharmacological standpoint, there is no difficulty in differentiating amitriptyline from Ludiomil.

We have seen that Ludiomil is a somewhat less powerful reserpine antagonist than imipramine. Whether or not this implies a weaker clinical effect is a complex question. It is not yet clear whether the prevention of reserpine-induced ptosis is due to a purely central effect or whether peripheral effects are also involved. On the other hand, the doses of Ludiomil and imipramine required to antagonise tetrabenazine were roughly the same.

I believe that conclusions as to the general clinical efficacy of a drug can, in principle, be drawn from differences in its relative potency in animal experiments, provided a variety of factors are taken into account and, in particular, provided the manifestations observed in the animal can be equated with corresponding symptoms in man.

I find it difficult to comment on the clinical cases in which Ludiomil is said to have exerted a stimulant effect and even to have induced aggressiveness. We have observed an anti-aggressive effect in several animal species. It is, however, conceivable that in clinical use the drug's stimulant action on the adrenergic system may predominate in certain cases. This would depend on the patient's symptomatology, on his constitution, and perhaps also on genetic factors. The fact that some patients may react differently, though, should not invalidate in any way the general expectation that the drug will exert an anti-aggressive, and possibly also an anxiolytic, effect.

The chemistry of polycyclic psycho-active drugs – serendipity or systematic investigation?

by M. WILHELM*

In the field of the psycho-active drugs—probably to a greater extent than in any other branch of pharmaceutico-chemical research—the path of progress is strewn with chance discoveries: the major tranquillisers—or neuroleptics, as they are sometimes called—owed their development to the hypothesis that substitution of the phenothiazine framework with basic side chains would give rise to histaminolytic agents; the discovery of the antidepressant properties of dibenzazepine derivatives was due to the assumption that preparations of this kind, besides possessing histaminolytic activity, might also display hypnotic effects[7]; and monamine-oxidase inhibitors of the hydrazine type represent the fruits of a research programme whose original aim was to develop tuberculostatic drugs. Psycho-active agents thus appear to furnish a classic example of the principle of serendipity in medicine[6].

Subsequent analysis, a process to which all new discoveries are subjected, as well as attempts to relate new findings to what was already known and to expand these findings, seemed in the initial phase of psycho-active drug development to confuse the issue rather than clarify it. Chemists found it difficult to understand why even very minor modifications to compounds that were closely related in structure should apparently produce considerable qualitative alterations in their pharmacological and clinical activity. Not until BENTE et al.[2] had published their studies on the structure-activity relationships of tricyclic drugs was the way open for systematic analysis. We shall try in this paper to summarise the results of investigations carried out over the past few years into structure-activity interrelationships in this field and to indicate the direction that future developments might take. We shall confine ourselves here simply to those few groups of substances that display definable antipsychotic effects (Figure 1).

Among these groups, the neuroleptic derivatives of phenothiazine and thioxanthene, as well as the thymoleptics from the dibenzazepine and dibenzocycloheptadiene series, are the most important from both the practical and the theoretical standpoint. All these substances seem to display, in principle, the same kind of structure: they consist of a tricyclic primary framework or skeleton, a usually aliphatic side chain, and a basic substituent. Depending on the way in which these various elements are put together, the molecule as a whole exhibits a particular type of steric configuration which apparently determines its site of action and thus its properties.

BENTE et al.[2] had already discovered that tricyclic psycho-active drugs with "flat" molecules possess neuroleptic effects, whereas an "angled" framework

* Research Department, Pharmaceutical Division, CIBA-GEIGY LIMITED, Basle, Switzerland.

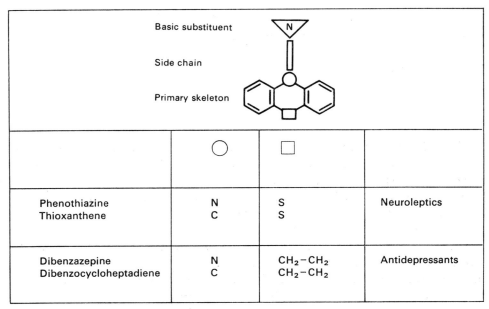

		○	□	
Phenothiazine Thioxanthene		N C	S S	Neuroleptics
Dibenzazepine Dibenzocycloheptadiene		N C	CH$_2$–CH$_2$ CH$_2$–CH$_2$	Antidepressants

Fig. 1. Structure of the tricyclic psycho-active drugs.

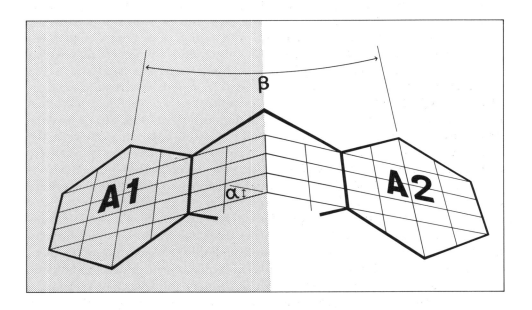

Fig. 2. Steric parameters: α = angle of flexure; β = angle of annellation.

results in molecules displaying antidepressant properties. WILHELM and KUHN[10] then worked out parameters by which the stereochemistry of the primary skeleton could be clearly defined—i.e. the angle of flexure α, the angle of annellation β, the angle of torsion γ, and the distance δ.

130

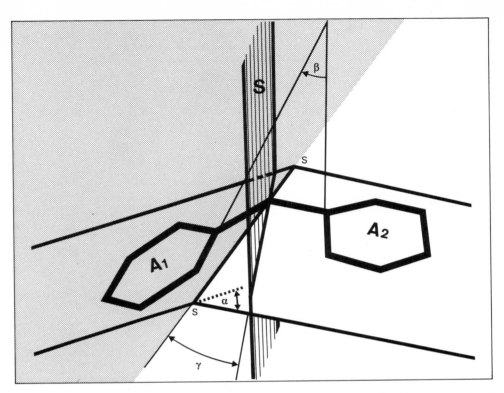

Fig. 3. Steric parameters: α = angle of flexure; β = angle of annellation; γ = angle of torsion.

A1, A2 = aromatics
s—s = axis of flexure
S = plane of symmetry

The angle of flexure α is the angle of intersection between planes A1 and A2, in each of which one of the basic framework's aromatic systems is located (Figure 2). The angle of annellation β is the angle at which the two aromatics are attached to the central ring. The angle of torsion γ represents the extent to which the molecule is twisted out of a symmetrical constellation (Figure 3), and δ is the distance between the two centre points of the aromatics.

Figure 4 shows the steric parameters—measured with the aid of Dreiding stereo models—of the most important primary skeletons of psychotropic drugs. These measurements are based on the assumption that the topography of the tricyclic structure approximates to that of the molecular model constructed on the principle of minimal angular tension. The values thus obtained are largely in agreement with those calculated by means of Hückel's molecular orbital method[12] and with experimental data derived from X-ray structural analyses[9].

If, in the case of preparations which differ from one another only in respect of their primary skeleton and possess the same side chain, the same basic group, or the same nuclear substituents, steric coefficients are compared with clinical

Primary skeleton	Angle of flexure α	Angle of annellation β	Angle of torsion γ	Distance δ
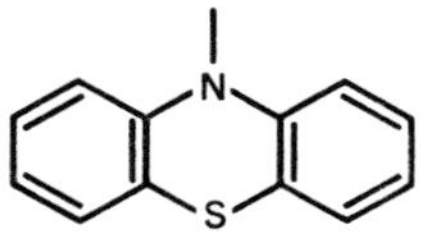	25°	10°	0°	5.1Å
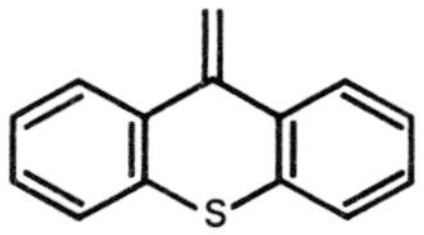	25°	10°	0°	5.1Å
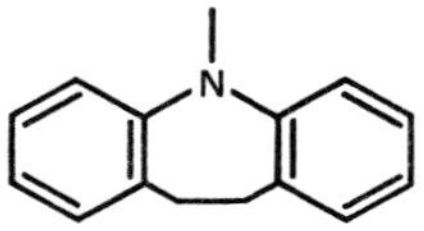	55°	40°	20°	5.1Å
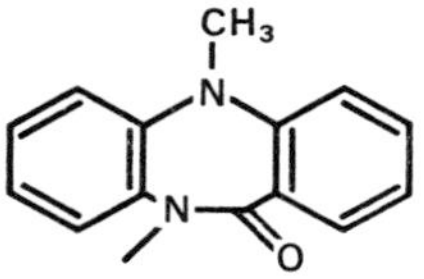	65°	−30°	15°	4.8Å

Fig. 4. Steric parameters of tricyclic primary skeletons.

activity, confirmation will be found for the hypothesis that the skeletons of relatively flat tricyclic substances (angle of flexure $\alpha = 35° \pm 10°$) exhibit predominantly neuroleptic properties, whereas angles of flexure of around 55° are characteristic of thymoleptic agents. The angles of annellation and torsion have much less bearing on clinical activity.

The effect exerted by the side chain on clinical activity is apparently to modulate the main action produced by the primary skeleton. Experience to date suggests that non-branching, three-membered carbon chains are preferable if the substance is to display neuroleptic or antidepressant properties of the purest type. Modification of the side chain, either by shortening it or by adding a branch, seems to enhance the sedative and hypnotic component in the activity of neuroleptics belonging to the phenothiazine series, as a comparison of methopromazine and levomepromazine indicates. In the antidepressants, an analogous change in structure leads to a diminution in the antidepressant effect and to the additional appearance of a sedative component.

From the standpoint of stereochemistry, these structure-activity correlations can be interpreted as a sign that the main effect of the substance, which is dictated by the topography of the primary skeleton, is influenced by the distance between the tricyclic framework and the basic centre, as well as by their position in relation to each other. This positional relationship is determined by the structure and constellation of the side chain. As the side chain is freely rotatable, the

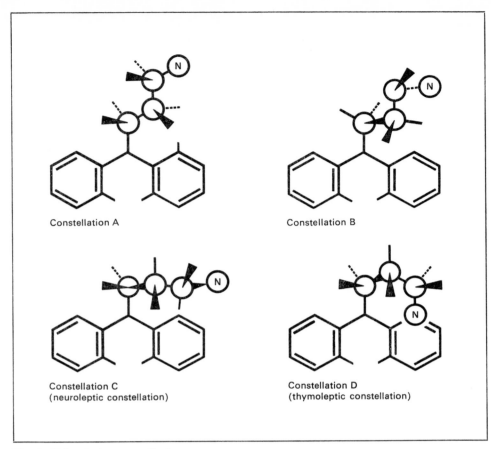

Constellation A

Constellation B

Constellation C
(neuroleptic constellation)

Constellation D
(thymoleptic constellation)

Fig. 5. Side-chain constellations.

active substance could in principle adopt any number of different constellations at its site of attack. The possibilities, however, are reduced to a reasonable figure if it is assumed that the side chain is most likely to adopt a thermodynamically favourable constellation at the site of attack. In the case of a non-branching, three-membered carbon chain the principal constellations that have to be borne in mind, therefore, are those illustrated in Figure 5.

Furthermore, from the X-ray structural analysis of chlorprothixene[3], as well as from the electron paramagnetic resonance (E.P.R.) analyses conducted on phenothiazine derivatives by FENNER[4], it can be deduced that in neuroleptic drugs the side chain most often adopts Constellation C. Additional backing for this hypothesis is to be found in the shifts in activity observed by GALANTAY et al.[5] following modification of the side chain in studies on the amitriptyline series.

In compounds displaying thymoleptic effects, on the other hand, the side chain seems to prefer Constellation D. This conclusion is based on the fact that in the dibenzo[b,e]bicyclo[2.2.2]octadiene series both the l-aminopropyl derivatives

133

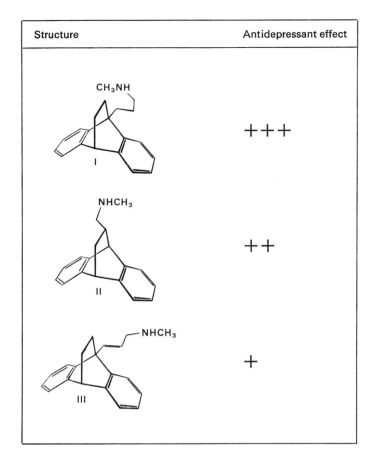

Structure	Antidepressant effect

CH₃NH

I

+++

NHCH₃

II

++

NHCH₃

III

+

Fig. 6.
Relationship of
side-chain
constellation
to activity.

(Figure 6, Formula I) and the 10-aminomethyl derivatives (Formula II) exhibit antidepressant properties; it is thus safe to assume that in both instances
the molecule's primary skeleton and basic centre are similarly positioned relative
to each other at the site of attack—which presupposes that the side chain adopts
Constellation D in compounds of the Formula I type. Compounds, however,
in which the side chain has been forced to adopt Constellation A (e.g. Formula
III) have been shown to exhibit minimal antidepressant properties.

To try to interpret the influence exerted by basic substituents on a compound's
spectrum of activity is by no means an easy task. The interaction of factors such
as basicity, hydrophilism, and stereochemistry, which all affect the compound's
activity, is so complex that it is difficult to analyse. As regards stereochemistry,
the same principle applies as before—namely, that those factors which favour
adoption of Constellation C by the side chain enhance the neuroleptic potency
of the molecule as a whole, whereas structural elements showing a preference
for Constellation D enhance the thymoleptic component.

The systematic correlations between stereochemical structure and activity
which have been deduced from studies of the classic tricyclic compounds can

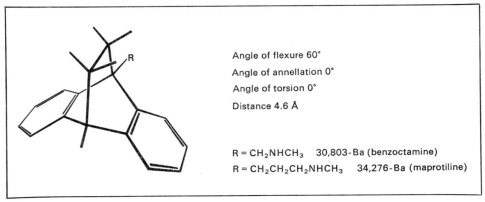

Angle of flexure 60°

Angle of annellation 0°

Angle of torsion 0°

Distance 4.6 Å

R = CH₂NHCH₃   30,803-Ba (benzoctamine)

R = CH₂CH₂CH₂NHCH₃   34,276-Ba (maprotiline)

Fig. 7. Steric parameters of dibenzo[b,e]bicyclo[2.2.2]octadiene.

be checked and corroborated by reference to the derivatives of dibenzo[b,e]-bicyclo[2.2.2]octadiene. Such corroboration is, in fact, desirable because the classic tricyclic compounds display a certain flexibility and their steric parameters can therefore only be defined if several marginal conditions are assumed to exist; furthermore, the plasticity of the molecule helps it to adapt itself to various receptors or substrates, which once again may considerably complicate the drug's biochemical and, especially, therapeutic pattern of effects. Dibenzo-[b,e]bicyclo[2.2.2]octadiene, by contrast, is a rigid structure which can be clearly defined sterically (Figure 7). Besides steric transparency, this carbocyclic system also has the advantage that basic side chains can be substituted in a variety of different ways. Of all the available possibilities, those involving substitution at the bridge-head have been subjected to particularly extensive investigation[11].

Benzoctamine, which features a short methylaminomethyl group as a substituent at the bridge-head, displays chiefly tranquillising and anxiolytic effects[1]. When the side chain is lengthened by adding two carbon atoms, the resultant compound (maprotiline, Ludiomil®) exhibits clear-cut antidepressant properties. Hence, the structure-activity hypotheses postulated for the classic tricyclic drugs can be confirmed and supplemented by examples taken from the polycyclic series of the dibenzo[b,e]bicyclo[2.2.2]octadienes. These examples show once again that the basic psychotropic activity of a polycyclic compound is dictated chiefly by the topography of the primary skeleton, the exact nature of this activity depending on the angle of flexure of the polycyclic framework. Relatively flat molecules produce a neuroleptic effect, whereas a more marked flexure of the primary skeleton tends to give rise to preparations displaying antidepressant properties.

Transmission of this basic psychotropic activity depends largely on the constellation adopted by the side chain. Side chains displaying Constellation C are optimal transmitters of neuroleptic effects, while side chains of Constellation D ensure optimal transmission of thymoleptic properties.

Table 1. Physico-chemical properties of some polycyclic psychopharmaceuticals.

| | Physico-chemical properties | |
	pK_a	$\log p_u$
Imipramine	9.5	4.66
Desipramine	10.0	4.12
Maprotiline	10.5	4.49
Benzoctamine	9.1	3.75

pK_a = acidity constant
p_u = distribution coefficient, in water and octanol, of the undissociated base

In the series of antidepressant polycyclic compounds, reducing the angle of annellation may have the effect of damping down the central stimulant component.

Among the numerous factors influencing the effectiveness of a drug, steric properties constitute only one element, albeit an essential one. They would seem—especially in neurologically active drugs—to have a decisive bearing on the selection of the drug's site of attack. Solubility and basicity, on the other hand, chiefly influence absorption and transport to the site of attack, and it is probably no mere chance that the compounds under discussion here have largely similar physico-chemical properties[8] (Table 1).

One of the most promising lines of pharmaceutico-chemical research is based on endeavours to pinpoint the influences exerted by structural factors on biological processes. These interconnections should be evaluated as quantitatively as possible, and they should eventually provide a basis for the designing of new active substances. In the field of the psycho-active drugs, our present knowledge already enables us to draw some far-reaching conclusions concerning the relationships between structure and activity. The phase of serendipity has thus given way to a period of systematic investigation which will in the future reveal many other connections between chemistry, biology, and medicine and will facilitate advances in the treatment of mental diseases. It is to be hoped, however, that, in addition to this logically planned progress, serendipity—which has virtually governed psychiatric drug research in the past—will continue to play a role and will again unexpectedly open up some fascinating new territory which can then be systematically explored by chemists, biologists, and physicians.

References

1 BEIN, H.J.: Pharmacological aspects of the activity of Tacitin. Anxiety and tension—new therapeutic aspects, Int. Symp., St. Moritz 1970, p. 36

2 BENTE, D., HIPPIUS, H., PÖLDINGER, W., STACH, K.: Chemische Konstitution und klinische Wirkung von antidepressiven Pharmaka. Arzneimittel-Forsch. *14*, 486 (1964)

3 DUNITZ, J.D., ESER, H., STRICKLER, P.: Die Konfiguration des physiologisch wirksamen 2-Chlor-9(ω-dimethylaminopropyliden)-thioxanthens. Helv. chim. Acta *47*, 1897 (1964)

4 FENNER, H.: Structure-activity relationship in the field of phenothiazine drugs. Pharmakopsychiat. Neuro-Psychopharmakol. *3*, 332 (1970)

5 GALANTAY, E., HOFFMAN, C., PAOLELLA, N., GOGERTY, J., IORIO, L., LESLIE, G., TRAPOLD, J.H.: Dibenz[c,d,h,]azulenes. II. "Bridged" amitriptyline analogs. J. med. Chem. *12*, 444 (1969)

6 GOLIN, M.: Serendipity—big word in medical progress. J. Amer. med. Ass. *165*, 2084 (1957)

7 KUHN, R.: The imipramine story. In Ayd, F.J., Jr., Blackwell, B. (Editors): Discoveries in biological psychiatry, p. 205 (Lippincott, Philadelphia/Toronto 1970)

8 MOSER, P.: Personal communication

9 MÜLLER, R.: Personal communication

10 WILHELM, M., KUHN, R.: Versuch einer stereochemisch-strukturellen Klassifizierung der Trizyklus-Psychopharmaka mit Einschluss der Dibenzo-bicyclooctadiene. Pharmakopsychiat. Neuro-Psychopharmakol. *3*, 317 (1970)

11 WILHELM, M., SCHMIDT, P.: Synthese und Eigenschaften von 1-Aminoalkyldibenzo[b,e]bicyclo[2.2.2]octadienen. Helv. chim. Acta *52*, 1385 (1969)

12 WOHL, A.J.: Molecular orbital analysis of conformational factors which affect the pharmacology of the tricyclic antidepressants. Pharmacologist *12*, 215 (1970); abstract of paper

Discussion

H. HIPPIUS: It is very gratifying for a clinician to hear his views backed up by a chemist. I should like to thank Dr. WILHELM for this support and to congratulate him on his paper. I believe that in the long run optimum results can only be achieved by the joint efforts of chemists, pharmacologists, and clinicians aided and abetted by a regular feedback system.

F. FREYHAN: It was a real pleasure to listen to Dr. WILHELM. I think that my comments in the discussion following Dr. HIPPIUS's paper may have been misunderstood by Dr. HIPPIUS himself and possibly also by others. In my view, we would do better to speak of "respect for scientific knowledge" rather than to use words such as "optimism" and "pessimism". There has never been any question of my not feeling respect for the progress that has been made in pharmacology and chemistry. What saddens me is the cleft between our clinical knowledge and capabilities, on the one hand, and what is actually being done day by day in general psychiatric and medical practice, on the other. Science has made great advances and has furnished valuable basic data for the clinician. We, however, in the light of our clinical experience, should realise the difficulties involved in reconciling scientific knowledge with the day-to-day work of the practising physician.

I. SANO: I myself am not really so optimistic. In fact, I almost believe that the thymoleptics will soon be a thing of the past. It is already possible to treat depressive patients very successfully with 5-hydroxytryptophan.

W. PÖLDINGER: Perhaps it would be possible to take the angles of flexure, annellation, and torsion, to which Dr. WILHELM referred, and to form from them a factor on the basis of which some prediction could be made. This prediction could then be proved right or wrong by both pharmacological tests and clinical trials. In my opinion, it is easier for the pharmacologist to devise a factor of this kind. What we clinicians can offer as our contribution is the quotient obtained from the results of treatment in retarded and in agitated depression. If you calculate this quotient, as we have done, you will find that it is approximately 1 for substances such as imipramine, 0.3 for drugs of the amitriptyline type (because they are effective chiefly in cases of agitated depression), and about 1.6 for desipramine. I think that this approach might be of value inasmuch as it would highlight certain aspects to which we clinicians could then devote special attention.

N. MATUSSEK: Dr. WILHELM's impressive paper showed how carefully and exactly the chemist sets about studying the problem of the molecular structure of psycho-active drugs. I think, Dr. WILHELM, that your work will provide molecular biologists with valuable suggestions as to how to elucidate the structure of receptors and will enable them to tackle this important problem, which is still far from having been solved, in a more effective manner than is at present possible. Just one question, Dr. WILHELM: in one of your slides you showed us extremely clear pictures of constellations C and D. Constellation C is indicative of neuroleptic activity and D of thymoleptic activity. There are a number of reasons for assuming that neuroleptic agents exert their effect via dopamine—i.e. by influencing dopamine metabolism—whereas the thymoleptics may possible act via serotonin or noradrenaline. The propylamino side chain is present in the molecules of all these three biogenic amines. Can you tell us whether dopamine tends to adopt Constellation C, and noradrenaline and serotonin Constellation D? Is it possible at present to venture any conclusions on this point, or do the side chains oscillate so freely that their positional relationships to the phenyl ring cannot be established?

R. KUHN: First of all, I should like to join with Dr. FREYHAN and Dr. HIPPIUS in stressing the exceptional importance of collaboration between chemists, pharmacologists, and clinicians. This collaboration draws one's attention to problems that one would otherwise never have thought about. Dr. WILHELM made a brief reference to the rigidity of the chemical structure of Ludiomil. The more inflexible the stereochemical structure of a thymoleptic agent, the easier it is to demonstrate its clinical activity. In the case of some thymoleptics it is impossible to say whether the effect is due to a particular stereochemical constellation of the drug itself or to the constitution of the individual patient. It is important for the future to develop molecules that are stereochemically stable. Besides the purely chemical aspects, however, the way in which the drug is formulated is also a major factor.

M. WILHELM: I am most grateful to the medical specialists here for having welcomed me, a chemist, so warmly in their midst. As regards Dr. PÖLDINGER's suggestion that our findings should be expressed in mathematical terms, we have in fact begun to do this with the steric parameters and the physico-chemical properties of various drugs, and we are trying to correlate these parameters and properties with biological effects. One difficult problem, however, especially with psychopharmaceuticals, is to find the corresponding biological parameters. What is the counterpart to our chemical parameters? In the case of the antidepressants, we considered first of all their ability to inhibit the uptake of noradrenaline, because this is something that can be accurately measured. Although the interaction of thymoleptic agents with other centrally acting drugs is studied in pharmacological experiments, the values obtained are hardly accurate enough to be correlated with exact geometrical data.

Dr. MATUSSEK likewise raised a very important point with his question about the receptors. We should be extremely grateful to him if in the course of his work he could give us more information about the nature, structure, and stereochemistry of the receptors. In the present state of our knowledge all we can do is to try, in the light of what we know about the topography of the agent, to draw conclusions as to the possible structure of the receptor. I think I am safe in saying that Constellation C does influence dopamine and Constellation D noradrenaline. MAXWELL has attempted to correlate the constellation of noradrenaline with that of thymoleptic agents, but all the hypotheses put forward in this field still lack a sound foundation.

Finally, I should like to thank Dr. KUHN for his suggestion that clinicians should work together with chemists. We chemists can only do our work properly if we have the opportunity of discussing our problems with pharmacologists and clinicians. As for the request for stable molecules, we shall certainly try to do our best.

The metabolism and pharmacokinetics of Ludiomil (maprotiline)

by W. Riess, T. G. Rajagopalan, and H. Keberle*

The behaviour of a drug in the body, i.e. its absorption, distribution, metabolism, and excretion, depend both on the physico-chemical properties of the active substance and on the way in which the organism reacts to it. Although these two factors constitute given data, about which much detailed information may already be available, it is still impossible at present to make on a purely theoretical basis any quantitative predictions as to how a new compound will behave in the body. The most that can be done is to venture a few imprecise qualitative presuppositions deduced from the physico-chemical and structural attributes of the substance.

Maprotiline, the active substance of Ludiomil® (Figure 1), is a strong base (pKa 10.5) with a primary skeleton of lipophilic nature. At physiological pH levels, it is protonised to the extent of almost 100 %. It can therefore be anticipated to display a distribution pattern characterised by higher concentrations in those tissues and organs which exhibit an affinity for lipophilic bases, e.g. the lungs, adrenals, kidneys, and brown fat. In view of the drug's high degree of ionisation, it is unlikely to penetrate all that rapidly through the lipophilic barriers, and thus, in comparison with neutral lipophilic substances, cannot be expected to attain particularly strong concentrations in the brain, in the spinal cord, or in the nerves.

The chemical structure of maprotiline is such as to suggest that its metabolites will take the form of products of de-alkylation, de-amination, aliphatic and aromatic hydroxylation, and combinations thereof. To what extent these qualitative predictions are accurate, and how the substance is in fact metabolised in quantitative terms, are questions which of course can only be answered by recourse to experimental research.

Essential for the success of such metabolic studies are methods of analysis by which it is possible, when investigating the drug's overall metabolism, to measure both the unchanged substance and its metabolites. For this purpose, use of the compound in a radioactively labelled form is the method of choice; in all our animal experiments, as well as in some specific studies undertaken in man, we thus employed a maprotiline preparation labelled with C^{14} or with H^3 at the positions indicated in the structural formula in Figure 1.

To investigate the kinetics of the active substance in a large number of subjects, a gas-chromatographic technique was elaborated whose high sensitivity is based on the formation and detection of the N-heptafluorobutyryl derivative of maprotiline.

* Research Department, Pharmaceutical Division, CIBA-GEIGY LIMITED, Basle, Switzerland.

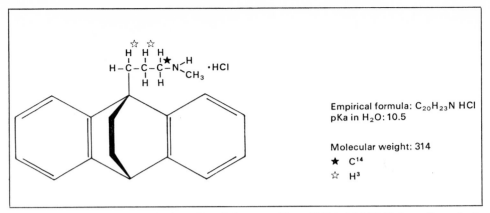

Empirical formula: $C_{20}H_{23}N$ HCl
pKa in H_2O: 10.5

Molecular weight: 314

★ C^{14}

☆ H^3

Fig. 1. The active substance of Ludiomil (maprotiline, CIBA 34,276-Ba), radioactively labelled for pharmacokinetic experiments: 1-(3-methylaminopropyl)-dibenzo[b,e]bicyclo[2.2.2]octadiene.

First of all, however, the fate of maprotiline was studied in the mouse, rat, and dog. The extent to which the drug penetrates into the various organs was determined by reference to autoradiograms of sagittal sections through the body of the mouse showing the distribution pattern of the radioactivity five minutes, 30 minutes, and 120 minutes after an intravenous dose (20 mg./kg.) of maprotiline labelled with C^{14}.

Shown in Figures 2 and 3 are negatives of these autoradiograms, in which the pale zones indicate where the radioactive preparation is located. From the distribution pattern five minutes after the injection (Figure 2) it can be seen that, as was to be expected, maprotiline displays a marked affinity for the lungs, adrenals, and kidneys.

Particularly deserving of interest is the distribution pattern in the brain (Figure 3), where high levels of radioactivity can be observed in the cortex of the cerebrum and cerebellum, in the thalamus, in the colliculi, in the cerebellar nuclei, and in the medulla. Two hours after the injection, the highest concentration is found in the hippocampus. This tendency for the drug to concentrate in the hippocampus has also been reported in the case of other psychopharmaceuticals, such as imipramine, amitriptyline, and chlorpromazine[1,2]. One distinctive feature of maprotiline is its very pronounced affinity for the adrenals, where the concentration two hours after the injection is highest in the region between the cortex and the medulla, i.e. in what appears to be the so-called zona reticularis.

In order to supplement the findings yielded by the method of whole-body autoradiography—a method which provides a very impressive but only qualitative picture of a drug's distribution in the organism—the concentration patterns in the tissues and organs were also studied quantitatively by radiometric combustion analysis in the rat. To obtain data on the distribution of the unchanged active substance, the organs were removed only five minutes after administration of an intravenous dose of 10 mg./kg., i.e. at a time when such metabolites

141

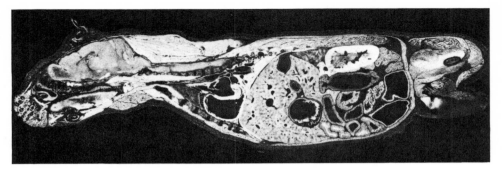

Fig. 2. Distribution of radioactivity in the mouse five minutes after intravenous administration of C^{14}-labelled maprotiline in a dose of 20 mg./kg.

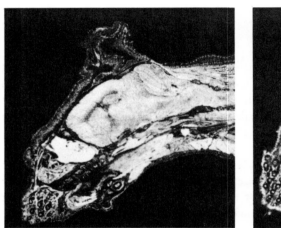
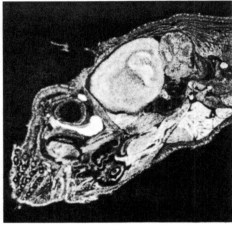

A   B

Fig. 3. Enlarged portions of autoradiograms taken 30 (A) and 120 (B) minutes after intravenous administration of C^{14}-labelled maprotiline, showing the distribution pattern of the radioactivity in the brain.

as had already been formed could have accounted for only an insignificant proportion of the total radioactivity measured.

From Figure 4, in which the concentrations thus recorded in 20 different organs are presented in graphic form, it can be seen that the highest tissue concentrations were found in the lungs and adrenals, and very low concentrations in the testes and in white fat. The brain showed a medium concentration. The lowest concentrations of all were measured in the blood only five minutes after the injection—a fact which indicates that maprotiline penetrates quite quickly into the tissues and that it has a large distribution volume. A study of the time course of the blood concentrations leads to the same conclusions.

In Figure 5, the blood concentrations of the unchanged substance are represented by the uninterrupted curve, and the sum of the metabolites by the interrupted

142

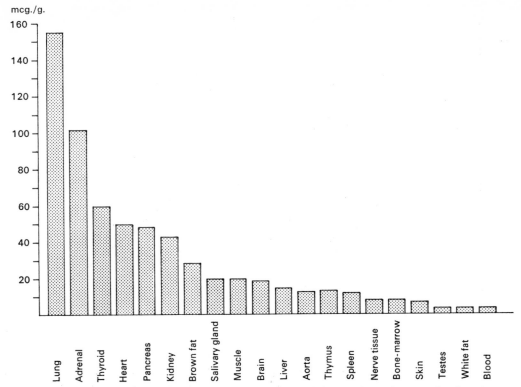

mcg./g.

Fig. 4. Distribution of H³-radioactivity in the organs of the rat five minutes after intravenous administration of H³-labelled maprotiline in a dose of 10 mg./kg. (N = 4).

curve. The rapid decrease in the concentration of the unchanged substance within the first hour corresponds to the distribution phase; the subsequent further diminution in the concentration is dependent upon the rate at which the drug is metabolised and excreted. From the slope in this part of the curve the half-life of maprotiline can be calculated. In the rat its biological half-life works out at 3.2 hours.

By extrapolating to the point in time t = 0, it is possible to determine the theoretical initial concentration. The distribution volume, i.e. the quotient calculated from the dose and the initial concentration, attains a value over ten times greater than the actual volume of the body.

The interrupted curve has two maxima. This finding suggests that the drug gives rise to various metabolites displaying complex kinetic features.

The total quantity recovered in the urine and faeces is equivalent to 89 % of the dose after the first 24 hours, and to no less than 98 % after 48 hours. Of the intravenously injected dose, 40 % is excreted in the urine, and 60 % in the faeces. From this it is evident that in the rat the major portion is eliminated via the bile. Although the excretion figures show that almost 100 % of the amount administered duly leaves the body again, the levels in the individual organs of the ani-

143

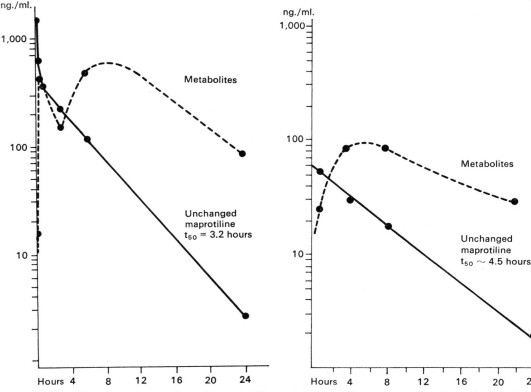

Fig. 5. Concentrations of unchanged H³-labelled maprotiline and its metabolites in the blood of rats following an intravenous dose of 10 mg./kg. (each point in the curves represents the concentration measured in pooled blood from four animals).

Fig. 6. Concentrations of unchanged C¹⁴-labelled maprotiline and its metabolites in the blood of the dog following an intravenous dose of 0.6 mg./kg.

mals were also measured following intravenous injection of the labelled substance in order to confirm that, after attainment of the respective maximal concentrations, the drug is steadily eliminated from all the tissues and organs; except in the case of the liver and kidneys, which actively participate in the drug's excretion, the concentrations in all the organs continuously diminished until, after 72 hours, they had reached levels of only ≤ 0.1 mcg./g.

In similar radiotracer experiments performed in the dog (Figure 6), it was found that, following an intravenous dose of 0.6 mg./kg., the half-life of the unchanged substance in the blood amounts to 4.5 hours. Dogs, too, excrete the bulk of the dose via the bile; only 23 % of the dose was recovered in the urine within the first 48 hours.

In certain specific studies resembling these animal experiments, C¹⁴-labelled maprotiline was also administered to test subjects in order to investigate the drug's fate in man, i.e. in order to determine the blood-concentration patterns

Clinical

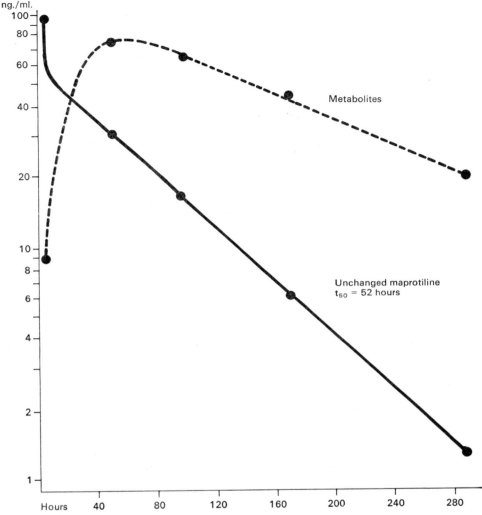

Fig. 7. Concentrations of unchanged maprotiline and its metabolites in the blood of man following intravenous administration of C^{14}-labelled maprotiline in a dose of 40 mg. (0.9 mg./kg.).

of the unchanged substance and the metabolites, their elimination rate, and the nature of the metabolites excreted in the urine.

In the experiment illustrated in Figure 7, the half-life of the unchanged active substance in the blood following an intravenous dose of 40 mg. worked out at 52 hours. The distribution volume of the active substance is roughly equivalent to ten times the subject's actual body volume; in other words, we can expect maprotiline to exhibit in man the same distributional behaviour as had already been found in animal experiments. In Figure 7, too, the concentrations of metabolites in the blood have been arrived at by calculating the difference between

145

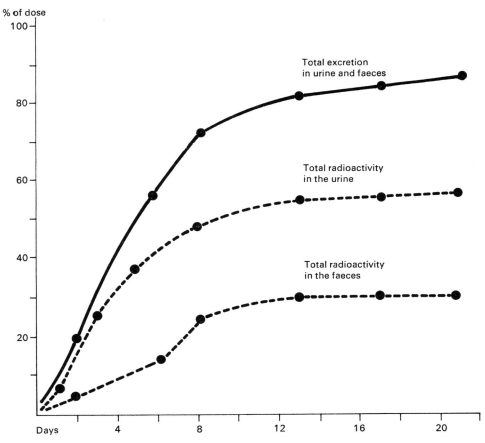

% of dose

Total excretion
in urine and faeces

Total radioactivity
in the urine

Total radioactivity
in the faeces

Days

Fig. 8. Excretion of radioactivity in the urine and faeces of man following intravenous administration of C^{14}-labelled maprotiline in a dose of 40 mg. (0.9 mg./kg.).

the concentration of total radioactivity measured and the concentration of unchanged active substance.

The excretion figures recorded in man showed that, following intravenous administration of maprotiline, 30 % of the dose is excreted in the faeces and 57 % in the urine over a period of up to 21 days; these findings reveal that in man, in contrast to rats and dogs, renal elimination outweighs biliary elimination of the drug (Figure 8).

The metabolites excreted in the urine were first preparatively enriched by physical means and then identified by resorting to a combination of gas chromatography and mass spectrometry, as well as high-resolution mass spectrometry. The metabolites found in man proved to be the same as those already traced in rats and dogs. As shown in Figure 9, all the metabolites identified result from simple and multiple hydroxylation of the primary skeleton and oxidative modification of the side chain. Most of these metabolites appear in the urine con-

146

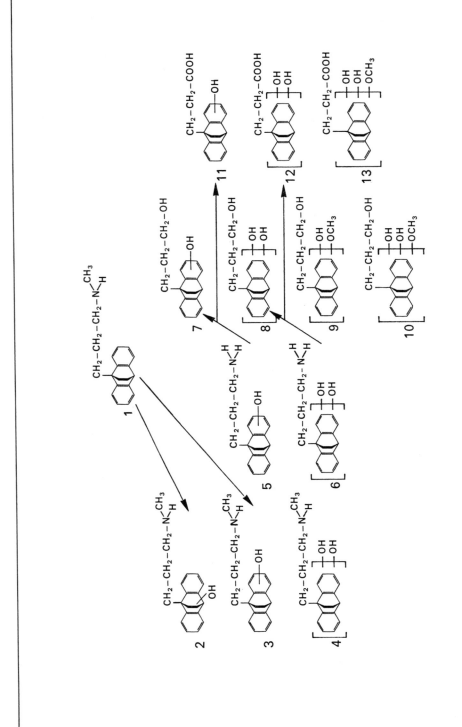

Fig. 9. Formulae of the maprotiline metabolites identified in the urine.

147

jugated with glucuronic acid. One peculiarity of the metabolism of maprotiline—a peculiarity which had already been noted in the course of studies on the dog—is the formation of monomethyl ethers of the polyhydroxylated derivatives. Probably responsible for these derivatives are methyltransferases of the type which also participate in the metabolism of biogenic amines.

Another extensive study was concerned with the kinetics of maprotiline following single intravenous or oral doses, as well as following repeated oral administration. In order to assess the drug's absorption by the oral route, a comparison was made between the blood-concentration curves obtained in response to an intravenous and an oral dose of identical size.

As shown in Figure 10, the surface areas beneath the concentration curves plotted from the averages for a group of six persons are the same after oral as after intravenous treatment with doses of 50 mg. each. It may therefore be concluded that the oral dose is fully absorbed. Analysis of the six individual blood-concentration curves obtained following the intravenous dose yielded half-life values for the active substance ranging from $t_{50} = 27.4$ hours to $t_{50} = 57.6$ hours.

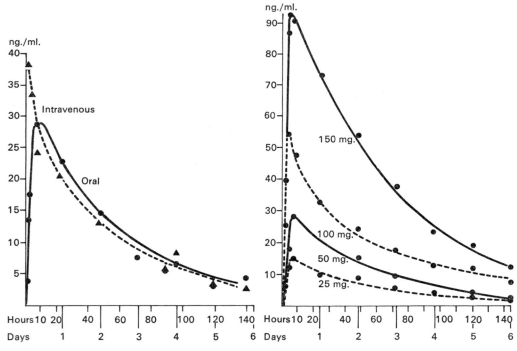

Fig. 10. Concentrations of unchanged maprotiline in the blood of man following oral and intravenous doses of 50 mg. (each point in the curves represents the mean value obtained from the same six subjects).

Fig. 11. Concentrations of unchanged maprotiline in the blood of man following single oral doses of 25 mg., 50 mg., 100 mg., and 150 mg. (each point in the curves represents the mean value obtained from nine subjects).

In order to determine the degree to which the blood concentrations are dependent on the size of the dose administered, each person in a group of nine test subjects was given single oral doses of 25 mg. and 100 mg. with a 14-day interval between the two doses; in a second group of nine test subjects the same procedure was adopted with single oral doses of 50 mg. and 150 mg.

As can be seen from Figure 11, the surface areas beneath the average concentration curves are roughly proportional to the size of the respective doses—a finding which indicates that all the four doses were absorbed in their entirety and that the pharmacokinetic constants operating at such dosage levels remain the same.

The chief practical value of pharmacokinetic studies lies in the fact that, by mathematically analysing the concentration patterns obtained in experiments in which a single dose of a given size has been administered, it is possible to predict what concentration patterns can be expected in response to a proposed dosage schedule in which the active substance is to be given repeatedly.

Mathematical analysis of the experimental data is preferably carried out using an electronic analogue computer. The analysis is based on a model set-up yielding values which tally with the kinetic data resulting from the experimental measurements.

The pharmacokinetics of maprotiline can be well simulated by using the three-chamber model illustrated in Figure 12 together with the rate constants indicated.

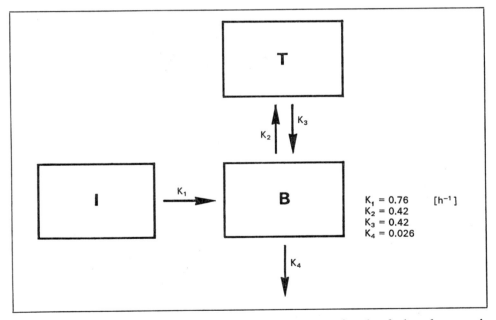

Fig. 12. Kinetic model, comprising three compartments, for simulating the experimentally determined kinetics of maprotiline in the blood of man. I = intestine, B = blood, and T = tissues; K_1 = invasion constant, K_2 and K_3 = rate constants for the exchange between compartments B and T, and K_4 = elimination constant.

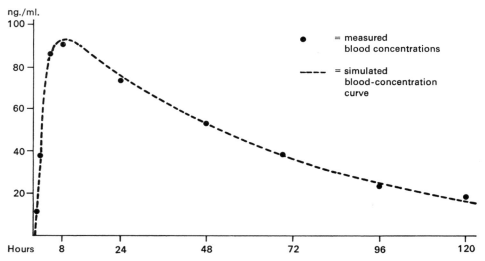

Fig. 13. Correlation between experimentally determined and simulated blood concentrations of maprotiline in man following an oral dose of 150 mg.

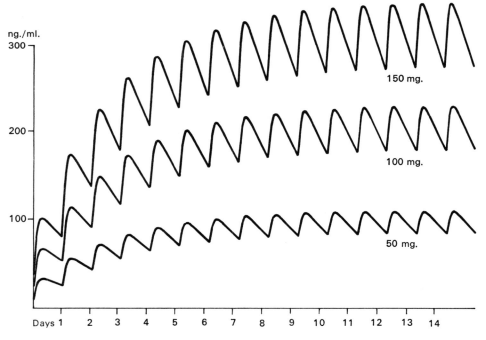

Fig. 14. Theoretically predicted blood-concentration patterns for maprotiline in man resulting from repeated oral doses of 50 mg. daily, 100 mg. daily, and 150 mg. daily.

The extent to which the simulated blood concentrations match the values actually recorded in experiments is revealed in Figure 13. Calculations based on this model show that, in patients receiving prolonged medication with repeated daily doses of maprotiline, the blood concentrations initially rise, whereupon—

150

in the second week of treatment—a state of equilibrium is reached in which the minimal and maximal blood concentrations measured during each dosage interval are the same as in the preceding dosage interval.

In Figure 14, the anticipated blood concentrations have been simulated for average cases given repeated daily doses of 50, 100, and 150 mg. It can be seen

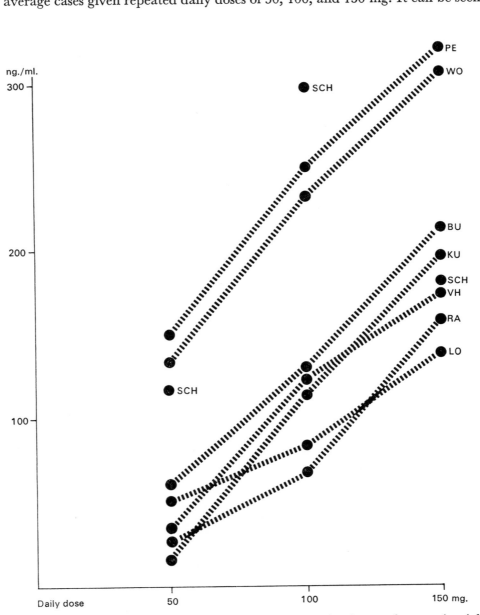

Fig. 15. Dose-dependence of the blood concentrations in the steady state in eight subjects treated with maprotiline in oral doses of 50 mg. daily for 14 days, followed by 100 mg. daily for 14 days, and finally 150 mg. for 14 days. In test subject SCH the blood samples taken following treatment with 100 and 150 mg. daily were presumably interchanged by mistake.

that the concentrations reached in a state of equilibrium, i.e. in the so-called steady state, show the same ratios between one another as the daily doses.

To ascertain whether the blood concentrations in the steady state are indeed dose-dependent as predicted, eight test subjects were given a dose of 50 mg. daily for two weeks, followed by 100 mg. daily for two weeks, and then 150 mg. daily for another two weeks. During the second week of each of the three periods, blood samples (minimum: three; maximum: seven) were taken immediately prior to the first dose of the day and analysed for unchanged active substance. As shown in Figure 15, the minimal concentrations measured in the blood samples obtained from the individual test subjects in the steady state do in fact tally with the doses administered, just as had been predicted on theoretical grounds.

To find out if an influence is exerted on the steady state, depending on whether the daily dosage of 150 mg. is administered in a single dose or in two or three fractional doses divided over the day, and also to discover whether there are

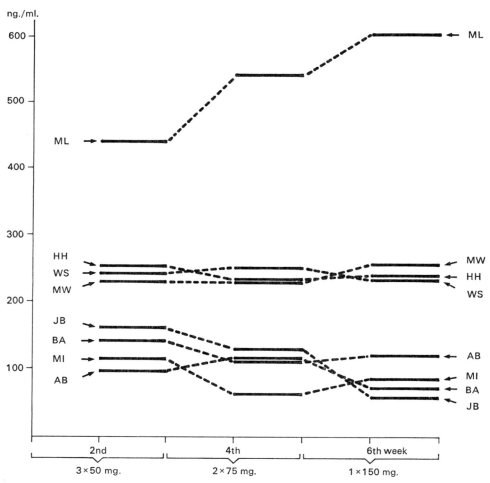

Fig. 16. Blood concentrations of maprotiline in the steady state in eight normal subjects receiving 150 mg. daily in three different dosage schedules.

differences in the pharmacokinetics of maprotiline in normal subjects as compared with patients suffering from depression, the following experiment was undertaken: eight normal persons and six depressive patients were given 50 mg. maprotiline three times daily (intervals between doses: 5, 5, and 14 hours) for two weeks, followed by 75 mg. twice daily (intervals between doses: 10 and 14 hours) for two weeks, and then 150 mg. once daily for two more weeks; as in the previous experiment, the blood concentrations of maprotiline were measured immediately prior to the first dose of the day during the second week of each period.

Statistical evaluation of the results failed to reveal any significant difference at the 95 % probability level between the blood concentrations obtained with the three different dosage schedules within the same groups of subjects or between the blood concentrations measured in the healthy as compared with the depressive group (Figures 16 and 17).

When the averages for all the individual blood-concentration measurements made over the total six weeks' period of the experiment were worked out, the mean values obtained and the 95 % confidence limits for the steady-state blood concentrations, recorded in each instance at the end of the daytime intervals, were as indicated in Figure 18. The mean values for the individual concentra-

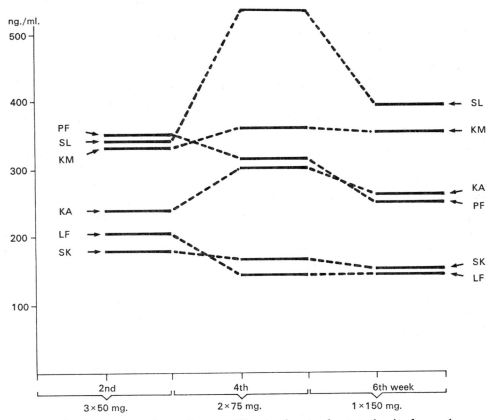

Fig. 17. Blood concentrations of maprotiline in the steady state in six depressive patients receiving 150 mg. daily in three different dosage schedules.

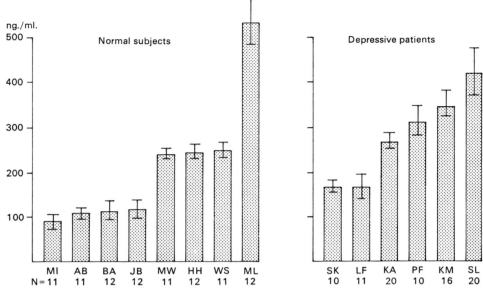

Fig. 18. Mean values and 95 % confidence limits for the blood concentrations of maprotiline recorded in the steady state in 14 persons treated with 150 mg. maprotiline daily (N = number of blood samples analysed during the six weeks' period of treatment).

tions measured in the total series of subjects were found to range between approximately 100 ng./ml. and 500 ng./ml.

Illustrated in Figure 19 are the theoretically predicted blood-concentration patterns resulting from two different dosage schedules. The upper curve indicates the pattern in response to a daily dosage of 150 mg., given in three fractional doses of 50 mg. divided over the day. The lower curve represents the pattern when the same daily dosage is administered in a single dose.

Viewed from the pharmacokinetic standpoint, both dosage schedules appear to be equivalent to each other. Here, only clinical experience can reveal which of the two dosage schedules in fact yields better results in practice.

Before concluding, we should like to add that pharmacokinetic studies in man such as have been described in this paper can only be successfully conducted given close cooperation between those engaged on experimental research and those working in the field of clinical research. For all that they have done to make possible the studies on the maprotiline blood concentrations in man which have been outlined here, the Research and Medical Departments of CIBA-GEIGY LIMITED are particularly indebted to Prof. FÜNFGELD and his colleagues at the University Clinic of Homburg (Saar), as well as to Dr. MATUSSEK of the University Neurological Clinic in Munich.

References

1 CASSANO, G.B., HANSSON, E.: Autoradiographic distribution studies in mice with C^{14}-imipramine. Int. J. Neuropsychiat. *2*, 269 (1966)
2 HANSSON, E., CASSANO, G.B.: Distribution and metabolism of antidepressant drugs. Antidepressant drugs, Proc. 1st int. Symp., Milan 1966, p. 10. Int. Congr. Series No. 122 (Excerpta med. Found., Amsterdam etc. 1967)

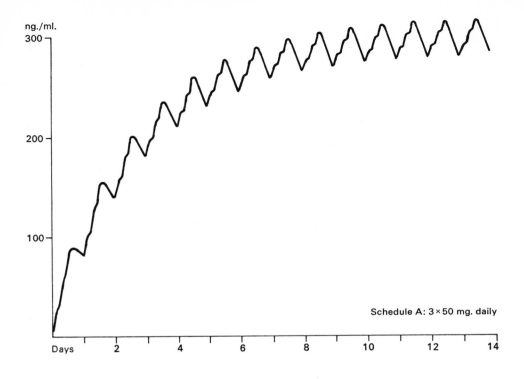

Schedule A: 3×50 mg. daily

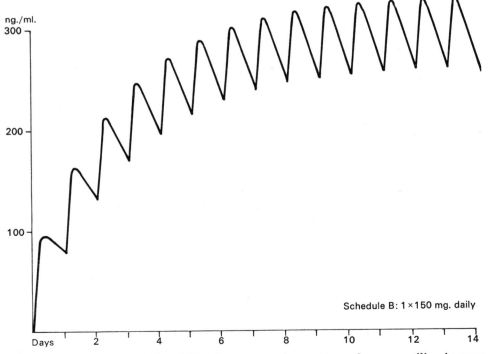

Schedule B: 1×150 mg. daily

Fig. 19. Theoretically predicted blood-concentration patterns for maprotiline in man resulting from two different dosage schedules.

Discussion

W. Pöldinger: Dr. Keberle, can you explain why the blood concentrations in the steady state remained the same irrespective of the dosage schedule employed? This feature is, after all, not encountered with other drugs displaying an antidepressant effect.

A. Coppen: I should like to emphasise that, when one is doing drug trials, one is essentially looking at the effect of a certain concentration of the drug in the biological fluids of a patient, and there are, I think, two groups of factors which may affect this. First of all, there's the very elementary question as to whether the patient is in fact taking the drugs that one gives him, and I believe quite a lot of evidence exists to suggest that a substantial proportion of patients don't in fact take the drugs that you prescribe for them; perhaps 20 or even 30% of the patients in a trial won't be taking the drugs at all. Secondly, of course, there is the problem of the tremendous variation that one finds in the plasma concentrations following a standard dose of a drug. With some drugs the variation may be a twenty-fold one, and I think I am correct in saying that with the compound we are now discussing we have found a five-fold variation in the concentration. So in certain respects it is meaningless to give a standardised dose of a drug until one has data on what plasma levels one is getting. I should therefore like to make the plea that—whenever any drug is undergoing trials, including especially initial trials—data on the concentrations in the plasma should be regularly obtained. Even this, of course, is very elementary information, because what we are really interested in is the concentration of the drug in the central nervous system, and the plasma concentrations don't tell us anything about that. A high proportion of the drug may in fact be inactive, bound to protein, and so on. I think one should at least have these data. When one bears in mind the misinformation that is liable to arise from this sort of error, coupled with the difficulties encountered in collecting clinical material and in rating the patient, I can't help feeling how remarkable it is that we obtain any meaningful results from our drug trials at all.

R. Kuhn: I, too, was particularly struck by the fact that the blood concentrations in the steady state were the same regardless of whether the daily dosage was administered in a single dose or in two or three fractional doses. In clinical practice, there are always patients who alter their dosage schedule of their own accord and who, for example, instead of taking two tablets three times daily as prescribed, swallow the entire daily dosage in the morning or in the evening. Now, I have noticed that when patients did this with Ludiomil, no complications arose, whereas they certainly would have done with Tofranil®. It is simply not possible to take 150 mg. imipramine in a single dose without severe disturbances occurring. Is this merely a question of the side effects of imipramine, or are other factors involved? Does Ludiomil perhaps differ from imipramine pharmacokinetically as well? In the case of imipramine, another special aspect has to be considered—namely, the times at which the divided doses should be given during the day, e.g. before or after meals. We know of course that the effect may be completely different, depending on the time of administration.

J. Welner: The paper presented by Dr. Keberle prompts me to say a few words on behalf of Dr. Kragh-Sørensen, who is working at the State Mental Hospital in Glostrup (Denmark) and who unfortunately wasn't able to attend this symposium. He is one of the investigators for the North European trial group. In connection with our trials he administered our standard dosage of Ludiomil (150 mg. daily) to five patients, and amitriptyline to four patients, over periods ranging from three to 11 months, the average being six months. Eight of these nine patients showed no disturbing or unexpected side effects, but the ninth, a nurse aged 55 years, had to stop treatment with Ludiomil because of unwanted effects. After the medication had been in progress for two weeks she became somewhat dizzy, and during the second month of treatment she suffered from spells marked by a very sudden loss of muscle tone described as a sort of cataplexy. This symptom disappeared for three weeks when the dosage was reduced to 75 mg. daily, but it then reappeared although the dosage had not been increased. Dr. KRAGH-SØRENSEN would like me to ask those present here whether any similar observations have been made by anybody else in the course of long-term medication. He also asked me to mention that the pharmacokinetic studies he performed with nortriptyline—especially those relating to measurement of the plasma concentrations in the steady state—revealed that some patients never reached a steady state. The plasma concentration continued to rise even when the dosage was decreased.

M. HAMILTON: Concerning the statements made by Dr. R. KUHN and Dr. COPPEN, I should like to emphasise that, both in clinical trials and in clinical practice, the best way to solve the problem of the patients who do not take their drugs is to establish a relationship of confidence and trust between them and the physician—and not by spying on them, i.e. monitoring their blood or urine. I must stress once again the importance of spending sufficient time with the patients. I find that if I warn them that they may have severe side effects, they come back in a fortnight's time and report that, to their great surprise, they have indeed had some of these side effects. They even begin to respect me when they realise that I actually knew what was going to happen to them! To win their confidence is essential in the handling of patients, and I even feel I can congratulate myself on my success if a patient comes back to me after two weeks with a full bottle of tablets and says "I couldn't take them". At least this means that he can trust me and that he does not have to conceal his sin of omission. Usually I can persuade him to make another effort. This also underlines the importance of another aspect of drug trials, i.e. that the trial should not be carried out with a fixed dosage of drug, but that the physician giving the medication should adjust the dose until he obtains some sort of evidence that it is having an effect on the patient's metabolism, as reflected either by a clinical change in the symptoms or by the development of side effects. In this way it is possible to compensate for the fact that the concentration in the blood or the effective concentration in the brain may differ so widely from patient to patient. A clinical trial should be a practical affair and should be designed to furnish information of practical use to the clinician.

C.R.B. JOYCE: The undesirable effect seen by Dr. KRAGH-SØRENSEN, to which Dr. WELNER referred, has not been observed in the standard 21 or 28-day trials carried out with the drug. Of course, in Dr. KRAGH-SØRENSEN's patient, this effect manifested itself outside that 28-day period; I should therefore like to stress that if anybody has any information—whether positive or negative—on long-term follow-up studies which has not otherwise come to our attention, we should be interested to hear about it.
Dr. R. KUHN has remarked that it appears to make no difference whether Ludiomil is administered in a single daily dose or in three divided doses. However, given the present state of our clinical—as distinct from our pharmacokinetic—knowledge, we do not yet know for certain if this is true, but we suspect that it is. Controlled trials involving a close clinical study of the effect of altering the regime in this way are now in progress.
Dr. R. KUHN's observation does seem to have been very satisfactorily borne out by the information Dr. KEBERLE has just given.

N. MATUSSEK: Dr. KEBERLE, could you tell us how the half-life of Ludiomil compares with that of other antidepressants, and also whether it is likely to decrease following prolonged administration, as happens with other drugs? The half-life of cannabinols, for example, is shorter in users than in non-users*.
In addition, it is a pity that the number of patients treated so far is too small for correlations to be drawn between blood level and clinical effect, because I feel that this is a

---

* LEMBERGER, L., TAMARKIN, N.R., AXELROD, J., KOPIN, I.J.: Delta-9-tetrahydrocannabinol: metabolism and disposition in long-term Marihuana smokers. Science *173*, 72 (1971)

point we should always bear in mind. Perhaps the findings would be similar to those obtained by SJÖQVIST's group* in a study on nortriptyline, in which the therapeutic effect was shown to be dependent on the blood level.

One last question for the pharmacologists: do the metabolites of Ludiomil discovered to date include any biologically active compounds, or is it considered safe to assume that the drug owes its entire pharmacological and clinical activity to the unchanged substance?

R. KUHN: I can only concur with what Dr. HAMILTON has said. It has always been a principle of ours to adapt the total dosage, the number of divided doses, and all other necessary measures to the patient's individual requirements. This, I am sure, is one of the reasons why we have encountered relatively few side effects with Ludiomil, although other authors have reported fairly severe ones in some cases. Admittedly, we ourselves have observed epileptic seizures, albeit very rarely. As soon as the first signs of any hyperactivity appear, we reduce the dosage and, if necessary, administer appropriate drugs, such as anti-epileptic agents. By refusing to give the patients a dosage that is fixed from the very outset, one can usually also avoid the other danger mentioned by Dr. HAMILTON, i.e. the danger that the drug will not be taken at all. Precisely in the field of the psychopharmaceuticals, the success of treatment depends to a considerable extent on a relationship of trust between doctor and patient; only if the patient is absolutely sure that the doctor understands something about the disease and about the drugs prescribed, is drug treatment—whether with Ludiomil, imipramine, or any other psycho-active agent—likely to be of genuine value. But the first prerequisite for success is that the dosage should not be fixed from the outset. This may not always be very satisfactory from the pharmacological or scientific standpoint, but, as Dr. HAMILTON has already emphasised, it is in conformity with medical experience and thus also with the requirements which we as doctors have first and foremost to fulfil.

K. RICKELS: I should also like to support the statement made by Dr. HAMILTON. I think that flexibility of dosage, even in controlled double-blind studies, is most important. An I believe that there are basically two criteria which should be used: these two end-point criteria are the presence of disturbing side effects or the absence of an improvement. If side effects are encountered, or if no improvement is observed, the physician should certainly adjust the dosage.

If the physician has the patient's confidence, and if the patient feels free to talk to him about side effects, he doesn't need to hide the fact that he may not have taken his medication. In our experience poorly educated persons sometimes have great difficulty in conveying to the doctor that the drug isn't helping them; they often simply default because they are afraid to return and inform their doctor that the medicine doesn't help them or causes side effects. Having the patient become a cooperative participant in the project, and not just an object, will certainly decrease drop-out rates and will enable the patient to provide accurate information about his drug intake.

Another point I'd like to mention concerns the question of dosage, i.e. once daily versus three times daily. When employing amitriptyline it is quite a common practice in the United States, and probably in Europe too, to start depressed patients on a high dose at night so as to reduce the problem of side effects; a few days later, a morning dose may be added. After about a week, the dosage pattern can be altered, because by then the patient will have adjusted to his treatment and will consequently have less side effects.

W. R. DARROW: I should like to comment briefly on the side effect which occurred in Dr. KRAGH-SØRENSEN's patient. The trials being carried out in the United States

---

* SJÖQVIST, F., ALEXANDERSON, B., ÅSBERG, M., BERTILSSON, L., BORGÅ, O., HAMBERGER, B., TUCK, D.: Pharmacokinetics and biological effects of nortriptyline in man. Acta pharmacol. (Kbh.) 29, Suppl. 3: 255 (1971)

include two studies involving continued administration over prolonged periods. In neither of these trials have we seen any side effects of the kind Dr. WELNER described. We have some 10 patients who have been treated for a three-month period. In the second trial only three patients have completed the seven-month period of treatment. One thing we have noted, however, is that the therapeutic response, as assessed at the end of the first month of medication, frequently continues to improve under maintenance treatment.

F. FREYHAN: Of course, I agree with Dr. HAMILTON about the value of a relationship of trust and confidence with the patient. I have in fact stressed on many occasions that the physician-patient relationship should never be allowed to suffer because of the requirements imposed by a clinical experiment. But I disagree with his view that monitoring implies spying on the patient. I believe there is a growing need for objective monitoring of drug intake. In the case of lithium treatment, for example, effectiveness depends solely on ensuring that the plasma drug levels are within the therapeutic range. The need for drug monitoring is being more and more strongly emphasised by investigators employing controlled methods of evaluation. You can no longer depend on what the patient tells you, no matter how much you trust him. We need not have a guilty conscience about monitoring in psychiatric treatment; after all, the quantitative effects of treatment with anticoagulants or antidiabetic drugs are regularly monitored. I should like to make a strong plea that, to ensure accurate dose determination, reliance on the physician-patient relationship should be replaced by objective monitoring. Dr. COPPEN has already stressed that we must correlate plasma levels with therapeutic effectiveness. Lithium offers a good example in point, since it is essential to know whether the plasma levels of this drug are below, within, or above the therapeutic range.

M. HAMILTON: I'd like to ask Dr. FREYHAN one question. How does he deal with the patient who takes a dose of drug only on the morning when he is going to be monitored?

F. FREYHAN: May I ask whether you are referring only to lithium?

M. HAMILTON: No, any drug.

F. FREYHAN: I don't have any exact quantitative correlations. It is not difficult to distinguish between a single dose taken on the day of the patient's visit to the clinic and a regular drug intake. Furthermore, we use the services of a nurse who collects urine and blood specimens in the course of unscheduled visits to the patient's home. While I agree with you, Dr. HAMILTON, that there may be quite a number of patients who just take a dose on the night or on the morning before, I think the methods of drug-level determination available today are sufficiently accurate to distinguish the occasional from the regular dose-taker.

H. KEBERLE: In this discussion of our paper two speakers have asked if there is any explanation for the fact that the blood concentrations of Ludiomil in the steady state remained the same irrespective of the dosage schedule employed, and whether this property is peculiar to Ludiomil. I would answer briefly as follows:
In the case of substances displaying a short half-life great importance attaches, firstly, to the time at which the dose is given and, secondly, to the time at which blood is sampled for the purpose of determining the plasma levels. The plasma levels may, in fact, vary considerably depending on these two times. If a substance has a long, or relatively long, half-life—as in the case of Ludiomil, for example—this time factor is of much less significance, because the steady-state concentrations attained following repeated doses are far higher than the maximum levels reached after a single dose; hence, even the omission of treatment for one day does not have a particularly striking effect on the steady-state concentrations. Individual variations in these concentrations—I am thinking here, for instance, of the exceptional case reproduced in our Figure 16 (page 152)—depend not so much on the substance concerned as on the

159

patient's ability to metabolise that substance. In my opinion, therefore, it would be very important, as a means of finding out why a particular patient had failed to respond or had developed an unusual side effect, to check, where possible, the blood levels attained by the drug.

May I now try to answer Dr. MATUSSEK's request for data on the half-life of other psycho-active agents. The best-documented drugs in this respect are those which, like desipramine and nortriptyline, are secondary amines, since relatively sensitive methods of analysis have been developed for such compounds. The half-life of desipramine has been reported to range from a few hours to 54 hours, while that of nortriptyline is said to be about 29 hours*. In the case of tertiary amines—such as imipramine or amitriptyline, for example—sufficiently reliable methods of analysis are not yet available, and I should therefore be reluctant to give any hard and fast figures. As for the question of whether the half-life of Ludiomil becomes modified following repeated administration of the drug, all I can say is that we have not observed anything of this kind in our long-term experiments.

Lastly, I am unfortunately unable at present to state definitely whether the metabolic products of Ludiomil also include biologically active compounds, because most of the metabolites so far discovered have only been identified in very small quantities.

A. DELINI-STULA: I should like to comment briefly on this last point from the pharmacological angle. A few potential metabolites of Ludiomil have in fact been prepared by synthesis and subjected to pharmacological testing with the aim of finding out whether they have any antidepressant activity. They have proved in these tests to be either much less active than Ludiomil or else completely inactive.

H. KEBERLE: Before discussing the question of whether metabolites are active, one should really know which metabolites are at all relevant from the pharmacokinetic point of view, i.e. which metabolites occur in the blood in the requisite concentrations. On this point we have no information, and I'm afraid it will take some time for us to acquire the necessary experimental data.

* SJÖQVIST, F., ALEXANDERSON, B., ÅSBERG, M., BERTILSSON, L., BORGÅ, O., HAMBERGER, B., TUCK, D.: Pharmacokinetics and biological effects of nortriptyline in man. Acta pharmacol. (Kbh.) 29, Suppl. 3: 255 (1971)

Haemodynamic studies with CIBA 34,276-Ba (Ludiomil)

by A. REALE* and M. MOTOLESE**

This study is presented as a detailed investigation of the central and peripheral haemodynamic effects of intravenously administered Ludiomil® in man.

The cases studied consisted of 10 patients undergoing diagnostic heart catheterisation, whose ages ranged from 13 to 43 years (median age: 32 years) and who weighed between 31 and 66 kg. (mean weight: 54 kg.). The patients were selected on the basis of an essentially normal circulation and normal left ventricular function. Five of them had innocent murmurs, three trivial to moderate mitral stenosis, one a hyperkinetic syndrome, and one primary pulmonary hypertension of slight degree.

The patients were investigated in the post-absorptive state and received no pre-medication. Local anaesthesia for venous and arterial cut-down was performed at least 30 minutes before actual administration of the trial preparation. Venous and retrograde arterial catheterisation was performed in every case, and the following variables were measured or calculated: minute ventilation (VM 1./min.), oxygen consumption ($\dot{V}O_2$ ml./min.), oxygen saturation in the pulmonary artery (PA O_2%) and in the brachial artery (BA O_2%), arterio-venous difference (a–v difference in O_2 vol. %), heart rate (HR), left ventricular systolic pressure (LVSP) and left ventricular end-diastolic pressure (LVEDP), brachial artery systolic pressure (BASP) and brachial artery mean pressure ($\overline{BAP}$), first derivative of left ventricular pressure (max. LV dp/dt mm. Hg/sec.), which is an index of the contractile state of the ventricle, cardiac index (CI 1./min./m.²), stroke volume index (SVI ml./m.²), systemic arterial resistance (SAR dynes sec. cm.⁻⁵), left ventricular stroke work index (LVSWI g.m./m.²), which is an estimate of left ventricular function, and the product of left ventricular peak systolic pressure times heart rate (LVSP × HR), which is an index of myocardial oxygen consumption.

All measurements were first obtained under basal conditions, then repeated 10 and 20 minutes after intravenous administration of Ludiomil in a dose of 25 mg. in the first five patients and of 50 mg. in the other five. The dose per kg. body-weight ranged from 0.38 mg. to 0.52 mg. (mean: 0.44 mg.) for the first group and from 0.80 mg. to 1.61 mg. (mean: 1.03 mg.) for the second group.

The findings are presented in Table 1, which shows the mean values and the standard errors of the means, and in Figures 1–7. No significant changes occurred in left ventricular systolic, brachial artery systolic, or brachial artery mean pressures (Figure 1). Maximum dp/dt of left ventricular pressure was

* Divisione Cardiologica, Istituto di Chirurgia del Cuore, University of Rome, Italy.
** Medical Department, CIBA-GEIGY S.P.A., Viale di Villa Massimo 29, Rome, Italy.

Table 1. Haemodynamic variables before, as well as 10 and 20 minutes after, intravenous administration of Ludiomil in a dose of 25 or 50 mg. Mean values for 10 patients. The figures in brackets represent in each case the standard errors of the means.

Variables	Basal	10 min. after	20 min. after	Basal	10 min. after	20 min. after
		25 mg. Ludiomil i.v.			50 mg. Ludiomil i.v.	
$\dot{V}O_2$ (ml./min.)	230.20 (28.61)	235.40 (27.37)	232.60 (24.56)	219.20 (29.89)	236.00 (25.45)	232.00 (23.45)
VM (l./min.)	6.56 (0.35)	7.18 (0.66)	7.46 (0.46)	7.56 (1.07)	8.02 (0.95)	7.94 (0.79)
PA O_2 (%)	67.00 (4.92)	69.20 (4.81)	69.20 (4.81)	64.60 (3.41)	68.20 (3.92)	67.20 (3.20)
BA O_2 (%)	93.00 (2.42)	93.40 (2.04)	92.80 (2.22)	90.80 (1.90)	91.00 (1.22)	91.00 (1.51)
a–v diff. (O_2 vol.%)	4.64 (0.51)	4.41 (0.65)	4.31 (0.58)	4.88 (0.34)	4.34 (0.47)	4.54 (0.30)
LVSP (mm. Hg)	110.60 (11.28)	109.40 (9.87)	106.20 (9.11)	111.20 (9.81)	113.40 (10.96)	110.40 (10.85)
LVEDP (mm. Hg)	7.20 (1.24)	6.80 (0.86)	6.60 (0.97)	8.60 (1.96)	8.00 (1.92)	7.20 (1.65)
BASP (mm. Hg)	117.80 (10.16)	119.80 (8.38)	118.00 (9.02)	117.20 (7.41)	123.80 (9.04)	120.40 (8.85)
$\overline{BAP}$ (mm. Hg)	83.00 (7.10)	84.40 (6.36)	81.00 (7.19)	78.20 (6.75)	80.40 (6.72)	79.40 (6.01)
LV dp/dt (mm. Hg/sec.)	1,904.20 (386.85)	1,958.20 (386.19)	1,961.20 (407.25)	1,862.80 (179.72)	1,990.20 (284.98)	1,913.80 (282.36)
CI (l./min./m.²)	3.30 (0.73)	3.60 (0.72)	3.58 (0.66)	2.74 (0.23)	3.54 (0.38)	3.26 (0.26)
SVI (ml./m.²)	32.40 (5.19)	36.40 (6.00)	37.40 (5.39)	32.40 (3.32)	42.40 (4.53)	37.80 (2.90)
LVSWI (g.m./m.²)	34.20 (8.38)	38.40 (7.70)	38.00 (7.04)	29.80 (2.17)	41.00 (4.70)	36.60 (3.05)
LVSP x HR (units)	11,052.00 (1,659.27)	10,597.20 (1,389.99)	10,119.20 (1,356.84)	9,403.60 (784.98)	9,610.00 (900.40)	9,344.40 (901.39)
SAR (dynes sec. cm.⁻⁵)	1,332.40 (193.45)	1,321.00 (220.06)	1,246.40 (195.06)	1,584.20 (338.28)	1,204.40 (146.46)	1,343.00 (180.12)
HR (beats/min.)	98.00 (5.47)	95.60 (5.49)	94.00 (6.16)	84.80 (1.62)	85.20 (3.26)	84.80 (2.24)

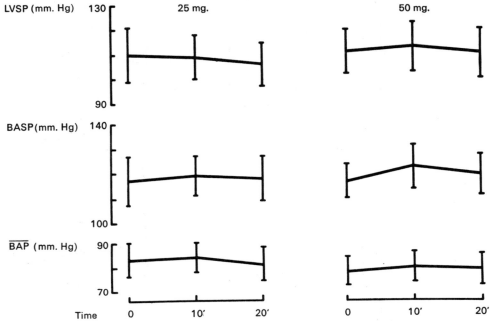

Fig. 1. Left ventricular systolic pressure (LVSP), brachial artery systolic pressure (BASP), and brachial artery mean pressure ($\overline{\text{BAP}}$) before (Time 0), as well as 10 and 20 minutes after, intravenous administration of 25 or 50 mg. Ludiomil.

unchanged. Left ventricular stroke work index increased in all cases, the mean change being significant ($P < 0.05$) for the group of patients who received 50 mg. Left ventricular end-diastolic pressure tended to decrease, and the mean change was significant ($P < 0.05$) for the 50 mg. group (Figure 2). Thus, left ventricular function, as expressed by the relationship between LVSWI and LVEDP, was generally improved. Myocardial oxygen consumption, derived from the product of left ventricular pressure times heart rate, was practically unaffected because heart rate either showed no change or decreased slightly, while left ventricular peak systolic pressure remained practically unchanged (Figure 3).

Mean values for cardiac index and stroke volume index tended to increase, although the changes were not statistically significant (Figure 4). Evaluation of individual cases showed that, when cardiac output increased noticeably, it did so as a result of an increase in oxygen consumption and/or a decrease in arteriovenous difference, the latter being due to increased O_2 saturation of mixed venous blood (Figure 5). Minute ventilation appeared to be enhanced in all but one case (Figure 6).

Systemic arterial resistance decreased, but the mean changes were not statistically significant (Figure 7).

Statistical analysis of the data failed to reveal any differences in the behaviour of the variables with respect to the two doses of Ludiomil administered, with the exception of the effect upon LVEDP and LVSWI.

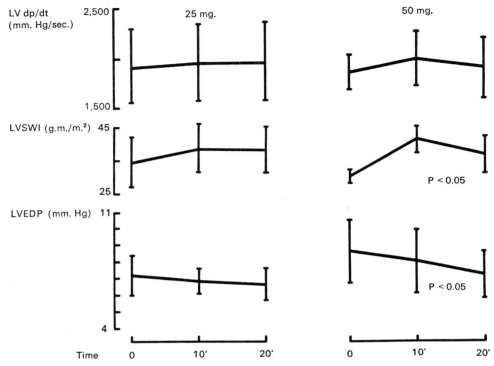

Fig. 2. First derivative of left ventricular pressure (max. LV dp/dt), left ventricular stroke work index (LVSWI), and left ventricular end-diastolic pressure (LVEDP) before (Time 0), as well as 10 and 20 minutes after, intravenous administration of 25 or 50 mg. Ludiomil.

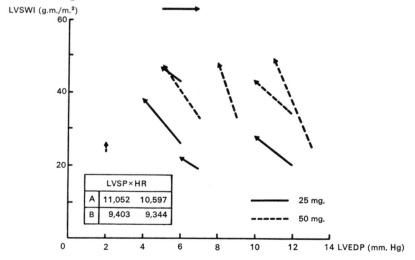

Fig. 3. Improvement in left ventricular function, as expressed by the relationship between left ventricular stroke work index (LVSWI) and left ventricular end-diastolic pressure (LVEDP), in response to 25 and 50 mg. Ludiomil. Inset: the product of left ventricular systolic pressure (LVSP) times heart rate (HR) showed that Ludiomil had virtually no effect on myocardial oxygen consumption; A = before and 10 minutes after 25 mg. Ludiomil, B = before and after 50 mg.

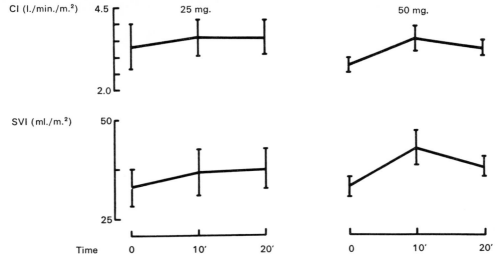

Fig. 4. Cardiac index (CI) and stroke volume index (SVI) before (Time 0), as well as 10 and 20 minutes after, intravenous administration of 25 or 50 mg. Ludiomil.

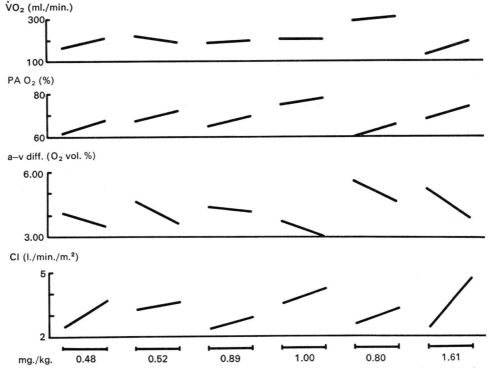

Fig. 5. Increase in cardiac output in individual cases. This increase was due to a rise in oxygen consumption ($\dot{V}O_2$) and/or a decrease in arteriovenous difference (a-v diff.), the latter being caused by increased O_2 saturation of mixed venous blood (PA O_2).

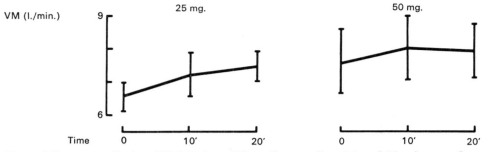

Fig. 6. Minute ventilation (VM) before (Time 0), as well as 10 and 20 minutes after, intravenous administration of 25 or 50 mg. Ludiomil.

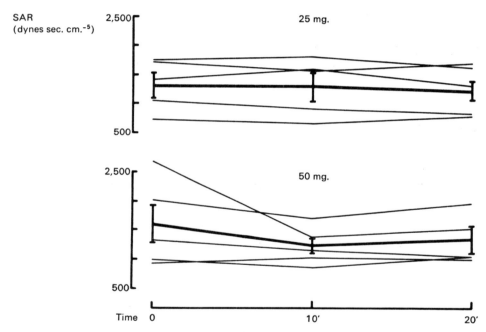

Fig. 7. Systemic arterial resistance (SAR) before (Time 0), as well as 10 and 20 minutes after, intravenous administration of 25 or 50 mg. Ludiomil.

Where deviations from control values did occur, the change was sometimes more marked after 10 than after 20 minutes, but no definite pattern emerged.

Two additional patients were studied using a 100 mg. dose (1.38 mg./kg. and 2.15 mg./kg.) (Table 2). The effects were similar to those observed with the lower doses and apparently more pronounced, although no statistical elaboration could be attempted on such a numerically limited group.

No side effects or subjective discomfort of any kind were noted in the entire series.

Table 2. Haemodynamic variables in two patients before, as well as 10 and 20 minutes after, intravenous administration of Ludiomil in a dose of 100 mg.

Variables	Patient No.	Basal	10 min. after	20 min. after
			100 mg. Ludiomil i.v.	
$\dot{V}O_2$ (ml./min.)	11	240	247	258
	12	231	240	260
VM (l./min.)	11	6.7	6.9	7.4
	12	9.6	10.0	10.8
PA O_2 (%)	11	46	53	53
	12	62	66	70
BA O_2 (%)	11	87	87	86
	12	93	95	95
a–v diff. (O_2 vol.%)	11	6.54	5.42	5.26
	12	5.77	5.40	4.66
LVSP/LVEDP (mm. Hg)	11	98/7	102/6	97/4
	12	87/4	95/4	90/4
BASP (mm. Hg)	11	103/53	107/57	103/54
	12	96/52	102/58	96/52
$\overline{BAP}$ (mm. Hg)	11	72	75	74
	12	66	71	68
LV dp/dt (mm. Hg/sec.)	11	2,287	2,261	2,261
	12	1,143	1,119	1,107
CI (l./min./m.^{2})	11	2.0	2.5	2.7
	12	2.6	2.8	3.6
SVI (ml./m.^{2})	11	22	27	29
	12	26	25	32
LVSWI (g.m./m.^{2})	11	19	25	27
	12	22	23	28
LVSP × HR (units)	11	9,016	9,384	9,322
	12	8,700	10,640	10,080
SAR (dynes sec. cm.$^{-5}$)	11	1,599	1,332	1,216
	12	1,332	1,411	974
HR (beats/min.)	11	92	92	96
	12	100	112	112

On the basis of the haemodynamic data, the following conclusions can be drawn:

1. The tendency of the systemic arterial resistance to decrease, although not to a statistically significant extent, might indicate that the compound initiates some degree of vasodilatation in certain vascular beds. Whether or not this vasodilatation is a direct or an indirect effect of Ludiomil was not investigated in the present study. Arterial hypotension, however, was never encountered; as a matter of fact, the average brachial artery mean pressure showed a slight increase during the first 10 minutes. This finding is consistent with animal experimental data[1].
2. The contractile state of the ventricle was unaffected by the drug, and overall cardiac performance tended to improve, the ventricle being capable of more work at a lower end-diastolic pressure and at the same level of myocardial oxygen consumption.
3. Ludiomil had no depressant influence on respiratory function.
4. Deviations from control values, in particular for LVEDP, cardiac index, LVSWI, and systemic arterial resistance, appeared to be somewhat more pronounced with the higher doses.
5. Most of the changes observed were still present after 20 minutes, which was the maximum duration of our observation period.

Reference

1 BRUNNER, H., HEDWALL, P.R., MEIER, M., BEIN, H.J.: Cardiovascular effects of Preparation CIBA 34,276-Ba and imipramine. Agents and Actions *2*, 69 (1971)

Discussion

H. J. BEIN: It has been shown by P. IMHOF (unpublished data) that in seven subjects Ludiomil in intravenous doses of 35–65 mg. reduced heart rate slightly, and neither changed resting blood pressure nor impaired orthostatic blood-pressure regulation. Furthermore, it was found that the effects of intravenously injected noradrenaline (5 mcg.) are enhanced by Ludiomil. It seems reasonable to assume that the slight haemodynamic changes seen by Dr. REALE are due not to a direct effect of Ludiomil but rather to an indirect effect resulting from potentiation of the action of endogenous catecholamines.

P. KIELHOLZ: One question from the clinical point of view, Dr. REALE: you suggest that some degree of vasodilatation may occur following intravenous injection of the drug. Have you observed any complications which might be connected with this vasodilatation?

R. KUHN: I used Ludiomil to treat one youth, aged about 17 years, who was a racing cyclist. He said that when he took the drug he was unable to carry on with his training. Could this possibly be connected with the fact that the training subjected his circulatory system to an exceptional strain? In view of what Dr. BEIN has just said, I could imagine that this might be the explanation; or is some other cause likely to be involved?

J. J. LÓPEZ IBOR: We have noticed that imipramine and clomipramine can give rise to postural hypotension when injected intravenously. In such cases, we now administer pressor agents as a compensatory measure. It would certainly be very interesting if Ludiomil did not cause postural hypotension. I believe that some, though not all, of the epileptic seizures attributed to imipramine are in fact forms of hypotension-induced syncope. Since we started administering drugs to compensate for this postural hypotension, we have never encountered any "epileptic seizures" in response to these antidepressants.

R. KUHN: I should like to add something to what Dr. LÓPEZ IBOR has just said. There are cases in which the blood pressure tends quite spontaneously to be reduced during the depressive phase. In some of these patients Ludiomil may eliminate the hypotension, while in others the hypotension becomes more pronounced; in these latter instances it is absolutely essential—and, incidentally, very easy—to combat the hypotension by administering a suitable drug. In this respect, too, the circumstances vary tremendously from one patient to another and must be carefully evaluated in each individual case.

N. MATUSSEK: May one conclude from your studies, Dr. REALE, that Ludiomil can also safely be given to patients suffering from heart failure? It has repeatedly been stressed, particularly in recent months, that other antidepressants—especially amitriptyline—should be used with caution in such patients. Would this restriction cease to apply in the case of Ludiomil?
One question for Dr. KUHN: for how long was your racing cyclist treated with Ludiomil? We very often noticed that our normal test subjects became tired and lethargic at the beginning of treatment; their performance also declined in many tests. After the medication had been continued for 8–10 days, however, this effect was reversed, and the drug even exerted an action resembling, in some respects, that of amphetamine. The tennis players and athletes among our subjects then found that they did better at their respective sports; did your racing cyclist also experience similar phases?

C. R. B. JOYCE: As you will see later from the observations made in the series of international trials to be reviewed towards the end of this meeting, some investigators reported a small number of cases of so-called "hypotension". I think it is worth pointing out that the definition of hypotension differs from one clinical situation, or one clinical speciality, to another, and depends to a marked extent on the method by which the hypotension is assessed. With amitriptyline and imipramine, the two main comparative drugs used in the trials, the incidence of this effect was roughly the same as that usually reported and was higher than in the patients treated with Ludiomil. Amitriptyline showed the highest incidence of this so-called hypotension, imipramine figured second, and Ludiomil had the lowest incidence.

R. OBERHOLZER: Do you think, Dr. REALE, that any conclusions as to the effects of long-term treatment can be drawn from the short-term experiments which you have described in your paper?

W. WALCHER: So far we have used Ludiomil, in an open clinical trial, chiefly to treat patients suffering from depression associated with somatic symptoms. Rewarding though these cases may be as regards their response to specific thymoleptic medication, it is difficult to bring them successfully through the initial stage of treatment, because they find the anticholinergic side effects of thymoleptic agents so troublesome. Tachycardia in particular, with its overtones of anxiety, often causes these patients to drop out because it makes them afraid that their condition is becoming worse. Our clinical experience to date fully confirms Dr. REALE's findings. I feel that, in view of the small number of side effects it provokes, Ludiomil really does constitute an exception among the antidepressants, precisely with regard to cardiac disturbances. Hardly any of our patients complained of tachycardia, and the absence of this side effect substantially facilitates the treatment of depression in cases where the principal symptoms are of a somatic nature. The same applies to the absence of a hypotensive effect. A sedating action, on the other hand, is desirable in these patients, who tend to be of the hypochondriacal, complaining type, because it helps to carry them through the first few days of treatment.

R. KUHN: In answer to Dr. MATUSSEK's question, the difficulties encountered by the racing cyclist I mentioned occurred at the commencement of treatment with Ludiomil. This patient, however, had a family history not only of endogenous psychosis, but also of epilepsy, and epilepsy potentials were found in his E.E.G. There may perhaps be a connection here with the point raised by Dr. LÓPEZ IBOR. It is extremely difficult to say in such cases whether the complication is purely of an hypotensive nature or whether it is associated with cerebral disorders.
On the subject of heart failure, I would mention that we have recently used Ludiomil in the treatment of two patients suffering from cardiac insufficiency, and no complications whatever occurred in either of them.

A. REALE: In reply to your comment, Dr. BEIN, our findings are in agreement with those of my good friend PETER IMHOF inasmuch as we didn't observe any tachycardia or hypotension either. I can't say anything about postural hypotension, because all our studies were done in the recumbent position on the catheterisation table. As for the question of whether Ludiomil has a vasodilator effect, if you have an increase in cardiac output and an unchanged mean pressure, you therefore get a calculated decrease in systemic resistance. Whether or not this means that a vasodilator effect occurs, I'm afraid I can't say. But if there is a decrease in systemic resistance, this must presumably imply that there has been some vasodilator effect somewhere in the vascular bed. Dr. KIELHOLZ asked whether, in view of this apparently mild vasodilator effect, we have encountered any complications. The answer is that we have not, either during the study itself or after the patients had been brought back to the ward. None of them ever complained of anything out of the ordinary.
Dr. R. KUHN asked whether the results of our studies suggest that people taking Ludiomil should possibly not indulge in exercise. I would say "why not"? As far as I am concerned, they can certainly take exercise.
Dr. LÓPEZ IBOR mentioned postural hypotension with reference to other drugs. As I said before, we cannot make any statement about postural hypotension.

As regards Dr. Matussek's question, it would seem from our data that the drug can safely be given to cardiac patients; as a matter of fact, it should be even good for them, because if anything Ludiomil actually improves ventricular function. The end-diastolic pressure goes down and the stroke work index goes up—which is a very favourable state of affairs.

As for Dr. Joyce's comment, there's nothing much I can say in this connection; I can only repeat that Ludiomil did not give rise to hypotension in our studies.

I have no idea, Dr. Oberholzer, whether my results are applicable to long-term therapy. As you will of course realise, these are studies which can be carried out only in an acute form. It is not feasible to prolong this type of study for more than a couple of hours at the most, and repeated catheterisation does not appear to be justified. Haemodynamic effects of long-term therapy should be investigated with non-invasive techniques.

Studies on the influence of CIBA 34,276-Ba (Ludiomil) on respiratory function in man

by L. Geisler and H.-D. Rost*

Recent investigations have shown that there are various psycho-active drugs which, when administered in therapeutic doses, may exert a by no means negligible depressant effect on respiration. In studies undertaken together with Herberg[2,5,6], we ourselves have observed that diazepam and clomethiazole, for example, have a negative influence on respiration. Since the psychopharmaceuticals constitute, both pharmacologically and chemically, an extremely varied group of substances, there is *a priori* no reason to suppose that they all produce the same type of repercussions on respiratory function. On the contrary, even psycho-active drugs displaying relatively similar activity—such as tranquillisers, for instance—may well differ radically from one another as regards their influence on respiration. A good example in point is the difference in the respiratory response following treatment with diazepam and benzoctamine. As already reported earlier by us[3,4], diazepam has a distinctly depressant effect on respiration, whereas benzoctamine actually exerts a mild central stimulant action on respiration. So far as we are aware, no systematic studies have ever been carried out to determine the way in which respiration reacts to antidepressants. Wiener[15], who undertook trials with doxepine in asthmatics, found that the drug slightly increased the respiration rate while at the same time diminishing the respiratory minute volume and eliciting a mild bronchospasmolytic effect. He nevertheless utters a warning against the drug's use in the presence of advanced respiratory failure.

The conditions under which antidepressants are employed are of a somewhat special nature, and this for two reasons: firstly, because such drugs tend to be required chiefly in elderly patients, a certain percentage of whom will inevitably be suffering from manifest or latent respiratory insufficiency; and, secondly, because the treatment usually has to be given over a prolonged period. Consequently, it would seem not only reasonable, but in fact essential, also to study the influence which the new antidepressants exert upon respiratory function.

Methods

We began our investigations on Ludiomil® by carrying out tests in healthy volunteers. After it had been found that the drug had no negative repercussions on respiration in these subjects, further tests were conducted in patients with partial or global respiratory failure due to obstructive diseases of the airways. The CO_2-sensitivity of the respiratory centres was determined by reference to

* Medizinische Kliniken und Polikliniken der Justus-Liebig-Universität, Giessen, Germany.

the CO_2-response curves plotted during a rebreathing experiment. Provided the lungs are mechanically intact, the steepness of the CO_2-response curves offers a useful parameter by which to assess the CO_2-sensitivity of the respiratory centres[2, 6-11]. This steepness can be expressed in terms of the so-called excitability quotient (E.Q.), which is arrived at by dividing the increase in respiratory minute volume (in litres) by the rise in CO_2 tension (in mm. Hg) in the arterial blood. Measurement of the excitability quotient before (E.Q. I) and after (E.Q. II) administration of a drug indicates whether the CO_2-sensitivity of the respiratory centres has undergone any change, i.e. whether respiration has been stimulated (E.Q. I < E.Q. II) or depressed (E.Q. I > E.Q. II).

The spirometric measurements were performed in a closed spirometric system, using a special model of the 602A Repo-Test apparatus manufactured by Dargatz. To determine the blood gases (pO_2, pCO_2, pH), samples of capillary blood were taken from the ear after prior hyperaemisation and the blood gases analysed by the micro-analytical method[1, 12-14]. All tests of pulmonary function were first carried out at rest in order to obtain pre-treatment values. The tests were then repeated 30–60 minutes after intravenous injection of Ludiomil. The volunteers studied consisted of healthy individuals, most of whom were either students or members of our staff aged between 20 and 30 years. Details of the tests performed in the various groups were as follows: determination of the excitability quotient in 10 healthy subjects before and after intravenous administration of 25 mg. Ludiomil; complete gamut of spirometric measurements (static and dynamic pulmonary volumes) in 10 healthy subjects before and after intravenous injection of 25 mg. Ludiomil; analysis of the arterial blood gases in 10 healthy subjects before and after 25 mg. Ludiomil i.v. and in five healthy subjects before and after 50 mg. Ludiomil i.v.; and analysis of the arterial blood gases in five patients with obstructive diseases of the airways before and after 25 mg. Ludiomil i.v.

The statistical calculations (analysis of variance) were kindly undertaken by the Institute for Medical Statistics and Documentation in Giessen (Director: Prof. J. DUDECK).

Results and discussion

The values obtained are listed in detail in Tables 1 to 5. In response to 25 mg. Ludiomil i.v., the excitability quotient showed a slight but not statistically significant increase from 1.8 ± 0.63 to 2.2 ± 0.74 (l./mm. Hg). There is thus no reason to suppose that Ludiomil depresses respiration by adversely affecting the CO_2-sensitive central receptors.

The spirometric measurements made in 10 healthy subjects before and after intravenous injection of 25 mg. Ludiomil revealed no significant changes in any of the parameters studied [vital capacity, $F.E.V._1$ (forced expiratory volume in the first second following maximal inspiration), and maximal breathing capacity]. In other words, no obstructive or restrictive disorders of ventilation were observed in response to the intravenous administration of Ludiomil. These findings in themselves were sufficient to suggest that the drug would be unlikely

173

Test subjects	E.Q. I (l./mm. Hg)	E.Q. II (l./mm. Hg)
1. Z.	2.27	3.08
2. W.	1.23	1.49
3. P.	1.62	2.03
4. R.	2.06	1.85
5. L.	1.47	2.34
6. U.	1.50	2.20
7. N.	1.23	3.41
8. K.	3.09	2.68
9. W.	2.38	2.02
10. F.	1.14	0.88
$\bar{x}$	1.799	2.198
s	0.6329	0.7392

Table 1. Excitability quotient before (E.Q. I) and after (E.Q. II) intravenous administration of 25 mg. Ludiomil in 10 healthy subjects.

Table 2. Spirometric values recorded in 10 healthy subjects before and after intravenous administration of 25 mg. Ludiomil.

Test subjects	Vital capacity (ml.)		F.E.V.$_1$ (ml.)		Maximal breathing capacity (l./min.)	
	Before	After	Before	After	Before	After
G.	3,700	3,640	3,270	3,410	77	74
H.	3,690	3,590	3,420	2,930	70	47
R.	3,800	4,250	3,750	3,980	82	84
Z.	3,800	3,900	3,500	3,000	102	80
R.	5,020	4,900	4,220	3,470	75	67
H.	5,500	4,860	4,600	4,500	129	137
W.	5,460	5,300	3,750	4,130	77	88
W.	5,300	4,560	4,070	4,350	115	117
M.	3,760	3,700	3,070	3,160	74	86
F.	4,330	4,620	4,030	4,040	87	98
$\bar{x}$	4,436	4,332	3,768	3,697	89	88
s	791	605	469	572	19	25
$s_{\bar{x}}$	255	191	148	181	6	8

to exert any influence on the arterial blood gases. Analysis of the blood gases 30, 60, 90, and 120 minutes after an intravenous dose of 25 mg. Ludiomil in 10 healthy subjects, and after 50 mg. in five healthy subjects, did in fact show that neither the arterial oxygen tension or arterial carbon dioxide tension nor the pH underwent any significant change in response to Ludiomil. The blood-gas analyses which were later performed in five patients suffering from chronic obstructive diseases of the airways indicated that the drug likewise has no deleterious effect on the arterial blood-gas levels in cases of manifest respiratory insufficiency.

Table 3. Arterial blood gases and pH in 10 healthy subjects before and after intravenous administration of 25 mg. Ludiomil.

	Test subjects	At rest		Following 25 mg. Ludiomil i.v.			
		After 30 min.	After 60 min.	After 30 min.	After 60 min.	After 90 min.	After 120 min.
pO$_2$ (mm. Hg)	1. W	100	95	100	88	92	90
	2. Z.	104	100	76	94	92	94
	3. N.	106	100	93	98	101	100
	4. B.	98	86	88	86	88	90
	5. J.	94	76	96	92	82	94
	6. W.	94	88	96	90	94	93
	7. M.	90	92	91	88	92	90
	8. E.	82	94	82	90	88	88
	9. M.	104	104	104	106	102	104
	10. H.	94	96	100	100	96	98
x̄		96.6	93.1	92.6	93.2	92.7	94.1
s		7.36	8.14	8.65	6.33	6.03	5.13
sx̄		2.32	2.57	2.73	2.00	1.90	1.62
pCO$_2$ (mm. Hg)	1. W.	47	46	43.8	47	45	46
	2. Z.	38	39.5	37.5	39.9	40.8	36.7
	3. N.	33	37	41	34	34.5	38
	4. B.	35.5	35.5	35	34.3	33.5	34
	5. J.	41	42.3	34.5	47.5	43.5	47.5
	6. W.	37.5	40	40	38	40	39.8
	7. M.	42	44.2	42	44	41.5	44.2
	8. E.	42	41	38.5	43	43	42.5
	9. M.	38	38	41.5	42	39	40
	10. H.	41	41	41.5	42	43	42.5
x̄		39.5	40.4	39.5	41.1	40.5	41.1
s		3.94	3.20	3.08	4.67	3.80	4.22
sx̄		1.24	1.01	0.97	1.47	1.20	1.33
pH	1. W.	7.38	7.41	7.40	7.38	7.40	7.41
	2. Z.	7.40	7.40	7.40	7.40	7.39	7.42
	3. N.	7.44	7.43	7.40	7.44	7.43	7.43
	4. B.	7.43	7.43	7.43	7.45	7.47	7.47
	5. J.	7.43	7.44	7.47	7.37	7.39	7.37
	6. W.	7.43	7.41	7.40	7.42	7.40	7.41
	7. M.	7.42	7.42	7.43	7.41	7.43	7.42
	8. E.	7.43	7.39	7.43	7.40	7.39	7.38
	9. M.	7.41	7.41	7.39	7.40	7.42	7.41
	10. H.	7.41	7.41	7.40	7.39	7.39	7.39
x̄		7.42	7.42	7.42	7.41	7.41	7.41
s		0.017	0.014	0.025	0.024	0.026	0.026
sx̄		0.005	0.004	0.008	0.008	0.008	0.008

Table 4. Arterial blood gases and pH in five healthy subjects before and after intravenous administration of 50 mg. Ludiomil.

	Test subjects	At rest		Following 50 mg. Ludiomil i.v.			
		After 30 min.	After 60 min.	After 30 min.	After 60 min.	After 90 min.	After 120 min.
pO_2 (mm. Hg)	1. P.	96	92	86	88	88	84
	2. C.	96	102	102	94	90	86
	3. P.	80	92	76	84	94	90
	4. M.	86	80	86	88	90	86
	5. H.	80	80	86	80	94	88
$\bar{x}$		87.6	89.2	87.2	86.8	91.2	86.8
s		8.0	9.3	9.3	5.2	2.6	2.2
$s\bar{x}$		3.6	4.2	4.2	2.3	1.2	1.0
pCO_2 (mm. Hg)	1. P.	43.5	41	43.5	42	41.5	42
	2. C.	38	40	37.5	42.5	40	42
	3. P.	44	41.5	43	38.5	41.5	44
	4. M.	45	42	46	45	45	45
	5. H.	44.5	43.5	45	45	39.5	45
$\bar{x}$		43	41.6	43	42.6	41.5	43.6
s		2.8	1.2	3.2	2.6	2.1	1.5
$s\bar{x}$		1.3	0.5	1.4	1.2	0.9	0.6
pH	1. P.	7.38	7.40	7.36	7.38	7.39	7.38
	2. C.	7.43	7.42	7.45	7.41	7.40	7.40
	3. P.	7.39	7.40	7.41	7.41	7.39	7.40
	4. M.	7.38	7.39	7.38	7.39	7.39	7.39
	5. H.	7.39	7.39	7.39	7.40	7.43	7.39
$\bar{x}$		7.39	7.40	7.40	7.39	7.40	7.39

Summary

Our investigations have furnished proof that, when given in a single intravenous dose of 25 or 50 mg., Ludiomil exerts no negative influence on respiration either in healthy subjects or in patients with respiratory insufficiency. In particular, the results obtained virtually exclude any possibility of the drug's depressing respiratory function.

Table 5. Arterial blood gases and pH in five patients with obstructive diseases of the airways before and after intravenous administration of 25 mg. Ludiomil.

	Patients	At rest		Following 25 mg. Ludiomil i.v.			
		After 30 min.	After 60 min.	After 30 min.	After 60 min.	After 90 min.	After 120 min.
pO_2 (mm. Hg)	1. R.	70	66	73	70	72	68
	2. W.	58	75	58	58	57	58
	3. H.	64	66	64	61	59	59
	4. N.	66	66	68	72	68	68
	5. K.	62	62	58	60	62	62
$\bar{x}$		64.0	67.0	64.2	64.2	63.6	63.0
s		4.47	4.79	6.49	6.34	6.26	4.79
$s\bar{x}$		2.00	2.14	2.91	2.84	2.80	2.14
pCO_2 (mm. Hg)	1. R.	47	46	45	41	46	47.5
	2. W.	35	38	33	35.5	32	33
	3. H.	30.5	33	35.5	36.5	36.5	32.5
	4. N.	43	44	44	45	46	45.5
	5. K.	46.5	48	44	43.5	45	45
$\bar{x}$		40.4	41.8	40.3	40.3	41.1	40.7
s		7.32	6.18	5.60	4.19	6.46	7.31
$s\bar{x}$		3.28	2.77	2.51	1.87	2.89	3.27
pH	1. R.	7.43	7.43	7.43	7.45	7.42	7.42
	2. W.	7.42	7.42	7.42	7.41	7.43	7.42
	3. H.	7.43	7.42	7.43	7.42	7.42	7.43
	4. N.	7.43	7.42	7.42	7.43	7.42	7.43
	5. K.	7.39	7.40	7.43	7.45	7.43	7.43
$\bar{x}$		7.42	7.42	7.43	7.43	7.42	7.43

References

1 ASTRUP, P., JØRGENSEN, K., ANDERSEN, O.S., ENGEL, K.: The acid-base metabolism. Lancet i, 1035 (1960)
2 GEISLER, L., HERBERG, D., CEGLA, U., UTZ, G.: Untersuchungen über die CO_2-sensible zentrale Atmungsregulation an Lungengesunden und bei verschiedenen Krankheitsbildern. Schweiz. med. Wschr. 99, 144 (1969)

3 GEISLER, L., ROST, H.-D.: Studies on the influence of Tacitin on respiration in man. Anxiety and tension—new therapeutic aspects, Int. Symp., St. Moritz 1970, p. 57

4 GEISLER, L., ROST, H.-D.: Untersuchungen am Menschen über den Einfluss des neuen Psychopharmakons 1-[(Methylamino)methyl]-dibenzo-[b,e]bicyclo[2.2. 2]octadien-hydrochlorid auf die CO_2-sensible zentrale Atemregulation. Arzneimittel-Forsch. *20*, 957 (1970)

5 GEISLER, L., ROST, H.-D.: Hyperkapnie – Pathophysiologie, Klinik und Therapie der CO_2-Retention (Thieme, Stuttgart; printing)

6 HERBERG, D., GEISLER, L., BOHR, W., UTZ, G.: Untersuchungen am Menschen über den Einfluss verschiedener Pharmaka auf die CO_2-sensible zentrale Atmungsregulation mittels CO_2-Antwortkurven. Pharmacol. clin. *1*, 54 (1968)

7 JULICH, H.: Die Bedeutung des Sauerstoffrückatmungsversuches für die Beurteilung atemwirksamer Arzneimittel. Med. Klin. *58*, 337 (1963)

8 JULICH, H.: Die Veränderung der Erregbarkeit des Atemzentrums durch erregbarkeitssenkende Arzneimittel, mit einem Beitrag zur Methodik der Erregbarkeitsbestimmung. Z. ges. exp. Med. *117*, 539 (1963)

9 JULICH, H.: Die Sensibilitätsprüfung des Atemzentrums. Ärztl. Forsch. *19*, 352 (1965)

10 LOESCHKE, H.H., KATSAROS, B., LERCHE, D.: Differenzierung der Wirkungen von CO_2-Druck und Wasserstoffionenkonzentration im Blut auf die Atmung beim Menschen. Pflügers Arch. ges. Physiol. *270*, 461 (1960)

11 LOESCHKE, H.H., SWEEL, A., KOUGH, R.H., LAMBERTSEN, C.J.: The effect of morphine and of meperidine (Dolantin, Demerol) upon the respiratory response of normal men to low concentrations of inspired carbon dioxide. J. Pharmacol. exp. Ther. *108*, 376 (1953)

12 ULMER, W.T., REICHEL, G., NOLTE, D.: Die Lungenfunktion (Thieme, Stuttgart 1970)

13 ULMER, W.T., REIF, E., WELLER, W.: Die obstruktiven Atemwegserkrankungen (Thieme, Stuttgart 1966)

14 ULMER, W.T., THEWS, G., REICHEL, G.: Klinische Anwendbarkeit einer Mikroanalysenmethode zur Bestimmung des Sauerstoff- und Kohlensäuredruckes im arteriellen Blut aus hyperämisierten Capillaren. Verh. dtsch. Ges. inn. Med. *69*, 670 (1963)

15 WIENER, K.: Ergebnisse einer klinischen Prüfung von Doxepin bei Asthma bronchiale. Med. Welt (Stuttg.) *22*, 1343 (1971)

Discussion

W. PÖLDINGER: What effect do tricyclic antidepressants have on respiration when given in doses equivalent to those of Ludiomil?

R. KUHN: With regard to the treatment of depression in particular, studies on the effect exerted by drugs on respiration are also of considerable clinical importance, not only because respiration may be objectively impaired in depressive patients but also especially because of the unpleasant subjective sensations often experienced by such patients. These subjective respiratory symptoms are known to respond quite well to conventional antidepressants, and they no doubt also respond to Ludiomil. But I should like to ask one question: in clinical practice we used to differentiate very carefully between the expiratory and inspiratory type of respiration, and—as regards the use of hypnotics, for example—we used to adapt our therapeutic approach accordingly. Some hypnotics tend to promote an inspiratory type of respiration, and others an expiratory type. I have noticed that appreciably better responses can be elicited if this factor is borne in mind. It would interest me to know, Dr. GEISLER, whether you also take clinical observations of this kind into account?

E. HEIM: From psychosomatic studies we know that a patient's emotional state has a marked influence on his respiratory function. In cases of depressed mood, for example, the respiration rate may be increased, but the respiratory minute volume is reduced because the amplitude flattens off. This has been demonstrated by DUDLEY in blood-gas analyses, and we ourselves have confirmed his findings in our studies on respiration during speech. I should like to ask you, Dr. GEISLER, whether you think that an improvement in the mood of depressive patients would be likely to lead to a corresponding improvement in respiratory function.

L. GEISLER: First of all, let me take Dr. PÖLDINGER's question about the effect of other antidepressants on respiration. I'm afraid I have no data on this subject, as we have not carried out any investigations of our own. Although we have tested a very large number of psycho-active drugs with regard to their effect on respiration, these drugs have not included any other antidepressants. Moreover, as far as I am aware, no systematic studies of this nature have been published in the literature.

As for Dr. KUHN's comment, I certainly agree that attention should be paid to the type of respiration and to the clinical phenomenology, and we, too, bear these factors in mind. However, I believe that such great advances have now been made in the study of pulmonary function that, in the interests of accuracy, respiratory status should no longer be assessed merely on the basis of clinical observations, but that recourse should be had to the data furnished, for example, by whole-body plethysmography, spirometry, and analysis of the blood gases.

As to whether the respiration of depressive patients can be improved by brightening their mood, I cannot venture an opinion here, because we have investigated only non-depressive subjects. I can imagine, though, that a change in mood might well account for the effects observed by Dr. HEIM in depressive patients.

The effect of maprotiline (Ludiomil) on the waking state and on sleep patterns in normal subjects and in patients suffering from depression

by U.J. Jovanović*, E. Brocker*, V. Dürrigl**, F. Hajnšek***, D. Kirst*, V. Rogina**, J. Rouik*, V. Stojanović**, and B. Tan-Eli*

Following the completion of studies designed to shed light on the effect exerted by Ludiomil® [CIBA 34,276-Ba; 1-(3-methylaminopropyl)-dibenzo[b,e]bicyclo[2.2.2]octadiene; maprotiline] on the cortical electro-encephalogram in normal subjects (Jovanović and Tan-Eli[11]), we decided to continue our investigations on a broader front.

Test procedure

The findings reported in the present paper relate to 80 adults of both sexes whose ages ranged from 20 to 48 years. Sixty of them were normal subjects aged between 20 and 45 years, while the remaining 20 were men and women aged between 21 and 48 years suffering from depression.
The 80 subjects were divided into three groups. The preparation under study and, in two of the three groups, a comparison substance were invariably administered by mouth.

Group I comprised 50 normal subjects of both sexes aged between 20 and 45 years. In each of them an E.E.G. (over the frontal, parietal, occipital, and temporal regions) was recorded in the waking state on three separate occasions— prior to the administration of maprotiline, following a single dose of 50 mg., and following two days of treatment with a dose of 50 mg. three times daily (i.e. 300 mg. altogether). On each occasion only tracings obtained after the first 10 minutes of the 40-minute recording period were evaluated. The method of evaluation employed was that of Jovanović (cf. Dürrigl et al.[1]; Hajnšek et al.[2]; Jovanović[3-7]; Jovanović et al.[8-10]; Jovanović and Tan-Eli[11]), the parameters examined being the *wave counts*, *wave frequencies*, and *wave amplitudes*. Certain quotients of the wave counts were also calculated. The data were subjected to statistical analysis in the Computer Centre of the University of Würzburg.

Group II was made up of 10 normal subjects aged between 20 and 34 years, whose sleep patterns were studied by reference to polygraphic recordings made continuously throughout the night (for altogether 20 nights per subject). The polygraphic record included the following data: electro-encephalogram, electro-oculogram, electromyogram, electrocardiogram, respirogram, electrodermato-

* Universitäts-Nervenklinik und Poliklinik, Würzburg, Germany.
** Psychiatrisches Krankenhaus "Vrapče", Zagreb, Jugoslavia.
*** Neuro-Psychiatrische Klinik der Universität, Zagreb, Jugoslavia.

gram, phallogram, and response to arousal stimuli. Tape-recordings of dream content, as well as the results of direct observation and answers to questionnaires, were also analysed.

In this group of subjects, as well as in Group III, the effect of maprotiline was compared with that of imipramine, the procedure adopted being that of a double-blind, cross-over trial. In Group II, the active substances were administered in a dose of 50 mg. three times daily for two periods of five days each, and placebo was given for three days before and two days after each period; an interval of 10 days was allowed to elapse before the subjects crossed over from one side of the trial to the other (Table 1). Half the subjects received maprotiline first and then imipramine, and the other half imipramine first and then maprotiline. A randomisation table was used to allocate the subjects to the two subgroups.

Group III comprised the 20 patients suffering from depression, 10 of whom received maprotiline first and the other 10 imipramine first. The patients were allocated to the two sub-groups at random. The first side of the trial lasted 10 days, the patients being given placebo for the first three days, active substance for the next five, and placebo again for the last two (cf. Table 1). In the second side of the trial—following a treatment-free interval of 10 days—placebo was not employed. During this 10-day period of medication with the active substances only, the sleep patterns of each patient were again polygraphically recorded for five nights; clinical examinations were then performed for a further five days. In the depressive patients a reduced programme of tests was carried out (E.E.G., E.O.G., E.M.G., E.C.G., and direct observations), because we were not allowed to wake the patients while they were sleeping. On the other hand, the results of clinical examinations and the answers to special questionnaires were also taken into account in the assessment of these cases (cf. HAJNŠEK et al.[2]; JOVANOVIĆ[6]). The polygraphic records obtained in this group thus covered 300 man-nights. *NB 5 days is too short a period to observe the drug effect in its therapeutic phase.*

The sum total of man-nights studied in Groups II and III was therefore 500, yielding no fewer than 250,000 metres of polygraphic sleep curves weighing 3,500 kg.!

The visual evaluation of this material was extremely time-consuming. It took 10 working days to evaluate one sleep curve and therefore 5,000 working days to evaluate all 500 records. The parameters considered were as follows: 1. Counts, frequency, and amplitude of the E.E.G. waves in all stages of sleep, as described by LOOMIS et al. (cf. JOVANOVIĆ[5]); 2. Rapid and slow eye movements (upwards, downwards, to the right, to the left, predominantly upwards, predominantly downwards, predominantly to the right, predominantly to the left); 3. Motor activity during sleep—i.e. turning in bed with or without waking up, change of position in bed without turning over and with or without waking up, body movements involving no change in position in bed, coarse limb movements (left arm or leg, right arm or leg, predominantly left arm or leg, predominantly right arm or leg, both arms or legs to the same extent), fine movements and

181

Table 1. Plan of trial and dosage used.

Group		No. of subjects	Dose in mg	Days 1	2	3	4	5	6	7	8	9	10	11	12	13	14	15	16	17	18	19	20	21	22	23	24	25	26	27	28	29	30
II	Normal subjects	5	3×50	P	P	P	X	X	X	X	X	P	P	I	—	—	—	—	—	—	—	—	P	P	P	P	Y	Y	Y	Y	P	P	P
		5	3×50	P	P	P	Y	Y	Y	Y	Y	P	P	I	—	—	—	—	—	—	—	—	P	P	P	P	X	X	X	X	P	P	P
III	Depressive patients	10	3×50	P	P	P	X	X	X	X	X	P	P	I	—	—	—	—	—	—	—	—	Y	Y	Y	Y	Y	Y	Y	Y	Y	Y	Y
		10	3×50	P	P	P	Y	Y	Y	Y	Y	P	P	I	—	—	—	—	—	—	—	—	X	X	X	X	X	X	X	X	X	X	X

P = placebo; X = maprotiline; Y = imipramine; I = interval (no treatment given)
Note: on Days 3 and 23 of the trial the normal subjects received placebo in the morning and at midday, but active substance in the evening. In the case of the depressive patients, this procedure was adopted only on Day 3.

twitching of the limbs (with or without differences between left and right arm or leg, as for coarse limb movements); 4. Heart rate; 5. Respiration rate; 6. Bio-electrical activity of the skin (one-peaked, two-peaked, positive and negative skin potentials); 7. Erections (weak, moderately marked, and marked); 8. Duration of acoustic arousal stimuli (successful, unsuccessful); 9. Dream content (transcribed from tape-recordings and processed by a special system); 10. Assessment of subjective status before, during, and after administration of the preparations; 11. Evaluation of completed questionnaires on the test subjects' mood before and after sleep. The results will be reported in full elsewhere.

For the purposes of the present paper only a fairly small proportion of the data has been processed—i.e. the data relating to *depth of sleep, latency times (time taken to fall asleep and time elapsing before onset of deep sleep), number of waking episodes during the night, total duration of waking episodes, and sleep periodicity.* Thanks to the design of the trial it was possible to make various within-patient and between-patient comparisons. In addition, the findings obtained in depressive patients were compared with those recorded in normal subjects.

E.E.G. tracings recorded in normal subjects in the waking state

In response to both single doses of 50 mg. maprotiline and total doses of 300 mg., the E.E.G. revealed a rise in the alpha-wave counts, a reduction in alpha-wave frequency, and an increase in alpha-wave amplitude (Figure 1). All these findings indicate that oral treatment with the drug exerts a tranquillising

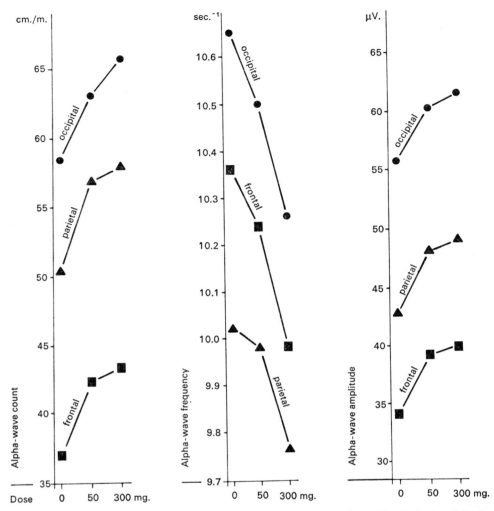

Fig. 1. Changes observed in alpha-wave count, frequency, and amplitude in the E.E.G. of normal subjects following administration of maprotiline in a single dose of 50 mg. and in repeated doses of 50 mg. three times daily for two days (= 300 mg.).

effect, as previously reported by us (JOVANOVIĆ and TAN-ELI[11]). Compared with the activity of an analeptic agent (JOVANOVIĆ et al.[10]), or of a tranquilliser (JOVANOVIĆ et al.[9]), the effect of maprotiline was to produce psychomotor relaxation. Examination of the test subjects' past history confirmed these E.E.G. findings. Slight drowsiness was observed in only six of the 50 test subjects 30–60 minutes after they had taken the first dose of 50 mg.; one subject fell asleep for three hours. All the subjects reported feeling a little tired after this first dose, but the tiredness was already considerably less marked after the second dose, and did not occur at all after the third dose.

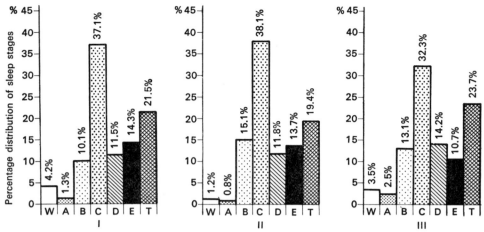

Fig. 2. Effect of maprotiline on depth of sleep in normal subjects; distribution of sleep stages. I = before, II = during, and III = after treatment with maprotiline (I and III = during medication with placebo).

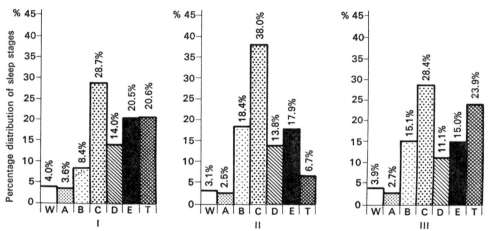

Fig. 3. Effect of imipramine on depth of sleep in normal subjects; distribution of sleep stages. I = before, II = during, and III = after treatment with imipramine (I and III = during medication with placebo).

Effects on sleep patterns in normal subjects

Figure 2 illustrates the distribution of the various *stages of sleep*, expressed as percentages of the total duration of sleep*, during treatment with maprotiline. There are several points worth noting here: *Stage W* (total duration of waking episodes) was shortened; so was *Stage A* (stage marked by tiredness and drowsiness), but to a slightly lesser extent. *Stage B* (very light sleep) was appreciably prolonged, and *Stage C* (light sleep) hardly prolonged at all. *Stages D* (moderately deep sleep) and *E* (deep sleep) remained almost unchanged, while the *R.E.M.*

---

* "Total duration of sleep" is defined as the time elapsing between going to bed at night and getting up in the morning.

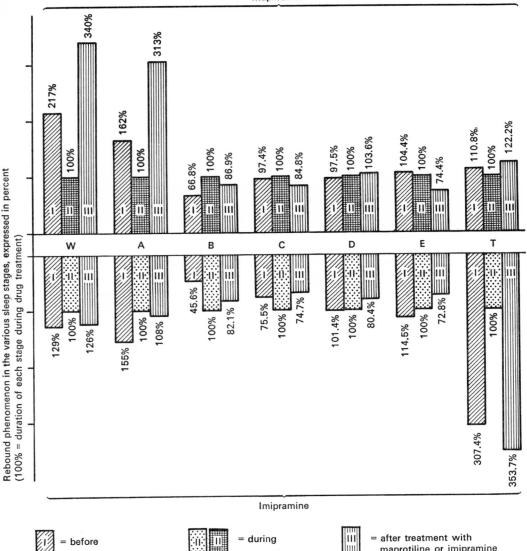

Fig. 4. Rebound phenomenon in normal subjects following withdrawal of treatment with either maprotiline or imipramine. A marked rebound phenomenon was observed in Stages W (waking episodes) and A (tiredness and drowsiness) following the withdrawal of maprotiline, and in Stage T (R.E.M. phases, dreaming sleep) following the withdrawal of imipramine.

phases T (dreaming phases = R.E.M. sleep = paradoxical sleep = desynchronised sleep) were somewhat shortened. Despite this reduction, the duration of the R.E.M. phases was still within normal limits (cf. Jovanović[5]). Following the withdrawal of maprotiline, *Stages W and A* increased again, as did the *R.E.M. phases*, whereas the other stages of sleep either tended to become still further reduced, or increased slightly, or remained unchanged.

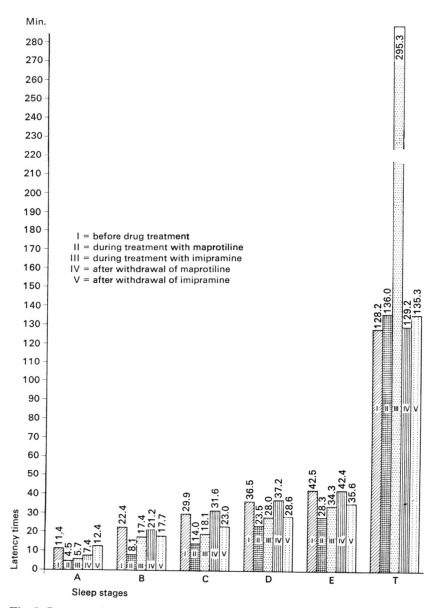

Fig. 5. Latency times (i.e. time elapsing before onset of each stage of sleep) in normal subjects.

The effect of imipramine (Figure 3) differed from that of maprotiline in several respects. During treatment with imipramine *Stages W and A* were less reduced than in response to maprotiline, *Stages B and C* increased to a greater extent, and *Stage E* decreased. Of particular importance is the difference between the two drugs as regards their effect on the length of the *R.E.M. phases*, expressed as a percentage of total duration of sleep. Whereas the reduction in the *R.E.M. phases* was only slight in response to maprotiline, it was very pronounced during treatment with imipramine (compare Figure 3 with Figure 2). The withdrawal of imipramine was followed by an increase in *Stages W, A, and T*, and a decrease in the duration of *Stages B, C, D, and E*.

A comparison of the *rebound* phenomena observed following the withdrawal of treatment (Figure 4) reveals the differences in the effects of the two drugs still more clearly. During treatment with maprotiline *Stage W* decreased considerably, and a marked rebound phenomenon was observed following withdrawal of the drug. In *Stage A*, a similar rebound phenomenon was apparent. The other stages either did not display this phenomenon to the same extent or else they exhibited what might be termed a negative rebound phenomenon—that is to say, stages which had become longer during treatment with the drug increased still further following its withdrawal and those that had become shorter during treatment decreased still further after the drug had been discontinued. The *R.E.M. phases* showed only a slight rebound phenomenon, since their duration had in any case not undergone a very marked reduction in response to maprotiline. Imipramine yielded different findings. Here, no great change occurred in *Stages W and A*, but a clear-cut rebound phenomenon was observed in the *R.E.M. phases*—roughly as clear-cut, in fact, as the rebound in *Stages W and A* following the withdrawal of maprotiline. The effects of imipramine on *Stages B, C, and E* were a mirror-image of those produced by maprotiline. *Hence, maprotiline displays thymoleptic and euhypnic properties which appear to be more favourable than those of imipramine.* It should be borne in mind, incidentally, that a thymoleptic effect is not produced by the same mechanism as a euhypnic effect (cf. JOVANOVIĆ[5,7]; JOVANOVIĆ and TAN-ELI[11]).

The influence exerted by the two substances on *time taken to fall asleep* in normal subjects can be seen in Figure 5.

Effects on sleep patterns in depressive patients

The total duration of sleep in depressive patients was roughly the same during and after treatment with maprotiline as it had been before. Imipramine likewise did not cause any change in total duration of sleep. This parameter, however, is of no great value because it does not show whether the patients slept continuously or not. It is therefore more informative to examine the distribution of the various *stages of sleep* (Figure 6). Prior to the administration of maprotiline *Stage W* (total duration of waking episodes) was much longer in the depressive patients than in the normal subjects, amounting in fact to almost two hours. During five days' treatment with maprotiline, the total duration of waking episodes fell from almost two hours to less than one hour. Imipramine, administered in the same dosage, not only did not reduce but even prolonged *Stage W* in the depressive patients. Following the withdrawal of maprotiline, the total duration of waking episodes increased again, but without attaining the figure recorded prior to treatment with the drug. In the depressive patients, *Stage A* was relatively short before treatment and was even a little further reduced by both drugs. *Stage B*, before treatment, was likewise somewhat shorter in the depressive patients than in normal subjects; in response to maprotiline, it in-

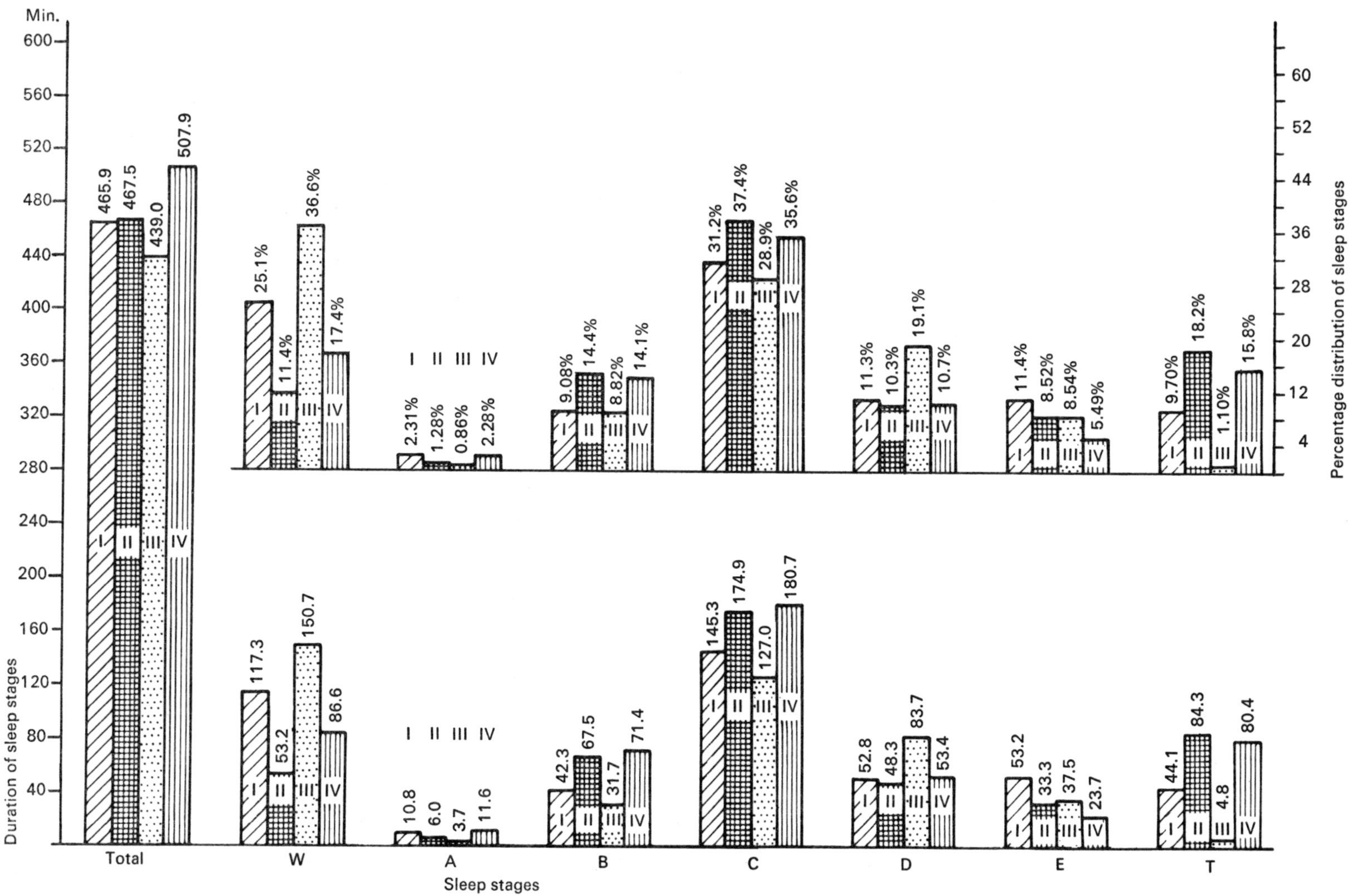

Fig. 6. Distribution of sleep stages in depressive patients before drug treatment (I), during (II) and after (IV) treatment with mapro-

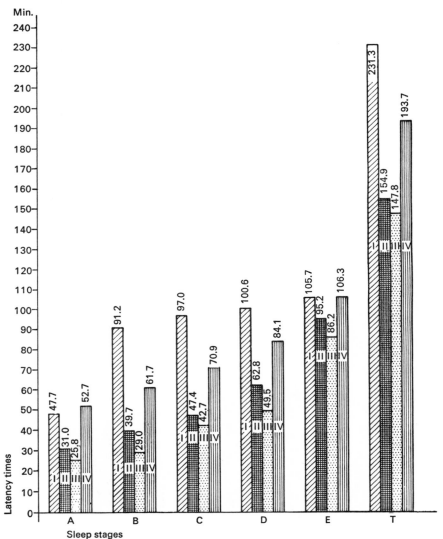

Fig. 7. Latency times (i.e. time taken to fall asleep and time elapsing before onset of each stage of sleep) in depressive patients before drug treatment (I), during (II) and after (IV) treatment with maprotiline, as well as during treatment with imipramine (III).

creased and even attained the same percentage figure as in normal subjects, whereas in response to imipramine it tended to become even further reduced. *Stage C*, before treatment, was just as long in the depressive patients as in the normal subjects. In response to maprotiline its duration increased a little, while in response to imipramine it decreased. The increase recorded during treatment with maprotiline tended to persist even after the drug had been withdrawn. *Stage D* in the depressive patients was at the lower limit of the normal range prior to treatment. Its duration decreased still further, though not to a significant extent, in response to maprotiline, whereas it increased in response to

189

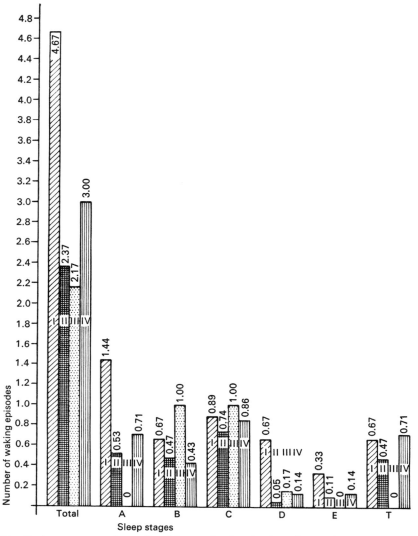

Fig. 8. Average number of waking episodes during the various stages of sleep in the course of one night in depressive patients before drug treatment (I), during (II) and after (IV) treatment with maprotiline, as well as during treatment with imipramine (III).

imipramine. Following the withdrawal of maprotiline the duration of *Stage D* tended to increase. Both drugs reduced the duration of *Stage E*. The *R.E.M. phases* were extremely short in the depressive patients prior to treatment. During medication with maprotiline, their duration returned almost to normal, whereas they became even shorter in response to imipramine. Following the withdrawal of maprotiline the duration of the dreaming phases decreased again, but only to a slight extent.

The latency times—i.e. the time taken to fall asleep and the time elapsing before the onset of deep sleep—were extremely long in the depressive patients prior to treatment

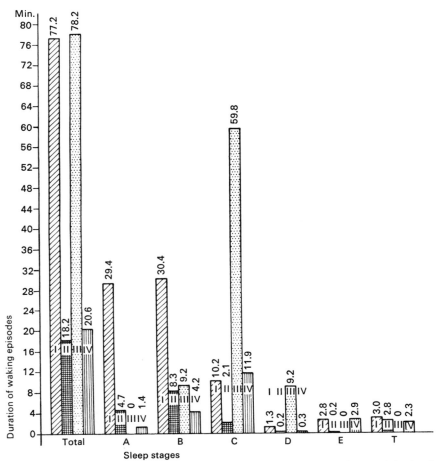

Fig. 9. Average duration of waking episodes in the course of one night in depressive patients (total duration of wakefulness and duration of waking episodes in each stage of sleep) before drug treatment (I), during (II) and after (IV) treatment with maprotiline, as well as during treatment with imipramine (III).

(Figure 7). Both drugs exerted a positive influence on these latency times, the effect of maprotiline being somewhat less marked than that of imipramine. Following the withdrawal of maprotiline the latency times increased again, but without, as a rule, becoming as long as before treatment.

The number of waking episodes (Figure 8) during the night was much higher among the depressive patients than among normal subjects of the same age. During treatment with both drugs, the number of waking episodes decreased. The effect of maprotiline in this respect was more marked than that of imipramine in *Stages B, C, and D,* and less marked in the other stages. Following the withdrawal of maprotiline the total number of waking episodes increased again in the depressive patients, but did not reach the figure recorded prior to treatment.

Of particular interest are the findings relating to the *duration of the waking episodes* (Figure 9). When not receiving any treatment, the depressive patients

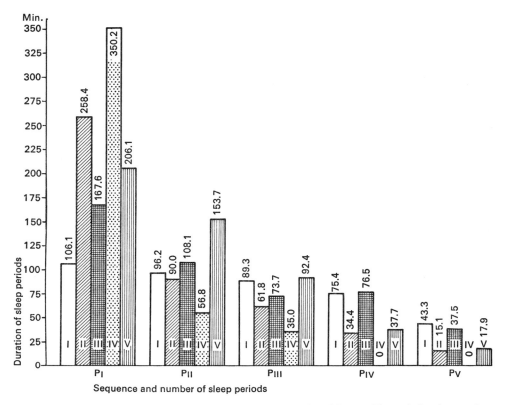

Fig. 10. Duration of sleep periods (P_{I-V}) in normal subjects (I) and in depressive patients not receiving drug treatment (II), and changes in their duration during (III) and after (V) treatment with maprotiline, as well as during treatment with imipramine (IV). During five days of treatment with maprotiline, sleep disturbances occurring after midnight and towards morning were eliminated or improved, so that the periods of sleep were more equally distributed throughout the night. During five days of treatment with imipramine, on the other hand, the periods of sleep were concentrated in the first half of the night.

stayed awake for long periods during the night (cf. also JOVANOVIĆ et al.[8])—for much longer, in fact, than normal subjects. Maprotiline reduced both the total duration of waking episodes and the duration of waking episodes in each of the various stages. Imipramine, on the other hand, may even prolong wakefulness during the night, as can be seen from the figures for the total duration of waking episodes and for the duration of waking episodes in *Stage C*. Only in *Stages A, E, and T* was imipramine more effective than maprotiline in reducing the duration of waking episodes.

It is a well-known fact that, in patients suffering from depression, sleep is particularly likely to be disturbed after midnight (cf. JOVANOVIĆ[7]; JOVANOVIĆ et al.[8]) and towards morning. In the present study, too, this phenomenon became clearly apparent when we subjected the duration of the various *periods of sleep* (P) to statistical analysis. Here, once again, the effect of the two substances differed in certain respects (Figure 10). Prior to treatment, *Sleep period I (P_I)* was extremely long in the depressive patients. During medication with maprotiline, it was considerably reduced. *Sleep period II (P$_{II}$)*, before treatment, was somewhat shorter in depressives than in normal subjects. During treatment with maprotiline it became longer. *Sleep period III (P$_{III}$)* likewise increased in response to maprotiline—from 61.778 to 73.687 minutes (s $\pm$ 38.638). *Sleep period IV (P$_{IV}$)*, which was very short prior to treatment, also increased during medication with maprotiline. *Sleep period V (P$_V$)* increased from 15.111 to 37.474 minutes during treatment with maprotiline, but did not attain the duration observed in normal subjects. Depressive patients, however, are apt to wake up earlier in the morning than normal subjects, with the result that this last sleep period in the morning varies greatly in length. The effect of imipramine differed from that of maprotiline in all sleep periods. *Our findings show that in the depressive patients sleep periodicity returned to normal—or tended to do so—during five days of treatment with maprotiline; this was not yet the case with imipramine, administered under the same conditions.*

Conclusions

1. In *normal subjects* maprotiline, administered orally in a dose of 50 mg., produced an increase in the alpha-wave count in the cortical E.E.G., a decrease in alpha-wave frequency, and an increase in alpha-wave amplitude. These electro-encephalographic findings were consistent with the feeling of psychomotor relaxation reported by the subjects themselves and with the results of previous trials. The first dose of 50 mg. gave rise to slight tiredness, but this effect was less apparent after the second dose. Following two days of treatment with the drug in a dose of 50 mg. three times daily, the alpha-wave counts in the cortical E.E.G., as well as the alpha-wave amplitude, showed a further, but less steep increase, and the alpha-wave frequency a further, but less marked reduction. These findings suggest that the brain was beginning to adapt itself to the drug. According to the subjects themselves, tiredness did not recur, but the feeling of psychomotor relaxation and equanimity persisted. On the first day, 12 % of the normal subjects felt drowsy, and one person fell asleep. Maprotiline was not compared with imipramine in this group.

2. In *normal* young and middle-aged adults, maprotiline reduced the total duration of waking episodes during the night, reduced the duration of *Stage A*, increased the duration of *Stage B*, caused no appreciable changes in the duration of *Stages C, D, and E*, and slightly reduced the length of the *R.E.M. phases*. Imipramine, on the other hand, reduced the length of the *R.E.M. phases* to a much greater extent, but did not reduce the total duration of waking episodes as much as maprotiline. *Both drugs exert a thymoleptic and euhypnic effect, but that of maprotiline is much more pronounced and more beneficial.*

3. In *patients suffering from depression*, neither of the two drugs produced any change in the total duration of sleep. The total duration of waking episodes during the night was reduced by maprotiline and increased by imipramine. In depressive patients, too, both drugs slightly reduced the duration of deep sleep. The duration of the *R.E.M. phases* was restored almost to normal by maprotiline, but reduced by imipramine.

4. Both drugs reduced the time taken to fall asleep—an effect of positive value in the case of *depressive patients*. This effect was more pronounced with imipramine than with maprotiline.

5. Both drugs reduced the number of waking episodes in most stages of sleep. Imipramine was generally more effective than maprotiline in this respect, but did lead to an increase in the number of waking episodes in *Stages B and C*.

6. The duration of waking episodes was considerably reduced by maprotiline, but not by imipramine. In *Stages C and D* the duration of waking episodes even increased in response to imipramine.

7. An essential difference between maprotiline and imipramine is to be found in their effect on sleep periodicity in *depressive patients*. Maprotiline lengthened the short periods of sleep after midnight and shortened the long periods immediately after the onset of sleep, with the result that sleep periodicity as a whole became similar, or largely similar, to that of normal subjects. *Hence, sleep disturbances occurring after midnight and towards morning in the depressive patients were improved or eliminated—a finding of considerable clinical importance.* In response to imipramine the depressive patients slept mainly during the first few hours, and even after five days of treatment with the drug their sleep periodicity had still not returned to normal.

In the light of all our findings, maprotiline compares favourably with known thymoleptic agents such as imipramine.

References

1 DÜRRIGL, V., ROGINA, V., STOJANOVIĆ, V., HAJNŠEK, F., GUBAREV, N., JOVANO-VIĆ, U.J.: Sleep depth of depressed patients under the influence of antidepressive drugs—A study of two substances. The nature of sleep, Int. Symp., Würzburg 1971 (Fischer, Stuttgart; printing)

2 HAJNŠEK, F., DOGAN, S., GUBAREV, N., DÜRRIGL, V., STOJANOVIĆ, V., JOVANO-VIĆ, U.J.: Some characteristics of sleep in depressed patients—Polygraphic studies, loc. cit.[1]

3 JOVANOVIĆ, U.J.: Das Elektroenzephalogramm des Menschen unter Wirkung von 2-Diäthylamino-5-Phenyl-Oxazolinon-(4). Ärztl. Forsch. *19*, 640 (1965)

4 JOVANOVIĆ, U.J.: Der normale, abnorme und pathologische Schlaf. Polygraphische Registrierungen. Verh. dtsch. Ges. inn. Med. *71*, 807 (1965)

5 JOVANOVIĆ, U.J.: Normal sleep in man (Hippokrates, Stuttgart 1971)

6 JOVANOVIĆ, U.J.: Problems of the visual evaluation of sleep curves, loc. cit.[1]

7 JOVANOVIĆ, U.J.: Disturbed sleep in man (1971; in preparation)

8 JOVANOVIĆ, U.J., DOGAN, S., DÜRRIGL, V., GUBAREV, N., HAJNŠEK, F., STOJANO-VIĆ, V., SCHELLER, H., SCHRAPPE, O.: Changes of sleep patterns in manic-depressive patients depending on the clinical symptoms, loc. cit.[1]

9 JOVANOVIĆ, U.J., DÜRRIGL, V., ROGINA, V.: Studies on the bio-electrical activity of the brain and results of psychological tests following the ingestion of Tacitin and alcohol. Relaxation therapy for psychosomatic disorders, Int. Symp., St. Moritz 1971, p. 146

10 JOVANOVIĆ, U.J., STOJANOVIĆ, V., ROGINA, V., DÜRRIGL, V.: Elektroencephalographische und Test-psychologische Untersuchungen mit Tradon. Zugleich ein Beitrag zur Auswertung des EEG (1971; in preparation)

11 JOVANOVIĆ, U.J., TAN-ELI, B.: The effect of compound CIBA 34,276-Ba on the cortical encephalogram of healthy people. Europ. Neurol. *4*, 39 (1970)

Clinical experiences with a new antidepressant

by R. Kuhn*

1. General aspects of depression and its treatment

The treatment of those disorders which are nowadays normally referred to as "depressive conditions" still poses numerous riddles that have yet to be solved. The reasons for this lie partly in the manner in which we are accustomed to consider and investigate these depressive conditions, and also partly in the extremely complex nature of the whole question as such. Medico-historical studies reveal that some of the problems and difficulties still encountered in this connection can even be traced back to classical antiquity. Down through the years they have given rise to many different theories, but now—thanks to the new possibilities opened up by drug therapy in the management of depressive disorders—they have come to assume increasing practical significance.

Since man has a somewhat naïve propensity to seek causes for everything that happens in and around him, it is hardly surprising that he has also attempted to do the same in the case of abnormal experiences and behavioural patterns. Consequently, it has become customary to make a distinction between those forms of depressive illness—known as *reactive*, neurotic, or symptomatic depression—which can be ascribed to causes that are either genuine or merely putative, and those so-called *endogenous* forms for which there is no apparent cause. Having drawn such a distinction, we tend to assume that we have achieved something positive, which absolves us from the onus of determining *what a depressive illness really is*. Research on the hereditary factors involved in depressive disorders and on the course which such disorders may take in an individual patient over a period of decades, coupled with meticulous analysis of the psychopathology of depressive conditions, has shown, however, that reactive, neurotic, symptomatic, and endogenous forms of depression are in fact very closely related. This suggests an underlying bio-organic anomaly which may manifest itself with or without the intervention of recognisable external or internal influences, and which, depending on the circumstances, may perhaps sometimes remain concealed.

If, as all the evidence seems to indicate, this is indeed the case, then these aspects must be taken into consideration not only when carrying out research on such illnesses, but also when studying their response to drug therapy. Thus, in contrast to the usual practice, which is to concentrate primarily on identifying those characteristics that distinguish one sub-group from another, the first task to be tackled is that of pinpointing the *underlying disorder common to all types of depressive disease*. In this way, by proceeding inductively, it is possible to establish the

---

* Kantonale Psychiatrische Klinik, Münsterlingen, Switzerland.

indication for antidepressive medication, which should be arrived at on the basis of the following features: evidence of an inherited susceptibility to depressive disorders, diurnal fluctuations in the severity of the condition (marked by aggravation of the symptoms in the morning), lassitude, difficulty and sluggishness in thinking, deciding, and acting, feelings of physical and mental constriction and oppression, and inability to take an interest in or enjoy life. On the other hand, the patient's age, the aetiology of the condition, the manner in which it was triggered off, its psychic symptomatology, its degree of severity, and whether it runs a phasic or a chronic course are all factors which have only a secondary bearing on the decision as to the indication for drug therapy and, as such, can often be largely ignored.

A strict distinction must be drawn between the decision to *initiate* medicinal treatment and the decision regarding the *form which the treatment should take*. It is in this latter connection that the *aetiology*, the *individual picture* presented by the disease, and the patient's *mode of reaction* to the drugs in question are of decisive importance. The *choice of drug* and its possible *combination* with other agents, the *method of administration*, the *dosage* and its *fractionation*, the *duration of treatment* and the *modifications* to be made in it during the course of the illness, and especially also the problem of *whether to combine pharmacotherapy with psychotherapy* and, if so, with what type of psychotherapy, are factors which all have to be considered together and which necessitate constant attention to numerous biological and psychological aspects of the pathological process in general, as well as to the requirements of the individual sufferer in particular.

An *optimum response to treatment* presupposes fulfilment of the conditions outlined above and, hence, a requisite measure of knowledge, experience, and practical skill on the part of the psychiatrist treating the case, who, in turn, must also be able to count on a certain degree of cooperation from the patient and from the members of his family or—in the case of an hospitalised individual—from those with whom he comes into contact in the hospital. An interplay of various related factors is thus involved, which the practising psychiatrist always has to bear in mind in the course of his work. To aid him in his task, he must rely upon his psychiatric training and his knowledge of psychopathology, upon regular interpretation of what his patients tell him, and upon the conclusions he can draw from their response to treatment. A great deal of information which would prove of value to him, however, has not yet found its way into the medical literature that is generally available, let alone into the text-books. Consequently, these documentary sources often convey an impression of diseases, indications, and methods of treatment which is already out of date. The old and familiar "clinical pictures" do not necessarily provide reliable indications for the use of new therapeutic methods. If new methods of treatment are to be discovered, it is therefore essential that conventional concepts of pathology should be revised; and if the maximum benefit is to be derived from such new discoveries, doctors must be willing to accept them and act upon them. This, of course, is a demand which it is difficult to meet. Once they have adopted a given diagnostic and therapeutic schedule, adherence to it becomes for many doctors an existen-

tial imperative upon which the stability and security of their professional—and perhaps even their personal—life depends! But psychiatry was never a dogmatic science, and is certainly not one today. It should constantly strive to remain dynamic and flexible: while retaining all that has stood the test of time, it must also be ready to accept what is new and good, to learn from day-to-day contacts with patients, and to take due note of any changes affecting the psychiatric field.

2. A few general principles applicable to clinical research on psychopharmaceuticals

In a clinical context, the term *"psychopharmaceutical"* is understood to mean a drug which acts primarily on psychic functions. In the light of such knowledge as is currently available, drugs of this type can be divided into the following three groups on the basis of their modes of action:

Group I   Substances displaying only *indirect* psychopharmacological activity:
  a) Sedative, hypnotic, narcotic, or anxiolytic substances.
  b) Activating, euphoriant, and stimulant substances.
  c) Psychotoxic substances which interfere with psychic functions and cause a radical alteration in the relationship between ego and environment.
Group II Relatively non-specific neuroleptic substances.
Group III a) Relatively specific antidepressant-thymoleptic substances.
  b) Substances which are effective in manic states and capable of influencing the clinical course of depressive and manic-depressive psychoses.

Most of the psychopharmaceuticals now either in use or undergoing clinical trials display effects appertaining to the first two groups, but not to the third group, although the substances in this latter group exhibit properties which to some extent also overlap into Groups I and II.

The more *general* the type of activity exerted by a drug, the easier it becomes to ascertain its pharmacological and clinical effects and to administer treatment with it. But the aim should be to provide as *specific* as possible a form of treatment for certain clearly delineated conditions and processes; this, however, makes the pharmacological and clinical characterisation of a psycho-active drug far more difficult. One and the same substance may often possess various properties which differ in their intensity and interact differently with one another depending on factors such as size and fractionation of dosage, mode of administration, and individual situation of the patient.

3. Clinical trials with a new antidepressant: procedure adopted and results obtained

The following prerequisites are essential to the success of *clinical trials* with an antidepressant:

Firstly, a meticulously thorough clinical diagnosis should be established on the basis of the patient's heredity, general case history, and current psychopathological status. Secondly, the effect of the drug under study should be exactly determined by observing the patient's behaviour, performance, and reactions to his environment as elicited by systematic questioning over an adequate period of time, i.e. over a period of at least three months. Observations of less than three months' duration are inevitably so subject to misinterpretation as to be valueless.

The dosage and its fractionation, the mode of administration, and such combination with other drugs as may be resorted to should be individually adapted in the light of the patient's requirements as ascertained by observing the course of the illness and the response to medication. Due attention must also be paid to the effects resulting from attempts at withdrawal of drug therapy, as well as to influences exerted by factors unrelated to the treatment, e.g. biological, environmental, and psychological factors such as situations of conflict or the patient's social and familial circumstances.

Trials carried out on hospitalised and on ambulant patients both have their advantages and disadvantages, as well as their own particular sources of error. Despite all the arguments in favour of trials conducted in a hospital setting, which are in fact indispensable, it must be borne in mind that only by administering treatment on an ambulant basis is it possible to ensure that the patient remains exposed to the stresses and strains of everyday life; and, though this means that many other disturbing and distorting factors have to be reckoned with, it is only from such ambulant trials that a relatively unadulterated picture of a drug's antidepressant activity *per se* emerges.

It is possible, and indeed probable, that a *clinical effect of an antidepressant type* can be achieved in a variety of ways and, depending on the circumstances, also by employing drugs of very different kinds. Of interest in this connection, for instance, is the problem posed by the monamine-oxidase inhibitors, which even today is still far from having been solved. A clinical investigator who has experimented with many different antidepressants, however, gains in the course of time a certain insight into possible correlations between chemical structure and specific antidepressant activity. Despite their highly problematical nature, such correlations have certainly proved of value in the course of trials with CIBA 34,276-Ba (Ludiomil®).

Whether or not a compound displays antidepressant activity can be determined by *carefully observing its effect in individual cases;* this enables one not only to form a general impression of its properties, but also to assess the potency of its action and the extent to which it provokes side effects. Attention must of course also be paid to possible *sources of error.* For example, a sedative effect, an activating and euphoriant effect, or a neuroleptic effect may simulate antidepressant activity. Alternatively, the clinical investigator may also be misled in his assessment of a drug by the spontaneous course which the illness takes, by biological factors such as menstruation, or by the intervention of some psychological or situational influence. Another possible source of error may be the patient's failure to take the drug as instructed.

When studied in the manner outlined above, *34,276-Ba was found to be a good specific antidepressant* endowed with mild, but clearly identifiable sedative-hypnotic and stimulating properties. Both its antidepressant effects and its side effects may differ from patient to patient. When administered to patients in whom previous types of antidepressant therapy had proved inadequate, 34,276-Ba yielded a better response in certain cases, whereas occasionally imipramine produced better results. When employed in individually adapted dosages ranging from 30 to 200 mg. daily, 34,276-Ba is capable of relieving depressive mood disorders characterised by loss of vitality, as well as of combating their repercussions on higher psychic functions and reactions; in other words, it can eliminate lassitude, feelings of oppression and constriction, and sluggishness in thinking, deciding, and acting, and it can also restore the patient's ability to take an interest in life and to derive pleasure and emotional satisfaction from it. In this way, the patient recovers his physical, emotional, and intellectual capacities to the full, while at the same time the diurnal fluctuations that are typical of the condition also disappear.

Although cases do occur in which other antidepressants come close to eliciting this ideal type of response, their purely antidepressant effect is usually associated with influences which sometimes serve to reinforce the latter effect but which sometimes also take the form of an undesirable non-specific neuroleptic, sedative, or stimulant action. This is also liable to occur with 34,276-Ba, but tends to be less marked the closer the condition corresponds to the drug's proper indications. It is by no means uncommon for an antidepressant to exert a good initial effect, which then—after a few days or weeks—diminishes and cannot be restored by increasing the dosage; in such cases, as well as in patients showing very severe symptoms, treatment is indicated with a monomethylamino compound such as 34,276-Ba in combination with a dimethylamino compound such as imipramine or clomipramine, since combined therapy of this type produces a more rapid, prolonged, and intensive effect.

Our own assessment of 34,276-Ba is based chiefly upon the results obtained in a series of 320 patients, 83 of whom were treated in hospital and the remaining 237 on an ambulant basis. Also useful in supplementing and rounding off the impression we gained of the drug's pattern of activity were the observations made in a further group of 300 cases in which 34,276-Ba was administered only as supporting therapy in a combined treatment regimen. Studies on this group of patients were already completed early in 1970. As regards the diagnoses and ages of the patients, the latter group was similar in composition to the series of 320 patients, but it constituted a selection of relatively unpromising cases insofar as it largely comprised patients who had shown little or no response to the main drug employed. Moreover, many of the patients in this group received inadequate doses of 34,276-Ba, because at that time we were still gathering initial experience in the drug's use. For this reason, the results from the group of 300 patients have not been included in Tables 1 and 2.

The series of 320 patients, to which these two tables refer, also contained cases treated with combined medication; here, however, 34,276-Ba was used as the main drug. The supporting drugs most frequently resorted to in such combined regimens were Insidon®, Tofranil®, and Anafranil®; occasionally Pertofran® or a major tranquilliser was administered. Of the total of 320 patients, 139 received monotherapy and 181 combined therapy.

Table 1. Results of treatment with 34,276-Ba alone and in combination.

	Very good N	%	Good N	%	Improved N	%	No effect N	%	Total
Phasic depression	37	41.2	39	43.4	12	13.3	2	2.2	90
Manic-depressive psychoses	3	23.1	5	38.5	3	23.1	2	15.4	13
Chronic depression	19	17.1	54	48.7	32	28.8	6	5.4	111
Psychopathic states	1	2.5	13	32.5	15	37.5	11	27.5	40
Enuresis	5	50.0	1	10.0	1	10.0	3	30.0	10
Schizophrenia	1	2.6	14	35.9	20	51.3	4	10.3	39
Organic psychoses	–		5	45.5	5	45.5	1	9.1	11
Miscellaneous	–		2	33.3	2	33.3	2	33.3	6
	66	20.6	133	41.6	90	28.1	31	9.7	320

Table 2. Results of treatment with 34,276-Ba alone.

	Very good N	%	Good N	%	Improved N	%	No effect N	%	Total
Phasic depression	22	52.5	16	38.0	4	9.5	–		42
Manic-depressive psychoses	–		2		–		–		2
Chronic depression	14	23.0	25	41.0	20	32.8	2	3.3	61
Psychopathic states	1	6.7	5	33.3	4	26.7	5	33.3	15
Enuresis	4		–		–		1		5
Schizophrenia	–		1	10.0	6	60.0	3	30.0	10
Organic psychoses	–		–		1		–		1
Miscellaneous	–		2		–		1		3
	41	29.5	51	36.7	35	25.2	12	8.6	139

The results obtained with 34,276-Ba, which were evaluated in accordance with the principles already outlined, are presented in Tables 1 and 2, in which the various diagnostic sub-groups have been listed separately. In patients suffering from predominantly *phasic forms of depression*, the percentage of responses classified as "very good" was as high as 41.2%, and in those cases where 34,276-Ba was given alone it was even higher, i.e. 52.5%. An equally clear picture emerges when the responses assessed as "good" are also included, the percentage of good and very good results being 84.6% for combined treatment and no less than 90.5% for treatment with 34,276-Ba alone. From these findings it is obvious that 34,276-Ba is a potent antidepressant agent.

Only a small number of patients received treatment for *manic-depressive psychoses*. The majority of them were given combined medication—a fact which may be interpreted as indicating that, as already known from experience with imipramine, such patients respond less well than cases of monophasic depressive disease.

In *chronic depression* the percentages of good and very good responses were roughly the same for both combined treatment and monotherapy, i.e. 65.8% and 64%, respectively.

In the patients suffering from *psychopathic depressive conditions*, who were relatively few in number, the treatment proved unsuccessful in about one-third of cases, whereas in phasic depression the failure rate was minimal and in chronic depression it was just over 5% for the whole group of patients and only 3.3% for those receiving monotherapy. Incidentally, it is often difficult to distinguish between psychopathic depressive states and chronic forms of depression.

Particularly deserving of mention are the results obtained in *schizophrenic depression*. Here, 34,276-Ba—given usually in combination with a major tranquilliser—elicited good or very good responses in 38.5% of cases and brought about an improvement in a further 51.3%; failures were observed in only 10.3% of the patients.

Although it was not possible for us to make a direct comparison between 34,276-Ba and imipramine, and although the psychiatric cases which we are now called upon to treat are so radically different from what they were a few years ago that a retrospective comparison would be inadmissible, we should nevertheless like to point out that, purely on the basis of clinical impressions, we believe 34,276-Ba to have a *spectrum of activity somewhat different from that of imipramine*. Its therapeutic action seems to extend further into the field of *schizophrenic depression*, although—like imipramine—it is ineffective in patients suffering from non-depressive forms of schizophrenia. Above all, however, 34,276-Ba is an excellent drug for use in *functional disorders of the digestive apparatus* and is even capable of exerting a beneficial effect in patients with ulcers. In this particular field it has proved to be primarily indicated in the presence of eructation, aerophagy, heart-burn, flatulence, colic, vomiting, and diarrhoea of the type associated with psychic symptoms which frequently assume a depressive and especially chronic-depressive character.

In all conditions in which 34,276-Ba may be indicated, it is important with regard to *differential diagnosis* always to bear in mind the possibility of sideropenia —a disease in which it would seem that the R.B.C. remains normal, or almost normal, in a far higher percentage of cases than is commonly assumed. An antidepressant is unlikely to exert a satisfactory effect until such time as the patient's serum iron levels have been restored to normal. On the other hand, in patients suffering from iron deficiency, treatment with iron may in itself prove sufficient to eliminate a depressive state; often, however, specific antidepressant medication has to be given in addition to iron therapy.

At this point, a few words should be devoted to the problem of *side effects*. Anything that does not directly serve to combat the symptoms of depression and loss of vitality can be regarded as a side effect; alternatively, one can restrict the term "side effect" to those drug-induced manifestations which are actually undesirable. A distinction also has to be drawn between effects which are inherent in the nature of the patient's disease and effects conditioned by individual and constitutional factors. These two types of effect must be further differentiated from those that are attributable to the properties peculiar to the drug itself. In a given case it is admittedly often difficult, and sometimes even impossible, to decide to which category a side effect belongs, particularly since the causes involved, though they may differ fundamentally, nevertheless frequently overlap and interact with one another. So complex is the situation, in fact, that the statistical analysis of side effects becomes an extremely problematical task. When one also bears in mind that many side effects are largely dose-dependent, that they either disappear again after a short while or do not make their appearance until treatment has been in progress for some considerable time, that they often only come to light when the patient is closely and specifically interrogated, and— last but not least—that they may well simply be part and parcel of the symptomatology of the disease itself, it then becomes obvious that attempts at the statistical analysis of side effects not only involve great difficulties but yield data whose exactitude is bound to be somewhat illusory.

Among the side effects of 34,276-Ba that can be predominantly ascribed to the action of the drug itself are undoubtedly a certain degree of *central vertigo* in which the external world as perceived by the patient loses some of its concreteness (particularly when he is descending stairs for example), as well as an *increase in appetite* which often results in marked weight-gains. The drug also exerts *anticholinergic effects*, though these are certainly less frequent and less pronounced than in the case of imipramine and its derivatives. Often a peculiar interplay of *sedative* and *stimulant effects* is observed, the two either alternating with each other or the one assuming predominance over the other. When treatment with 34,276-Ba is initiated with small, gradually increasing doses, however, intolerability is rarely encountered. In younger patients we twice observed *epileptic attacks*. Though *allergic skin reactions* have been seen, they are very rare. *Nosebleed* may also occur. No *cardiotoxic effects* have so far been met with.

In 142 patients the usual *blood tests* were performed during—and in some cases also before—treatment with 34,276-Ba. In many instances the patient's *blood chemistry* was also studied. The findings obtained were compared with those from a largish number of untreated cases, as well as from a group of patients who had received other psycho-active drugs. No deviations from the norm were observed. Nor were any trends apparent which could not have been likewise encountered in any large group of patients undergoing psychopharmacological treatment. Here, once again, however, the situation is somewhat complex inasmuch as certain reactions—such as leucopenia, eosinophilia, or an increase in liver-enzyme activity—are liable to appear in very transitory form; it is possible that brief reactions of this type may have occurred with 34,276-Ba without our so far having detected them.

Discussion

P. PICHOT: In your paper, Dr. KUHN, you divided up cases of depression into the following categories: phasic, manic-depressive, chronic, psychopathic, and schizophrenic. What connection is there between this subdivision and the usual system of classification? Judging from the tables you presented, a large proportion of your patients had chronic depression—their numbers, in fact, exceeded those with phasic depression. Does this "chronic depression" of yours bear some relation to what we in France call "neurotic depression"?

H. HIPPIUS: The cardiotoxic effects of antidepressants have of course been known for some ten years*, but renewed interest has been focused on them in Germany during the past year as a result of several publications. The German Drug Committee has also issued an official warning about the cardiotoxic effects of the tricyclic antidepressants**. Particular attention must be paid to this problem when introducing new antidepressants. You said, Dr. KUHN, that you had not observed any cardiotoxic side effects with Ludiomil. Did you carry out any systematic E.C.G. studies?

M. HAMILTON: Two points, Dr. KUHN. Firstly, you comment on the diurnal fluctuation in severity of condition, and you describe this as a worsening—an aggravation of the symptoms—in the morning. You do not mention the fact that about 20% of the patients seem to have a worsening in the evening; some of my patients—though admittedly very few of them—even insist that they are worse in the middle of the day. Secondly, I very much agree with you in general that the distinctions between the endogenous and reactive depressions are invalid; they are useless. Even more useless, I think, is the differentiation between neurotic and psychotic depression, which in my opinion is meaningless.

J.J. LÓPEZ IBOR: In our long experience with many hundreds of patients we have observed severe cardiotoxic side effects in only one case. This was a patient who had a myocardial infarction after having completed a course of treatment with imipramine. We invariably do an E.C.G. on every patient who comes to our clinic, but we have so far found only slight abnormalities which, so our cardiologists tell us, are of no significance. Thus, we are not so pessimistic on this matter as our German colleagues.
As regards the question of diurnal fluctuations, we, too, have noted that some patients feel worse in the evening; what is more, these patients are more difficult to treat. I don't know, however, whether the percentage is as high in our cases as in Dr. HAMILTON's; I would be inclined to put it at about 11 or 12%.

H. HEIMANN: Both Dr. HAMILTON, in the discussion following Dr. KEBERLE's paper, and Dr. KUHN have pointed out that a great deal depends on the dosage in which antidepressants are given. I myself used to share this view until practical experience convinced me that with all conventional antidepressants you really need very few guide-lines in order to achieve effective results and avoid serious side effects. Having used drugs of this type for many years, I would say that subtle dosage schedules are largely unnecessary in the treatment of depression. In the case of Ludiomil, I think that in practice you can start with a dose of 25 mg. t.i.d., and then raise it quite safely to 50 mg. t.i.d.

P. KIELHOLZ: One conclusion that might perhaps be drawn from Dr. KUHN's paper is that masked depression and, possibly, psychosomatic disorders constitute major

---

* Cf. HIPPIUS, H., MALIN, J.-P.: Veränderungen des Elektrokardiogramms während der Behandlung mit trizyklischen Psychopharmaka. Pharmakopsychiat. Neuro-Psychopharmakol. *1*, 140 (1968)
** EDITORIAL: Zur kardiotoxischen Wirkung trizyklischer Pharmaka. Dtsch. Aerztebl. *68*, 2925 (1971)

indications for Ludiomil. If this were so, then dosage would probably be an important factor.

W. WALCHER: We have found the dosage of 50 mg. three times daily satisfactory in clinical use; the number of cases in which we have used the drug is admittedly small, but only in one patient—a fellow-doctor, incidentally, who was being treated on an ambulant basis—did I reduce the dose because he felt too tired to cope with his work. In a hospital setting, I feel that the suggested dosage of 50 mg. t.i.d. will probably prove satisfactory as a means of achieving a prompt effect. But in general practice this dose is too high for all those patients who have to carry on their daily occupations. These patients, as well as children and elderly subjects, require a lower dosage. However, we have not yet managed to try out this approach, because we did not have low-strength tablets available. I think that in the case of Ludiomil, as in that of other antidepressants, the procedure of choice is to begin with low doses and to increase them gradually.

B. POPKES: We started off by administering 25 mg. Ludiomil four times daily and usually found this dosage sufficient; in rare cases, we had to give 50 mg. three times daily. A gradual build-up proved necessary in a few ambulant patients, because they felt too tired in response to an initial dose of 25 mg. four times daily.

W. GRÜTER: The importance of adapting the dose to the needs of the individual case has been stressed by Dr. KUHN, and Dr. WALCHER has advocated a gradual raising of the dosage. Both these suggestions are admirable, provided the circumstances permit such an approach and provided time is not a major factor. I would point out, however, that the physician is obliged not only to avoid side effects as far as possible, but also to help his patients obtain prompt and effective relief from their symptoms. This can be especially important in cases of severe depression. In such instances, the desire to avoid side effects has to be carefully weighed against the need to elicit a rapid response. My own experience with Ludiomil in 562 patients tends to show that in severe depression a daily dosage of 150 mg. is usually required to produce optimum results. If you begin with the full dose, you get a particularly prompt onset of action and only a slight increase in side effects. Provided you make this clear to the patients beforehand and tell them what the possible side effects are, you find that they almost always tolerate them without complaining. I have therefore tended increasingly to prefer this approach, especially in cases of severe depression, and even in many ambulant patients.

H. HIPPIUS: There are a few points in Dr. KUHN's paper which I did not quite grasp. If I understood you correctly, Dr. KUHN, you don't want to see any clear line of demarcation drawn between endogenous and neurotic depression; I quite agree with you there. But then in your tables you subdivided your cases into phasic depression, manic-depressive psychoses, and chronic depression. Doesn't this mean that you are drawing precisely the type of distinction which you had previously rejected? And doesn't the term "chronic depression" raise a question of principle which, in a classification that is after all in the last analysis based on nosological factors, can only cause confusion? Aren't we running the risk here of mixing up completely different concepts and methods of classification?

I was a little puzzled, Dr. KIELHOLZ, by your comment on Dr. KUHN's paper. Is it really possible at this stage to pinpoint special indications for Ludiomil? Psychosomatic disorders, as they are called, certainly represent a most interesting group of diseases, but I rather feel that Ludiomil cannot be regarded as definitely indicated in such special cases until exact double-blind trials have been carried out in suitable patients suffering from these disorders. Has any accurate and, from the methodological standpoint, reliable double-blind study already been done in this field—a study that would entitle us to say that Ludiomil is evidently the drug of choice here? We are familiar with the results obtained with amitriptyline in similar studies. Perhaps someone in the audience is in a position to state whether Ludiomil is superior to, for example, amitriptyline in this indication?

And now just a few words about the cardiotoxic effects of the tricyclic antidepressants. Cases of myocardial infarction in the course of treatment with a drug of this type are rare. The problem lies rather in the fact that systematic E.C.G. studies in patients receiving various tricyclic psycho-active agents have revealed the presence of transient E.C.G. changes related to the duration of therapy and occurring even after comparatively low doses. We should therefore not try to play down the importance of these side effects from the outset, on the grounds that fatalities are rare.

P. KIELHOLZ: There is probably nobody in this room who would not agree with Dr. HIPPIUS's criticisms, demands, and general standpoint. I was merely trying, on the basis of the results presented by Dr. KUHN, to pick out certain disorders which might conceivably constitute major indications for Ludiomil.

W. PÖLDINGER: It is of course true that dosage is a very important factor in the treatment of masked depressions. In a double-blind study of the kind postulated by Dr. HIPPIUS, a special dosage schedule would have to be selected, because it is precisely patients with masked depression—i.e. with a disease chiefly marked by somatic symptoms—that react particularly strongly to any side effects which the drug used might have. This became apparent in investigations conducted in the Psychosomatic Ward at the Basle clinic. Quantitative measurements of saliva production, for example, showed that dryness of the mouth was aggravated by antidepressant therapy (for instance, by treatment with imipramine). Similar findings were obtained in respect of various other manifestations, and it was also noticed that the more severe the depression—as measured by means of a questionnaire—the higher the incidence of such symptoms. Dryness of the mouth, for example, is in any case already very pronounced in severe depression; it becomes worse in response to treatment, and the patients therefore refuse to continue the medication. For this reason, it is wrong to advise general practitioners, as is so often done, to use psycho-active agents as an aid to diagnosis in cases where the patient complains of symptoms for which no objective explanation can be found and which do not respond to somatic treatment. Antidepressants, in particular, should not be employed in such cases because, if they are, the patient will of course immediately complain that his somatic symptoms have become worse.

P. KIELHOLZ: I, too, am utterly against the idea of using an antidepressant as an aid to diagnosis.

U. J. JOVANOVIĆ: Besides the work I reported on in my paper, we have also carried out clinical studies on a double-blind basis in 60 patients, of whom 20 received amitriptyline, 20 imipramine, and 20 Ludiomil. The daily dosage of 150 mg. yielded roughly similar results in all three groups, and no significant differences were found. But our detailed neurophysiological investigations did reveal significant differences between the various drugs. Consequently, the considerable expenditure of time and labour involved in collecting the necessary neurophysiological data night after night was in fact justified from the standpoint of scientific research. The assessment of symptoms constitutes one of the major problems in cases of depression. Some physicians find the Hamilton scale too long, but I believe it to be too short. The various items on it can be scored 1–4, but it is very often hard to decide whether a particular symptom merits a "3" or a "4". What we need, perhaps, is a scoring system that runs from 1 to 10. The assessment would then take longer, but it would supply a more accurate picture.

I might add, incidentally, that we treated a further group of 35 ambulant patients with daily dosages of either 150 or 100 mg. Ludiomil, depending on the needs of the individual case. The daily dose of 100 mg. was divided as follows: 50 mg. in the morning, 25 mg. at midday, and 25 mg. in the evening. This dosage, too, was found to be effective, although it must of course be added that we administered it under open conditions.

W. BIRKMAYER: Some doctors, such as Dr. WALCHER and myself, see many cases of masked depression—probably because our departments belong to large hospitals. My own hospital in Vienna, for example, has a sum total of 6,000 beds. If you act as a consultant for other departments—internal medicine, surgery, dermatology, etc.— you are bound to come across numerous cases of masked depression. We emphasise time and again that masked depression falls into the province of the general practitioner, because patients suffering from this disorder do not feel mentally ill and do not therefore go to a psychiatrist. As regards the dosage of Ludiomil to be used by G.P.s for ambulant cases of masked depression, I would not recommend more than 25 mg. t.i.d. If the patient needs more, he must be referred to a psychiatrist, who can then adapt the dosage to the requirements of the case. But the great majority of such patients can be treated by the G.P. The G.P., moreover, has that close relationship to his patients to which Dr. HAMILTON attaches so much importance. We psychiatrists just don't have the same relationship to patients with masked depression.

C. R. B. JOYCE: May I make what is probably a very obvious point. Two themes have been exercising a number of the speakers in this discussion: one is the question of dosage, particularly in general practice, and the second is the question of the drug of choice in special indications. It seems to me that depression in general practice is a special indication. As Dr. BIRKMAYER has just reminded us, the patient who reaches the psychiatrist via the general practitioner differs from the one who never gets beyond the general practitioner. The patients, in fact, stop at different points on the way. Perhaps they have different diseases. In his comprehensive review of masked depression Dr. LÓPEZ IBOR mentioned that one of the synonyms often used, particularly in Anglo-Saxon countries, is "missed depression". It is surely expecting a great deal of the general practitioner to find "missed depression" at all; it is probably precisely the G.P. who is missing it, and it is precisely specialists like Dr. BIRKMAYER who are finding it and who may therefore not consider it to be either "missed" or "masked". The only recommendations about dosage that we can offer are dictated by the results of trials and clinical studies conducted in their own distinctive setting and with their own distinctive patient material. Up to now, our recommendations have been based upon controlled trials in university or other scientifically oriented hospitals. The only way to be sure that our further recommendations are correct is to find the appropriate patient group, or rather to find the scientifically motivated investigator who has a sufficiently large number of appropriate patients, and to secure his cooperation and help in discovering whether our predictions about the correct dosage—or even the correct drug—are right. We are at the moment setting up trials of this kind in general practice and, of course, in some special indications as well.

K. RICKELS: I think it is very important that work of the type described in Dr. KUHN's paper should be carried out in the early stages of a new drug's career in order to establish possible—and I would like to emphasise the word "possible"—indications which then may serve as hypotheses to be tested in well-controlled studies. But I doubt whether one needs hundreds of patients for this purpose; on the contrary, I can't help feeling that some of the patients treated by Dr. KUHN could already have been studied using a controlled trial design. Such an approach might well have yielded more meaningful information than has been provided today. I am particularly unhappy about the use of an experimental drug in combination with one or more known compounds in a clinical trial.

P. BERNER: I should like to revert to the question of what dosage should be recommended in cases of masked depression, and to emphasise once again what I said in the discussion following Dr. LÓPEZ IBOR's paper. I believe that we should first make up our minds as to what we understand by the term "masked depression". A characteristic feature of those depressions in which neurotic defence mechanisms appear to play a predominant role, and which also display symptoms of an endogenous psychosis, is their shallowness; where the depression is of a deeper type, neurotic defence mechanisms apparently fail to operate. Such patients do in fact require low doses—and this also applies to Ludiomil. The situation is not the same, however, in patients with retarded depression, in whom drive is severely impaired whereas mood may be only slightly affected. These patients, too, very often consult first of all a specialist in internal diseases or a general practitioner, but what they need is a higher dosage specifically designed to enhance their drive.

R. KUHN: This discussion has confirmed once again something which we have all known for a long time, but which cannot be repeated often enough—namely, the incorrectness of the widely held view that psychiatry has become easier thanks to the advent of the psycho-active drugs. The contrary is, in fact, the case.

And now let me try to answer the various questions that have been raised. To avoid any misunderstanding, I would emphasise that in my paper I was reporting on trials I had conducted with an entirely new substance belonging to a hitherto unknown class of compounds. Nobody could say at that time whether this substance would display psychotropic properties of any kind—let alone an antidepressant effect—in clinical use. In other words, the situation was almost the same as before the discovery of imipramine. All the data and findings reported in my paper must be viewed against this background. I think that this explanation already answers a number of the questions that have been put to me.

A word or two now about the classification of depressive states. It would really need not a 20-minute speech, but rather a 20-hour discussion to establish with some degree of clarity what each of us thinks about this subject. In my tables the heading "Chronic depression" simply covered all cases in which the depression was of long duration. Some of these patients may possibly have been cases of phasic depression in which the phase lasts more than one year, or even as much as two, five, or ten years but may perhaps eventually subside of its own accord. Even mania may sometimes run a similar course. In addition, the heading "Chronic depression" certainly includes a number of cases which may quite rightly be described as neurotic depression. Furthermore, the masked depressions already referred to on several occasions in this symposium also very frequently run a chronic course.

As regards the problem of double-blind trials, I certainly agree that in later stages in the investigation of a drug double-blind studies are perfectly justified in the field of the psycho-active agents as well, but I must say that they entail an extremely large number of additional problems. It is very difficult to form sufficiently large homogeneous and comparable groups. The patients who finally come to us psychiatrists for help cannot always be placed in standardised categories; moreover, many of them have already been treated unsuccessfully for years or even decades with every conceivable measure. For example, one of my patients—a woman—had been suffering from gastric disorders for ten years. She had been X-rayed several times from head to foot. She had consulted not one but several gastro-enterologists, but none of them could help her. Not until she received Ludiomil did her condition improve. I think that clinical results of this type also have to be taken into account, even though they may not necessarily be allowed for in certain cut-and-dried trial plans designed to demonstrate the effectiveness of a new psycho-active agent.

We did not carry out any systematic E.C.G. studies. E.C.G. tracings, however, were invariably recorded in cases where clinical examination aroused the least suspicion of a cardiac disorder. In none of our cases did the cardiac findings become worse during treatment with Ludiomil. In one patient with a conduction disorder, this disorder actually disappeared. Naturally, I do not wish to imply that Ludiomil is capable of curing heart disorders; such disorders can of course regress spontaneously. To shed light on this problem, one would really have to know the incidence of E.C.G. changes in patients who do not display any signs of a cardiac disorder.

One question of major interest, which was raised by Dr. HAMILTON among others, is that of the "morning trough". If you ask patients whether they feel worse in the morning, a certain percentage of them will say "Yes". Others will reply that they feel worse in the evening, and a few that they feel worse in the middle of the day. There will even be some who maintain that they always feel the same. It is also important to ask the patients which symptoms are worse in the morning and which in the evening. They will often reply that the feeling of oppression is worse in the morning, and the feeling of tiredness at night. That is quite possible. It all depends on how the patients sleep. After a sleepless night they are usually more tired in the morning than in the evening—and this is not necessarily what one would expect. Another point is that many patients are quite incapable of describing their own sensations during a depressive phase. After the phase has lifted, however, they say "Now I remember that I always used to feel much worse in the morning, because now I wake up with a completely different feeling". Complex though the problem is, there can be no doubt that diurnal fluctuations and the "morning trough" have a cardinal bearing on the indication for treatment. I fully agree with Dr. LÓPEZ IBOR that the prognosis as regards treatment is less favourable if the patient complains of feeling worse in the evening. The only question is: how many of these patients are really suffering from pure forms of depression? In many of them the depression is probably combined with organic disorders—especially cerebral atrophy—which are often not detected. Particularly in cases where the patient complains of feeling worse in the evening, one should always bear the possibility of schizophrenia in mind, especially in young subjects.

As for dosage, there seems to be no major conflict of opinion on this subject. We start treatment *as a rule* with a dose of 25 mg. three times daily, which is then raised, if necessary, to 50 mg. t.i.d.; some cases require 75 mg. t.i.d. There are also some patients, even adults, who are better stabilised on 10 mg. t.i.d. than on 25 mg. t.i.d. The possibility of reducing the dose to this lower level should always be considered in cases where 25 mg. t.i.d. fails to produce satisfactory results.

P. KIELHOLZ: I, too, have pointed out on many occasions that not only G.P.s but also psychiatrists are apt to neglect cases of chronic depression. Roughly one-third of all cases of depression run a chronic course.

A multinational, multi-centre, double-blind trial of a new antidepressant (CIBA 34,276-Ba)

by J. WELNER*

CIBA 34,276-Ba (Ludiomil®) is an antidepressant pharmacologically related to the conventional tricyclic drugs but chemically different from them in its stereo-chemically defined three-dimensional tetracyclic structure (Figure 1).

Preliminary uncontrolled clinical trials on some 400 depressed patients suggested that this compound might have some advantages over the usual tricyclic drugs; 34,276-Ba was thought to have a faster onset of action, better tolerability, greater efficacy in reactive depressions, and the ability to control agitation while simultaneously enhancing mood and drive.

Obviously, the drug deserved to be submitted to sophisticated, controlled trials, and such trials were in fact organised in a number of European countries and in America. Since standardised methods of evaluation and rating were employed, this series of trials afforded an opportunity of assessing the drug's efficacy and therapeutic profiles on a really large scale. Even more interesting, perhaps, are the possibilities which a multinational study offers as a means of elucidating cultural differences, ecology, and the urgent problem of taxonomy.

In the North-European group which I represent today, eight psychiatric centres participated in the trial: two in Denmark, one in Finland, two in the Netherlands, and three in Sweden. In the latter half of 1969 the investigators and the sponsors from the manufacturing company met several times in order to reach agreement on important practical questions.

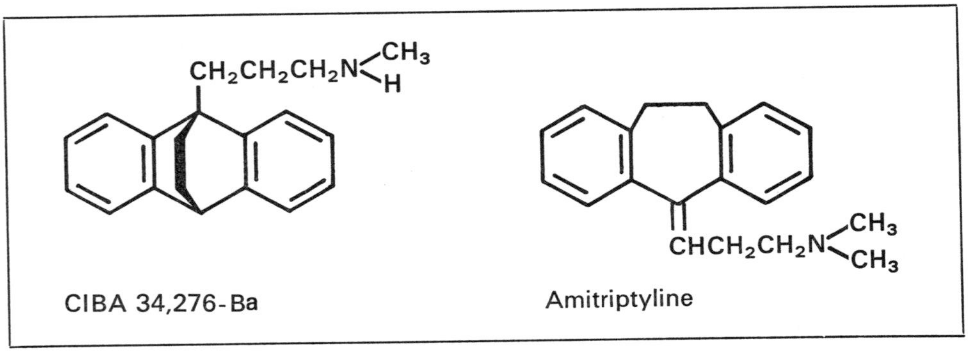

Fig. 1. Structural formulae of 34,276-Ba and amitriptyline.

* Psychiatric Department, Kommunehospitalet, University of Copenhagen, Denmark.

Amitriptyline was chosen as the standard preparation for comparison, the dosage schedule being 25 mg. t.i.d. on the first three days and 50 mg. t.i.d. on subsequent days. The dosage of 34,276-Ba was 50 mg. t.i.d. throughout the trial.

The duration of treatment was at least four weeks, and all patients were hospitalised during this period. For practical reasons, the drug-free wash-out period before treatment had to be as short as three days. During the trial minimum doses of benzodiazepines were allowed, but no other psycho-active drugs.

Discussions of diagnostic criteria were deliberately avoided, and the investigators agreed to include in the trial any patient suffering from depression who would otherwise have been treated with a full dosage of the tricyclic drug preferred by the centre in question. It was evident, however, that the investigators shared the continental European concept of endogenous versus reactive depression.

Ratings on the Hamilton Rating Scale for Depression were performed on Days 0, 7, 14, and 28. On the same days laboratory tests were carried out and the side effects of treatment quantitatively assessed. On Day 28, drug effect and treatment side effects were globally evaluated on five-point scales.

In this paper I shall restrict myself to a very short survey of the results of treatment. A detailed report will be published elsewhere. Thereafter I shall describe the status of the samples before treatment, with the principal aim of examining possible national differences.

Table 1 gives the eight centres and the number of patients treated in each of them. Out of the total of 211 patients, 20 did not complete the treatment. Table 2 lists the drop-outs and indicates the reasons for the discontinuation of treatment. The proportion of drop-outs was similar in the two treatment samples.

Of the 191 patients who completed the trial, 98 were treated with 34,276-Ba and 93 with amitriptyline. The sex and age distributions, as well as social and marital status, were not significantly different in the two groups.

Tables 3 and 4 show the global assessments of the effect of the two treatments, judged by investigator and patient respectively. No significant difference was found between 34,276-Ba and amitriptyline.

Table 5A indicates the incidence and degree of unwanted effects. The incidence was significantly greater in the amitriptyline sample (Table 5B). The frequency of side effects severe enough to interfere with the treatment, however, was low (7–8%) and not significantly different in the two samples. Blurred vision and sweating were significantly less often reported in the 34,276-Ba sample than in the amitriptyline sample. Other differences were insignificant.

Analysis of the Hamilton scores showed a mean of 21.2 for the total material before treatment, but the analysis of variance disclosed highly significant differences between centres ($P < 0.01$). The "before treatment" means of the two samples, however, did not differ.

The regression of the "after treatment" mean on the "before treatment" mean bordered on non-parallelism ($P = 0.01-0.05$). Hence, the basic prerequisites for a linear analysis of covariance were not completely fulfilled. Consequently, the covariance adjustment on the "before treatment" Hamilton score introduced some distortion, which, however, probably had little practical importance.

Table 1. List of investigators and number of patients treated. Trial period: January 1970 to February 1971.

Code	Investigator	Address	Number of patients treated
DK 1	J. Welner Hanne Madsen B.J. Lauritsen	Kommunehospitalet 1353 Copenhagen Denmark	35
DK 2	P. Kragh-Sørensen	State Hospital 2600 Glostrup Denmark	23
NL 1	P.A. Botter	Sinai-Klinik Amersfoort Netherlands	30
NL 2	H. Zwart	Alg. Psych. Ziekenhuis "Het St. Joris Gasthuis" Delft Netherlands	29
S 1	R. Sjöström	Ulleråkers Hospital Uppsala Sweden	30
S 2	G. Bernhardson	Ulleråkers Hospital Uppsala Sweden	29
S 3	B. Wetterholm	St. Annas Hospital Nyköping Sweden	9
SF 1+2	M. Kauppinen	Piirimirlisairaala Oulu Finland	26
		Total	211

Covariance analysis led to the following conclusions:

The total Hamilton score means decreased significantly during treatment.

This decrease was not significantly different in the two samples, or in the eight centres.

The means on Days 7, 14, and 28 did not differ in the two samples, but they *did* differ in the eight centres.

In other words, amitriptyline and 34,276-Ba had the same quantitative effect, measured by the Hamilton Rating Scale. Onset of action was similar with both drugs. The regional samples of treated patients did differ, at least with respect to severity of illness as measured by the total Hamilton scores. This difference may have been due wholly or in part to lack of inter-rater reliability.

Though some meetings took place at which the Hamilton items were discussed, it must be borne in mind that tests of inter-rater reliability were not performed. I do not intend to make excuses for this omission, since such a procedure would

Table 2. Patients who did not complete the treatment and reasons for their not doing so (or reasons why their response was not assessed).

Treatment	Centre	Patient No.	Sex	Age	Diagnosis	Days of treatment	Reasons for discontinuation
34,276-Ba	DK 1	211	M	51	Endogenous depression, retarded	14	Skin reaction (generalised exanthema)
	DK 1	216	F	46	Endogenous depression, retarded	3	Deterioration in patient's condition
	DK 1	233	M	57	Endogenous depression, agitated	13	Suicide
	DK 2	105	F	22	Endogenous depression, agitated	19	Deterioration in patient's condition
	DK 2	121	F	60	Endogenous depression, agitated	12	Skin reaction (generalised exanthema) and poor efficacy
	NL 2	110	M	44	Reactive depression, retarded	14	Refusal of medication; irregular intake
	S 1	115	M	64	Endogenous depression, retarded	15	Development of acute manic state
	S 2	136	F	49	Endogenous depression, agitated	2	Refusal of medication; poor cooperation
	S 3	203	F	35	Reactive depression, agitated	13	Poor cooperation; deterioration in patient's condition
	SF 1	111	M	46	Endogenous depression, hypochondriacal	6	Patient defaulted
Amitriptyline	DK 1	232	F	25	Endogenous depression, retarded	11	Deterioration in patient's condition
	DK 2	102	F	69	Endogenous depression, retarded	20	Deterioration in patient's condition
	DK 2	106	F	21	Endogenous depression, retarded	24	Deterioration in patient's condition
	DK 2	112	M	59	Endogenous depression, retarded	3	Deterioration in patient's condition
	NL 2	103	M	25	Endogenous depression, agitated	21	Development of a catatonic state
	S 1	120	F	39	Endogenous depression, retarded	12	Deterioration in patient's condition
	S 2	131	F	41	Endogenous depression, retarded	26	No assessment of patient's condition before treatment
	S 2	150	F	60	Endogenous depression, agitated	12	Intercurrent medical illness (cardiac infarction)
	SF 1	109	M	18	Reactive depression, hypochondriacal	13	Deterioration in hypochondriacal symptoms
	SF 2	143	M	34	Schizophrenia	15	Wrong diagnosis on admission

have been extremely time-consuming and difficult to work out with so many centres.

Many authors—the most recent being KLERMAN[6]—have advocated the use of multivariate techniques for the qualitative evaluation of drugs. These techniques are especially important whenever differences in sampling are suspected, as is the case in the present cross-national study. In order to assess these national differences, factor analyses, using the principal component method, were done.

Table 3. Global assessment of the therapeutic effect of the treatment. Investigator's judgment.

Response to treatment		34,276-Ba			Amitriptyline			Both treatments		
		N	%		N	%		N	%	
Effect observed	Marked	21	19.8		25	24.5		46	22.1	
	Moderate	45	42.5	85.9	40	39.2	87.2	85	40.9	86.5
	Minimal	25	23.6		24	23.5		49	23.5	
No effect observed	No change	12	11.3		10	9.8		22	10.6	
	Deterioration	3	2.8	14.1	3	2.9	12.7	6	2.9	13.5
Total reported		106		100.0	102		100.0	208*		100.0

* Data not available on three of the 211 patients
There is obviously no significant difference between the two preparations. 86.5% of the patients responded to treatment with either 34,276-Ba or amitriptyline (the 0.95 confidence limits are: 81.9–91.1).

Table 4. Global assessment of the therapeutic effect of the treatment. Patient's opinion.

Response to treatment		34,276-Ba			Amitriptyline			Both treatments		
		N	%		N	%		N	%	
Effect observed	Marked	25	23.8		29	28.4		54	26.1	
	Moderate	39	37.1	79.0	34	33.3	83.3	73	35.3	81.2
	Minimal	19	18.1		22	21.6		41	19.8	
No effect observed	No change	19	18.1		14	13.7		33	15.9	
	Deterioration	3	2.9	21.0	3	2.9	16.6	6	2.9	18.8
Total reported		105		100.0	102		100.0	207*		100.0

* Data not available on four of the 211 patients
The patient's opinion on the efficacy of the treatment did not differ much from the investigator's judgment. No significant difference could be detected between the two preparations: 81.2% of the patients felt they had benefited from treatment either with 34,276-Ba or with amitriptyline (0.95 confidence limits: 75.9–86.5).

Two centre populations were picked out from each of the countries Denmark (N = 58), Netherlands (N = 59), and Sweden (N = 59), and analyses were performed on each of these roughly equal national groups as well as on the total of 176 patients. The first 17 Hamilton items were chosen as variables, as HAMILTON did in his own work.

Table 6 lists the loadings on unrotated factors obtained from the total sample. Factor 1 shows only positive loadings of almost equal size, so it appears to be a general factor measuring severity of depression. This finding is identical to that reported by other authors, such as HAMILTON[3, 4], KILOH and GARSIDE[5], KLERMAN[6], and PAYKEL et al.[8].

The findings in respect of Factor 2 are likewise very similar to those previously reported. Factor 2 is bipolar—with retardation, depressed mood, impaired work and interests, and guilt feelings at one pole, and agitation, somatic anxiety, and general somatic symptoms at the other. This factor would appear to reflect the dimension retardation/agitation; on the other hand, it does not seem to be adequately covered by the terms "endogenous/reactive" or "psychotic/neurotic".

Table 5A. Global assessment of tolerability. Unwanted effects.

| | 34,276-Ba | | Amitriptyline | | Both treatments | |
	N	%	N	%	N	%
Side effects absent	45	41.7	26	25.2	71	33.6
No significant interference	54	50.0	70	68.0	124	58.7
Significant interference	8	7.4 ⎫ 8.3	6	5.8 ⎫ 6.7	14	6.6 ⎫ 7.5
Therapeutic effect nullified	1	0.9 ⎭	1	0.9 ⎭	2	0.9 ⎭
Total	108	100.0	103	100.0	211	100.0

In order to compare the incidences in the two treatment samples, the last two categories have been grouped together.

Table 5B. Analysis of the data presented in Table 5A.

Categories compared	d.f.	χ^2	P
Absent versus present	1	6.3696	0.01–0.02
No significant interference versus (signif. interf. + ther. eff. null.)	1	0.9150	0.30–0.40
Total	2	7.2846	0.02–0.05

The proportion of cases reported to have side effects was significantly greater in the amitriptyline sample (74.8%; 0.95 confidence limits: 66.4–83.2) than in the 34,276-Ba sample (58.3%; 0.95 confidence limits: 44.5–63.1).

Factor 3 is not immediately interpretable. The high loadings for agitation, loss of insight, and psychic anxiety, and the close to zero loadings for depressed mood, retardation, and guilt feelings are not clinically identifiable in terms of depressive states. The above-mentioned authors have all had similar difficulties in finding a term to describe Factor 3.

Rotation of the factors to the varimax, the oblimin, and an oblique criterion were of little interest as they resulted in hardly any change apart from the expected disappearance of the severity dimension.

Hence, we followed the advice of NUNNALLY[7] and used the unrotated solution in order to test the hypothesis that the three national materials represent the same dimensions of depressive illness—i.e. that identical, or near identical, factors can be derived from these materials.

The factor loadings in all three national data turned out to be very similar and closely resembled the pattern shown in Table 6.

In order to examine the degree of similarity between the national factors, the scores of the 176 individuals for the first three factors obtained from the total sample were correlated with the three sets of national factors. If the factors were reliable, i.e. if they measured the same dimensions in the different countries, the correlations between the four sets of scores should be close to unity. Table 7 shows this to be the case for Factor 1.

Table 8 shows that, of the four sets of scores for Factor 2, the Danish, the Swedish, and the one derived from the total sample are close to being identical to one another, whereas the set of scores for the Netherlands is different.

Table 6. Loadings on unrotated factors (principal components). Items arranged in order of loadings on Factor 2 (N = 176).

No. Items	Factor 1	Factor 2	Factor 3
1. Retardation	0.39	0.69	0.11
2. Depressed mood	0.56	0.45	0.18
3. Work and interests	0.45	0.41	0.30
4. Guilt	0.51	0.36	0.11
5. Suicidal tendency	0.50	0.13	−0.17
6. Hypochondriasis	0.37	0.12	−0.11
7. Loss of weight	0.55	0.10	−0.20
8. Insight	0.41	0.06	0.53
9. Insomnia, initial	0.47	0.03	−0.48
10. Insomnia, middle	0.53	−0.05	−0.41
11. Insomnia, delayed	0.64	−0.16	−0.33
12. Somatic symptoms, gastro-intestinal	0.56	−0.18	0.04
13. Anxiety, psychic	0.57	−0.25	0.39
14. Somatic symptoms, genital	0.49	−0.35	−0.10
15. Somatic symptoms, general	0.48	−0.42	0.03
16. Anxiety, somatic	0.39	−0.52	0.07
17. Agitation	0.25	−0.55	0.42
Percentage of variance	23.5%	12.0%	8.1%

Table 9 shows that Factor 3 does not at all meet the demand for cross-national identity.

These findings imply that we may safely evaluate drug efficacy cross-nationally by means of Factor 1. This factor's correlation with the investigators' rating of severity on a five-point scale is high—i.e. 0.45 (Table 10)—and its correlation with the total Hamilton score is 0.99.

Thus, Factor 1 does measure severity, as claimed for his Factor 1 by HAMILTON[4]. If, however, we are interested only in the quantitative effects of treatment, we could just as well use the total Hamilton score, and factor analysis would be superfluous.

Factor 2 is the most important group factor, containing two comparatively well-defined poles. In the present trial this factor is useful for the study of differential treatment outcome. Its use, however, is restricted by two facts:

1. The factor accounts for only 12% of the total variance.
2. Its cross-national reliability is limited. The Danish and Swedish samples can be pooled, but the Netherlands sample has to be treated separately.

Factor 3 cannot be used cross-nationally in this study, and the clinical significance of the factor is difficult to recognise.

Consequently, it must be concluded that factor analyses failed to confirm our hypothesis that the three national samples represent the same dimensions of depressive illness. In view of the findings of other authors, especially KLERMAN[6], suggesting that scores derived from factor analyses are potentially highly reliable, differences in raters seems to be a more likely explanation than differences in patients.

I would like to report briefly on our very preliminary attempts to use factor analyses for treatment evaluation. We used the total sample factors at Day 0 (shown in Table 6) and we calculated factor scores at Day 28 with respect to these factors. The analyses showed that Factor 1 scores decreased significantly and that Factors 2 and 3 were completely insensitive to the treatment given. From this we may conclude that either our method of assessment cannot detect qualitative changes, or that qualitative changes did not occur.

My associate B. HUTCHINGS proposed the use of M.C.A. (Multiple Classification Analysis[1]), also recommended by BLUMENTHAL[2]. This programme is constructed for sociological problems. It is a hybrid between multiple-regression analysis and discriminant-function analysis. It can handle a multivariate set of predictors insofar as they relate to a single dependent, two-class variable—e.g. improved versus not improved. The predictor variables might be a set of items of an ordinal scale, such as the Hamilton scale.

When using this programme, we are beating a strategic retreat. We are going back to the raw data—to the Hamilton items—which is a good thing to do. We simply test empirically the ability of Hamilton Day 0 items to predict improvement at Day 28. The result will thus be an expression of what happened in *our* patients, but will not enable us to test hypotheses concerning depressive illness as such. However, it would be interesting if hypotheses generated by this programme could be tested in other groups of patients.

Table 7. Correlations between scores obtained on the total sample using Factor 1 from the total sample and Factor 1 obtained from each country separately (N = 176).

	F_1	F_{1DK}	F_{1NL}	F_{1S}
(F_3)	(0.00)	(0.09)	(−0.12)	(0.07)
F_1	1.00	0.99	0.92	0.98
(F_2)	(0.00)	(0.04)	(0.35)	(0.05)
F_{1DK}		1.00	0.90	0.98
F_{1NL}			1.00	0.88
F_{1S}				1.00

Table 8. Correlations between scores obtained on the total sample using Factor 2 from the total sample and Factor 2 obtained from each country separately (N = 176).

	F_2	F_{2DK}	F_{2NL}	F_{2S}
(F_3)	(0.00)	(−0.18)	(0.58)	(−0.05)
F_2	1.00	0.78	−0.41	0.89
(F_1)	(0.00)	(−0.06)	(0.59)	(−0.03)
F_{2DK}		1.00	−0.41	0.73
F_{2NL}			1.00	−0.46
F_{2S}				1.00

Table 9. Correlations between scores obtained on the total sample using Factor 3 from the total sample and Factor 3 obtained from each country separately (N = 176).

	F_3	F_{3DK}	F_{3NL}	F_{3S}
(F_2)	(0.00)	(−0.50)	(−0.59)	(−0.08)
F_3	1.00	−0.45	−0.44	−0.88
(F_1)	(0.00)	(0.04)	(0.21)	(0.12)
F_{3DK}		1.00	0.50	0.45
F_{3NL}			1.00	0.38
F_{3S}				1.00

Table 10. Correlations between the three factors, investigator's rating of severity, and the total Hamilton score (N = 176).

	F_1	F_2	F_3	Investigator's severity rating (five-point scale)	Total Hamilton score (17 variables)
F_1	1.00	0.00	0.00	0.45*	0.99*
F_2		1.00	0.00	0.20**	0.04
F_3			1.00	0.11	0.05
Investigator's severity rating (five-point scale)				1.00	0.48*
Total Hamilton score (17 variables)					1.00

*P < 0.001   **P < 0.01
Mean severity rating = 3.06   Mean Hamilton score = 19.19

In conclusion, when considering ways and means of improving trial designs, careful attention should obviously be paid to the following points:

Firstly, attempts should be made to improve inter-rater reliability. This would call for a long preparatory period, and for the use of video-taped, translated interviews which should be circulated among the investigators until reliability has reached a high level.

Secondly, life history and pre-morbid personality ratings, reliably measured, are desirable if the best possible use is to be made of a cross-cultural study, especially where problems of typology and differential outcome of treatments are concerned.

Time does not allow me to discuss further results and other sources of information obtained from the study. The group of investigators will continue work on this trial, and other reports are in preparation.

References

1 ANDREWS, F., MORGAN, J., SONQUIST, J.: Multiple classification analysis (Survey Res. Center, Inst. soc. Res., Univ. of Michigan, Ann Arbor 1969)
2 BLUMENTHAL, M.D.: Heterogeneity and research on depressive disorders. Arch. gen. Psychiat. *24*, 524 (1971)
3 HAMILTON, M.: A rating scale for depression. J. Neurol. Neurosurg. Psychiat. *23*, 56 (1960)
4 HAMILTON, M.: Development of a rating scale for primary depressive illness. Brit. J. soc. clin. Psychol. *6*, 278 (1967)

5 Kiloh, G. L., Garside, R. F.: The independence of neurotic depression and endogenous depression. Brit. J. Psychiat. *109*, 451 (1963)
6 Klerman, G. L.: Clinical research in depression. Arch. gen. Psychiat. *24*, 305 (1971)
7 Nunnally, J. C.: Psychometric theory (McGraw-Hill, New York etc. 1967)
8 Paykel, E. S., Prusoff, B., Klerman, G. L.: The endogenous-neurotic continuum in depression: rater independence and factor distributions. J. psychiat. Res. *8*, 73 (1971)

Discussion

K. RICKELS: I first want to congratulate Dr. WELNER on his excellent study. It shows how controlled research can indeed be carried out in depression. I only wonder why unrotated and not rotated factors were used.

P. PICHOT: I want to make only a brief comment, because my friend MAX HAMILTON will certainly have much more to say. I'd just like to point out that the second factor cannot be regarded as closely similar to the second principal component in KILOH and GARSIDE's study and in similar factor analyses. As you know, the second principal component is usually bipolar, but the meaning of this second dimension depends on the items, and in most studies of the KILOH and GARSIDE type the items have been a selection of the symptoms classically linked either with the endogenous or with the reactive-neurotic aetiology of depression. A very striking feature of your results, Dr. WELNER, is that two of the items, which are classical markers of endogenous versus exogenous depression, have a practically zero saturation in the second factor. I am referring to "initial insomnia" with its 0.03, which is virtually zero, and "delayed insomnia", with its −0.16; this minus saturation is paradoxically more in the direction of what would be termed an exogenous depression. So I think that, since the items which constitute the Hamilton scale have not been selected for specifically revealing an endogenous/neurotic dimension, your second principal component is very dissimilar to the one of KILOH and GARSIDE and to the one which has been found by other authors, including myself.

M. HAMILTON: I am reluctant to take part in a long discussion on the problems posed by the interpretation of factors, but I think that the best approach to this probably lies somewhere between what Dr. PICHOT has said and what Dr. WELNER has said. The first thing one should always remember is that the factors obtained from an analysis of the correlations depend very much on the way in which the patients have been collected—in other words, on the selection of the patients. It is this which dominates the patterns of the factors. Nevertheless, even where there are great distortions in the method of selection—such as have occurred, for example, in the Netherlands group of patients—the patterns of loadings as shown here in Factors 1 and 2 do bear a close resemblance from one investigation to another. The factors I obtained, and those obtained by KLERMAN* in the U.S.A. and by HORDERN, BURT, and HOLT** who have used this scale in Australia, for example, are indeed very similar, and Factor 2 does more or less differentiate the pattern of symptoms which we as clinicians recognise as revealing the difference between the retarded versus the anxious (agitated) type of depression. As for the loadings for insomnia, they do vary considerably, but this is bound up with other problems as well. I think that factor rotation, which simply reveals a group of symptoms closely linked, merely gives us grouped symptoms as against individual ones. But in a scale like this the symptoms have already been grouped, and there is probably little to be gained by a rotation. However, as we say in England, the proof of the pudding is in the eating. What concerns us is not whether the loadings of the variables resemble another loading, or what sort of name we invent for a factor (naming factors is very much like naming children, it is very arbitrary), but whether these factors show any correspondence to clinical entities. Do they show some relation to the types of patient we have or to the outcome of treatment? And this is the point that I'm sure Dr. WELNER was trying to emphasise.

J. WELNER: May I first answer Dr. RICKELS. We tried to rotate, but the factors did not seem to be clinically all that meaningful, at least not more meaningful than before

---

* KLERMAN, G. L.: Clinical research in depression. Arch. gen. Psychiat. 24, 305 (1971)
** HORDERN, A., BURT, C. G., HOLT, N. F.: Depressive states. A pharmacotherapeutic study (Thomas, Springfield, Ill. 1965)

rotation. We therefore followed NUNNALLY, because we were not really interested in the factors or in typology, but in the similarities between centres and nations. There's not much I can say in reply to Dr. PICHOT's comment. As far as I know, insomnia is on the whole a very unreliable measure. By this I mean that the subjective complaint of insomnia does not correlate well with the neurophysiological measurements which some investigators have carried out. So I wouldn't place very much emphasis on it. Finally, it only remains for me to thank my friend, Dr. HAMILTON, for having explained so well what I was driving at.

A comparison of open and blind dosage in an antidepressant trial

by E. Heim*, C. R. B. Joyce**, and K. H. Martin*

In current psychopharmacological research, double-blind studies are given preference over open studies, above all because they allow better control of observer bias and placebo effects. Various studies of drug-set interaction have proved that the objectivity of the observer as a measuring instrument fluctuates very markedly. It is also well known that in initial open non-comparative studies with a new drug the investigator's enthusiasm frequently leads him to adopt an uncritical attitude. This may explain in part the disappointments that often occur subsequently when the new drug is submitted to careful comparative investigation, especially under single or double-blind conditions. However, not many studies have been reported in which the reliability of open and blind trials has been compared simultaneously in a single design, and there are even fewer studies—if any—in which the effect of blind versus open changes of *dosage* upon the subsequent evaluations has been compared, although knowledge that the dose has been changed is potentially as great a source of error as is knowledge of the identity of the treatment received by the patient.

In the first part of the present trial, two antidepressants were compared, using the classic double-blind between-patient technique, in 39 depressive patients. Dosages, however, could if necessary be changed at the discretion of the psychiatrists. The results of this study can be summarised as follows:

1. The two antidepressants—one of them a substance of a structurally new type (CIBA 34,276-Ba, Ludiomil®) and the other the well-known comparative drug amitriptyline—were not found to differ significantly in efficacy or tolerability, although in the patients receiving amitriptyline the scores on the Hamilton Rating Scale for Depression were consistently but insignificantly lower as from the seventh day of treatment.

2. There was a highly significant difference between the mean total Hamilton scores at the various assessments, the scores decreasing linearly from the seventh day of treatment. Both sub-samples followed this trend.

The two treatment sub-samples described were found not to differ significantly in any of the pre-treatment variables, with the exception of the item "retardation" on the Hamilton Rating Scale, which was significantly more frequent in the 34,276-Ba sub-group. As can be seen from Table 1, the diagnostic categories were not equal in the two sub-samples. Although, when assessing the effect of treatment, differences in numerical starting values can be—and indeed in the

* Psychiatrische Klinik "Schlössli", Oetwil am See, Switzerland.
** Medical Department, CIBA-GEIGY LIMITED, Basle, Switzerland.

present instance were—adjusted for by submitting the results to an analysis of covariance in which the pre-treatment value is used as a covariate, it has to be realised that covariance is a technical device and cannot take account of differences in diagnoses. It could therefore be argued that a Type II error might have occurred, i.e. that the instrument used failed to reject the null hypothesis because of diagnostic inhomogeneity in the treatment groups. The Hamilton Rating Scale is no doubt one of the best for measuring depressive illness, but there is no way of being sure that it was sensitive enough to detect differences in this particular sample.

There is a second point to be made: differences in diagnoses can be due to lack of operational definition of the diagnostic categories, but they can also be due to a bias in the observer in favour of one or other of the diagnoses. One of the objects of the second part of the study was to detect observer bias. During the first part, the principal observer and the responsible ward psychiatrists had already described in detail their opinions on the specific effects of the two drugs, and registered their guesses as to what treatment the patient had actually received. Before starting the second part of the study and without informing them about the actual outcome of the first part, the observers were also asked to give a lengthy description of the expected properties and effect of the two drugs.

In the second part of the trial, conducted in 72 depressive patients considered suitable for treatment with 150 mg./day of amitriptyline, but using a more complex factorial design, comparisons not only of the two drugs but also of

Table 1. Main diagnostic categories and types in the first part of the trial.

Main diagnostic categories	34,276-Ba		Amitriptyline		Total	
	f	%	f	%	f	%
Endogenous	6	31.6	6	30.0	12	30.8
Reactive	6	31.6	10	50.0	16	41.0
Other	7	36.8	4	20.0	11	28.2
Total	19	100.0	20	100.0	39	100.0

Main diagnostic types	34,276-Ba		Amitriptyline		Total	
	f	%	f	%	f	%
Agitated	4	21.0	6	30.0	10	25.6
Retarded	11	58.0	12	60.0	23	59.0
Other	4	21.0	2	10.0	6	15.4
Total	19	100.0	20	100.0	39	100.0

dosage increases up to 225 mg./day, where permitted by the trial design, were partly blind and partly open (Figure 1). There were thus 12 treatment sub-groups, each comprising six patients. As in the first part of the trial, assessments of the patients' progress were made at 0, 7, 14, 21, and 28 days by reference to the Hamilton Rating Scale for Depression, as well as to other conventional psychiatric measurements. In addition, information was collected about so-called unwanted effects (which were also enquired for on Day 0, in order to reduce the risk of their being falsely attributed to treatment).

Such a design is intended to enable one to ascertain the influence of bias on the part of the observers, and, in particular, to compare the attitude of the principal observer—from whom greater objectivity is expected—with that of other observers responsible for treatment. Differences between open and blind designs in respect of number of dosage changes and of drop-outs can also be evaluated. Indicated below are some of the hypotheses to be tested when the trial has been completed. (The allocation to the various treatments was made in blocks of 12, and the present report deals with the observations made on the first 36 patients treated.)

1. With regard to differences between open and blind conditions:
   a) More unwanted effects were expected to occur under blind than under open conditions, and this difference was expected to be more marked in the case of the drug preferred by the observer than in the case of the other substance.
   b) More drop-outs were expected when either treatment or dosage was blind, and more were expected when the dosage was changed blindly during blind treatment than when it was changed blindly during open treatment.
   c) Inter-rater reliability (Hamilton scale) was expected to be greater when patients were receiving blind treatment than when they were receiving open treatment.
   d) Finally, it was expected that patients' evaluations would show smaller differences between open and blind conditions than would those of the physicians.

2. With regard to differences between observers:
   a) Since the principal observer, although completely unaware of which group the patient belonged to, had already been responsible for the first part of the trial, it was anticipated that his ratings, when compared with those of various observers responsible for the treatment of individual patients, would be less subject to bias and would show smaller differences between the two parts of the experiment.
   b) The less experienced observers were expected to show a more marked appreciation of the new drug under open conditions.
   c) Bias in favour of the drug preferred by the observers would be more apparent under open than under blind conditions; this bias would also be more apparent when the dosage was changed openly than when it was changed blindly.

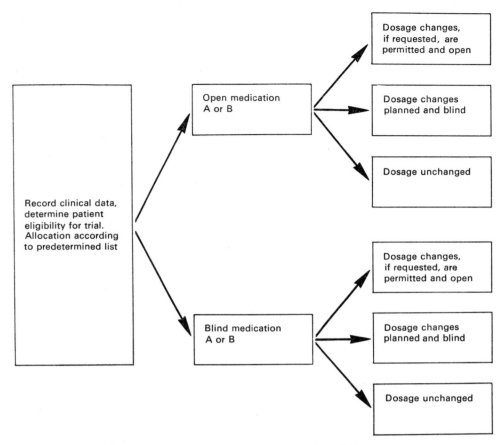

Fig. 1. Block diagram of experiment (second part of the trial).

A = amitriptyline: 50 mg. (2 tablets of 25 mg.) t.i.d.
B = 34,276-Ba: 50 mg. (2 tablets of 25 mg.) t.i.d.
Assessment at Day 0, 7, 14, 21, and 28
Dosage increased on Day 7 to 75 mg. (25+50 mg.) t.i.d. (if permitted or planned)

Results

This was a multivariate, multifactorial study in which only 36 patients have so far been observed. It is not to be expected that conventional levels of significance will be obtained with such small numbers and therefore only trends are reported (Table 2):

– There has been a slight trend in favour of 34,276-Ba over amitriptyline in all the variables reported here. As judged by the Hamilton Rating Scale, the improvement in response to both drugs was slightly greater when treatment was open, as well as when changes in dosage were made openly; under blind conditions, the difference in favour of 34,276-Ba was more marked.

– So-called "drug-related" unwanted effects were in the predicted direction when the dosage was changed blindly (i.e. the total of unwanted effects observed

225

Table 2. Results obtained in the first 36 patients in the second part of the trial.

	Medication		Treatment		Dosage change		Medication and treatment				Medication and dosage change			
							A		B		A		B	
	A	B	Blind	Open	Blind	Open	Blind	Open	Blind	Open	Blind	Open	Blind	Open
Patient's evaluation	3.0	3.4	3.4	2.8	3.5	2.9	3.9	2.1	3.3	3.4	3.2	2.8	3.6	3.0
Doctor's evaluation	3.2	3.5	3.6	3.1	3.2	3.5	3.6	2.7	3.4	3.5	3.2	3.4	3.4	3.5
Hamilton change*	18	21	19	20	19	20	17	19	20	21	17	19	20	21
Unwanted effects change*	0.2	0.6	0.6	0.3	0.1	1.1	0.7	+0.3	0.4	0.9	0.1	0.4	0.1	1.7
Onset of effect (days)	12	9	10	11	10	10	11	13	9	9	13	10	9	8

* Day 0–Day 28   A = amitriptyline   B = 34,276-Ba

during the 28-day period was lower than at Day 0, though the extent of the reduction was less marked following blind changes in dosage than following open changes), but they were in the non-predicted direction when treatment was blind (i.e. although the total of unwanted effects observed during the 28-day period was lower than at Day 0 for both treatments, the reduction was less when treatment was open).

– Treatment was discontinued before 28 days had elapsed in eight cases, of which six had shown an inadequate effect. Of these six, five were on the blind dosage change regime; this difference had been predicted. Four were receiving amitriptyline and the other two 34,276-Ba. Four were on open treatment and two on blind treatment; this was in the reverse direction from the prediction.

– The doctor's and the patient's overall evaluations of the effect of treatment did not show the expected difference between blind and open conditions. Whereas both ratings were better when treatment was blind, the patient's evaluation was better when dosage was changed blindly and the doctor's was more favourable when dosage changes were made openly.

Discussion

Detailed comments on these results would be premature and must clearly await the completion of the projected study of 72 patients. In particular, no attempt can be made at the moment to draw any conclusions with regard to inter-rater reliability or observer bias. However, it seems likely that knowledge of the actual dosage increase does modify the doctor's perceptions of the effect of treatment. Unwanted effects also are somewhat less likely to be reported when the dosage is changed openly, and treatment is more likely to be discontinued prematurely when the dosage is changed blindly than when it is changed openly.

On the face of it, therefore, it appears that blind dosage changes may be as important for "objective" drug evaluation as blind treatment; but it should be noted that, since medication was always given in the form of two tablets of identical appearance three times daily, the blindness and openness with which this report has been concerned are really applicable only to the doctor. The patient had no *direct* information at all about his treatment or his dosage schedule. The word "direct" should perhaps be emphasised, because there is no lack of evidence from other studies that much information is unwittingly communicated, often by non-verbal means, from the experimenter to his subjects. Thus, it is just conceivable that the apparently greater sensitivity of the patient, as compared with the doctor, to differences in a regime about which he is supposed not to have any information, may have represented a form of "amplification" of signals generated by the doctor. The doctor himself, possibly under the influence of his scientific training, may have been less responsive to these signals in his own reports.

If this is true, it is possible that the results of current practice in dose-finding, much of which is performed "openly", may owe more to the doctor's expectations of what is an effective and what is a toxic dose than to carefully obtained clinical evidence.

Conclusions

Preliminary analysis of results from a trial of two antidepressants, using a multivariate and multifactorial design, suggests that to evaluate the effect and optimal dose of a new drug by comparing it with a standard under conditions which allow the dosage to be varied blindly is no less important than to ensure that the traditional blind evaluation of treatments themselves is observed. This, and the trend in favour of 34,276-Ba in comparison with amitriptyline, will be examined in the second half of the trial, which is being conducted along exactly the same lines as the first half. Once the whole trial, has been completed, moreover, it will be possible to assess inter-rater reliability under both blind and open conditions, as well as observer bias.

Discussion

H. HEIMANN: I assume that Dr. HEIM was the "principal observer" in this trial. As the trial has not yet been completed, I should like to ask him whether this preliminary analysis might not markedly influence his own judgment—as well as that of his assistants, who have probably also seen the interim results—and whether it might not therefore have a decisive effect on the second half of the trial.

M. HAMILTON: I would like to congratulate Dr. HEIM on having examined some of the practical aspects of trials which we all talk about or take for granted without ever having properly evaluated them. This question of the variation of dosage is fundamental. As I said earlier today, the practising clinician always varies the dosage of a drug to suit the patient, and I think it is important that a drug trial should also try to evaluate a drug in exactly the same way. But this problem of varying the dosage can give rise to difficulties, and it is these difficulties that Dr. HEIM has been investigating. I have always made sure in my trials that, where the dosage of the drug can be altered, the routine procedure should be that two physicians work together, that one physician looks after his own group of patients, observes them clinically, and alters the dosage as he thinks fit, but that he makes the assessment on his colleague's patients, and vice versa. In this way an attempt can be made to alter the dosage so as to achieve the optimum effect, but without influencing the actual assessment of the effect that has been produced.

E. HEIM: In answer to Dr. HEIMANN's question I would point out that, although I planned the trial, I am not the principal observer. The principal observer is, in fact, a colleague of mine at the clinic, who is keeping the patients under continuous surveillance. Moreover, he is not aware of the results obtained hitherto, although we did consider the possibility of informing him and our other colleagues about the trends observed in the first half of the trial in order to see whether this would have any effect on the further course of the study.

As regards Dr. HAMILTON's comment, I should like to add that the suggestion to plan a trial in this way came indirectly from him during a discussion on the differences between open and blind studies.

Results obtained with a new antidepressant in children

by V. Kuhn-Gebhardt*

In the field of child psychiatry, the use of drugs to treat depression has not yet gained the recognition it deserves. Until a few years ago, only a very limited number of child psychiatrists were prepared to consider the possibility of such a form of therapy. But at the IVth Congress of the Union of European Paedo-psychiatrists, which was held in Stockholm from 30th August to 3rd September 1971 and which was devoted exclusively to an exchange of views and ideas concerning the management of depressive states in children and adolescents, it was apparent that a clear-cut change in attitude had taken place. Despite this, there are still two diametrically opposed schools of thought, with the result that the discussions in Stockholm were sometimes marked by wide divergences of opinion. One group of child psychiatrists is still inclined to look for the classic symptoms of melancholia as postulated by KRAEPELIN, but seldom succeeds in actually finding typical cases displaying delusions of culpability, depressive phases alternating in some instances with episodes of mania, suicidal tendencies, and severe plaintive inhibitions. Many of the younger child psychiatrists, by contrast, have adopted a modified nosological classification similar to that which has been found necessary in adults since the advent of the antidepressant drugs. That is to say, they have widened the concept of depression to embrace all conditions associated with depressive mood disorders which are more marked in the morning and which are characterised by loss of vitality. In children, however, disorders of this type do not give rise to the same signs and symptoms as in adults. Such extremely common phenomena as tiredness and/or poor per-formance at school, tendency to weeping, anxiety, quarrelsomeness, irritability, and, in particular, radical changes in personality of a generally episodic nature which cannot be attributed to situational, psychological, or pathophysiological factors, are more often than not the outward manifestations of depressive mood disorders, the psychic equivalents of which take the form of capriciousness, discontentedness, and absence of the carefree cheerfulness normally encountered in children. Cases of this type account on an average for 10–15 % of the patients seen by a child psychiatrist—and it is this 10–15 % that could derive benefit from treatment with antidepressant drugs.

One of the drawbacks to treating children with antidepressants lies in the side effects which these preparations are liable to provoke. To be sure, imipramine or its derivatives can also be prescribed for children, but they frequently give rise to nausea and vomiting, with the result that treatment has to be discon-tinued. For this reason, any drug that is not only effective but also seems to be

---

* Kantonale Psychiatrische Klinik, Münsterlingen, Switzerland.

better tolerated by children is to be welcomed. One such drug is CIBA 34,276-Ba (Ludiomil®), which has shown itself to be a useful antidepressant in children. It is also effective against enuresis and encopresis.

The general principles concerning the indications and administration of this drug are the same in children as in adults. The appropriate dosage varies greatly from one patient to another. As a rule, treatment should be initiated with 10 mg. tablets, the dosage being gradually increased to a level which—in older children, at least—may often approach that employed in adults.

Preparation 34,276-Ba is better tolerated than imipramine and its derivatives. Occasionally—especially at the start of treatment—it may cause tiredness, and in quite a number of our cases it led to a progressive increase in irritability, which in some patients was so severe as to amount to aggressiveness. Two patients—one a child and the other an adolescent—reacted with epileptiform seizures. As these seizures were definitely due to the drug, medication was discontinued.

A more detailed picture of the preparation's effectiveness can be gathered from statistical data covering 100 cases (75 boys and 25 girls). The average age of these patients was 12 years; 95 of them were treated on a purely ambulatory basis, whereas the remaining five also received hospital treatment. (These patients are included in the 320 cases mentioned in the paper by R. KUHN.) As in the case of adult patients, our primary concern was to obtain a satisfactory therapeutic result in each individual case. Consequently, we adhered to the above-mentioned principle of a gradual increase in dosage, but we varied the amount given to each patient until we found a dosage which, while exerting an optimum antidepressant action, provoked as few side effects as possible. For the same reason, we employed combined therapy, when necessary, in a large proportion of the patients (42%); in these patients, too, however, 34,276-Ba was

Table 1. Results of treatment with 34,276-Ba alone and in combination.

	Very good		Good		Improved		No effect		
	N	%	N	%	N	%	N	%	Total
Phasic depression	3	23.1	6	46.2	3	23.1	1	7.7	13
Manic-depressive psychoses	–		–		1		–		1
Chronic depression	6	13.3	24	53.3	12	26.6	3	6.6	45
Psychopathic states	1	4.6	4	18.2	8	36.4	9	40.9	22
Enuresis	4	44.4	1	11.1	1	11.1	3	33.3	9
Schizophrenia	–		–		2		1		3
Organic psychoses	–		2		1		1		4
Miscellaneous	–		2		1		–		3
	14	14.0	39	39.0	29	29.0	18	18.0	100

invariably the main drug used. "Very good" or "good" results were recorded in 53 % of the total collective (Table 1). This figure was even higher (58.7 %) in the patients who received only 34,276-Ba (Table 2). As with the adults, the cases that responded best were those of "pure" depression—i.e. of phasic and chronic depression—whereas psychopathic conditions proved, as expected, more refractory. The results obtained in enuresis struck us as being encouraging, although the number of cases involved was small.

Taking all the indications together, 18 % of the total collective failed to show any response to treatment; the corresponding figure for the group treated with 34,276-Ba alone was 12.1 %.

It is interesting to compare these statistics with those obtained in another group of 100 patients treated in 1964. Then, the majority of the patients had received imipramine or desipramine. Their average age was 11 years and four months, and the distribution of the various indications was comparable to that in the present group. In 1964 very good and good responses were elicited in only 38 % of the cases, and some 15 % failed to show any improvement at all. The success rate has therefore improved markedly over the last eight or nine years—thanks no doubt to the increased effectiveness of the drugs available.

In conclusion, it can be said that 34,276-Ba is a very good drug which, in the field of child psychiatry, can be used to excellent effect to treat many behavioural disorders associated with depressive moods. The treatment, however, must be carefully adapted to the needs of the individual case, and close supervision of the patient is essential. Preparation 34,276-Ba should, moreover, be given in combination with other drugs and should be backed up by appropriate psychotherapeutic measures as well as by advice on questions concerning the child's upbringing.

Table 2. Results of treatment with 34,276-Ba alone.

	Very good		Good		Improved		No effect		
	N	%	N	%	N	%	N	%	Total
Phasic depression	3	30.0	4	40.0	3	30.0	–		10
Manic-depressive psychoses	–		–		1		–		1
Chronic depression	4	14.3	15	53.5	8	28.6	1	3.6	28
Psychopathic states	1	9.1	2	18.2	4	36.4	4	36.4	11
Enuresis	3		–		–		1		4
Schizophrenia	–		–		1		1		2
Organic psychoses	–		–		–		–		–
Miscellaneous	–		2		–		–		2
	11	19.0	23	39.7	17	29.3	7	12.1	58

Discussion

W. WALCHER: I consider Dr. KUHN-GEBHARDT's paper to be extremely important chiefly because it draws attention in a most impressive way to the fact that depression does indeed occur in children, even though it is frequently just not recognised as such. If you examine the past history of adult depressives, you quite often find that even in childhood they already displayed the somatic equivalents typical of infantile depression—a form of depression, incidentally, which is almost invariably somatised. The clinical picture of depression in children is in many cases marked simply by a failure to cope with school-work—often interpreted as laziness—or by a certain degree of listlessness or gloominess. When I talked about clinical pictures of this type at the World Congress of Psychiatry held in Madrid a few years ago, I found that very few of my colleagues backed me up; most of the participants felt that there was no such thing, but I remember that Dr. KUHN lent me considerable support in the ensuing discussion. Today, it is already far more widely acknowledged that this type of underlying depression really does occur in children and that it may respond to appropriate treatment. Hitherto, we have been in the habit of using as a rule small doses of amitriptyline or imipramine. Only in one case of juvenile depression have we so far had the opportunity to employ Ludiomil; the patient was a 15-year-old girl, and she showed a very prompt and satisfactory response to the medication. The important thing, however, is that, when confronted with certain somatic manifestations in children and adolescents—our youngest patient was only four and a half years old—one should bear in mind the possibility of depression.

M. LORGÉ: You said, Dr. KUHN-GEBHARDT, that the average age of your patients was 12 years. Could you also tell us the median age? How many were over 12?
One other question: can you offer any explanation as to why Ludiomil proved less effective in children than in adults? A comparison of your tables with those of Dr. KUHN, which of course also contain the children treated by you, reveals the striking fact that his success rates were higher—and would have been higher still if the children had not been included. It would be interesting to know whether and, if so, to what extent this difference is significant.

N. MATUSSEK: What was the average duration of treatment in the case of the children you reported on, Dr. KUHN-GEBHARDT? Do you think that Ludiomil could also be used for the long-term treatment of children? And one last question: is anything known about the therapeutic and prophylactic value of lithium therapy in children—who, of course, may also suffer from phasic depression?

B. POPKES: What was the age of the youngest children you treated, Dr. KUHN-GEBHARDT? Were you able to differentiate between endogenous phasic depression and neurotic depression?

J. J. LÓPEZ IBOR: I have been particularly surprised in recent years at the prevalence of depression in children and adolescents. For some time now I have therefore been trying to establish in a methodical way how often endogenous factors are involved in the pathogenesis of these depressions and psychosomatic disorders. In the case of children, questioning the patient cannot be expected to yield any clues as to the nature of the depression. In many cases you find that the child has a morbid fear of school and that he suffers from sleep disturbances and nightmares; these are possible symptoms which I always ask about. In the case of adults, too, I do all I can to discover whether they have displayed depressive equivalents in childhood. In addition, I endeavour to obtain information about the patient's family circumstances and about hereditary factors. In my experience, it is often possible to help children suffering from depression.

P. SCHMIDLIN: How would you define depression in children, Dr. KUHN-GEBHARDT? Do you consider it to be a condition marked by a specific symptomatology? I ask this because it is conceivable that, depending on the child's development, there might not be any outward manifestations of depression at all. Or do you think that infantile depression is simply ordinary depression occurring in childhood?

R. KUHN: May I add a brief word about the important role which Ludiomil in particular could play in the management of adolescent drug addicts. Though we don't have time to discuss this problem in detail now, I think we can safely assume that the preparation offers possibilities in this indication, even if it is still too soon for us to assess their exact scope.

P. KIELHOLZ: In connection with the diagnosis of depression in children, I should like to mention an additional factor which is doubtless familiar to a wide circle of doctors and to which I drew attention 20 years ago: if we question patients with endogenous depression very carefully about their past history, going right back to their childhood, many of them tell us that there were frequent occasions in their youth or adolescence when they had to stay at home because of a sore throat, stomach ache, or some other pain, and that only now, when they know what depression is, do they realise that these symptoms were really of a depressive nature. Loss of contact with other children of the same age is a frequent clue to the presence of depression. One of the reasons why depression in childhood is so often not recognised is, I am sure, the fact that children are not yet in a position to express their state of mind in words; even adults are very frequently incapable of doing this, so how can we expect children, who have no idea what depression is, to manage it?

V. KUHN-GEBHARDT: As regards the age of the children I reported on in my paper, I would point out that most of them were schoolchildren, because the majority of my patients are referred to me by schools or school psychologists. The children, then, were for the most part aged between seven and 12 years. Of course, we also had a large number of younger patients, most of whom had been sent to us by their family doctors, the commonest reason for referral being sleep disturbances. Generally speaking, these children responded quite well to Ludiomil. Two of them were between one and two years old. One child, who is now three years of age, has been treated with relatively large doses of Ludiomil for about a year. This is probably a case of infantile schizophrenia marked by severe depressive moods which run a phasic course. During the phases of severe depression the dosage has to be increased.
As for the duration of treatment, we treated one boy with Ludiomil uninterruptedly for six years. Towards the end of this period he had made such an improvement that we were able gradually to reduce the doses and finally to withdraw the drug altogether. The boy is now going through puberty and can manage without any medication. The treatment enabled him to attend school like a normal child. We have not so far had any experience with lithium therapy.
In order to diagnose depression in children, you have to enquire specifically about depressive symptoms. This is not always easy. Often the typical manifestations of depression are absent. Moreover, children are usually incapable of describing a diurnal fluctuation or a depressive mood, even if it were a feature of their illness. But, as their parents tell us, they have difficulty in falling asleep and don't want to get up in the morning. Another question you can ask is whether the children eat more in the morning or in the evening. If their appetite increases in the evening, the chances are that antidepressant treatment will yield good results. Although it is much more difficult in children than in adults to distinguish between neurotic and endogenous depression, the distinction has, in fact, no bearing on treatment, because both forms respond well. Neurotic disorders, which one comes to recognise in the course of time, should be treated by psychotherapy. Besides treating the children with drugs, we generally try to ensure that both they and their parents receive psychotherapy.
In reply to Dr. LORGÉ, who asked why Ludiomil proved less effective in children, I would say that the difference is probably due to the fact that the diagnosis is far more difficult to establish in children and that therefore the drug is sometimes used in cases where it is not indicated.

233

A controlled, double-blind, between-patient trial comparing CIBA 34,276-Ba and imipramine in depressive states

by I. Guz*

Presented in the following paper are observations relating to 57 patients suffering from depressive illness who were treated under a double-blind regime. The patients, all of whom were considered suitable for treatment with imipramine, were randomly allocated to one of the following treatment groups:

CIBA 34,276-Ba (Ludiomil®) = 28 cases
Imipramine (Tofranil®)   = 29 cases.

Before treatment was initiated, all the patients were submitted to a wash-out period of one week.

The Hamilton Rating Scale for Depression was employed to assess the severity of the depressive illness before treatment, and subsequent assessments using the same scale were made during treatment on the 3rd, 7th, 14th, 21st, and 28th days of the treatment period. A check-list of signs and symptoms which might be related to conventional antidepressant therapy was used at all interviews, including the pre-treatment one. Blood and urine samples were taken at each examination, so that laboratory investigations could be performed in order to determine the hepatic, renal, and haematological tolerability of the two drugs. Since the object of the trial was to compare the overall efficacy and tolerability as well as the onset of action of both drugs in the treatment of depression, the two preparations were administered in identical daily dosages of 150 mg. (2 × 25 mg. tablets t.i.d.) for a period of 28 consecutive days. All the patients were hospitalised and were treated at the "Hospital das Clínicas" of São Paulo University.

1. Description of sample

1.1. General characteristics

The patients treated comprised 49 males and eight females, aged between 18 and 72 years. The mean age of the total sample was 40.14 years. Twelve patients in the imipramine sub-sample and 17 in the 34,276-Ba sub-sample were below the mean age (Table 1).

The sub-samples were analysed by reference to the patient's concomitant medical condition and familial history of mental illness. As can be seen from Table 1, there was a significantly (5 % level) higher incidence of familial depression in the 34,276-Ba sub-sample than in the imipramine sub-sample, but this was the

* Head of the Adult Male Ward at the Psychiatric Clinic, Neuropsychiatric Department (Head: Prof. Fernando Oliveira Bastos), "Hospital das Clínicas", Medical School of São Paulo University, Brazil.

Table 1. General characteristics of the two treatment sub-samples.

	34,276-Ba N = 28		Imipramine N = 29	
	f	%	f	%
Age: (mean age 40.14 years) Below mean	17	60.7	12	41.4
Sex: Males	24	85.7	25	86.2
Race: White Caucasian	24	85.7	25	86.2
Concomitant medical condition: Present	5	17.9	7	24.1
Family history of mental illness:				
Depression*	7	25.0	1	3.4
Alcoholism	7	25.0	3	10.3
Schizophrenia	–	0.0	–	0.0
Other	4	14.3	5	17.2
Patient's attitude towards treatment: Cooperative	23	82.1	17	58.6
Patient's condition in previous two weeks: Deteriorated	11	39.3	18	62.1

* P = 0.05–0.01
N = number of patients
f = absolute frequencies
% = relative frequencies

only significant difference between the sub-samples as far as general character-istics were concerned.

70.2 % of the patients in the sample were regarded as "cooperative" in their attitude towards treatment. In 50.9 % of all the cases the depressive illness had "deteriorated" in the two weeks prior to the start of antidepressant treatment. As revealed in Table 1, there was no significant difference between the two sub-samples in these two respects.

1.2. Diagnosis
As indicated in Tables 2 and 3, there was also no significant difference between the sub-samples with regard to either the type or the category of the depressive illnesses from which the patients were suffering.

1.3. Individual Hamilton items before treatment
When analysing the 21 items of the Hamilton Rating Scale, it was found that at the beginning of treatment significantly more patients in the 34,276-Ba sub-sample had diurnal (i.e. matutinal) variations than in the imipramine sub-

235

Table 2. Main diagnostic categories and types in the two treatment sub-samples.

Category/Type	34,276-Ba N = 28		Imipramine N = 29	
	f	%	f	%
Endogenous:	11	39.3	11	38.0
Agitated	1	3.6	5	17.2
Retarded	5	17.8	4	13.8
Other	5	17.8	2	6.9
Reactive:	5	17.9	4	13.7
Agitated	–	0.0	1	3.5
Retarded	1	3.6	–	0.0
Other	4	14.3	3	10.3
Other:	12	42.8	14	48.3
Agitated	1	3.6	2	6.9
Retarded	4	14.3	5	17.2
Other	7	25.0	7	24.1

N = number of patients
f = absolute frequencies
% = relative frequencies

Table 3. Main diagnostic types in the two treatment sub-samples.

Types	34,276-Ba N = 28		Imipramine N = 29	
	f	%	f	%
Agitated	2	7.2	8	27.6
Retarded	10	35.7	9	31.0
Other	16	57.1	12	41.4

N = number of patients
f = absolute frequencies
% = relative frequencies

sample. With this exception, there was no significant difference between the sub-samples as regards the remaining 20 items.

Matutinal variation was registered in 57.1 % of the cases treated with 34,276-Ba and in only 17.2 % of the group treated with imipramine. This difference was significant at a level of $P < 0.005$.

2. Effect of treatment

Item per item of the Hamilton Rating Scale registered at each interview was analysed so as to detect any possible difference in target symptoms between the two treatment groups. Improvement for any item is defined as a degree of severity

Table 4. Analysis of improvement in Hamilton scale items: "Depressed mood", "Initial insomnia", and "Delayed insomnia".

Symptom	Day	34,276-Ba		Imipramine	
		f/N	%	f/N	%
Depressed mood	3	14/27*	51.8	9/29	31.0
	7	20/28	71.4	17/29	58.6
	14	19/28	67.9	18/29	62.1
	21	20/28	71.4	19/29	65.5
	28	22/28	78.6	23/29	79.3
Initial insomnia	3	13/18	72.2	7/18	38.9
	7	17/18	94.4	15/18	83.3
	14	15/18	83.3	16/18	88.9
	21	15/18	83.3	16/18	88.9
	28	16/18	88.9	16/18	88.9
Delayed insomnia	3	12/20*	60.0	8/19	42.1
	7	10/21	47.6	10/19	52.6
	14	16/21	76.2	16/19	84.2
	21	17/21	80.9	17/19	89.5
	28	16/21	76.2	17/19	89.5

* One patient not assessed on Day 3
N = number of patients reporting symptom before treatment, including two patients in 34,276-Ba sub-sample and four in imipramine sub-sample, who have been excluded from the final analysis because of variable assessment dates or wrong dosage (one case in imipramine sub-sample)
f = absolute frequencies; % = relative frequencies of patients improved

less than that recorded at the pre-treatment interview. No significant difference in improvement for any item at any time was found between the two sub-samples. However, during the first week of treatment, a clear tendency towards better results in the 34,276-Ba sub-sample than in the imipramine sub-sample was observed for the following items: depressed mood, initial insomnia, psychic and somatic anxiety, and gastro-intestinal symptoms (cf. Tables 4 and 5). No similar tendency in favour of imipramine was observed with respect to any of the remaining items.

The total scores on the Hamilton Rating Scale for each patient who completed the 28-day treatment period were taken at each of the five interviews and submitted to covariance analysis, the pre-treatment score being used as a covariate. Tables 6 and 7 summarise the results of the covariance analysis, which shows a significant logarithmic decrease in the total Hamilton scores from the 3rd to the 28th day of treatment. Although no significant difference is apparent at any time between the two sub-samples, there is nevertheless a tendency for the scores in the 34,276-Ba sub-sample to decrease more quickly at the beginning of treatment than in the imipramine sub-sample.

The cumulative frequencies and proportions of cases which began to respond to treatment after the second day exhibit a difference in favour of 34,276-Ba

237

Table 5. Analysis of improvement in Hamilton scale items: "Psychic anxiety", "Somatic anxiety", and "Gastro-intestinal symptoms".

Symptom	Day	34,276-Ba		Imipramine	
		f/N	%	f/N	%
Psychic anxiety	3	14/27*	51.8	7/26	26.9
	7	19/28	67.9	12/26	46.1
	14	19/28	67.9	17/26	65.4
	21	18/28	64.3	19/26	73.1
	28	21/28	75.0	16/26	61.5
Somatic anxiety	3	10/26	38.5	6/24	25.0
	7	12/26	46.1	11/24	45.8
	14	14/26	53.8	15/24	62.5
	21	16/26	61.5	15/24	62.5
	28	20/26	76.9	13/24	54.2
Gastro-intestinal symptoms	3	8/16	50.0	3/19	15.8
	7	8/16	50.0	5/19	26.3
	14	11/16	68.7	11/19	57.9
	21	12/16	75.0	11/19	57.9
	28	11/16	68.7	14/19	73.7

* One patient not assessed on Day 3
N = number of patients reporting symptom before treatment, including two patients in 34,276-Ba sub-sample and four in imipramine sub-sample who have been excluded from the final analysis because of variable assessment dates or wrong dosage (one case in imipramine sub-sample)
f = absolute frequencies; % = relative frequencies of patients improved

Table 6. Mean total Hamilton scores at the various times indicated.

Treatment	Before		Days of treatment			
			3	7	14	28
34,276-Ba	27.1	u	19.3	17.0	14.3	11.1
		a	19.6	17.3	14.6	11.4
Imipramine	28.6	u	24.5	19.8	16.7	12.3
		a	24.2	19.5	16.4	12.0
Total treatments	27.9		21.9	18.4	15.5	11.7

u = unadjusted mean total Hamilton scores
a = adjusted mean total Hamilton scores
Covariance adjustment: $\bar{y}'_{it} = \bar{y}_{it} - 0.42\,(\bar{x}_i - 27.9)$

Table 7. Covariance analysis of total Hamilton scores.

Source of variation	d.f.	Σx^2	Σxy	Σy^2	$(\Sigma xy)^2/\Sigma x^2$	Σy^2 adj.	d.f.	Adj. m. sq.	F
Main units:									
Treatments	1	112.598	218.844	425.340	–	256.996	1	256.996	1.569
Patients within treatment	49	11,508.578	4,896.215	9,940.846	2,083.048	7,857.798	48	163.704	–
Treatments + patients	50	11,621.176	5,115.059	10,366.186	2,251.392	8,114.794	–	–	–
Sub-units:									
Days of treatment	3	–	–	2,836.642	–	2,836.642	3	945.547	30.881*
Linear regression term	1	–	–	2,830.000	–	2,836.000	1	2,830.000	92.426*
Quadratic regression term	1	–	–	1.416	–	1.416	1	1.416	0.046
Cubic regression term	1	–	–	5.224	–	5.224	1	5.224	0.170
Treatments × days of treatment	3	–	–	110.105	–	110.105	3	36.701	1.198
Residual (sub-units error)	147	–	–	4,501.004	–	4,501.004	147	30.619	–
Total	203	–	–	17,813.937	–	–	–	–	–

* $P < 0.001$

x = values recorded before treatment

y = scores during treatment

[Scores from the 4th treatment assessment (on 21st day) have been omitted in order to obtain equal ratios between times]

Table 8. Onset of drug effect (cumulative frequency record).

Day of treatment	34,276-Ba		Imipramine	
	f	%	f	%
1	–	0.0	–	0.0
2	1	4.3	–	0.0
3	3	13.0	1	4.2
4	3	13.0	1	4.2
5	8	34.8	5	20.8
6	8	34.8	5	20.8
7	9	39.1	5	20.8
8	9	39.1	6	25.0
9	13	56.5	10	41.7
10	16	69.6	12	50.0
11	16	69.6	12	50.0
12	16	69.6	12	50.0
13	16	69.6	12	50.0
14	16	69.6	13	54.2
15	17	74.0	13	54.2
16	18	78.3	15	62.5
17	19	82.6	18	75.0
18	19	82.6	19	79.2
19	19	82.6	21	87.5
20	20	86.9	22	91.7
21	20	86.9	22	91.7
22	21	91.3	23	95.8
23	22	95.6	23	95.8
24	23	100.0	24	100.0

f = absolute frequencies
% = relative frequencies

Note: five cases not reported in both the 34,276-Ba and the imipramine sub-samples

Table 9. Investigator's assessment of therapeutic effect.

Assessment	34,276-Ba		Imipramine	
	f	%	f	%
Treatment effective				
Moderate or marked improvement	20(1*)	76.9	16(2*)	64.0
Minimal improvement	3(1*)	11.5	6(2*)	24.0
Treatment failed				
No change, or deteriorated	3	11.5	3	12.0
Total	26(2*)	100.0	25(4*)	100.0

f = absolute frequencies
% = relative frequencies
* The figures in brackets refer to patients excluded from the final analysis because of variable assessment dates or wrong dosage.

until the 18th day, the largest difference in the response occurring on the 15th day; but the difference of 19.8 % (34,276-Ba = 74 %; imipramine = 54.2 %) is not significant in the Kolmogorov-Smirnov two-samples test (Table 8).

Tables 9 and 10 present the results of the investigator's and patient's assessment of the therapeutic effect. There was no significant difference between the two

Table 10. Patients' assessment of therapeutic effect.

Assessment	34,276-Ba		Imipramine	
	f	%	f	%
Treatment effective				
Moderate or marked improvement	19(1*)	73.1	15(2*)	60.0
Minimal improvement	3(1*)	11.5	6(1*)	24.0
Treatment failed				
No change, or deteriorated	4	15.4	4(1*)	16.0
Total	26(2*)	100.0	25(4*)	100.0

f = absolute frequencies
% = relative frequencies
* The figures in brackets refer to patients excluded from the final analysis because of variable assessment dates or wrong dosage.

Table 11. Clinical diagnoses (according to the International Classification of Diseases, 1965 Revision, Vol. 1, W.H.O., Geneva 1967) and results obtained.

I.C.D. No.	Clinical diagnosis	34,276-Ba		Imipramine	
		Response Marked/ Moderate	Minimal/ None	Response Marked/ Moderate	Minimal/ None
		f/N	f/N	f/N	f/N
296.1–3	Manic-depressive psychosis	7/10	3/10	5/7	2/7
300.4	Depressive neurosis	9/11	2/11	5/9	4/9
298.0	Reactive depressive psychosis	2/2	0/2	2/2	0/2
296.0	Involutional depression	1/1	0/1	2/5	3/5
299	Psychosis (involutional), not otherwise specified	0/1	1/1	0/0	0/0
296.9	Manic-depressive reaction, not otherwise specified	0/1	1/1	0/0	0/0
300.0	Anxiety neurosis	0/0	0/0	1/2	1/2
295.8	Schizophrenia of specified type	1/1	0/1	1/1	0/1
295.8	Schizophrenia, childhood type	1/1	0/1	0/0	0/0
295.3	Schizophrenia, paranoid type	0/0	0/0	1/1	0/1
295.7	Schizo-affective psychosis	0/0	0/0	1/2	1/2
	Total	21/28 (75%)	7/28 (25%)	18/29 (62%)	11/29 (38%)

f = absolute frequencies; N = number of patients

sub-samples either in the investigator's or in the patient's assessment of the therapeutic effect. However, viewed in the light of the absolute figures and of the clinical diagnoses, the results obtained in the group treated with 34,276-Ba may be regarded as better than those for the imipramine group (Table 11).

3. Tolerability

All signs and symptoms reported by the patients during at least one of the five treatment interviews were carefully registered. Signs and symptoms reported only at the pre-treatment interview were not considered in the overall analysis of tolerability. A significant difference (at the 1% level) in the incidence of sweating during treatment was observed, a significantly greater proportion of patients having reported this symptom in the imipramine sub-sample. Although tolerability generally seemed better with 34,276-Ba than with imipramine, no statistically significant difference between the two sub-samples was encountered with respect to any of the other signs and symptoms.

Of the 23 signs and symptoms reported, there were only three (13.0%) which showed a higher incidence in the 34,276-Ba sub-sample, i.e. dystonic symptoms, other autonomic nervous symptoms, and skin reactions. In the imipramine sub-sample, eight (34.8%) of the 23 signs and symptoms showed a higher incidence, i.e. tremor, hypotension, dry mouth, blurred vision, nausea/vomiting, dysphagia, dizziness/faintness/weakness, and sweating (Table 12).

The incidence of the remaining symptoms registered was roughly equal for both sub-samples: insomnia (~7%), drowsiness (~8.8%), excitement (~12.3%), rigidity (~1.7%), akathisia (~10.5%), tachycardia (~24.6%), nasal congestion

Table 12. Signs and symptoms reported only during treatment, showing the difference in their incidence between the two sub-samples.

Sign or symptom	34,276-Ba		Imipramine	
	f	%	f	%
Tremor	5	17.9	10	34.5
Hypotension	1	3.6	4	13.8
Dry mouth	7	25.0	13	44.8
Blurred vision	9	32.1	13	44.8
Nausea/vomiting	1	3.6	5	17.2
Dysphagia	2	7.1	4	13.4
Dizziness/faintness/weakness	4	14.3	7	24.1
Sweating*	0	0.0	8	27.6
Dystonic symptoms**	3	10.7	1	3.4
Other (autonomic nervous system)	4	14.3	2	6.9
Skin reactions	5	17.9	3	10.3

f = absolute frequencies; % = relative frequencies
* $P < 0.01$
** Negative change, i.e. fewer patients reported these symptoms during treatment than before

Table 13. Global assessment of tolerability (based on investigator's assessments).

Side effects	34,276-Ba		Imipramine	
	f	%	f	%
No side effects	5	19.2	3	12.0
No significant interference	20*	76.9	21*	84.0
Significant interference	1	3.8	1	4.0
Total	26*	100.0	25*	100.0

f = absolute frequencies; % = relative frequencies
* Excluding two patients in 34,276-Ba sub-sample and four in imipramine sub-sample, because of variable assessment dates or wrong dosage

($\sim$12.3%), increased salivation ($\sim$8.8%), diarrhoea ($\sim$14.0%), constipation ($\sim$24.6%), headache ($\sim$22.8%), and miscellaneous ($\sim$5.3%).
In the global assessment of tolerability, no significant difference between the two sub-samples was found (Table 13).

4. Laboratory findings

Decreases in the white blood count or abnormalities in the differential blood count were noted in seven patients (five in the 34,276-Ba sub-sample and two in the imipramine sub-sample) who had shown normal pre-treatment values, but these changes proved to be unspecific and clinically insignificant. Transient elevation of serum transaminases (S.G.O.T. and S.G.P.T. or both) was observed during treatment in 13 patients (22.8%) who had had values within the normal range before treatment (maximum values registered: 34,276-Ba sub-sample—64 units; imipramine sub-sample—78 units). This transient elevation of serum transaminases was found in 25% of the cases in the 34,276-Ba sub-sample and in 20.7% of those in the imipramine sub-sample. Increases in blood urea nitrogen were observed in 11 patients (19.3%); these alterations, however, did not provoke any clinical manifestations calling for additional measures.
With regard to the incidence of abnormal laboratory findings, no significant differences were observed between the two sub-samples.

5. Conclusions

a) Preparation 34,276-Ba has proved to be a very effective drug in the treatment of depressive states of varied aetiology. The results obtained in endogenous, reactive, involutional, or psychotic forms of depression were practically the same. 34,276-Ba seems to exert a better influence on anxiety symptoms, particularly at the beginning of treatment, i.e. at the time when it is actually

243

possible to detect this effect. Somato-hypochondriacal forms of depression, as well as organic and symptomatic forms, responded equally well to treatment with 34,276-Ba.

b) A definite improvement in depressed states can usually be seen in response to 34,276-Ba after only 2–3 days of treatment. The drug's mood-elevating effect precedes, or at least coincides with, its drive-enhancing effect—which means that there is no danger of a dissociation between these two therapeutic responses. Preparation 34,276-Ba appears to have a bipolar action, i.e. it dampens agitation and also enhances drive.

c) Unwanted effects provoked by 34,276-Ba were of minor importance, and the drug was in general well tolerated. The incidence of sweating was significantly higher in patients treated with imipramine than in those receiving 34,276-Ba. Dystonic symptoms, other autonomic nervous symptoms, and skin reactions were more frequently observed in the 34,276-Ba sub-sample, whereas tremor, hypotension, dry mouth, blurred vision, nausea/vomiting, dysphagia, dizziness/faintness/weakness, and sweating were more common in the imipramine sub-sample. In the global assessment of tolerability, no significant difference between the two sub-samples was found.

d) No significant difference was observed between the two sub-samples with respect to the incidence of abnormal laboratory findings. Such alterations as occurred in the serum transaminases, blood urea nitrogen, and haematological values recorded were of no clinical importance.

6. Summary

No significant difference was found between 34,276-Ba and imipramine as regards either their tolerability or their efficacy, although 34,276-Ba showed a slight tendency to be more effective and better tolerated and to have a more rapid onset of action than imipramine.

A double-blind comparative study on the effectiveness of maprotiline (Ludiomil) and imipramine (Tofranil) in endogenous depression

by J. Angst, M. Frei, M. Lehmann, A. Padrutt, and P. Vetter*

I. Aim of the trial and methods used

As extensive clinical data on maprotiline (Ludiomil®) were already available, the aim of our double-blind trial was merely to determine whether the effect of this drug differed qualitatively from that of imipramine (Tofranil®).

The trial was conducted in altogether 22 patients suffering from endogenous depression, who were allocated at random to the two treatment groups. These two groups were homogeneous in respect of diagnosis, and did not differ significantly as regards sex or age (Table 1).

The duration of treatment was invariably 20 days, and both drugs were given by mouth in a daily dosage of 150 mg. The patients were submitted to physical and psychiatric examinations prior to the start of medication (Day 0), as well as on the 10th, 15th, and 20th days of treatment, and the findings were recorded by applying the A.M.P. system (A.M.P. = *Arbeitsgemeinschaft für Methodik und Dokumentation in der Psychiatrie*) and the Hamilton scale. An I.B.M. 370-155 computer and an electronic desk calculator were employed to process the data. Only non-parametric procedures were used for the statistical analysis of changes in psychic symptoms and for the comparative evaluation of the two groups.

The trial ran from 1st June to 31st October 1971.

Table 1. Composition of the two treatment groups.

		Maprotiline	Imipramine
Diagnosis	Endogenous depression	11	11
Sex	Male	4	2
	Female	7	9
Age	Mean	56.55	55.73
	Standard deviation	11.61	7.60

II. Results

1. Global assessment of response after 20 days

There was, at the most, a slight tendency for imipramine to produce a better effect than maprotiline, but it must be borne in mind that the number of patients treated was small. The detailed results are reproduced in Table 2.

* Psychiatrische Universitätsklinik, Zurich, Switzerland.

Table 2. Global results in the two treatment groups.

	Maprotiline	Imipramine
Symptom-free	2	3
Marked improvement	2	3
Slight improvement	3	1
No improvement	3	4**
Deterioration	1*	–
	11	11

* Treatment discontinued on Day 10 because of delirium
** Treatment in one case discontinued by the patient's ophthalmologist on Day 10 because of pre-existing glaucoma

Table 3. Symptoms showing a significant degree of improvement during treatment.

	Maprotiline			Imipramine		
Days	10	15	20	10	15	20
Poor concentration	o	*	*		o	o
Constriction of thought	o		o		o	*
Autism			o			
Feeling of helplessness					o	o
Impaired emotional vitality					*	o
Depressed/dejected						o
Hopeless/despairing	*	*	**			*
Feeling of inadequacy					o	
Lack of drive					*	*
Drive inhibited					*	*
Sociability decreased						o
Feeling of illness		*				*
Initial insomnia	o					*
Middle insomnia			*		o	*
Duration of sleep reduced			*		o	o
Loss of appetite	***	**	**		o	o
Feeling of pressure in the head (or similar sensations)		*	o	o		

Significance levels: o = P < 0.10
      * = P < 0.05
      ** = P < 0.01
      *** = P < 0.001

2. Effect on psychic symptoms, assessed by reference to the A.M.P. system
The A.M.P. system (Sheets 3 and 4) enables one to assess the psychic and somatic symptomatology of depression, as well as clinically detectable side effects. The signs and symptoms are graded as a rule in terms of their severity (i.e. mild, moderate, or severe).
Table 3 lists those symptoms which showed a significant change during treatment. Changes were considered to be significant even at the 10 % level because

the trial groups were very small. Despite their smallness, however, quite a large number of depressive symptoms decreased significantly in each group.
Maprotiline clearly had a more rapid onset of effect, inasmuch as five symptoms had already diminished by the 10th day. Most impressive of all was the improvement in appetite, which was significant at the $1^0/_{00}$ level on the 10th day. Initial insomnia, poor concentration, constriction of thought, and hopeless/despairing mood likewise improved. In the further course of treatment, the other forms of insomnia associated with depression, as well as the patients' feeling of illness, also regressed in response to maprotiline (cf. also Figures 1–3).

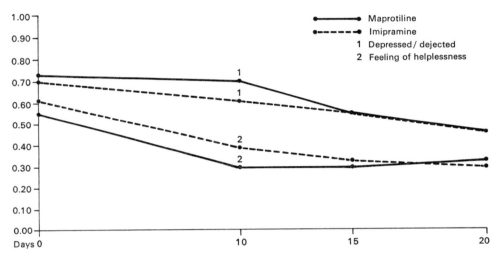

Fig. 1. Changes in two psychic symptoms of depression during treatment with either maprotiline or imipramine. Ordinate: coefficient of severity (A.M.P. system).

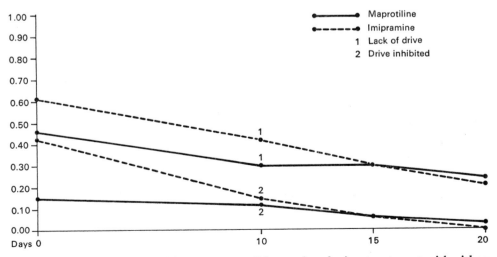

Fig. 2. Changes in two psychic symptoms of depression during treatment with either maprotiline or imipramine. Ordinate: coefficient of severity (A.M.P. system).

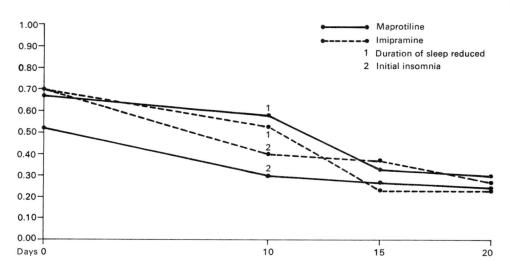

Fig. 3. Changes in two somatic symptoms of depression during treatment with either maprotiline or imipramine. Ordinate: coefficient of severity (A.M.P. system).

In the imipramine group the effect of treatment did not become statistically significant until 15 days had elapsed. By this time, however, virtually the entire depressive syndrome (i.e. the disorders affecting mood, emotional vitality, thought, sleep, and appetite) had regressed in a fairly uniform manner. This trend was particularly marked by the 20th day, at which time nearly all the depressive symptoms had improved in response to imipramine. In this respect, moreover, there appeared to be a qualitative difference in the action of the two drugs: in response to imipramine both lack of drive and inhibited drive improved to such an extent that the change was already significant at the 5% level by the 15th day of treatment; in the patients receiving maprotiline, these symptoms showed no significant change even by the 20th day (Figure 2).

Hence, imipramine led to an improvement in a wider range of depressive symptoms (excluding agitation, which was present in too few patients for it to be taken into account). Maprotiline displayed a somewhat more rapid onset of effect and acted chiefly on the somatic symptoms of depression (loss of appetite, sleep disorders), as well as on mood, whereas its influence on drive was less clearly marked in the present trial. It should be stressed, however, that the group of patients treated with maprotiline had displayed fewer disturbances in drive on Day 0 than the group given imipramine; consequently, maprotiline was bound to have less effect on these target symptoms. In other words, caution is indicated when interpreting the findings.

The slight differences found between the two drugs cannot be regarded as more than vague trends, to which—owing to the small number of patients studied—no statistical significance can be attached. When the groups were compared by applying the median test across all the A.M.P. items, no difference could be detected between the two preparations. It should be borne in mind, however, that the discriminatory capacity of this test is relatively low.

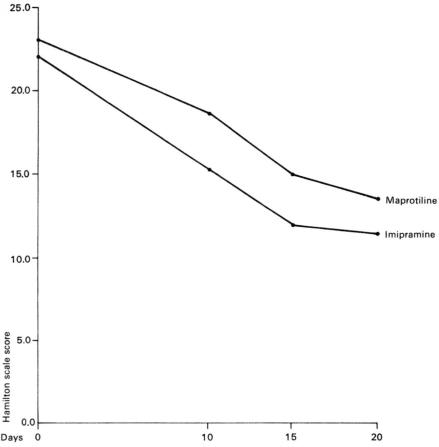

Fig. 4. Global improvement during treatment with either maprotiline or imipramine, as assessed by using the Hamilton scale.

Due allowance being made for these reservations, the response as assessed by reference to the Hamilton scale tended to be more favourable in the patients receiving imipramine (Figures 4 and 5). This applies not only to the total scores but also to Factor 1 (general factor). Factor 1, the value for which was the same in both groups prior to treatment, showed a more consistent decrease in the imipramine patients than in those receiving maprotiline, with the result that the gap between the two curves steadily widened in the course of treatment. With respect to Factor 2 (agitation/retardation), the Hamilton scale indicated that the patients were suffering from retarded depression, but the values for this factor hardly changed at all in the course of treatment. Hamilton's Factor 2 does not seem to measure lack of drive and inhibited drive with the same precision as the A.M.P. system, nor does it appear capable of differentiating so sharply between these two parameters.

249

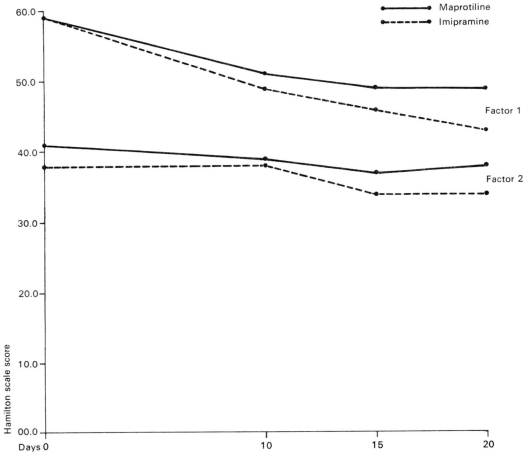

Fig. 5. Factors 1 and 2 during treatment with either maprotiline or imipramine.

III. Global assessment of tolerability

No essential differences were found between the two drugs in respect of tolerability. The principal side effects consisted of autonomic nervous manifestations which were as a rule fairly mild. In one patient receiving maprotiline and in two receiving imipramine, however, they assumed a moderately severe form (tremor, disorders of micturition, and dizziness). Also worth noting is the course taken by those autonomic nervous symptoms that are commonly regarded as side effects of treatment. Dryness of the mouth, disorders of accommodation, constipation, and the like did not show any significant changes during treatment with either of the two drugs. Only in the case of constipation was a slight, but still not significant, increase in severity noted during medication with maprotiline; during treatment with imipramine, on the other hand, this "side effect" tended, if anything, to improve (Figure 6). In both groups, the patients often

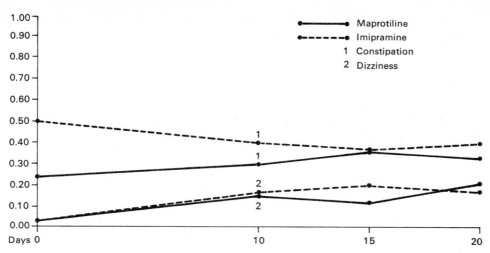

Fig. 6. Changes in two somatic "side effects" during treatment with either maprotiline or imipramine. Ordinate: coefficient of severity (A.M.P. system).

Table 4. Global assessment of tolerability in the two treatment groups.

Side effects	Maprotiline	Imipramine
None	2	3
Doubtful	3	1
Mild	4	5
Moderate	1	2
Severe	1	–
Total	11	11

complained of dizziness and of a feeling of pressure in the head—two subjective side effects of no great importance. In one case, treatment with maprotiline gave rise to delirium, which necessitated the drug's withdrawal on the 10th day. One patient on imipramine dropped out on the instructions of an ophthalmologist because she was suffering from pre-existing glaucoma.

The severity of the side effects caused by the two drugs is indicated in Table 4.

IV. Summary

A double-blind trial was carried out in 22 in-patients suffering from endogenous depression in order to compare the effect of maprotiline (Ludiomil) with that of imipramine (Tofranil). The 11 patients in each group were treated for 20 days, the daily dosage in both instances being 150 mg. by mouth. The patients

251

were examined on Days 0, 10, 15, and 20, and the findings were recorded using both the A.M.P. system and the Hamilton scale. After 10 days' medication one patient had to be withdrawn from the maprotiline group because of drug-induced delirium, and one from the imipramine group because of pre-existing glaucoma.

Both drugs had an antidepressant action. They appeared to differ in the quality of their effect, but this difference could not be shown to be statistically significant. Maprotiline displayed a more rapid onset of effect (within 10 days) and acted chiefly on the somatic symptoms of depression (loss of appetite and sleep disorders). Particularly impressive was the extent to which it improved appetite. Imipramine acted somewhat more slowly, but influenced a wider range of signs and symptoms. Unlike maprotiline, it also led to a significant improvement in lack of drive and inhibited drive.

Despite the more rapid onset of action of maprotiline, therefore, imipramine tended to have a more pronounced antidepressant effect, as revealed both by the A.M.P. system (greater improvement in psychic symptoms) and by the Hamilton scale (global assessment). Both drugs were well tolerated.

It might perhaps be possible to differentiate more clearly between the two drugs by giving them in higher daily doses and by studying them in a larger number of patients.

International experience with Ludiomil*

by O. DE S. PINTO, S. P. AFEICHE, E. BARTHOLINI, and P. LOUSTALOT**

Introduction

One of the most stimulating things about clinical research is that the evaluation of a drug is never complete. As methods and techniques become more and more sophisticated, the amount of information that can be collected about both new and old therapeutic preparations is constantly increasing; and as the volume of such information grows, it becomes increasingly important to remember that such knowledge is of little practical value unless the facts obtained can be correctly interpreted and communicated.

This is of special significance when a new drug is being evaluated before being made available for general use. It is during this period that the basis is laid down both for treating patients under the normal conditions prevailing in hospital and in practice, and also for future research.

During the earlier stages in the evaluation of a new drug, one must of necessity proceed cautiously. The drug's safety has to be demonstrated and its potential value assessed. After comprehensive open clinical trials and other studies had shown that Ludiomil® met our requirements in both respects, we set about planning further investigations on an international basis. Shortly after these trials had started, a special issue of *Psychopharmacology*, a publication of the U.S. National Institute of Mental Health[4], reviewed 2,000 papers on the effectiveness of antidepressant drugs. It was concluded that significantly lower improvement rates are reported for antidepressant drugs under the conditions shown in Table 1.

Table 1. Factors associated with lowest improvement rates in clinical trials with antidepressants. (From: SMITH et al.[4])

Hospital setting
Strictly regulated fashion
Short duration
Control group
Evaluator of effectiveness unaware of the treatment provided
Conclusions of investigator based on statistical analysis rather than clinical overview

* This paper was read by Prof. C. R. B. JOYCE.
** Medical Department, CIBA-GEIGY LIMITED, Basle, Switzerland.

The series of clinical trials with Ludiomil which will be surveyed in the present paper did in fact fulfil all these stringent criteria. They were carried out in a hospital environment and were strictly regulated and controlled, being double-blind between-patient studies based on a common, defined trial plan and using a sophisticated patient-data recording system; in addition, the main trial was usually preceded by a dummy run on a few patients to correct any initial errors in operating procedure. The trial period was relatively short. Control groups with comparative compounds were included. Neither the treating physicians nor their ancillary staff knew which treatment was being given, and the conclusions were based upon statistical analysis.

The trials were all carried out according to the same plan and employing the same data-recording system, so that results from different centres could be compared at least in some important respects. For the evaluation of drug effects the Hamilton Rating Scale for Depression was used; this rating scale has been internationally validated and is widely accepted. In addition, unwanted effects were assessed by means of a check-list. Both therapeutic efficacy and side effects were also globally rated.

The series of international trials to be described here was carried out in 12 countries; 850 patients were included, of whom 412 were given Ludiomil. During the planning of the trials, discussions with participating investigators revealed that amitriptyline and imipramine—the basic tricyclic antidepressants—were still generally thought to be the most useful compounds in this class. Because of this, and also because so much is known about imipramine and amitriptyline, these two drugs were chosen as the comparative compounds, each investigator being asked to select the one he preferred or regarded as most suitable. The only exception has been in France—where clomipramine was chosen as the comparative agent—but from France we have so far received the results of only one completed controlled trial on a small number of patients (two groups of 15 cases each). The criterion for patient selection was defined as any depressive state considered suitable for treatment with tricyclic antidepressants.

Ludiomil was given in a fixed dose of 50 mg. three times daily from the start of treatment, because in earlier probing trials this dosage had proved to be safe and effective. It has long been recommended that amitriptyline and imipramine should initially be administered to patients in a relatively low dosage which can subsequently be increased. The decision about initial treatment with the comparative compounds was made by each investigator. Generally, treatment was started with a dose of 25 mg. three times daily, which was increased to 50 mg. three times daily after three or seven days. In six trials, however, treatment with imipramine or amitriptyline was initiated and continued with a dosage of 50 mg. three times daily.

Efficacy

The results of such a trial series can be evaluated either by pooling the findings from different centres or, alternatively, by analysing the individual trials separately. The first of these methods is open to some criticism, and pooled results must indeed be interpreted with caution. However, the data emerging from individual trials have in general been the same, and the differences have in most instances been minor ones.

Pooled results relating to 639 patients were analysed while we were awaiting completion of individual trials. There was no statistical difference between the efficacy of Ludiomil, amitriptyline, and imipramine, as judged by the investigator's overall assessment after 28 days. Covariance analysis of the total Hamilton scores in all the cases treated showed a highly significant decrease in the mean score in each of the three treatment groups ($P < 0.001$) from Day 7 to Day 28, i.e. there was a significant improvement in the depressive state in response to treatment with any of the three drugs.

The scores for the individual items rated by the Hamilton scale were also analysed separately for each of the three treatments. Statistically significant differences were found with respect to six of the individual items (Table 2).

Amitriptyline was more active than Ludiomil and imipramine in the relief of *initial insomnia* (but not in other sleep disturbances), and this can of course be ascribed to its sedative properties.

By the end of the first week, the proportion of *retarded* patients improving on Ludiomil was significantly larger than in response to amitriptyline or imipramine. Although this difference disappeared during the remaining part of the treatment period, the more rapid response to Ludiomil in such patients may well be of practical importance.

At the end of the second week of treatment, the patients on Ludiomil and, perhaps surprisingly, those on imipramine showed a significantly higher improvement rate—when they were *agitated* or when they had *obsessive or compulsive symptoms*—than those on amitriptyline. In the case of agitation, this difference persisted until the end of treatment, but was no longer statistically significant. With regard to obsessive and compulsive symptoms, the first place on the 28th

Table 2. Six individual items on the Hamilton scale for which statistically significant differences between the three treatments were found.

Target symptoms	Imipramine	Amitriptyline	Ludiomil
Initial insomnia	Less good	Better	Less good
Retardation	Less good	Less good	Better
Agitation	Better	Less good	Better
Obsession and compulsion	Better	Less good	Better
Depressed mood	Less good	Better	Better
Work and interests	Less good	Better	Better
Total score: better	2	3	5
Total score: less good	4	3	1

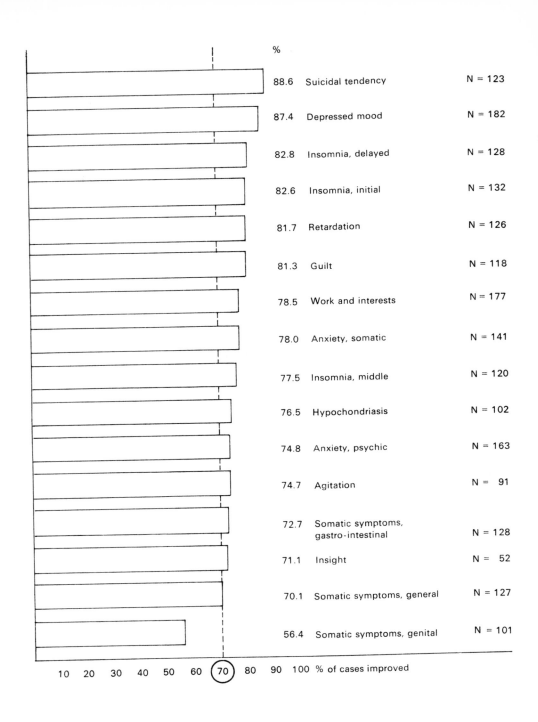

Fig. 1. Percentage of patients showing improvement on Ludiomil at the end of a four-week period by reference to 16 items from the Hamilton scale that are most specific for depression. N = number of patients with a particular symptom at the start of treatment and completing the trial period; these are drawn from a total population of 238 patients.

day of treatment was held by imipramine, followed by Ludiomil and then by amitriptyline.

At the end of the treatment period, *depressed mood* as well as *work and interests* were shown to have improved in a higher proportion of the patients on Ludiomil or amitriptyline.

Depression is a picture of many colours, mostly subdued in tone, which blend to form various patterns on a poorly defined but clinically understandable background. It is difficult to isolate a single part, examine it out of context, and draw any useful conclusions. At the same time, if the various components of the depressive picture and the response of each component to treatment are examined separately, worthwhile information may be obtained. It is certainly useful to show that Ludiomil covers an unusually wide range of depressive manifestations, especially when—as was the case here—the information has been obtained from strictly regulated clinical trials.

When a given form of treatment is prescribed, the proportion of patients that can be expected to respond, and also the proportional pattern of the response, is obviously of great interest.

The percentages of patients showing a response to treatment with Ludiomil is shown in Figure 1 by reference to 16 symptoms from the Hamilton scale, all of which are specific for depression. *Depressed mood, suicidal tendency, initial and delayed insomnia, retardation,* and *feelings of guilt* were improved in over 80% of cases, while the other symptoms—with the single exception of those referable to the genital system—showed an improvement in over 70% of cases. Genital symptoms, which improved in only 56% of patients, are often problem symptoms and not enough information is available for any detailed comment to be ventured here.

Before leaving these considerations on the efficacy of Ludiomil as evaluated from pooled results, a brief reference should be made to the drug's onset of action. The response to antidepressant drug therapy can be dramatic, but more often it is rather gradual. In such cases it may be very difficult to define the onset of action with any degree of precision. However, during these trials an attempt was made to assess the onset of action on the basis of clinical judgment, and the findings showed a trend in favour of Ludiomil. The more rapid response of retarded patients, which has already been commented upon, should also be noted.

Some of the results from individual trials in this series have been presented during this meeting, and findings from others will be published elsewhere. Thirteen individual trials—carried out in Austria, Brazil, France, Germany, Great Britain, Italy, Northern Europe, Spain, and Switzerland—will be considered here. Some basic information about them is given in Table 3. Two of these studies were multi-centre trials, the first of which was undertaken in Italy and the second in Northern Europe (with centres in Denmark, Finland, the Netherlands, and Sweden).

It is well known that under rigorous trial conditions somewhat variable results have been obtained with all the antidepressant drugs in common use today. Indeed, some investigators have occasionally found it hard to differentiate between such drugs and a placebo.

A global assessment of efficacy, made at the end of each trial period for each patient, would seem to be a coarser method of measurement than the use of a validated rating scale, but it is nevertheless worth examining.

The histogram in Figure 2 shows the percentages of cases in each of the trials that improved on each treatment, as revealed by an overall assessment at the end of the trial period. As would be expected, the differences between drugs are generally small.

From the decrease in the mean Hamilton scores (i.e. from the degree of improvement) in individual trials (Figure 3) a similar general picture emerges. Viewed in conjunction with the findings reported in other antidepressant trials, this pattern confirms the potent antidepressant effect of Ludiomil. Between-centre or

Table 3. International Ludiomil trials: double-blind, between-patient.

Country	Investigator	Ref. No.	Total No. of patients	Comparative compound(s)
Austria	*Tschabitscher,* Vienna	A 18	50	Amitriptyline
Brazil	*Paprocki,* Belo Horizonte	BR 1	60	Imipramine
	Campos, Rio de Janeiro	BR 2	60	Amitriptyline
	Guz, São Paulo	BR 3	57	Imipramine
France	*Kammerer,* Strasbourg	F 3	30	Clomipramine
Germany	*Jovanović,* Würzburg	D 15	47	Amitriptyline, imipramine
	Schmitt, Homburg	D 17	34	Amitriptyline, imipramine
Great Britain	*Forrest* and *Hay,* Edinburgh	GB 1	28	Imipramine
Spain	*Obiols,* Barcelona	E 1	49	Imipramine
Switzerland	*Heim,* Oetwil am See	CH 1	39	Amitriptyline
	Heimann, Lausanne	CH 3	50	Amitriptyline
	Multi-centre			
Italy	*Benassi,* Reggio Emilia			
	Cassano, Pisa			
	Giberti, Genoa	I 4	135	Amitriptyline, imipramine
	Muratorio, L'Aquila			
	Nistri, Florence			
North-European				
Denmark	*Kragh-Sørensen,* Glostrup			
	Welner, Copenhagen			
Finland	*Kauppinen,* Oulu			
Netherlands	*Botter,* Amersfoort	N-E	211	Amitriptyline
	Zwart, Delft			
Sweden	*Bernhardson,* Uppsala			
	Sjöström, Uppsala			
	Wetterholm, Nyköping			

even between-investigator differences are notoriously difficult to analyse and may be due to a wide variety of factors, as the papers by Dr. HEIM and Dr. WELNER have suggested.

Tolerability

Having demonstrated the antidepressant activity of Ludiomil, it becomes important to examine the drug's tolerability as well. This was done by means of a check-list of unwanted effects emerging during treatment, including those side effects commonly observed during tricyclic therapy[2, 3].
It is well known that subjective reports of undesirable drug effects are difficult to evaluate. In this series, some symptoms which might otherwise have been

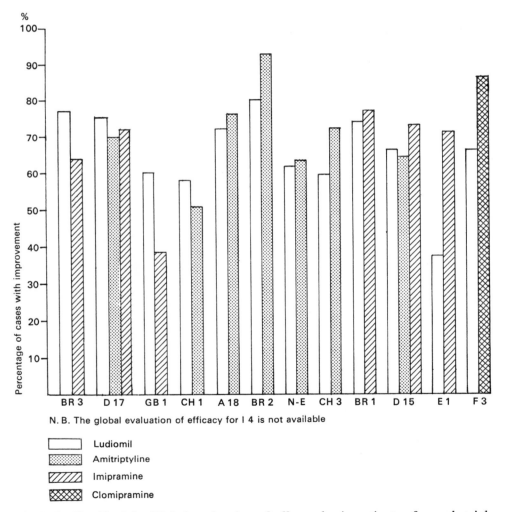

N. B. The global evaluation of efficacy for I 4 is not available

☐ Ludiomil
▨ Amitriptyline
▨ Imipramine
▨ Clomipramine

Fig. 2. Ludiomil trials. Global evaluation of efficacy by investigator for each trial. Individually analysed percentage of cases showing a "moderate or marked" improvement at the end of treatment.

reported as side effects were eliminated by having the check-list for side effects completed at the first patient interview, i.e. before treatment was initiated. It is now widely recognised that many depressed patients receiving no treatment complain, for instance, of dry mouth, dizziness, sweating, or constipation. And, of course, if antidepressant therapy is effective, such symptoms very often improve. On the other hand, once this risk of error has been reduced, the use of a detailed check-list tends to increase the reported incidence of side effects.

Certain side effects are commonly regarded as a problem with tricyclic compounds. Figure 4 shows some of these unwanted signs and symptoms emerging during treatment, in instances where statistically significant differences appeared with respect to the tolerability of one or more of the treatments; the good tolerability of Ludiomil is self-evident. It should also be remembered that all the patients on Ludiomil started treatment with 50 mg. three times daily (continuing without change), whereas in many of those on the comparative treatments medication was initiated with 25 mg. three times daily.

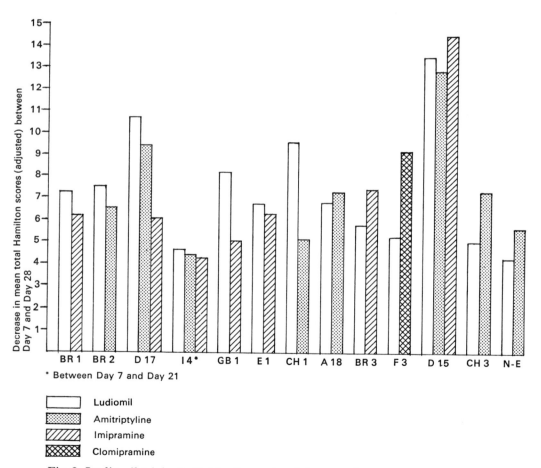

Fig. 3. Ludiomil trials. Individually analysed decrease in mean total Hamilton scores (adjusted) between Day 7 and Day 28.

However, Ludiomil proved to be less well tolerated than the comparative compounds as far as skin rashes are concerned. The problem of skin reactions occurring in association with psychopharmaceuticals is a complex one[1]. It is known that a wide range of skin reactions may be encountered with tricyclic antidepressants[2]. In order to determine the true incidence of such side effects, very large numbers of patients are needed, as well as a placebo control group[1]. During this series of trials skin rashes occurred in response to all three compounds;

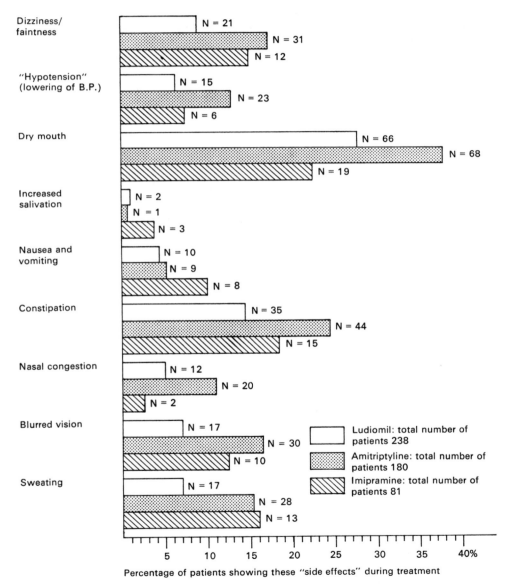

Fig. 4. Unwanted signs and symptoms emerging during treatment and showing a significant difference of incidence between the treatment groups (see also text).

irrespective of whether Ludiomil, amitriptyline, or imipramine was administered, they were of essentially the same nature, consisting mainly of localised or generalised exanthema, with or without itching. In the patients on Ludiomil, they occurred approximately twice as often as in the patients receiving the two tricyclics. In certain instances they disappeared spontaneously, whereas in the remaining cases the rash did not subside until after one or more of the following measures had been taken: reduction in dosage, administration of antihistamines, or discontinuation of treatment. In all cases where treatment was stopped, the skin reaction resolved rapidly and completely. When reactions of this kind are at all severe, the treatment should be withdrawn; but if they are mild and do not disturb the patient, then the medication can be cautiously continued and perhaps an antihistamine added to the regime.

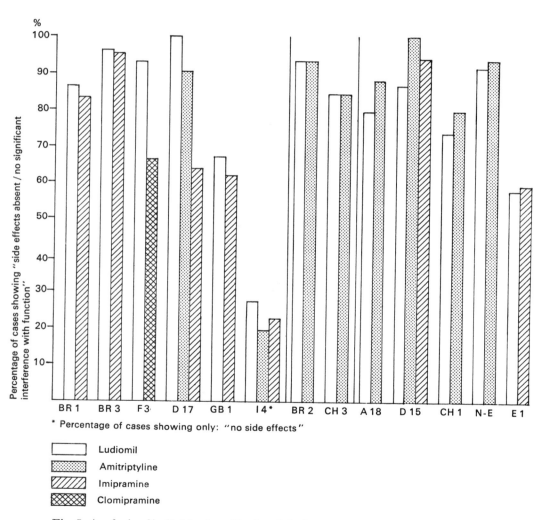

Fig. 5. Analysis of individual studies for global assessment of tolerability by the investigator. Percentage of cases showing "side effects absent/no significant interference with function".

The global assessment of tolerability presented in Figure 5 was based on all unwanted effects and was made at the end of the trial period. It is apparent from this figure that the tolerability of Ludiomil was equal to that of the comparative drug in two trials, whereas in the rest the trend favoured Ludiomil in six instances and the comparative compound in five. Hence, Ludiomil is certainly as well tolerated as the other drugs. In addition, as has been pointed out earlier in connection with various individual symptoms, the incidence of unwanted effects following Ludiomil was—with the single exception of skin rashes—either similar to that noted with the other compounds or even appreciably lower.

Laboratory screening

As part of our evaluation of Ludiomil during these trials, the lack of toxicity demonstrated during earlier studies has been confirmed by carrying out appropriate laboratory tests wherever possible. These included haemoglobin and haematocrit estimations, total and differential white blood counts, serum transaminase and alkaline phosphatase estimations, blood urea nitrogen determinations, and routine urine examinations. The tests—which were done at the beginning and end of the treatment period, and sometimes also during treatment—were performed in 10 different centres on 319 patients treated with Ludiomil. Full details of the results are available; it is sufficient to mention here that only occasional and transient changes were found and that these were generally within the range of normal values. In no case was medication stopped because of abnormal laboratory findings during treatment with Ludiomil; moreover, a retrospective analysis of the results has failed to reveal any case in which one could say with the benefit of hindsight that treatment ought to have been discontinued for this reason.

Long-term follow-up

Some comments on long-term follow-up studies have already been made in the course of this meeting. Patients are often treated either continuously or intermittently for long periods with antidepressant medication. Both the efficacy and the tolerability of Ludiomil have been good under such conditions. As is to be expected, subjective side effects tend to diminish and often disappear during treatment, and there has been no suggestion of toxic effects appearing in response to prolonged therapy.

Indications

In these trials, the criterion for patient selection was that all cases considered suitable for treatment with a tricyclic antidepressant should be admitted. The resultant sample of treated patients included those with reactive and neurotic depressive illnesses as well as the various types of affective psychotic disorder and mixed depressions. Ludiomil was shown to display very good activity in non-psychotic depressive states. For instance, in the Italian multi-centre trial the mean total decrease in the Hamilton score for patients with neurotic depression treated with Ludiomil was 14.3, as compared with 9.2 for patients on amitriptyline and 9.4 for those on imipramine. While it would be inappropriate here to discuss the classification of depression, there can be no doubt that Ludiomil represents a valuable form of treatment for both psychotic and non-psychotic depressive illnesses.

It should be added that some 20% of the subjects treated in these trials were out-patients. The efficacy and tolerability of Ludiomil was as good in these as in the larger group of in-patients.

Finally, as far as indications are concerned, it is important with any antidepressant medication to know whether it is at all likely to cause or encourage the development of mania. This, too, is not easy to elucidate in depth: mania may not only be precipitated by treatment, but may also develop because of lack of response to therapy. This, however, has not been a problem with Ludiomil; only in one patient, in fact, was the medication withdrawn because a manic state had become manifest.

Dosage

Opinions still differ somewhat as to the dose in which tricyclic antidepressants should initially be given and as to where the desirable upper dosage limits lie. It seems likely that at least in many depressed patients the dosage should be individually adjusted, and this is in fact being done in the trials with Ludiomil that are now in progress in the United States. But in the investigations described here, Ludiomil was given in a fixed dose of 50 mg. three times daily from the start of treatment, and was well accepted by the patients. The use of fixed doses makes prescribing simpler for the doctor and—what is even more important—enables the patient to understand the dosage schedule more easily.

Once a patient has shown a good and a continued response to this regime, the dose can be lowered to 25 mg. three times daily. Under such circumstances, the antidepressant effect will usually be maintained; but if it is not, then the original daily dose of 150 mg. should be resumed. In some patients, maintenance treatment has been stabilised on as little as 10 mg. three times daily.

It is known that tricyclic antidepressants can sometimes cause convulsions when given in very high doses, and that even when they are employed within the normal dosage range fits may occur in patients with epilepsy or with an epileptic diathesis[3]. The same is true of Ludiomil. Some psychiatrists nevertheless prescribe tricyclic antidepressants in high doses, although usually for in-patients. Our present experience indicates that oral treatment with Ludiomil in patients without organic disease is generally well tolerated when the drug is given in daily doses of up to 225 mg. This has also been confirmed by results obtained with intravenous therapy, which seems to be acquiring an increasingly important place in the treatment of depressive states.

In severely depressed patients, it is often considered desirable to initiate treatment parenterally—a procedure which may often avoid the necessity for electro-convulsive therapy. Circumstances also sometimes arise in which parenteral administration proves preferable because, for example, it is thought that the patient is unlikely to take tablets. Patients have been treated with intravenous infusions of Ludiomil in doses of up to 250 mg. daily (administered in 250–500 ml. physiological saline), and the infusions have been excellently tolerated. The average duration of such infusions in the cases thus far treated has been 90 minutes. Higher doses of Ludiomil, i.e. doses of up to 800 mg., have also been given by infusion, but there is a strong impression that the drug's tolerability decreases above the 250–300 mg. level. Another possibility is to administer Ludiomil by slow intravenous injection; doses of 50 mg. have been given intravenously without provoking unwanted systemic effects.

Conclusions

The trials described in this paper were carried out under conditions known to be particularly stringent and hence unlikely to favour the emergence of dramatic differences between the efficacy of the various treatments. Despite this, Ludiomil has shown itself to be effective in combating the classic signs and symptoms of depression, and we now know that it is suitable for use in a broad range of depressive illnesses, including reactive and neurotic as well as endogenous or psychotic depressions. Ludiomil can be given orally, by intravenous infusion, or by intravenous injection. When administered in a fixed dosage from the start of treatment, it is well tolerated; however, such dermatological manifestations as may occur should be treated with respect.

The evaluation of a new drug is indeed never complete. A firm foundation of clinical research with Ludiomil has already provided us with a good working knowledge of the compound. As was to be expected, the trials have resulted in various new ideas, which are being actively followed up with the intention of assessing the value of additional ways of using the compound in the treatment of depression and associated disorders.

Acknowledgments

We should like to express our appreciation to Prof. C. R. B. Joyce for his advice on methodology during the progress of these trials, to Prof. M. Turri for statistical advice during the planning stage and also for analysing the results, and to Dr. A. Yakabow and Miss R. Wilcox for their great help in designing the patient-data recording system.

References

1   Appleton, W. S., Shader, R. I., DiMascio, A.: Dermatological effects. In Shader, R. I., DiMascio, A., et al.: Psychotropic drug side effects, p. 77 (Williams & Wilkins, Baltimore 1970)
2   Ban, T.: Tricyclic antidepressants; adverse reactions and their treatment. In: Psychopharmacology, p. 283 (Williams & Wilkins, Baltimore 1969)

3   Jarvik, M.E.: Drugs used in the treatment of psychiatric disorders. Imipramine, amitriptyline, and related antidepressants; toxicity and precautions. In Goodman, L.S., Gilman, A. (Editors): The pharmacological basis of therapeutics, IVth Ed., p. 189 (Macmillan, New York/London/Toronto 1970)
4   Smith, A., Traganza, E., Harrison, G.: Studies on the effectiveness of anti-depressant drugs. Psychopharmacology, Special Issue (March 1969; Psycho-pharmacol. Res. Branch, Nat. Inst. ment. Health, Chevy Chase, Md)

Discussion

N. MATUSSEK: One thing that surprised me in this review of the clinical results was that during the first seven days of treatment Ludiomil appeared to be more effective in retarded depression. How can this be reconciled with the animal-experimental finding that Ludiomil has a more marked sedative action than imipramine?

K. RICKELS: I have one question, Dr. JOYCE. You mentioned that every patient started with 50 mg. of the experimental compound three times a day, but later you said that the investigators were given the option to start treatment with the control compound at a dosage of 25 mg. three times a day. If this was to be a controlled trial, surely you should also have initiated treatment with the experimental compound at a dosage of 25 mg. three times a day.

J. WELNER: I only have a minor point to make concerning reduction of the dosage when the patient responds satisfactorily. I myself would prefer to reduce the dosage very slowly, especially since we know from the "natural history" of depressive illness that the average duration of a phase will be at least six months. Usually I lower the total daily dose by 25 mg. every second week, and I increase it again at once if the signs of depression begin to reappear. I'd like to hear what my clinical colleagues have to say about this.

P. KIELHOLZ: We, too, Dr. WELNER, reduce the dosage step by step at 10-day intervals.

C. R. B. JOYCE: We have suggested that a reduction in the dose could be made if the patient was responding satisfactorily. The remarks that Dr. WELNER and Dr. KIELHOLZ have just made concerning the speed, or rather the caution, with which such a reduction should be effected are very valuable.

On the question raised by Dr. RICKELS, let me clear up a slight misunderstanding. The option to start the comparative drug at a lower dose than that of Ludiomil was discussed with each investigator before the commencement of his trial. He had to decide whether to use—for *all* his patients in the trial—either the lower or the higher starting dosage of the comparative drug only. There was no question of his being free to vary the starting dosage for individual patients. If he decided to begin with the lower dosage and then, after either three or seven days, to increase it, blindness was preserved by using the placebo-loading technique; despite the change in dosage, the same number of tablets was taken throughout the trial, the total being made up on the first few days with identical strip-packed placebo tablets.

In reply to Dr. MATUSSEK, I would only like to repeat that, as pointed out in our report, we too found it rather surprising that the response of retarded patients to Ludiomil was more striking in the first seven days than the response seen in other types of depression, particularly in view of the fact that this observation deviates somewhat from what might have been expected in the light of findings obtained in animal studies. But this apparent discrepancy is something which Dr. BEIN can perhaps clarify.

H. J. BEIN: I don't think that we should talk of a discrepancy between experimental and clinical findings in connection with certain specific symptoms of depression. We all know, of course, that an experimental model for depression just doesn't exist, and therefore we cannot make any correlations in respect of these symptoms. Although the influence which Ludiomil quite definitely exerts on serotonin may well be of importance in retarded patients, we do not know definitely that it is, and so we have to rely on "feedback" from the clinic. On the other hand, there are some correlations which we can draw—correlations which, I might almost say, are surprisingly good. You are familiar, for example, with the sedative effect of amitriptyline, which is more pronounced than that of Ludiomil—even though an effect on sleep disorders cannot simply be equated with a sedative effect. Finally, in double-blind trials it was observed that Ludiomil produced a certain anxiolytic effect, which again correlates very positively with pharmacological findings.

A. DELINI-STULA: In some experimental procedures we noticed that Ludiomil exerted a sedative action when given in doses which, in other experimental models in animals, elicited what might be called "antidepressant" effects. Hence, the drug exhibits two types of activity at roughly the same dosage levels. Its beneficial action in retarded patients is most probably due to stimulation of the adrenergic system. The reason why this action is so clear-cut is perhaps that a patient of this kind is, so to speak, "waiting" for just such an effect—that is to say, the effect supplied by the drug meets the patient's "demand".

N. MATUSSEK: Dr. KIELHOLZ, where would you insert Ludiomil in your classification of antidepressants? We have heard from Dr. JOYCE that, in the clinical trials reviewed by Dr. PINTO and his associates, imipramine had a better effect than Ludiomil in cases of agitated depression. You, however, would probably agree with most clinicians that it is better to use imipramine for retarded depression than for agitated depression.

P. KIELHOLZ: A general examination of the results obtained with Ludiomil suggests that this drug displays a novel profile of activity: it appears to be an antidepressant that possesses both anxiolytic and anti-aggressive properties, while at the same time influencing psychomotor retardation. As for the question of where I would insert Ludiomil in my classification, I can only say that to do this I should have to convert my classification into a three-dimensional one.

Concluding discussion

J. ANGST: The information presented in this clinical part of our symposium does, I think, give us food for thought. It reveals, after all, that Ludiomil does not differ significantly from imipramine or amitriptyline, irrespective of whether the results achieved are assessed by reference to a global evaluation of efficacy or of side effects, or by reference to the Hamilton scale. Should we derive satisfaction from this? Not one double-blind trial has disclosed significant differences between Ludiomil and the comparison drug. Are we content with this outcome? Perhaps we are. At least, it demonstrates that the new drug is as effective as the two comparison preparations. But is that enough? When we consider that the pooled results from 13 studies involving a total of 850 patients yielded only six Hamilton scale items for which statistically significant differences between the three drugs could be found, doesn't it seem that we may have lost a certain amount of information by restricting ourselves to the Hamilton scale? That is the question I should like you to reflect on. I would point out that Dr. HEIMANN, as he will shortly be telling us, used in his trial an additional instrument, the Structured Psychological Interview devised by BURDOCK and HARDESTY, which did reveal differences between the drugs employed. We ourselves, using the A.M.P. system, have also found that various symptoms tended to show different responses. I have a deep respect for Dr. HAMILTON and I know how reliable his scale is, but, in view of the findings I have just mentioned, wouldn't it really have been useful if, in addition to the Hamilton scale, other instruments had been resorted to in an attempt to obtain a somewhat more comprehensive picture of the new drug's spectrum of activity? I think it would be worthwhile to try to find out whether the failure of all the individual studies to reveal differences between the drugs administered was perhaps simply due to the fact that the instrument used was not sufficiently capable of detecting such differences.

C. R. B. JOYCE: Of course our methodology was inadequate. One always comes to this conclusion at the end of an experiment, or at least one should do. But I hope it was not so inadequate as the necessarily brief account we had to give of these trials may have implied. The time we have so far been able to devote to the full analysis and examination of the observations reported to us has been limited, and we are still far from having completed our task. It might indeed have been desirable to use other measuring scales or other rating instruments than the Hamilton scale, and fortunately in some trials the investigators—including Dr. HEIMANN—have used instruments in which they themselves are particularly interested. By employing the Structured Psychological Interview, for instance, Dr. HEIMANN in fact achieved a more sensitive demonstration of the effect of Ludiomil than with the Hamilton Rating Scale. But to get clinical trials done at all, one has—to express it bluntly—to decide not only what to put in but also what to leave out. And it was the general consensus of opinion that the Hamilton scale would stand the best chance of meeting with widespread international agreement. At the end of this phase of our investigations I think that, by and large, we would still have no cause to change this decision.

P. BERNER: I would like to report briefly on a preliminary study we carried out prior to embarking on a controlled trial. The study was an open one, of the type routinely performed in our clinic in order to obtain general information about a new drug's range of activity. The 20 patients involved comprised 14 women and six men; nine were under 45 years of age and the rest were older. Twelve of them were suffering from endogenous depression or, in a few instances, depression of late onset, while the other eight had psychogenic-reactive depression. The duration of treatment was 21 days, and the daily dose ranged in most cases from 75 to 150 mg.; the lowest daily dose administered was 30 mg. and the highest 300 mg., both these doses being given to only one patient each. As a rule, the drug was administered intramuscularly for the first six days, and thereafter by mouth. The response was evaluated by means of the A.M.P. system, the remission quotients for various symptoms being calculated on Days 3, 10, and 21. The corresponding items were quantitatively assessed as mild, moderate, or severe, and scored 1–3. On Days 3, 10, and 21 the scores of the individual patients for each particular symptom were added up and the sum was expressed as a percentage of the initial value (initial value = 100%).

The results obtained in this way for depressive mood, anxiety, and suicidal tendency are illustrated graphically in Figure 1. The curves for these three symptoms show that the effect of the drug set in promptly within the first three days, became steadily more marked until the 10th day, and then flattened out a little. As the residual values lay between 20 and 40%, the remission quotient for the items mentioned was 60–80% within 21 days—a result that can be regarded as satisfactory.

The effect of the drug on the psychomotor target symptoms of agitation and retardation is illustrated in the same way in Figure 2; as can be seen, agitated forms of depression responded more favourably than retarded forms, particularly between Day 3 and Day 10, although the difference was not statistically significant.

Finally, Figure 3 shows the effect of the drug on early insomnia and on two psychosomatic symptoms, i.e. cardiac sensations and feelings of pressure in the head. The effect exerted on early insomnia was recorded only on Days 10 and 21. Depressive

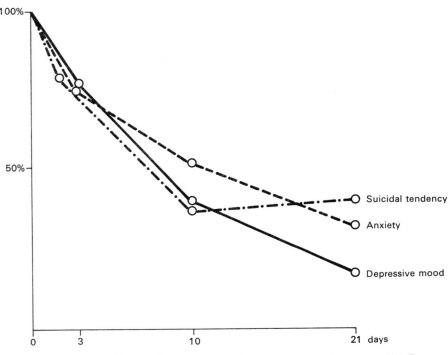

270   Fig. 1. Regression of depressive symptoms during treatment with 34,276-Ba.

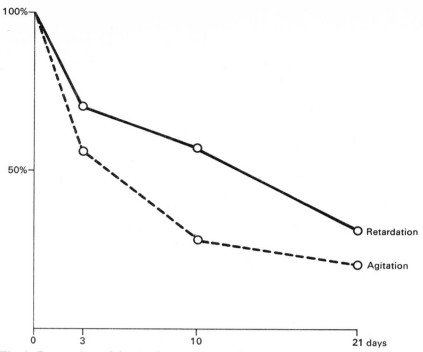

Fig. 2. Regression of depressive symptoms during treatment with 34,276-Ba.

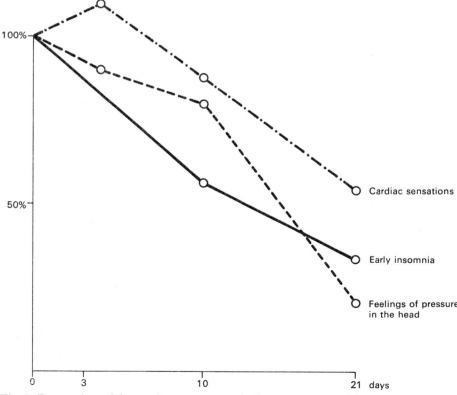

Fig. 3. Regression of depressive symptoms during treatment with 34,276-Ba.

patients usually suffer from severe sleep disturbances, and therefore the plan of treatment, even in scientifically conducted trials, has to allow for the additional administration of hypnotics. On the ninth and 20th nights, however, the hypnotic was replaced by placebo and the patients were asked on Days 10 and 21 how they had slept the previous night. It was found that early insomnia did not improve to the same extent as depressive mood. As regards the two psychosomatic symptoms, cardiac sensations in the form of "palpitation" actually increased a little at the commencement of treatment, but then regressed, though not to the same extent as the psychic and psychomotor symptoms. Feelings of pressure in the head showed only a very moderate response initially, but became appreciably less marked in the second half of the treatment period. We know from experience, of course, that in depressive patients psychosomatic syndromes often prove more refractory to treatment than psychic or psychomotor manifestations. One further point worth underlining is that elderly patients responded well to the new drug and usually required only small doses. Moreover, we found it generally more suitable not to spread the doses evenly over the day, but to give a larger dose in the evening than in the morning or at midday. It is my belief that, administered in this way, the drug exerted a better effect on sleep disturbances and also on the "morning trough".

The local and systemic tolerability of 34,276-Ba can be described as good. The side effects included occasional instances of tiredness at the start of treatment, dryness of the mouth, palpitation, sensations of pressure in the head, and, in one case, a disorder of micturition.

F. FREYHAN: In our study at St. Vincent's Hospital and Medical Center the daily dose of Ludiomil has ranged from 150 to 400 mg., with an average of 300 mg. All patients have been started on 150 mg. In contrast to what certain other speakers have reported today, we have found that the onset of improvement has been rather slow. The earliest onset has been during the second week, but more often it occurred at the end of the second or beginning of the third week. It may be of interest to note that one patient on a dosage of 400 mg., although a therapeutic failure, did not develop a single side effect. More than half of the patients undergoing treatment with Ludiomil developed E.E.G. changes similar to those reported from Dr. HIPPIUS's clinic in Berlin in patients receiving lithium.

Our therapeutic results have been assessed as either "maximal" or "moderate" in 76.8% of the cases. Our clinical impression of the antidepressant potency of Ludiomil is therefore favourable. We found no obvious correlation between the dosage level and the occurrence of side effects.

To sum up, I would say that we are encouraged by our initial experiences with Ludiomil. While we have not yet identified the syndrome-specificity of its action, we feel confident that Ludiomil represents a highly potent antidepressant compound.

W. GRÜTER: In Treysa (West Germany) we started an open trial with Ludiomil in November 1966. Although this trial was originally intended to be merely a pilot study, the new preparation proved to display such valuable properties that it very soon became, both for my colleagues at the Treysa clinic and for myself, the drug of choice in the treatment of depression. Thus, one and a half years later we had already used the drug in 562 patients, including 534 suffering from depression. I shall confine myself here to selecting from among the analysed results certain findings which relate to problems already discussed at the present symposium and which shed light on some of the particular advantages of Ludiomil. I can, in fact, summarise what I want to say under two headings: the first concerns the ambulatory treatment of depressive patients. It has already been mentioned that the overall incidence of depressive states is increasing and that, at the same time, progress has been made in the diagnosis of these conditions. Furthermore, patients are becoming less embarrassed at the idea of consulting a doctor because of psychic disorders. As a result of all these factors, we are faced with an increasing disproportion between, on the one hand, the number

Table 1. Data on patients treated with Ludiomil.

		Hospitalised	Ambulant	Total
Depressive	Endogenous depression, including menopausal and involutional depression	131	241	372
	Endo-reactive depression	17	19	36
	Reactive depression	16	15	31
	Depression associated with neuroses and personality disorders	15	20	35
	Symptomatic and organic depression	39	6	45
	Depression associated with schizophrenia	9	6	15
Non-depressive	Psycho-asthenic states unaccompanied by depressive symptoms; neuroses; or personality disorders	–	21	21
	Mania	2	2	4
	Weight deficit	–	3	3
	Total	229	333	562

Table 2. Response to Ludiomil in all forms of depression.

	N	Response nil (N) %	Moderate (N) %	Good/Very good (N) %
Hospitalised patients	227	(10) 4.4	(26) 11.5	(191) 84.1
Ambulant patients	307	(17) 5.6	(35) 11.4	(255) 83.0
Total	534	(27) 5.1	(61) 11.4	(446) 83.5

of depressive patients in need of treatment, and, on the other, the number of psychiatrists and, in particular, of psychiatric hospital beds available. In a steadily growing percentage of cases, therefore, depressive patients have to be treated on an ambulatory basis—and by doctors who are not psychiatrists.

The pattern of activity of Ludiomil encouraged us to use the drug to an increasing extent in out-patients, even in cases of severe depression and even where there was a definite risk of suicide. As you can see from Table 1, the number of out-patients treated with the drug eventually exceeded the number of cases treated in hospital. Table 2 shows that the results were largely the same in both groups. If we pick out the cases of endogenous, menopausal, and involutional depression and consider them as forming a special group (Table 3), we notice that ambulant treatment even tended to produce better results than treatment in hospital. The reasons why we felt more and more encouraged to use the drug on an ambulatory basis were as follows:

Table 3. Response to Ludiomil in cases of endogenous depression (including menopausal and involutional depression).

	N	Response nil (N) %	Moderate (N) %	Good/Very good (N) %
Hospitalised patients	131	(5) 3.8	(14) 10.7	(112) 85.5
Ambulant patients	241	(8) 3.3	(17) 7.1	(216) 89.6
Total	372	(13) 3.5	(31) 8.3	(328) 88.2

Table 4. Response of various syndromal types to Ludiomil.

	N	Response nil (N) %	Moderate (N) %	Good/Very good (N) %
Predominantly retarded depression	153	(11) 7.2	(19) 12.4	(123) 80.4
Predominantly agitated depression	107	(2) 1.9	(8) 7.5	(97) 90.6
Hypochondriacal and somatised depression	78	(2) 2.6	(6) 7.7	(70) 89.7

1. Its prompt onset of effect. A clear-cut improvement, which, though obviously not reflecting the full capabilities of the drug, was nevertheless often of decisive importance as regards the course of the disease, set in after an average of two days in ambulant patients, as against four days in hospitalised cases. Incidentally, may I add that, apart from the global measurable effect of a drug, its latency period is also a very important factor; if a drug succeeds in rapidly eliminating such major symptoms as suicidal thoughts, it may well be regarded as having accomplished something decisive, even though the influence it exerts on certain other symptoms may at this stage still be only slight.

2. In none of our cases did retardation improve before mood. Either both improved simultaneously, or else brightening of the mood preceded the improvement in retardation. We could therefore be relatively confident that any dissociation between the two effects was unlikely to have dangerous consequences.

3. The side effects were few in number and not very marked, although, as I mentioned in the discussion following Dr. KUHN's paper, we very often gave a dose of 50 mg. t.i.d. right from the outset of treatment.

4. It was relatively easy to select the right dosage, and the question of how the daily dose should be divided did not raise any problems.

5. The drug exerted a more or less equally good effect on the various depressive syndromes (Table 4). In our series, as can be seen from this table, the agitated patients responded somewhat better than the retarded ones. The fact that, as Dr. JOYCE has pointed out, this finding was not invariably confirmed in other studies, merely underlines, in my opinion, the bipolar nature of the drug's effect. This bipolar effect, of course, is only apparent upon clinical examination and is therefore very

Table 5. Effect of Ludiomil on the cardinal target symptoms of depressive states.

Symptom	Percentage of patients in whom the symptom was completely eliminated	Average degree of improvement (in %)
Mood:		
Basic mood dejected	74.6	82.5
Episodes of cheerfulness reduced	74.2	82.2
Episodes of sadness increased	75.4	83.2
Drive:		
Increased drive (agitation)	74.4	82.2
Retarded drive	63.7	76.1
Mental restlessness, tension	66.6	80.1
Anxiety	75.1	81.1
Suicidal tendencies and suicidal thoughts	93.9	96.5
Inability to concentrate and loss of memory	73.0	84.2
Sleep disturbances	73.9	85.1
Loss of appetite	87.0	89.6
Hypochondria	62.4	75.1
Diffuse somatic disorders	69.4	81.1

Table 6. Response to Ludiomil in chronic depression.

	N	Response nil (N) %	Moderate (N) %	Good/Very good (N) %
Hospitalised patients	39	(1) 2.6	(7) 17.9	(31) 79.5
Ambulant patients	52	(3) 5.8	(4) 7.7	(45) 86.5
Total	91	(4) 4.4	(11) 12.1	(76) 83.5

difficult to explain in pharmacological terms. It can be claimed that Ludiomil combines in a single preparation the advantages of both imipramine and amitriptyline.

6. Finally, the drug produced an excellent effect on suicidal thoughts and intentions (Table 5). Table 5 reveals, in fact, that these symptoms showed the highest improvement rate of all. Other symptoms, too, which loom particularly large in ambulant treatment—such as sleep disturbances, anxiety, inability to concentrate, and somatic disorders—likewise responded well. But the high success rate in the case of suicidal tendencies and suicidal thoughts strikes me as being especially impressive. This effect of the drug facilitates ambulant therapy quite considerably.

The second of my two headings relates to the question of protracted and chronic depression, which has already been discussed today. Impressed as we were by the effectiveness of Ludiomil, we picked out at the end of our study all the cases in which, prior to therapy, the depressive phase had lasted more than one and a half years without a remission and we analysed these cases separately (Table 6). They accounted for 91 of the 534 patients—that is to say, for 16%, which works out at one patient in every six. This surprised us; nevertheless, we have heard from Dr. KUHN that 16% is apparently still a low figure. The longest phase of all was 27 years without a remission. Another thing that surprised us was that when we collated our results we found that the chronic cases had not done at all badly; this really was astonishing, because all psychiatrists will agree that the longer the phase has persisted, the less likely it is that the depression will respond to treatment. It seems that Ludiomil does not obey this maxim.

May I just add that we did not observe a single epileptic seizure in our patients, or even the first manifestation of a hitherto latent tendency to convulsions. This is astounding, considering the size of the series and the fact that the average duration of treatment in these ambulant patients was 80 days. Skin reactions developed in six patients, i.e. in 1.1% of cases.

No untoward effects on the cardiovascular system were encountered. Ludiomil often even reduced an accelerated heart rate. Some of our patients, moreover, had been referred to us by the head of the internal diseases department at the clinic. Altogether 30 patients, suffering from organic heart disease, including severe disturbances of cardiac rhythm, received Ludiomil because of concomitant psychic symptoms. In all these cases Ludiomil had a beneficial effect on the heart rate. Atrioventricular tachycardia in particular improved during treatment with the drug, and in some cases of arrhythmia the heart beat became much more regular. The head of the internal diseases department felt that in cases of organic heart damage Ludiomil was not only not contra-indicated, but could even exert a positive effect.

P. KIELHOLZ: I feel that Dr. GRÜTER's remarks confirm once again that chronic depression—an important, albeit somewhat neglected, form of the disease—seems to respond better to Ludiomil than to other drugs.

H. HEIMANN: Since both Dr. ANGST and Dr. JOYCE have referred to the double-blind trial we carried out in 50 depressive patients at the Lausanne University Clinic, may I briefly report on the method employed and the results obtained in this study. First of all, the question of methodology: in addition to evaluating the patients by means of a global assessment and by reference to the Hamilton scale, we also used four other instruments. These were as follows: 1. The Structured Psychological Interview (S.P.I.) devised by BURDOCK and HARDESTY*; 2. The subjective status rating scale of VON ZERSSEN et al.** (a questionnaire to be completed by the patient, the questions being formulated in such a way that, in answering them, the patient portrays, as it were, his depressive state); 3. The polarities list, which we employ in all our pharmacopsychological studies; and 4. An analysis of speech, devised by FRIEDA GOLDMAN EISLER***, which provides an objective measure of the patient's subjective status and in which speed of speech is assessed by reference to the following factors: a) Total

---

* BURDOCK, E. I., HARDESTY, A. S.: Psychological test for psychopathology. J. abnorm. Psychol. *73*, 62 (1968)

BURDOCK, E. I., HARDESTY, A. S.: SCI-structured-clinical-interview-manual (Springer, New York 1969)

** ZERSSEN, D. VON, KOELLER, D.-M., REY, E.-R.: Die Befindlichkeits-Skala (B-S) – ein einfaches Instrument zur Objektivierung von Befindlichkeitsstörungen, insbesondere im Rahmen von Längsschnittuntersuchungen. Arzneimittel-Forsch. *20*, 915 (1970)

*** GOLDMAN EISLER, F.: Psycholinguistics. Experiments in spontaneous speech (Acad. Press, London/New York 1968)

speaking time; b) Relative length of pauses; and c) Rate of articulation. For the purposes of this analysis we used one of the items in the Structured Psychological Interview.

In order to obtain measurements that were not influenced by initial values, we performed our evaluation on so-called "residual gain scores"—that is, on regression-transformed data, as proposed by LIENERT*.

And now a few words about the results we obtained: whereas the Hamilton scale scores recorded 14 and 21 days after the commencement of treatment failed to reveal any differences between the two drugs used (Ludiomil and amitriptyline), the Structured Psychological Interview carried out on the same days showed that Ludiomil had produced better results, the difference being significant at the 5% level on Day 14 and at the 1% level on Day 21. The more favourable response to Ludiomil was reflected in particular in the factor "retardation/dejection"—a finding which appears especially important in view of everything we have heard about the drug today. The von Zerssen subjective status rating scale showed a tendency at the 10% level for Ludiomil to produce a greater degree of improvement after 14 days, whereas after three weeks the difference had become significant at the 5% level. The polarities list failed to reveal any differences between the two drugs. GOLDMAN EISLER's speech analysis likewise disclosed no differences between the drugs, but it did show that both total speaking time and the duration of pauses, expressed as a percentage of total speaking time, improved in the course of treatment, which indicates a brightening of depressive mood.

These results, however, must be interpreted with caution, because the fact that the instruments we used showed Ludiomil to produce a better response is not tantamount to saying that Ludiomil was invariably superior to amitriptyline. In our study we were concerned not only with comparing the two drugs, but also with examining the question of whether the additional instruments employed might possibly be better indicators of therapeutic effectiveness. The subjective status rating scale and the S.P.I. did, in fact, prove to be better.

In conclusion, I should like to make a brief comment on the subject of dosage, a comment that might perhaps be of some interest in the light of Dr. HEIM's studies on the dosage of antidepressants in open and double-blind trials. In a preliminary discussion on the trial I have just described, I suggested to my colleagues at the clinic that the comparison substance used should be amitriptyline in a dosage of 50 mg. three times daily, but they were very sceptical about this because they thought they would then always be able to detect from the side effects which patients were receiving amitriptyline, with the result that double-blind conditions could thus not be maintained. Their misgivings, however, were not borne out; neither of the two preparations was recognised either by the assistant doctors or by their chiefs. In other words, the "clinical experience" on which my colleagues based their doubts did not apparently stand up to the test of a double-blind trial.

B. POPKES: In 1966 ENGELMEIER and I started using Ludiomil in a few cases at the Psychiatric Clinic in Essen. In the course of time, we decided to administer it to almost all our in-patients and out-patients suffering from depression, with the result that we have so far treated about one thousand cases with the drug. The daily dose amounted on the average to 100 mg., and only in rare cases was 150 mg. daily required. The same dosage was given to patients with depressive syndromes caused by treatment with major tranquillisers and in cases of schizophrenia marked by depression; in no instance did we observe any provocation of symptoms. In depression of late onset we administered doses of up to 50 mg. daily, and often found that this produced a satisfactory brightening of mood. Side effects were rare in response to daily doses of up to 100 mg., but increased appreciably following higher doses. The most common

---

* LIENERT, G.A.: Über die Anwendung von Variablen-Transformationen in der Psychologie. Biomet. Z. *4*, 145 (1962)

side effect consisted of a considerable increase in appetite which regularly preceded the improvement in mood by a few days or even by as much as a week. This side effect, though desirable *per se*, occasionally gave rise to complications in cases where the patient gained a great deal of weight. We noticed that these patients developed a sudden desire for sweet things. In elderly, listless patients we then began to administer doses of up to 30 mg. Ludiomil daily in order to improve their appetite. Delirious states were encountered in a few elderly subjects during treatment with the drug. On several occasions we continued treating women with Ludiomil during early pregnancy, because we had not known they were pregnant when we started the medication or because we were afraid to withdraw the drug owing to the risk of a relapse. All these women gave birth to healthy infants. We have not observed any epileptiform seizures or any severe changes in blood chemistry.

In cases of agitated depression we found that the sedative effect of Ludiomil was not sufficient. This may have been a question of dosage, but at any rate we combined the drug in these cases with other agents, usually with diazepam. One striking feature of this combined therapy was that initially Ludiomil considerably reinforced the relaxing effect of diazepam. The marked sedation produced by this combined medication generally disappeared after only a few days. In none of the cases treated by us did Ludiomil prove incompatible with other drugs.

To sum up, Ludiomil, in our opinion, is at present the most reliable and most effective thymoleptic available—even for the treatment of depressive schizophrenia and depressive states induced by medication with major tranquillisers. We believe that Ludiomil is particularly suitable for the treatment of ambulatory patients for the following reasons: 1. It has a prompt onset of effect; 2. It exerts a good drive-enhancing action which, however, does not set in abruptly; and 3. It causes little or no impairment of the patient's subjective status.

We have also found the drug most satisfactory as an adjuvant in the psychotherapy of depressive neuroses. In such cases, we usually employed a dosage of 10–25 mg. t.i.d., which as a rule brought about a considerable brightening of mood. Quite often, in fact, proper psychotherapy would have been impossible without this prior medication.

W. PÖLDINGER: The open pilot trial on which I should like to report here was carried out when I was still at the Basle clinic. In this trial Ludiomil was given to 20 depressive patients in a dosage of 75–150 mg. daily. The A.M.P. system of documentation was employed and we calculated the remission quotients for various symptoms. May I perhaps very briefly describe the procedure: each symptom can score a maximum of three points; the points scored per symptom in all the patients before treatment were added together (= 100%), and the percentage decrease in the score was then calculated on Days 3, 6, and 10. As can be seen from Figure 1, the symptom "Depressive mood" responded best of all to Ludiomil, followed by "Psychomotor agitation". "Psychomotor retardation" also improved, but not quite so markedly as agitation. There was likewise an appreciable reduction in anxiety.

We were of course particularly interested in the effect exerted by the drug on suicidal tendencies, a factor which is of cardinal importance in the case of out-patients. Moreover, in Dr. KIELHOLZ's clinic suicidal tendencies and sleep disturbances were the only indications in which additional drugs were permitted, because the aim was to use monotherapy wherever possible. The results we obtained in two different groups of patients with suicidal tendencies are reproduced in Figure 2. In this study we merely recorded whether or not the symptom was present, and we did not score it. The upper curve, representing 16 patients, shows that suicidal tendencies improved in response to monotherapy with Ludiomil in a dosage of 50–75 mg. t.i.d. The lower curve, representing 14 patients, relates to combined treatment in which Tacitin®, a drug exhibiting marked relaxing and anxiolytic properties, was added to the regimen in a dose of 10 mg. t.i.d. As might be expected in view of the interrelationship between agitation, anxiety, and suicidal tendencies, a drug such as Tacitin is eminently suit-

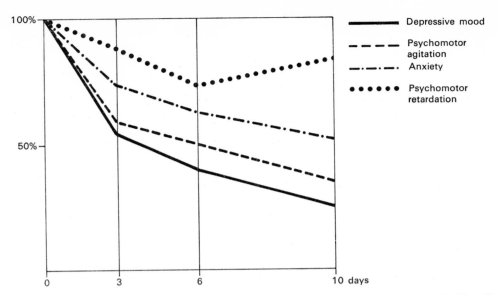

Fig. 1. Remission quotients for various symptoms during treatment with Ludiomil (N = 20).

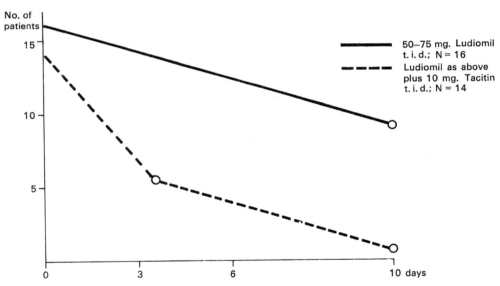

Fig. 2. Decrease in suicidal tendencies during treatment with Ludiomil and with Ludiomil + Tacitin.

able as a means of reinforcing the effect exerted by an antidepressant of the Ludiomil type on suicidal tendencies.

I. SANO: In recent years the view has steadily been gaining ground that the pathogenesis of endogenous depression is connected chiefly with a disturbance in the biosynthesis of serotonin—that is to say, with reduced serotonin levels in the brain. As far back as 1963 Dr. COPPEN reported on the effectiveness of oral L-tryptophan treatment—with or without the addition of an M.A.O. inhibitor—in these cases, but we were unable to obtain clear-cut confirmation of his results at that time. It was KLINE and SACHS who in 1963–1964 first used 5-hydroxytryptophan (5-H.T.P.). The DL-form employed, however, almost regularly gave rise to malaise, nausea, abdominal pain, and diarrhoea, which were usually so severe that DL-5-H.T.P. could not be given in large doses—i.e. in doses of the size commonly used in dopa medication. It therefore seemed to me very important to give the L-form of 5-H.T.P. a trial, but it was not until November 1970 that we had sufficient quantities of L-5-H.T.P. available with which to conduct clinical trials designed to establish whether its use is justified as causal treatment for endogenous depression. I cannot go into our results in detail now, but I was most interested to hear today that conventional antidepressants, including Ludiomil as well, likewise appear to influence serotonin metabolism.

W. WALCHER: In the past few months we have carried out a small open study which was designed more as a pilot trial for a subsequent double-blind investigation. For this pilot study we selected patients in whom "vitalisation symptoms" predominated. By no means all of them had masked depression; some were suffering from frank depression of moderately severe or severe degree, in which of course one often also encounters somatic equivalents. All the patients, however, were of the hypochondriacal, plaintive, anxious, and agitated type. Their ages ranged from 16 to 66 years. We began the study in rather a sceptical mood and without much enthusiasm, but we were pleased to find that our scepticism was not justified. Six patients, for example, all of whom had been admitted to the clinic over the same week-end, were started simultaneously on Ludiomil, and after only one or two days all six stated that they felt much better. The effect was exactly the same in all of them: they felt a good deal calmer, they experienced a pleasant sensation of tiredness, and they noted an improvement in their sleep disturbances.

One striking feature was the rapidity with which mood brightened and somatic "vitalisation symptoms" improved. After about a week the regression in the various symptoms seemed to stagnate a little in some of the cases, but in the third week the drug's thymoleptic effect became more marked again and the somatic "vitalisation symptoms" improved still further. Nine patients eventually became completely symptom-free, while the others showed an improvement—except for three who failed to respond at all. One of these three was a fellow-doctor who discontinued the drug because of its sedative effect (sedation, incidentally, was a very prominent feature in all the patients). The other two failures were patients suffering from neurotic depression who likewise showed no response at all to any of the other drugs commonly employed in our clinic.

As regards side effects, peripheral anticholinergic manifestations, including tachycardia in particular, were undoubtedly much less pronounced with Ludiomil; only in one patient did we have to administer a beta-blocker. Sweating, too, a side effect of conventional antidepressants which can be very tormenting for the patient, was also far less marked. Following intramuscular injection of Ludiomil some patients complained of neuralgic pain in the leg after a few days, with the result that we changed over to administering the drug by intravenous injection or infusion or by mouth. The dosage employed was invariably 50 mg. three times daily. Some of the patients had chronic depression; one of these chronic cases responded very well and became free of symptoms after three weeks, whereas the others improved as long as they were receiving infusions of the drug. These infusions, however, had to be discontinued after a while because we did not have a sufficient stock of ampoules.

Particularly impressive was the case of a patient with chronic depression who had been complaining of abdominal discomfort for years; as a result of these symptoms, for which no explanation could be found, he had undergone altogether five operations, but none of them had revealed any organic lesions. Since his last operation one year previously he had displayed in addition clear-cut psychopathological symptoms. After three weeks of oral treatment with Ludiomil he became completely symptom-free.

Closing addresses

P. KIELHOLZ: Ladies and Gentlemen, now that we have come to the end of our richly laden programme, I have the pleasant duty of expressing to all those who have presented papers or spoken in the discussions my most sincere gratitude for the hard work they put into preparing their most informative contributions. A vote of thanks is due also to CIBA-GEIGY LIMITED, as well as to Dr. ADAMS and his staff, who chose this magnificent venue for the symposium and who have organised it so brilliantly. I should also like to thank Mr. PHILPS and Mr. BIGLAND for their excellent translations, and Mr. CASTY for ensuring that all the technical equipment functioned so smoothly.

A source of particular satisfaction to me is the fact that all those who were asked to attend this symposium accepted the invitation, and it gives me great pleasure to think that we have succeeded here in gathering together in one room what, I feel, might justly be called an "international élite" in the field of research on depression. This is undoubtedly one of the main reasons why the symposium has been so successful and fruitful.

A wealth of new data, as well as a host of well-founded results, have been presented, and it is not easy to summarise and review all this material in just a few words.

We began by considering various problems that are currently exercising the minds of those engaged in research on depression—problems relating in particular to biochemical aspects, diagnosis, assessment, and statistical evaluation—and we then finally proceeded to discuss the results obtained in clinical trials with a new antidepressant. The findings recorded in these world-wide trials, especially in those conducted under double-blind conditions, as well as the highly informative and searching reports presented in the concluding discussion, justify the verdict that this antidepressant displays a new profile of activity which appears to me to be characterised by the following three properties:

1. More rapid onset of action.
2. Fewer side effects.
3. Suitability for use in all forms of depressive illness.

In addition, it is my impression that the drug could be particularly valuable in such special indications as masked depression and chronic depression. Having listened to what Drs ANGST, FREYHAN—the originator of the term "target symptom"—GRÜTER, and HEIMANN had to say in the last part of the symposium, I believe that I could after all assign a place to this antidepressant, too, in my classification: I would position it in the middle, between the two poles formed by anxiety-reducing and drive-enhancing effects. I would emphasise, however, that this is merely a provisional placing, a kind of working hypothesis. Before a final decision could be reached, the drug would have to be compared under double-blind conditions with all the other major antidepressants, including in particular those possessing pronounced drive-enhancing or potent anxiolytic properties.

May I, in conclusion, say a word about future prospects. Having had the opportunity at this symposium of improving my acquaintance with prominent investigators in the field of biochemistry, I am convinced that it will not be all that long before the biochemical factors underlying endogenous depression at least are elucidated, thus providing us with a foundation on which to base an approach to causal therapy. I am also optimistic in another respect: I believe that collaboration between the various disciplines, which has now been in progress for 15 years, will make it possible to develop new therapeutic agents displaying more specific effects.

I am not so optimistic, alas, as regards the standardisation we have long been hoping for in the definition, nomenclature, and classification of depressive illnesses. And yet no international collaborative research, no transcultural study in any field can be successfully conducted without a uniform classification and nomenclature. What we need is a standardised glossary, and unfortunately that is precisely what we do not yet possess. The lack of such a glossary is the reason why it is so difficult to reduce the results of trials to a common denominator and why we so often find ourselves trying to compare like with unlike.

This symposium has made it clear to us once again that decisive advances in research on depression can only be accomplished by interdisciplinary collaboration. Only by adopting this approach and by constantly endeavouring to understand one another better—that is, to speak the same scientific language—will we succeed in achieving our objectives.

R. OBERHOLZER: Ladies and Gentlemen, I feel sure I am speaking on behalf of all of you when, at the end of this symposium, I take the opportunity of thanking our Chairman, Dr. KIELHOLZ, most cordially for having presided over the proceedings. That we have had such an harmonious and fruitful scientific meeting is due in no small measure to his objectivity and consummate skill as a chairman.

One particularly gratifying aspect of the symposium has been for me—and I say this not only as a medical man, but also as a spokesman for CIBA-GEIGY—the extensive and informative discussions. The latest research findings and the latest results of clinical trials have been presented, discussed, and compared with complete frankness. Both optimistic and pessimistic views have been expressed, and our attention has been drawn to a number of problems that still remain to be solved.

I must confess that I rank myself among the optimists—and, I believe, with good reason. This very symposium, after all, has furnished a shining example of how problems of communication can be overcome. Consider, for instance, the nomenclature of the psycho-active drugs: in your papers and contributions to the discussions you have quite spontaneously made frequent use of the word "thymoleptics", a term which was introduced recently and whose origin is probably known to very few of you. This word was, in fact, coined by a member of our staff for the purpose of characterising Tofranil®, and it has since gained wide acceptance. The inventor of the term, Dr. SCHMIDLIN, is here among us today.

Just as this term has stood the test of time, so I hope—and in this respect, too, I am optimistic—will the proceedings of the present symposium have fruitful repercussions on further developments in the various branches of science represented here today.

Finally, I am also optimistic about the possibility that the chemists will succeed in removing some of our worries. It is my belief that, as a result of their work, certain problems now being encountered in the treatment of depression and giving rise to pessimism will become steadily less important.

Dr. KIELHOLZ, Ladies and Gentlemen, I should like to thank you all for having taken part in this symposium and to wish each and every one of you a pleasant journey home.

Index

284

Rating scale items: work and interests
256, 257
– scales 74–79, 82, 83, 93, 100–106, 108
see also Scales
– – for assessment of personality 101
– – – depression 74–79, 82, 83, 100–106
– – – determining prognosis 101, 106
– – – – response to treatment 101
– – and questionnaires 76, 77, 79
– – , scope 77, 82, 83
– – , scoring system 102–106
– – , various types 104, 105
Rebound phenomenon following withdrawal of medication 185, 187
Receptors, structure of 138, 139
Reflex transmission, polysynaptic 110
Regression analysis, multiple 90–92, 95
Regression-transformed data (LIENERT) 277
Relaxation, psychomotor 183, 193
Reliability 82, 91
see also Inter-rater reliability
R.E.M. phases
see Clinico-experimental findings, sleep stages
Reserpine 113, 114, 118, 120, 126, 128
Residual gain scores (LIENERT) 277
– scores 106
see also Assessment
Resistance, arterial 161, 162, 166–168
Respiration 161, 162, 166–168, 172–177, 179
– , type of 179
– , unpleasant subjective sensations 179
Respiratory depression 168, 172–177
– failure 172, 177
"Restless legs" 43
Restlessness, mental 275
Retardation 55, 67, 68, 73, 87, 94, 102, 223, 244, 246–249, 252, 255–257, 268, 270, 271, 274, 275, 278, 279

Sadness, vital 39, 46, 47, 48
Scale
see Rating scale
– , analogue
see Analogue scales
Scales for assessing clinical status 101, 105, 106
– – – effects of treatment 105, 106
– , physician rating 105
– , self-rating 104, 105
Schizophrenia, depression associated with 125, 127, 200, 201, 208, 230, 231, 235, 273, 278

– and depression, comparison 60, 61
– , provocation of symptoms 125, 278
School, morbid fear of 232
– , poor performance at 229, 232
S.C.I.
see S.P.I.
Scores, difference between initial and final scores 105, 106
– , sums of
see Scores, total
– , total 103, 104, 106, 213, 214, 216, 218, 222, 237–239, 249, 255, 258, 260, 264
see also Assessment, global
– , vector of 88
Scoring system 102–106
Secondary cases in members of patient's families 34
Self-Rating Depression Scale (ZUNG) 75, 77, 93
– – – , modified
see Wakefield Self-Assessment Depression Inventory
Septal rats 120, 121, 128
Serotonin 13, 26, 120, 138, 267
– in the brain 13, 14, 18, 24, 26, 125, 126, 279
– deficit 18, 24, 26
– in the depressive phase 14, 18, 24
– hypothesis of depression 13, 21, 54, 62
– in mania 14
– metabolism 13, 14, 18–19, 24–26, 46, 55, 125, 126, 279
– synthesis increased by lithium 25, 26
Serotoninergic neurones 26
Severity 78, 79, 85–87, 91, 92, 102, 103, 211–215, 218
– scores 102, 103
Sideropenia 201
Similarities between centres and nations 213–215, 221
– – regions 213–218, 221
Sleep deprival 20, 50, 61
– disturbances 45, 48, 66, 69, 70, 73, 187–194, 220–221, 233, 237, 267, 272, 275, 278, 280
– – in early morning 87, 194
see also Insomnia, delayed
– , duration reduced 246, 248, 252
see also Clinico-experimental findings, sleep, duration of
– – Insomnia, delayed
– , requirement increased 73
– studies
see Clinico-experimental findings